THE ADVOCATE GENERAL AND EC LAW

The Advocate General and EC Law

NOREEN BURROWS
Jean Monnet Professor of European Law, University of Glasgow
and
ROSA GREAVES
Professor of Law, University of Glasgow

OXFORD
UNIVERSITY PRESS

OXFORD
UNIVERSITY PRESS

Great Clarendon Street, Oxford OX2 6DP

Oxford University Press is a department of the University of Oxford.
It furthers the University's objective of excellence in research, scholarship,
and education by publishing worldwide in

Oxford New York

Auckland Cape Town Dar es Salaam Hong Kong Karachi
Kuala Lumpur Madrid Melbourne Mexico City Nairobi
New Delhi Shanghai Taipei Toronto

With offices in

Argentina Austria Brazil Chile Czech Republic France Greece
Guatemala Hungary Italy Japan Poland Portugal Singapore
South Korea Switzerland Thailand Turkey Ukraine Vietnam

Oxford is a registered trade mark of Oxford University Press
in the UK and in certain other countries

Published in the United States
by Oxford University Press Inc., New York

First published 2007

British Library Cataloguing in Publication Data
Data available

Library of Congress Cataloging-in-Publication Data

Burrows, Noreen, 1951–
The advocate general and EC law / Noreen Burrows and Rosa Greaves,
p. cm.
Includes bibliographical references and index.
ISBN 978–0–19–929900–3 (hardback: alk. paper) 1. Court of Justice of the European Communities. Advocate-General. 2. Law—European Union countries. I. Greaves, Rosa, 1952– II. Title.
KJE5472.5.B87 2007
341.242′2—dc22

2006039349

Typeset by Newgen Imaging Systems (P) Ltd., Chennai, India

Printed in Great Britain
on acid-free paper by
Biddles Ltd., King's Lynn

ISBN 978–0–19–929900–3

1 3 5 7 9 10 8 6 4 2

Preface

This book originated in a conversation between the authors as to the difficulty in researching the European Court of Justice in terms of writing judicial biographies. The collegiate nature of the Court means that it is difficult to attribute views to individual judges. Even the Reporting Judge who is responsible for drafting the judgment in a case becomes invisible in the deliberations. The Advocate General, by contrast, is identifiable. He presents an Opinion in open court and is free from the constraints of collegiality. Thus an opportunity exists to study the Opinions of members of the Court who do not participate in the decision-making process but whose status is equal to those who do. This book should be seen as a contribution to the literature on the Court and we have anchored our studies in the work of the Advocate General in the Court rather than covering other bibliographic aspects of the Advocates General discussed in the book.

Both authors are indebted to the Advocates General who agreed to be interviewed for this project; Advocates General Gulman (who was a Judge in the Court at the time of the interview), Jacobs, Léger, Mischo, Ruiz-Jarabo Colomer and Saggio. Francis Jacobs has been generous with his time and his comments on various aspects of this book since the initial interview. David Edward, former Judge in the European Court of Justice, has always responded to questions about the Court whilst maintaining strict secrecy about deliberations. We are grateful to him.

Chapters 2, 3, 5, 8, and 10 were written by Noreen Burrows. Chapters 4, 6, and 7 were written by Rosa Greaves and Chapter 9 by Rosa Greaves and Emily Reid from the University of Southampton. Chapters 1 and 11 are the joint responsibility of Noreen Burrows and Rosa Greaves. Noreen Burrows wishes to thank Catherine Corr and Jennifer Hendry who assisted in the research for this book and Maria Fletcher for her helpful comments on draft chapters. On a personal note, she wishes to thank her husband, Alastair Swanson, for his patience and support. Rosa Greaves wishes to thank Sebastian Harter-Bachmann for his excellent research assistance, Francis Pritchard for reading the manuscript and Nicholas Hopkins for helpful comments on the draft chapters. In addition, she wishes to thank all the friends and colleagues who have helped in so many different ways to bring this project to fruition. She is also grateful to the AHRC for a Research Leave Award that facilitated the completion of this project.

The law is as it stands on 1 January 2006.

August 2006

Contents

Table of Cases

European Court of Justice: cases in number order

Court of First Instance: Cases in number order

European Court of Justice: Cases in alphabetical order

European Court of Human Rights

Cases from National Courts

Germany

Italy

UK

1

Introduction

This book is a study of the Advocate General in the European Court of Justice of the European Communities. By studying the Advocate General in the context of the Court it aims to contribute to the literature on the Court in several ways. First, it demonstrates the role of the Advocate General in the Court's procedure and explains the potential significance of the submissions of the Advocate General in the Court's reasoning and decision making. Second, and linked to the first aim, it tries to answer the question of whether the Advocate General does assist the Court as he is required to do by Article 222 of the Treaty (EC).[1] The Court of Justice is required to make decisions in the cases before it.[2] Some of these decisions are narrow and technical and the Court provides a narrow and technical response. Others are on the interpretation of provisions of Community law which have major significance for individuals or commercial undertakings. The European Court of Justice is also the supreme constitutional court of the European Union and its decisions create constitutional principles. In all of these cases the Court is required to 'ensure that in the interpretation and application of [the] Treaty the law is observed'.[3] In this variety of contexts, how can the Advocate General assist the Court and what does assisting mean? The book's third objective is to assess the contribution of the Advocate General in developing principles of European Community law. We see the book also as a contribution to the legal history of the Court and the Community legal order in an attempt to stimulate further research in this area.

[1] Consolidated Version of the Treaty Establishing the European Community, Art 222 (formerly Art 166).

[2] The term 'decision' is used in the Statute of the Court of Justice. However, the Court is required to give a 'preliminary ruling' under Art 234 EC. Art 228 EC uses the term 'judgment' in cases involving actions against Member States for infringements of Community law and the same term is used when the Court rules on a matter relating to an arbitration clause under Art 238 EC. Art 231 EC requires the Court to 'declare' an act to be void if the circumstances provided for in Art 230 EC are met and a similar term is used in Art 333 EC. It may 'order' that the application of a contested act be suspended. It may 'prescribe' interim measures according to Art 243 EC. In discussing decision-making any one of these forms of procedure might be under discussion.

[3] Art 220 EC (formerly Art 164).

Who is the Advocate General?

Background

The Advocate General is an institution unique to the European Court of Justice although, as is apparent from the cases decided by the European Court of Human Rights discussed in chapter 3, similar institutions exist in the legal orders of some of the Member States. The origins of the Advocate General role lie in the negotiations leading up to the Treaty of Paris (1951). Part of the institutional structure of the European Coal and Steel Community was to be a Court of Justice. According to former Advocate General Darmon, 'certain Member States would have preferred Judges of the Court to be able to hand down dissenting judgments', but that the proposal was not accepted.[4] Instead, a French compromise was agreed creating an institution similar, but not identical, to the French *Commissaire du Gouvernement.*[5] The French delegation argued that the *Commissaires du Gouvernement* had assisted both in the development of the case-law of the *Conseil d'Etat* and more generally of *doctrine.*[6] A similar institution would do for the fledgling European Court what the *Commissaire du Gouvernment* had done for the *Conseil d'Etat.*

The Protocol on the Court of Justice annexed to the Treaty of Paris provided for two Advocates General to assist the Court.[7] The Convention on Certain Institutions Common to the European Communities of 1957 created a single institutional structure for the Coal and Steel Community and the newly created European Economic Community and Euratom. The Treaty of Paris was amended by this Convention so that from 1957 the Advocate General featured in the provisions of the three Treaties: the Treaty of Rome (1957) providing that 'The Court of Justice shall be assisted by two Advocates General'.[8] In a Community of six Member States and with the necessity of having an odd number of judges, a political

[4] M Darmon, 'The Role of the Advocate General at the European Court of Justice' in Shimon Shereet (ed), *The Role of Courts in Society* (1988) 427.

[5] See ibid and K Borgsmidt, 'The Advocate General at the European Court of Justice: A Comparative Study' (1988) 13 ELR 106. Advocate General Lagrange was part of the delegation negotiating the Treaty.

[6] Borgsmidt quotes the French delegation which participated in the Treaty negotiations as follows: 'Nul n'ignore le haut degré d'indépendence dont le corps des Commissaires du Gouvernement du Conseil d'Etat est traditionellement animé, ni l'importance du rôle que ces magistrats ont exercé et continuent d'exercer, tant dans le développement de la jurisprudence que dans le collaboration que la publicité de leurs conclusions permet d'assurer avec ce qu'on est convenu d'appeler "la doctrine". C'est avec la conviction qu'une telle institution procurera à la nouvelle Cour ces mêmes effets bienfaisants que nos partenaires ont accepté de la faire profiter des fruits d'une expérience essentiellement française'.

[7] D Ruiz-Jarabo Colomer and M Lopez Escudero, 'L'institution de l'avocat général a la Cour de Justice des Communautés européennes' in GC Rodriguez Iglesias, O Due, R Schingten and C Elsen (eds), *Mélanges en hommage à Fernand Schockweiler* (1999) 523.

[8] Art 222 EC (formerly Art 166).

compromise appears to have been reached that the additional judge would be Italian and the Advocates General French and German, thus ensuring that the 'big' Member States had equal representation in the Court.

The number of Advocates General has increased as the Community has enlarged.[9] In 1973 the number was increased to four with each of France, Germany, Italy and the UK, the four large Member States, nominating one of their nationals as Advocate General. In 1981, with the accession of Greece, the number was raised to five and then to six with the accession of Spain and Portugal in 1985. In 1995 the number was raised to eight (temporarily nine). The Treaty of Nice (2001) fixed the number of Advocates General at eight, although the Court can request the Council to increase the number.[10] Therefore, at the time of the most recent enlargement; in 2005, the number of Advocates General was not expanded.

The French origins of the institution have often been cited in studies of the role of the Advocate General.[11] However, some caution should be exercised in making such comparisons, as the specific role of the Advocate General in the context of the work of the European Court of Justice is not entirely functionally equivalent to the work of the *Commissaire du Gouvernement* in the *Conseil d'Etat*. There are both procedural and jurisdictional differences between them.[12] Thus, although it is true that the origins of the institution of Advocate General in the European Court of Justice are French and the first Advocate General, Maurice Lagrange, had himself been a *Commissaire du Governement* in the *Conseil d'Etat*, it would be wrong to assume that the Advocate General is a carbon copy of the French model. Fennelly, himself a former Advocate General, insists that, while there are similar offices in some of the civil law systems 'the truth is, however, that the Advocate General is *sui generis*. His role cannot be compared to any judicial or legal being in the common law system'.[13]

Appointment

The European Court of Justice today consists of 25 judges, one judge for each Member State, who are assisted by eight Advocates General. Judges and Advocates General rank equally in precedence according to their seniority in office.[14] The

[9] For full details see K Lenaerts, D Arts and I Maselis, *Procedural Law of the European Union* (2nd edn, 2006) 5.

[10] Art 222 reads: 'The Court of Justice shall be assisted by eight Advocates General. Should the Court of Justice so request, the Council, acting unanimously, may increase the number of Advocates General'.

[11] Borgsmidt (n 5 above); see also A Barav, 'Le Commissaire du Gouvernement Près le Conseil D'Etat Français et L'Avocat Général Près La Cour De Justice Des Communautés Européennes' (1974) Revue Internationale de Droit Comparé 809, and P Gori, 'L'Avocat Général A La Cour De Justice Des Communautés Européennes' (1976) Cahiers de Droit Européen 375.

[12] AA Dashwood, 'The Advocate General in the Court of Justice of the European Communities' (1982)2 LS 202. The procedural differences are discussed in ch 3.

[13] N Fennelly, 'Reflections of an Irish Advocate General' (1996) *Irish Journal of European Law* 5.

[14] Rules of Procedure of the Court of Justice of the European Communities, Art 6.

qualifications are the same for both judges and Advocates General. Article 223 EC provides:

> The judges and Advocates General of the Court of Justice shall be chosen from persons whose independence is beyond doubt and who possess the qualifications required for appointment to the highest judicial offices in their respective countries or who are jurisconsults of recognised competence.[15]

Like judges, the Advocates General are appointed for a renewable term of six years by common accord of the governments of the Member States. There is a partial replacement of Advocates General every three years.

The Statute of the Court of Justice makes clear that all of its conditions applying to the judges are also applicable to Advocates General. So, for example, an Advocate General is immune from legal proceedings. He is not allowed to hold political office or engage in any occupation (although the Council can give permission for them to take up certain positions, such as Honorary Professorships in Universities). An Advocate General can only be removed from office if, 'in the unanimous opinion of the judges and Advocates General of the Court, he no longer fulfils the requisite conditions or meets the obligations arising from his office'.[16]

The reference in the Treaty and the Statute of the Court emphasizes the individual who is appointed to a particular post. However, in reality, both judges and Advocates General are supported by a legal team. Each judge and Advocate General has a *Cabinet* composed of three legal secretaries whose function is to assist the judge or Advocate General in their work. Each *Cabinet* will work in different ways depending on the personality of the judge or Advocate General. In some instances the legal secretaries will produce successive drafts of the Preliminary Report of the Reporting Judge or the Opinion of the Advocate General. They will always be involved in researching the case, perhaps requesting the Court's information service to source academic writings and previous case-law.

Function—to assist the Court

Article 222 EC states that the eight Advocates General 'assist' the Court of Justice and in doing so it is their duty, 'acting with complete impartiality and independence, to make, in open court, reasoned submissions on cases brought before the Court of Justice'.[17] The Statute of the Court of Justice requires that judgments of the Court be reasoned.[18] Given that the Treaty emphasizes the task of legal reasoning as being the central duty of the Advocate General, it is not surprising that the Treaty equates the characteristics of judges and Advocates General in terms of their qualifications. Both judges and Advocates General are chosen 'from persons

[15] Art 223 EC (formerly Art 167).
[16] Art 6 (n 14 above).
[17] Art 222 EC (formerly Art 166).
[18] Statute of the Court of Justice, Art 36.

whose independence is beyond doubt and who possess the qualifications required for appointment to the highest judicial offices in their respective countries, or who are jurisconsults of recognised competence'.[19] The capacity for legal reasoning is the essential quality for both.

The function of the Advocate General has been described in different ways by different authors. Writing in 1962, Bebr stated that 'their function is similar to that of the *Commissaire du Gouvernement* at the *Conseil d'Etat* . . . his sole but vital function is to prepare and present publicly reasoned conclusions for the advice of the Court . . . although technically not legally binding, his conclusions may strongly influence the development of Community law'. [20] It must be stressed that the Opinions of the Advocate General are not legally binding at all, despite journalists mistakenly quoting them as being decisions of the Court. They are advisory only. As Brown and Kennedy state:

> He is a member of the Court. But that term is itself ambiguous, being sometimes restricted to the Judges alone, as in the first paragraph of Article 222 which provides that 'the Court of Justice shall be assisted by eight Advocates General'. This ambiguity may reflect a certain ambivalence, in the minds of the authors of the Treaties, about the role of the Advocate General: although a member of the Court, he acts as an independent adviser. However unlike his counterpart in the French *Conseil d'Etat*, the *Commissaire du Gouvernement*, he does not attend the Judges' deliberations . . . even in a consultative capacity.[21]

In the Court of Justice it is therefore clear, the judges decide cases but they have the benefit of the advice of the Advocate General before doing so.

In 1976 Lasok and Bridge described the function of the Advocate General in the following terms: 'their task is a three-fold one: to propose a solution to the case before the Court; to relate that proposed solution to the general pattern of existing case-law; and, if possible, to outline the probable future development of the case-law'.[22] Because the Advocate General proposes a solution, it has sometimes been stated that his Opinion is akin to a judgment of a court of first instance.[23] Hartley suggests that the Opinion could be seen as 'a judgment of first instance which is subject to instant and invariable appeal. It is, however, an appeal of a special nature, since the parties have no opportunity to comment on the Opinion before the Court begins its deliberations'.[24] Mégret takes a different, although related, view, stating that the Opinion of the Advocate General is particularly useful in a Court such as the Court of Justice from which there is no appeal. In these circumstances

[19] EC Treaty, Art 223 (formerly Art 167).

[20] G Bebr, *Judicial Control of the European Communities* (1962) 24.

[21] Brown and Kennedy *Brown & Jacobs: The Court of Justice of the European Communities* (2000) 64

[22] D Lasok and JW Bridge, *An Introduction to the Law and Institutions of the European Communities* (2nd edn, 1976) 159.

[23] JP Warner, 'Some Aspects of the European Court of Justice' (1976) Society of Public Teachers of Law 15, 18.

[24] TC Hartley, *The Foundations of European Community Law* (5th edn, 2003) 57. The significance of the parties not being able to respond to the Opinion of the Advocate General is discussed in ch 3.

the Opinion provides the Court with an independent view of the case which plays an important role in the preparation of the deliberations.[25] Judge David Edward warns against thinking, however, that the Opinion plays a decisive role. Writing about the deliberation, he says:

> It is often supposed that, once the Advocate General has delivered his Opinion, the Court has little more to do than to decide whether or not to follow the Opinion and the draft judgment accordingly. This is a complete misconception. Judge Grévisse described the deliberations at the 'heart of our work' . . . Apart from all other considerations, every judge must make up his own mind how the cases should be disposed of. He cannot do so until he has all the material for judgment including the Opinion of the Advocate General. The Opinion is therefore the *starting point* for the Court's deliberation even if, in many cases, the end result turns out to be the same.[26]

The Advocate General's Opinion is, or should be, written for the benefit of the Court according to the Treaty. However, it is also has a wider audience. It is published in the European Court Reports with the judgment, and is also published on the Court's website on the day it is delivered. Craig and de Búrca suggest that one function of the Opinion is to shed light on what are, sometimes, rather obscure judgments. They state: 'the style and content of the Advocate General's Opinion are virtually always more readable than those of the Court's judgments, and often shed light on the meaning of an obscure judgment'.[27] This wider function is also recognized by Arnull who writes: 'the Opinions of the Advocates General also have value for others concerned with the Court's activities, be they practising lawyers or academics or simply members of the general public. Being the product of a single mind, the Opinions often have a clarity and directness which judgments of the Court, essentially committee documents, may lack'.[28]

Independence

The Treaty stresses the importance of the independence of the Advocate General without defining that term. It must certainly include independence from the influence of any of the Member States. It should also include independence from any of the parties to a dispute. It has been stated that the Advocate General acts 'not as a legal representative of one of the parties but as a legal representative of the public interest'.[29] However, this statement suggests that the task of the Advocate General is to discern the 'public interest' in any case. No mention has been made, in any of the Opinions of the Advocates General studied in this book, of the public interest as a factor in their reasoning. A better formulation is that of Lasok and

[25] J Mégret, *Le Droit de la Communauté Economique Européenne*, vol 10 (1993) 32.
[26] D Edward, 'How the Court of Justice Works' (1995) ELR 539, 555.
[27] P Craig and G de Burca, *The Evolution of EU Law* (1999) 94.
[28] A Arnull, *The European Union and its Court of Justice* (1999) 9.
[29] D Chalmers, C Hadjiemmanuil, G Monti and A Tomkins, *European Union Law* (2006) 123.

Bridge, who state that Advocates General 'function only as the spokesmen of the law and justice in the context of the Treaties'.[30] The Court itself has stated that the Advocates General 'are not entrusted with the defence of any particular interest'.[31] It went on to say that the role played by the Advocate General is not part of the proceedings between the parties but is part of the procedure of the Court.

Independence might also mean independence from the legal order from which the Advocate General originates. This suggests that they should develop a comparative perspective on the law—namely, to see a question from the point of view of the Community legal order rather than from the point of view of national law. This is not to say that an Advocate General might not suggest a solution based on a principle derived from a national legal order—proportionality and the German legal order for example—but that he should never take the position that a case must be answered in a particular way because that is what would happen 'back home'. It seems that the Advocates General are conscious of this sense of their independence without perhaps articulating it.

Studying the Advocate General—Methodology

Several authors have pointed to the difficulties inherent in assessing the contribution of the Advocate General to the work of the Court or to the development of principles of Community law. For example, Tridimas discusses the criteria to be used in assessing the influence of the Advocate General on the Court.[32] It is possible to examine the number of cases in a given period in which the Court followed the Opinion of the Advocate General.[33] He points out that this is a method liable to convey a fallacious understanding of the task which the Advocate General is required to perform, since the task of the Advocate General is not to give judgment but to assist the Court in reaching judgment. He suggests that it is not possible to measure how far a judgment has been followed. He also suggests that it might be possible to identify cases which mark major developments, including cases where the Court overrules its previous case-law, and to see whether, in these cases, the Court followed the Opinion of the Advocate General. However, the same problem arises: how can the contribution of the Advocate General be separated from the other influences that might be brought to bear on the Court in reaching its decision? Tridimas concludes that the Opinions of the Advocate General should be seen as an invisible influence on the Court. He suggests that one of the most important aspects of the work of the Advocate General is the explanatory value of the Opinion and that one of the most important functions of

[30] Lasok and Bridge (n 22 above) 159.
[31] Case C-17/98 *Emesa Sugar (Free Zone) NV v Aruba*, Order of the Court of 4 February 2000.
[32] T Tridimas 'The Role of the Advocate General in the Development of Community Law: Some Reflections' (1997) 34 CML Rev1349.
[33] Ibid, 1363.

the Advocate General is to consider the legal principles independently of the facts.[34]

Arnull also suggests that it is difficult to gauge empirically the influence of the Advocate General on the development of the case-law of the Court.[35] The deliberations of the Court are held in closed session and a single collective judgment is given. No dissenting judgments are given. In the past, the Court rarely made reference to the Opinion of the Advocate General (although that is now done more frequently). Arnull suggests that all these factors tend to conceal the influence of the Advocate General in any particular case.

The methodology chosen in this book is based on case-studies. It would be impossible to analyse all the Opinions of all the Advocates General in a single work without reducing the study to a very superficial level. We have chosen to pursue two types of case-study. In chapters 4, 5, 6 and 7, our study of selected Advocates General allows us to examine in some depth the engagement of Advocates General Lagrange, van Gerven, Warner and Jacobs with the Court, and with the Opinions of other Advocates General who have been involved in the selected area of law, in order to appreciate the influence, if any, of the Advocate General on the work of the Court. How far did these Advocates General assist the Court in its task of ensuring that in the interpretation and application of the Treaty the law is observed? This method also allows us to test some assertions about particular Advocates General. For example, Tridimas asserts that Advocate General van Gerven played a major role in developing sex discrimination law,[36] although no study of van Gerven's contribution in this area of law has been done to date. It also provides an opportunity to see how very different people occupying the same role might work in different ways and with different emphases.

The second set of case-studies in chapters 8, 9 and 10 are longitudinal studies insofar as they take a concept of Community law and trace its development through the prism of the Opinions of the Advocates General who have been involved in the key cases. It is not possible to discuss all the cases relating to a particular concept and therefore some choice has been exercised. These chapters allow us to make comparisons between the approaches of different Advocates General and to assess if some have had more influence on the development of Community law than others, or if they have provided more assistance to the Court. The benefit of this approach is that we are more clearly focused on the outcome of the Court's reasoning.

For both types of case studies we have used a well recognized research technique known as purposive sampling. '[t]his term is applied to those situations where the researcher already knows something about the specific people or events and

[34] Tridimas (n 32 above) is referring to the role of the Advocate General in the Court of Justice rather than the Court of First Instance where the role of the Judge acting as Advocate General (see ch 2) might be to establish the facts in a case.

[35] Arnull (n 28 above) 7.

[36] Tridimas (n 32 above).

deliberately selects particular ones because they are seen as instances that are likely to produce the most valuable data'.[37] Both the choice of Advocates General and the choice of concepts reflect our own expertise and knowledge in specific areas of Community law and our knowledge of the workings of the Court. Given the enormous potential research field this method is more likely to generate interesting and provocative data. The technique of triangulation, looking at a topic from different perspectives using different methods, is a clearly accepted research technique, and is also pragmatic given the methodological difficulties cited by writers such as Tridimas and Arnull. It is a method that might be replicated by other scholars since the literature on the Advocate General is minimal.

Choice of Advocates General

Advocate General Maurice Lagrange (Chapter 4) was chosen for analysis because he was the first appointed Advocate General. In addition he has been credited with defining the role based on his own experience as *Commissaire du Gouvernement* in the French *Conseil d'Etat*.[38] Thus Lagrange was pivotal in the shaping of the role and function of the Advocate General during the early stages in the creation of the Community's legal order. In particular, he delivered Opinions in cases where the foundations of this new legal order were established. These Opinions covered such fundamental questions as the methods of interpretation to be adopted, the extent of the *locus standi* of non-privileged applicants and the relationship between Community law and national law.

Advocate General Walter van Gerven is credited with making a major impact on sex discrimination law.[39] Chapter 5 tests this assertion by examining the cases in which he was involved. Sex discrimination law is an area where Burrows has some knowledge and expertise, an essential feature of the technique of purposive sampling. Van Gerven is the only one of our sample to come from a small Member State, although it is unlikely that that factor influenced his work at all. Like Lagrange he came to the Court from a civil law background, although he has a deep knowledge of the common law tradition and is respectful of both traditions. With a business background and a distinguished academic career, a study of his approach provides the opportunity to see how someone without a practitioner or judicial background approaches the task of assisting the Court.

There are two reasons why the Opinions of Advocate General Francis Jacobs have been chosen for analysis (chapter 6). First, Advocate General Jacobs was the second longest serving Advocate General, the longest was Advocate General Roemer. However, of these two Advocates General, only Jacobs was involved in

[37] M Denscombe, *The Good Research Guide for Small-scale Social Research Projects* (2000) 15.

[38] SJ Kenney, 'The Members of the Court of Justice of the European Communities' (1998) 5 Columbia Journal of European Law 112.

[39] Tridimas (n 32 above) at 1349.

cases relating to the three concepts discussed in chapters 8, 9 and 10. Second, during his period in office, fundamental changes occurred in the development of the Community's legal order and in the structure of the European Court of Justice. The increase of EC/EU competences, the establishment of the principle of State liability and the introduction of Community property rights, namely the Community Trade Mark and the Community Design Right, are clear examples of the former.

Jacobs' Opinions are widely read and influential, particularly in academic writings. His Opinions on some issues, such as those concerning the horizontal direct effect of directives and the EC Treaty conditions for establishing *locus standi* of individuals to challenge EU measures before the European Court of Justice, may not have been followed by the European Court of Justice but they have, nevertheless, given rise to polemical debates amongst practitioners and academics throughout Europe and beyond.

Although there are several areas of Community law on which Jacobs delivered significant Opinions, those on intellectual property rights have been selected for several reasons. First, these are private property rights which were deeply embedded in the legal systems of the original six Member States. The drafters of the EC Treaty foresaw conflicts between national laws protecting these rights and the fundamental principle of free movement of goods, but they failed to foresee the huge importance of these rights, not only for the individuals concerned, but also for the Community as a powerful market operating globally. As private property rights they are used by their owners ('exercised') in a manner which may be incompatible with two fundamental EC market rules: EC competition rules and EC free movement of goods rules. These rules are fundamental to the achievement of an integrated and competitive European market. Second, it is in the area of intellectual property rights that the EU created the first EU wide private rights by adopting a Community Trade Mark Regulation and a Design Right Regulation. A trade mark may now be obtained for the whole territory of the European Economic Area comprising the 25 EU Member States as well as Iceland, Liechtenstein and Norway. Disputes arising as to the grant of a Community trade mark are resolved by the Court of First Instance (CFI) with a right of appeal on law to the European Court of Justice. In parallel, the national courts are dealing with similar issues concerning the grant and the infringement of similar rights granted by their national legislation. The national courts, however, are dealing with national legislation, which has been enacted to implement the Trade Mark Directive, and the Design Right Directive adopted by the Community in order to harmonize national laws on the granting of these rights and on infringement actions. Where doubts arise in national litigation as to the interpretation or application of national law that was enacted to implement Community directives, the national judge may find it necessary to refer to the European Court of Justice questions of interpretation of the directives. The consequence is that there are a considerable number of cases coming before the European Court of Justice, either on appeal from the Court of First Instance on matters concerning the Trade Mark Regulation, or on preliminary references from national courts on questions of interpretation of the Trade Mark Directive. In both cases the European Court of Justice considers issues based on the same wording contained in different legislative measures. Jacobs has delivered a large number of Opinions in these cases which will be considered in chapter 6.

Jean-Pierre Warner was the first Advocate General appointed from a common law tradition, which made studying his Opinions an interesting excercise in studying how a common law trained lawyer reacted to the procedures and traditions of a civil law system (chapter 7). In addition, Warner held office during the 1970s, a period in the history of the Community when the European Court of Justice (and not the Community legislators) was active in promoting the development of the common market by delivering judgments considered by commentators as law-making rather than interpreting the law. The decision to narrow the research to the Opinions he delivered in cases involving issues on the implementation of the EC competition rules was based on a number of factors, not least the personal research interest of the author, a key factor in purposive sampling.

The EC competition rules are very much a creature of Community law, created and developed to meet the needs of the European market. At the time of the establishment of the common market, only Germany had embryonic national competition legislation.[40] It is true that the UK had restrictive practices legislation when it acceded to the Community, but that legislation was largely benign. The United States of America, with its long standing tradition of antitrust law,[41] had considerable influence in Europe after the end of the Second World War, and the US antitrust principles had been the role model for the German competition regime. However, the European market, unlike the US market, was fragmented and in bad shape. Thus the central objective of the founding fathers was the integration of the national markets of the Member States. The competition rules that were adopted for the European market reflected this objective and were interpreted by the European Court of Justice in that context. The consequence of this scenario is twofold. First, in the interpretation and application of the EC competition rules the key issues to come before the European Court of Justice did not involve conflicts with national legal orders but with creating a coherent body of law that was the product of EC legislation and European Court of Justice case-law. Second, the grant of investigative and decision-making powers to the European Commission brought natural and legal persons into direct contact with the Community's legal order and its procedures. Where the Commission adopts a decision prohibiting a practice incompatible with the EC competition rules, the addressee of that decision has direct access to the European Court of Justice to seek annulment of the decision or a reduction on the fine imposed. Warner was trained and practised in a

[40] *Gesetz gegen Wettbewerbsbeschränkungen* 1957.
[41] Sherman Act and Clayton Act.

common law system where advocacy is a well known feature of court proceedings, with judges asking questions of the lawyers appearing before them. Strict rules of evidence and procedure have been developed to protect the right of defence. Thus the Opinions of Warner were examined to find out what kind of influence he may have had on these competition law cases.

Choice of concepts

The selection of some key principles/concepts and the analysis of their origins enable us to understand how Community law has developed, sometimes incrementally and sometimes dramatically and suddenly. In this part of the book we examine whether we can attribute to that development the contributions of Advocates General in the Court.

It has been said that the cases which established the principle of direct effect, discussed in chapter 8, are some of the most important and revolutionary cases decided by the Court.[42] The concept of direct effect of Community law was developed and refined over a number of years and there are, to this day, unanswered questions as to its full scope and meaning. In chapter 8, the discussion is of key cases which show the kinds of problems that have been placed before the Court as the implications of the Court's case-law have become apparent to the judges in the national courts. Direct effect is of primary concern to national courts and tribunals, to individuals and undertakings, as it allows natural or legal persons to invoke provisions of Community law in these national courts. It is a concept that is central to the European project. Questions concerning direct effect have been referred to the Court from the 1960s to the present day, and this provides an opportunity to examine the contribution of a number of Advocates General over what is effectively the whole period of existence of the European Union.

This case-study also provides the opportunity to demonstrate the dialogue between the Advocates General and the Court on some very difficult constitutional issues. Vranken suggests that 'a special dialogue takes place between the Court and the Advocate General'.[43] We do not share with him, however, his conclusion that the Court should acknowledge in each case the extent to which the Court relies on his submissions in coming to its decision, and neither do we see the purpose in trying to assess whether an Opinion has more 'value' than a judgment, given the different purpose of both as outlined above. Nevertheless, the concept of the dialogic relationship is an important one and is best demonstrated over time. Choosing a concept such as direct effect provides the opportunity to follow the dialogue and to see where the Court and the Advocates General diverge

[42] Chalmers (n 29 above) at 365.

[43] M Vranken, 'Role of the Advocate General in the Law-Making Process of the European Community' (1996) 25 Anglo-American Law Review 39, 40.

and converge. Bengoetxea suggests that some cases can be read as a chain novel in the sense that the next case continues the story started in the previous case. In this process he suggests that the Court is 'reshaping the law of the Treaties and re-interpreting its own case-law in the best possible light'.[44] To study this phenomenon, it is important to see the twists and turns in the plot. Direct effect provides a useful example of this chain novel concept as there have been so many developments in the concept over time. From the point of view of a study of the Advocate General, without perhaps stretching the analogy too far: can he be seen as the 'ghost writer', assisting the Court by suggesting plots and sub-plots?

There are several legal and practical reasons why the principle of State liability (chapter 9) has been selected for an analysis of Advocates General's Opinions. First, the principle of State liability for infringements of Community law gained prominence in the Community's legal system only in the 1990s when the Community's legal order was already well established. In addition, a flurry of European Court of Justice preliminary rulings was delivered in a relatively short period, and this defined and refined the scope of the cause of action very quickly. This is rather unusual in the historical development of the Community's legal order; it is a fact that most, if not all, of the fundamental principles of Community law have been established in preliminary rulings. However, the very nature of the preliminary ruling procedure impedes the coherent development of law. The European Court of Justice is totally dependent on the national courts to refer questions of interpretation to it. As the procedure was devised as a mechanism for seeking interpretation and validity of Community law, the European Court of Justice is presented with specific questions requiring an interpretative answer, which are devised by national courts in the context of the litigation they have before them. The national courts are not concerned with the development of Community law. Rather, they require an answer to a question of law which they have no competence to interpret. Having received the ruling on Community law, the national judges' concern is to apply the ruling and reach a judgment on the case. The European Court of Justice is often subject to criticism for not determining precisely the scope, nature and limits of the rulings it delivers, yet it is the very mechanism itself which prevents this, requiring simply that the Court respond directly to specific questions.

Second, in establishing the principle of State liability the Court had to consider, in particular, the relationship between Community law and the national legal systems of the Member States. This was particularly evident in determining the substantive and procedural conditions which are sufficient for the Member States, found to be in breach of their Treaty obligations, to be required to make reparation for the resulting loss or damage. Needless to say, this exercise had to be undertaken within a wider context, namely ensuring that the cohesion of the operation of the Community's legal system is maintained.

[44] J Bengoetxea, *The Legal Reasoning of the European Court of Justice* (1993) 105.

Third, State liability for infringements of Community law is now well established in the Community's legal system. Although not often relied on by EU citizens and businesses, the mere existence of this cause of action is a powerful deterrent for the governments of the Member States. The potential financial consequences for governments where such liability is affirmed could be very costly indeed. The governments of the Member States are fully conscious of the importance of acting with care when the Member States exercise their legislative, executive and judiciary functions in any area of Community competence. It is also of increasing importance in view of Article 47 of the Charter of Fundamental Rights, and the continuing restricted standing for natural and legal persons under Article 230(4) EC.[45]

The concept of citizenship is a relatively new concept in Community law. The provisions on citizenship were inserted into the Treaty of Rome (1957) by the Treaty of Maastricht (1992). It could be argued that, because of the intensely political nature of the concept, the Court was faced with two choices as to their interpretation. Articles 17 and 18 EC[46] could be read as aspirational political objectives, devoid of legal content except to the extent of their literal interpretation. Alternatively, they could be read as a means of deepening political integration during a decade and more where the European projected is contested—both at the level of political elites and at grass-roots citizen level; witness the negative results in the French and Dutch referenda on the Constitutional Treaty. In retrospect we know that the Court has not read these provisions as being devoid of legal content but has interpreted them liberally so as to flesh out the concept of the rights of citizens in the EU. Citizenship, therefore, provides a test case for determining whether the teleological or purposive method of interpretation, which has become a characteristic of many of the Court's judgments, is a characteristic shared by the Advocates General. However, it could be argued that these cases have shown the Court as a deeply politicized institution and that, although its judgments are based on an expansive and constructivist interpretation of Treaty provisions, and, as such, are still rooted in the law, it has shown a determination to confront the governments of the Member States. In this context, a case-study of the contribution of the Advocate General provides an insight as to the extent of the politicization of the Advocate General. Have the Advocates General been complicit in the constructivist interpretation of Articles 17 and 18? If so, can it be said that the institution of Advocate General is a political role rather more than has been previously suggested? Was it the Court, in the sense of the judges, who decided to fill out the concept of citizenship or was it the Advocates General?

[45] Art 230(4) EC (formerly Art 173).
[46] Arts 17 and 18 EC (formerly Arts 8 and 8a respectively).

Structure

Although chapters 4–10 consist of case-studies, and they can be read as such, we have structured the book as a self standing work. The first part provides an overview of the role and function of the Advocate General in the context of proceedings both in the European Court of Justice and in the Court of First Instance. The second part examines the contribution of four Advocates General, chosen for the reasons listed above. The final part focuses on three important concepts of Community law and traces their development, in each case examining the contribution of the relevant Advocates General to the development of these three principles (chapters 8–10). In the conclusions we reflect on the contribution and influence of the Advocate General in shaping the Community's legal order and make some observations on the appropriate role of the Advocate General as a member of a Court with 25 or more judges.

Part I

The Advocate General as a Member of the ECJ

2

The place of the Advocate General in the procedure of the European Community Courts

Introduction

When Advocates General Lagrange and Roemer took up office as the first Advocates General in December 1952 and February 1953 respectively, Article 165 (EEC) provided that the Court of Justice of the European Communities, composed of seven judges at that time, should normally sit in plenary session. It was required to sit in plenary session when it heard cases brought by a Member State or one of the institutions and for preliminary references. The Court could form chambers of three or five judges to undertake preparatory enquiries or to adjudicate in certain categories of cases. Originally there were only two Chambers of the Court and the Advocates General were assigned one each to these Chambers. When the number of Advocates General was increased to four, two were assigned to each of the chambers.[1] The Advocate General was required to give an Opinion in each case before the Court.

Nowadays the judicial architecture of the European Union is more complex. 'The institution known as the "Court of Justice" consists at present of three Courts, the Court of Justice, the Court of First Instance and the European Union Civil Service Tribunal'.[2] In future new specialized panels may be created. There is thus a three tier system of Community courts.[3] In addition the European Free Trade Area (EFTA) Court was created in parallel to the Community courts. There is no role envisaged for an Advocate General in either the specialized judicial panels or in the EFTA Court.[4] Within the Court of First Instance one of the judges

[1] J Usher, *European Court Practice* (1983) 180.

[2] K Lenaerts, D Arts and I Maselis, *Procedural Law of the European Union* (2nd edn, 2006) 4.

[3] N Lavranos, 'The new specialised courts within the European judicial system' (2005) 30 ELR 261.

[4] S Norberg, 'The EFTA Court' in R Plender (ed), *European Courts Practice and Precedents* (1997) 3–26. Norberg explains the decision not to appoint an Advocate General to the EFTA Court in the following terms: 'The EFTA Court has no Advocates General. For various reasons, the EFTA States, in none of which such a function exists at a national level, decided not to equip the EFTA Court with any Advocates General'. It seems that the Scandinavian countries did not see the role

may be designated to act as Advocate General and therefore there are no separate Advocates General in that Court: the Advocates General assist only the Court of Justice.

It was originally envisaged that an Advocate General would give an Opinion in all cases before the Court. However during the lead-up to the Intergovernmental Conference (IGC) before the ratification of the Treaty of Amsterdam (1997) it was proposed to reduce the Advocate General's involvement in court proceedings.[5] The Reflexion Group on the Future of the Judicial System of the Communities concluded that the Nice IGC should consider whether it was necessary that each and every case before the Court of Justice should be submitted to the analysis of an Advocate General.[6] At that time concerns were being expressed as to the capacity of the Court to handle the increasing workload brought about by a combination of an expanded jurisdiction and the presumed imminent enlargement of the European Union. The Court itself had submitted two reports for the IGC[7] but in neither of these did the Court suggest any amendment to the role of the Advocate General, leading Rasmussen to believe that the Court had turned its face against the possibility of reform.

The debate on the European judicial architecture at the time of the Nice IGC centred on the ways in which to manage the workload of the Court and to reduce the time it took for the Court to give judgment. The increase in volume of the caseload had been astonishing. In 1975, 130 cases had been lodged before the Court, while in 1980, 279 cases were lodged. In 1988, the year it was decided to establish the Court of First Instance, 385 cases were lodged. In 1999, 543 cases were lodged with the Court of Justice and 384 with the Court of First Instance. The time taken to provide a preliminary ruling had increased from six months in 1975 to 17 months in 1988 and was 23.1 months in 1999. The Court complained that there was now a structural imbalance between the volume of incoming cases and the capacity of the Court to dispose of these. The problems related partly to procedures in the Court itself, and some steps were taken to ameliorate this by introducing, for example, an expedited procedure. Others were caused by the increasing problem of translation; in 1998, 325,000 pages of documents were required to be translated, and within three years that figure had risen to 450,000.

The Report of the Reflexion Group suggested that one way of reducing administrative and translation costs was to involve the Advocate General only in important cases, which were defined as: those presenting new points of law, those where some modification of the case-law of the Court might be necessary, or complex

of Advocate General as being necessary. There is certainly no tradition of an equivalent post in the Scandinavian countries.

[5] H Rasmussen, 'Remedying the Crumbling EC Judicial System' in 37 CML Rev 5, 1071–1112.

[6] *Report of the Reflexion Group on the Future of the Judicial System of the Communities*, 7 February, 2000.

[7] *The Future of the Judicial System of the EU (Proposal and Reflections)*, May 1999 and the *Contribution by the Court of Justice and the Court of First Instance to the IGC*.

cases where it was essential to ensure that the Court had not overlooked some significant legal point or argument. The President of the Court, the first Advocate General and the Reporting Judge should decide on whether to proceed without the benefit of an Opinion of the Advocate General. Rasmussen argued that proceedings in the Court could be shortened by between one and three months if the Court were to decide to hear the Advocate General in half the cases or less. According to Ramsey, by the time the Heads of State met in Nice there was 'almost unanimous agreement that it should not be compulsory for Advocates General to intervene in all cases before the European Court of Justice'.[8] Ramsey opposed this consensus, however, arguing that the nature of the single judgment given by the Court with no dissenting opinions and with only sparse reasoning meant that the Opinion of the Advocate General was helpful in understanding the case-law of the Court.

The solution chosen at Nice was to increase the number of judges to ensure that there would be one judge per Member State but to make no increase in the number of Advocates General. However, at the request of Court of Justice, the Council, acting unanimously, may increase the number of Advocates General. Thus the number of Advocates General was to remain at eight (Art 222 EC). A more radical change is found in the second paragraph of Article 222 EC which specifies the duties of the Advocate General. With the Nice amendments it now reads: 'It shall be the duty of the Advocate General, acting with complete impartiality and independence, to make, in open court, reasoned submissions on cases which, in accordance with the Statute of the Court of Justice, require his involvement'. Thus the Advocate General is no longer required to make a submission in every case before the European Court of Justice but only in those cases which require his involvement. The Statute of the Court was subsequently amended and a new Article 20 replaces former Article 18. It reads: 'Where it considers that the case raises no new point of law, the Court may decide, after hearing the Advocate General, that the case shall be determined without a submission from the Advocate General'.

It is difficult to determine in advance whether a case will raise a new point of law. The Rules of Procedure, however, ensure that both the Reporting Judge and the Advocate General assigned to the case will be involved in coming to that decision. Article 44(2) of the Rules of Procedure specifies that the Reporting Judge shall recommend in his Preliminary Report, whether to dispense with an Opinion of the Advocate General and the Court shall decide, after hearing the Advocate General, what action to take.

The Treaty of Nice came into force on 1 February 2003 and the amendments to the Statute and the Rules of Procedure shortly after. It is interesting to note the type of cases where the Court decided to proceed to judgment without an Opinion. For example, in the period from 22 June 2003 to 22 August 2004, the

[8] L Ramsey, 'Reforming the European Courts at the IGC' (2000) Juridical Review 213.

Court gave judgment without an Opinion of the Advocate General in some 58 cases. Of these, 45 cases were infringement proceedings against a Member State. Four were cases brought under Article 238 EC for an interpretation of an arbitration clause in contracts concluded by the Commission with companies pursuant to various European programmes. Four were requests for preliminary rulings regarding the interpretation of the Community Customs Code, for example on the definition of the term 'pen case'. Two were requests for preliminary rulings where the Court applied its previous case law on the direct effect of international agreements and on legitimate expectations, whilst two others were on the interpretation of specific words or phrases in Community legislation, for example, the meaning of the term 'commercial navigation'. Finally, one case was a reference under the Brussels Convention (1968) and related to an interpretation of 'matters relating to a contract'; a term which the Court had already interpreted on a number of occasions and therefore the Court applied its previous case-law.

Procedure in the European Court of Justice

The Treaty establishing the European Community provides that the Statute of the Court of Justice 'is laid down in a separate Protocol'.[9] The basic framework of the Statute was agreed in 1957, although there have been amendments to take into account the enlargement of the Community and the decision to establish a Court of First Instance. The Statute sets out the rules governing the judges and the Advocates General (Title I), organization of the Court (Title II), procedure (Title III) and the Court of First Instance (Title IV). The Court of Justice may adopt its own Rules of Procedure but these must be approved unanimously by the Council. Procedural rules are therefore governed both by the Statute and by the Rules of Procedure of the European Court of Justice.

The key procedural rule in the Statute is contained in Article 20, which stipulates that procedure before the Court consists of two parts, the written procedure and the oral procedure.[10] A third stage in the process is the deliberations by the judges. Only the judges participate in the deliberations. The Statute requires that these 'shall be and shall remain secret'.[11] The secrecy of the deliberations is underlined by Article 2, which requires each judge to take an oath in open court that he or she will preserve the secrecy of the deliberations. The involvement of the Advocate General is therefore limited, in the direct or active sense, to the written and oral procedures.

[9] EC Treaty, Art 245 (formerly Art 188). For the background to procedural issues see J Schwarze, 'The Origin of the European Courts' Statutes and Rules of Procedure' in R Plender (ed), *European Courts Practice and Precedents* (1997).

[10] EC Treaty, Protocol on the Statute of the Court of Justice, Title III.

[11] Ibid, Title III, Art 35.

Stage 1: The written procedure

Direct actions

Once an application initiating proceedings has been lodged with the Registrar, the President of the Court assigns it to a Chamber and designates one of the judges from that chamber as Reporting Judge.[12] As soon as this has happened, the First Advocate General assigns the case to one of the Advocates General or to himself.[13] There are no hard or fast rules as to how the First Advocate General allocates cases but there are certain conventions that are followed.[14] An Advocate General is never allotted a case where the Member State of which he is a national is directly involved in the case as a party. This is to preserve his independence and impartiality so that he cannot become subject to political pressure. The second convention is that the Reporting Judge and the Advocate General would not normally be of the same nationality, thus ensuring that a case is examined from the perspective of at least two individuals trained in different jurisdictions.[15] The third convention is that the First Advocate General distributes cases both by subject matter and type of action across his colleagues. In this way the Advocate General does not become a specialist although, as we will see from the studies of the Advocates General in this book, certain Advocates General do develop a specialist knowledge of a particular subject area. However, distributing the work across a variety of cases and types of action ensures that different voices can be heard and different approaches tested. Advocate General Léger is adamant on the point that the creative nature of the court benefits from 'du plus grand nombre d'avis et de réflexions de nature à l'aider a mener à son terme un delibéré'.[16] Finally, of course, the First Advocate General must ensure an equitable work-load.

In the case of a direct action an applicant must specify in writing the subject matter of the proceedings, a summary of the pleas in law and the nature of any evidence in support of the application.[17] The defendant in return must lodge a defence stating the arguments of fact and law relied on and the nature of any evidence submitted.[18] The application may be supplemented by a reply from the applicant and a rejoinder by the defendant.[19] After all these documents have been lodged the written procedure comes to an end.

Both the Reporting Judge and the Advocate General will examine the application and the defence, including the pleas in law, the facts and the evidence submitted.

[12] Court of Justice Rules of Procedure [1991] OJ L176/7, Title III, Art 9(2).

[13] Ibid, Art 10(2).

[14] This and what follows is taken from P Léger, 'De la Nature de l'Avocat Général à la Cour de Justice des Communautés Européennes' in Mélanges offerts au Professeur Jean-Claude Soyer (Librairie générale de droit et de jurisprudence). See also A Dashwood, 'The Advocate General in the Court of Justice of the European Communities' (1982) 2 LS 202.

[15] Information from the (then) First Advocate General Fennelly in an interview at the European Court of Justice, April 2000.

[16] Leger (n 14 above) at 6.

[17] Court of Justice Rules of Procedure (n 12 above), Art 38(1).

[18] Ibid, Art 40.

[19] Ibid, Art 41.

The Advocate General will consider at this stage any procedural issues but his key task is to read through the dossier and to begin the background research for his Opinion. The Reporting Judge will compile his Preliminary Report. Judge David Edward gives some indication of what is included in the Preliminary Report when he notes that it is a purely internal document designed to 'tell the other members of the Court what the case is about'. [20] It makes recommendations as to how the case should be dealt with. Edward provides an insight for the outsider into the form of the Preliminary Report: 'normally, after a brief introduction which seeks to encapsulate the point of the case, the Report summarizes the legal and factual background and the submissions of the parties and concludes with the personal observations and recommendations of the *Rapporteur*'. He adds that, in the past, some Reporting Judges offered a fairly full analysis but time constraints now mean that judges do not have the luxury of either writing or reading long reports. Léger also gives an indication of the content of the Preliminary Report: he states, 'Ce rapport décrit l'objet du recours, les dispositions normatives nationales et communautaires pertinentes, fait la synthèse des arguments des parties principales ainsi que des observations des parties intervenantes et propose la formation de jugement qui convient ainsi que, le cas échéant, des mesures d'instruction complémentaires'.[21]

Although it is not possible to verify this as an outsider, it is clear that the Preliminary Report must also indicate whether the parties are in agreement as to the facts of the case. Where facts are in dispute, or where they are unclear, the Reporting Judge can recommend that preparatory inquiries be undertaken. In the absence of such inquiries it would seem that the Preliminary Report sets out those facts deemed to be proved for legal purposes.

The Preliminary Report 'is intended for the administrative meeting of the Court of Justice (the Judges, the Advocates General and the Registrar) . . . where necessary, it proposes measures of organization of procedure or measures of inquiry'.[22] Judge David Edward gives a glimpse of these Tuesday evening meetings. He considers that the most important decision to be made in the General meeting is 'whether the case should be dealt with by the whole Court, a *petit plenum*, a chamber of five or a chamber of three'.[23] Not surprisingly, given the volume of cases, the Court prefers to refer cases to chambers, and Edward explains the factors that determine its decision. If the point at issue is covered by existing case-law or where it concerns the interpretation of highly technical rules it will be referred to a chamber of three judges. More difficult cases raising issues of principle but which are not likely to break new ground go to chambers of five. Ground-breaking cases go to the Grand Chamber and the Court, it seems, will prefer to hear a case in the Grand Chamber if there is any suggestion that a chamber would

[20] D Edward, 'How the Court of Justice Works' (1995) ELR 535 at 552.

[21] Léger (n 14 above) at 6. [22] Lenaerts (n 2 above) at 551.

[23] Edward (n 20 above) at 552. Edward was writing in 1995. Nowadays the Court routinely sits in Chambers of three or five. The Grand Chamber of 13 judges sits when the Court considers that a particular case raises an important legal issue or in certain cases specified in the statute. The Full Court sits very rarely and may decide a case if 15 judges are present.

be unable to decide the matter. It is the Reporting Judge who recommends the formation of the Court to hear the case. The Court makes its decision on such procedural matters after hearing the Advocate General. The Reporting Judge may recommend that the oral procedure may be dispensed with. In this case the Court, after hearing from the Advocate General, and with the express consent of the parties, may decide to go straight to deliberations.

In the view of some Advocates General, their involvement in the weekly administrative meetings ensures their full participation in the management of cases before the Court. For example, Advocate General Ruiz-Jarabo Colomer equates the role of the Advocate General and the Reporting Judge in procedural matters.[24] He explains the involvement of the Advocate General in these procedural questions as being active involvement ('l'avocat général intervient activement'). Advocate General Léger also stresses the role played by the Advocate General throughout this phase. He states that the consultation with the Advocate General leads to him being involved in the successive drafts prepared by the Reporting Judge and involvement in the general meetings ensures that the Advocate General has an equal say with the judges as to the definition of the relevant legal issues in the case ('la même voix déliberative pour prendre des décisions de mise en état des affaires sur le point d'être jugé').[25] Both the need for and the explanation of this collective and iterative approach are suggested by Advocate General Jacobs. The collective approach reflects 'the collegiate character of the Court' in which much of the work is done by committee.[26]

The Advocate General is also entitled to participate in any preparatory enquiries, the function of these being to establish the facts. Various measures of inquiry may be adopted, such as requesting information and documents, oral testimony or the commissioning of an expert's report but, whatever measures of inquiry are adopted, the Advocate General participates in them.[27] The Court is entitled to issue an Order requiring certain facts to be proved by witnesses. In this case the Court may summon a witness on its own motion, by an application of one of the parties or at the instance of the Advocate General.[28] The Advocate General has the same right to put questions to the witness as the judges. The participation of the Advocate General in preparatory inquiries gives him a key role in establishing the relevant facts of any case.

Preliminary references

The preliminary reference procedure commences with the receipt by the Court of an Order for Reference from a national court setting out the questions on which it

[24] D Ruiz-Jarabo Colomer, 'L'institution de l'Avocat Général à la Cour de Justice des Communautés Européennes' in G C R Iglesias, O Due, E Schintgen, and C Elsen (eds), *Mélanges en hommage à Fernand Schockweiler* (1999) 523, 530.

[25] Léger (n 14 above) at 8.

[26] F Jacobs, 'Advocates General and Judges in the European Court of Justice: Some Personal Reflections' in D O'Keefe and M Andenas (eds), *Liber Amicorum for Lord Slynn: Judicial Review in European Law*, vol 1, 17 at 23 (2000).

[27] Court of Justice Rules of Procedure (n 12 above), Art 45.

[28] Court of Justice Rules of Procedure (n 12 above), Art 47.

wishes the European Court to rule.[29] A preliminary reference is notified to all the Member States and the Commission as well as to the parties in the case, all of whom are invited to submit statements or observations on the issues raised in the case. Depending on the issues raised, the European Parliament, the Council or the European Central Bank might also be asked to submit observations or statements. The non-EU Member States of the European Economic Area are also notified, as is the EFTA Surveillance Authority and, where one of the fields of application of the EEA Agreement is concerned, they are invited to submit observations or statements. In similar vein, non-EU parties to international agreements concluded between the EU and third States are invited to submit observations if the subject matter of the reference arises from the terms of the agreement. The Court may also request an expert opinion.[30] There is no exchange of pleadings under this procedure since the 'preliminary ruling procedure is not, formally speaking, a dispute between "parties" '.[31] The Advocate General and the Reporting Judge will be furnished with all the documentation relating to the case once they have been assigned in the manner described above. On the basis of these documents the Reporting Judge will draw up his preliminary report. The procedures then continue in the same way for preliminary rulings as for direct actions.

Stage 2: The oral procedure

The oral procedure will normally take place a few weeks after the General Meeting of the Court where the Reporting Judge's Preliminary Report has been discussed or after completion of any preliminary enquiries. The parties will have received the Report for the Hearing prepared by the Reporting Judge. Immediately prior to the oral hearing, the Reporting Judge and the Advocate General have the opportunity to speak with the lawyers and inform them of the arguments that they would like to hear developed.[32] At this meeting the President takes a roll-call and checks how long each party is planning to speak. He then asks the Reporting Judge and the Advocate General whether there are particular points they wish to raise. Occasionally the Court convenes a separate pre-hearing meeting in particularly complex cases in order to decide the order of submissions or to discuss disputed matters of evidence and how these are to be resolved. The Advocate General sits to the right side of the judges. The ordering of the oral procedure is relatively straightforward: the presiding judge invites the parties to submit their oral arguments and, after they have done so, asks first the Reporting Judge, then the Advocate General, and then other members of the bench whether they wish to question either the parties themselves or interveners.[33] Ruiz-Jarabo Colomer suggests that the main questioning comes from the Reporting Judge and the

[29] EC Treaty, Protocol on the Statute of the Court of Justice (n 10 above), Art 23.

[30] Ibid, Art 25. [31] Lenaerts (n 2 above) at 611. [32] Ibid at 552.

[33] M Darmon, 'The Role of the Advocate General at the European Court of Justice' in Shimon Shetreet (ed), *The Role of Courts in Society* (1988) 430.

Advocate General since these individuals are more familiar with the case than others.[34] There is no cross-examination in the sense that lawyers working in the courts of England or Scotland would understand. Judge Edward notes that most of the counsels appearing before the court do not like to be interrupted whilst presenting their case and so questions tend to be left to the end of their presentations. Under the preliminary reference procedure, the oral hearing performs a different function. Given that there is no exchange of pleadings, the oral hearing is the only opportunity for the parties in the main action to comment on the submissions made to the Court. These statements and observations might be voluminous. The oral procedure therefore 'affords a full opportunity for explanations and counter-arguments'.[35] At the end of the oral hearing, the Advocate General occasionally issues his Opinion immediately but most often he will announce a date for the delivery of his Opinion, which will normally be four to six weeks later.[36]

It would be logical to assume that the oral phase of the procedure is the high point for the parties. Both Darmon and Lagrange support this position. Darmon uses the term 'high point' to describe the oral proceedings since it is the opportunity for the parties to give final shape to their arguments and also because of the public nature of the forum where the parties can plead directly in front of the judges.[37] Lagrange, meanwhile, viewed the oral procedure as 'essentially a supplement to a very full written procedure . . . the value . . . consists more in concentrating attention on essentials'.[38] Léger points out that the oral hearing is the only occasion on which Judges and Advocates General can enter into a dialogue with the parties and gives them the opportunity to make more precise the exact point of the case.[39]

From a symbolic point of view, this day in court would also be the opportunity for the citizens of Europe to hear, from time to time, the great constitutional arguments of the day. Léger agrees on the symbolic role of the oral proceedings, quoting the maxim, 'Justice has to be seen to be done'. He also refers to the pedagogic importance of the day since hearings are attended by students and lawyers interested in European Community Law.[40]

In reality, the oral hearing appears to have little effect on the overall outcome of a case. Judge Edward, for example, states that, in those cases where the procedure is dispensed with, 'there is no evidence, so far, that the Court has overlooked vital points in consequence'.[41] Having said that, however, he also admits that gifted pleaders can contribute to the judges' understanding of the issues. Unfortunately, though, it seems that gifted pleaders are not common in the Court.

Normally, the Advocate General will deliver his Opinion some weeks after the oral hearing. In practice only the conclusions are actually read out, as the judges will have the full text of the Opinion in front of them. The Opinion is not always

[34] Ruiz-Jarabo Colomer (n 24 above). Although this might depend on whether the case is being heard in chambers of 3, 5, or a Grand Chamber.

[35] Lenaerts (n 2 above) at 612.

[36] N Fennelly, 'Reflections of an Irish Advocate General' (1996) Irish Journal of European Law 5. Although Léger suggests a six to eight week period; see Léger (n 14 above) 10.

[37] Darmon (n 33 above) at 430.

[38] Quoted in Darmon, ibid.

[39] Léger (n 14 above).

[40] Ibid.

[41] Edward (n 20 above) at 555.

read by the author himself but by the Advocate General who happens to be sitting that day.[42] After the Advocate General has delivered the Opinion, the presiding judge will declare the oral procedure closed.[43] The Court does have the opportunity to re-open the oral procedure after hearing the Advocate General[44] or if further measures of inquiry are required.[45]

The Opinion of the Advocate General sets out the facts, the legal issues and the arguments of the parties and interveners as well as providing his analysis of the case and a suggested outcome.

It is useful to turn here to Bengoetxea's analysis of judicial decision-making to help us to understand the purpose behind the Opinion of the Advocate General.[46] Bengoetxea identifies four stages in judicial decision-making: the determination of the applicable rule, the determination of evidence, the formulation of the facts in the language of universals and, finally, the making of a binding determination of the legal consequences. Before he gives his Opinion, the Advocate General has been actively involved in the processes of the determination of the relevant law and facts. In formulating his Opinion, the Advocate General is clearly involved in the third stage. The Opinion is a formulation of the relevant facts into the language of the universals of European law. It is also a proposal to the judges as to how they may make a binding determination. The Opinion, therefore, 'assists' the judges in that it gives them an analysis of the case in terms of legal reasoning. The Opinion is 'judgment-like' in that sense, although it is rarely, if ever, like an actual judgment of the Court itself in terms of style. As noted in chapter 1, both judges and Advocates General are selected on the basis of their abilities to use the language and tools of legal reasoning. The most useful way in which an Advocate General can 'assist' the Court, as Article 222 EC requires, is to present in his Opinion 'an account of what [will make] a decision the right legal decision upon the legal question or case remitted to the Court for decision or answer. That is, [to] state justifying reasons'.[47]

This is how certain Advocates General have defined the purpose of the Opinion; for example, Advocate General Jacobs has written that:

> The Opinion usually sets out, in the same way as a full judgment—one might say as an English-style judgment—would do, the facts, the state of the law, the issues, and the submissions and will develop a line of reasoning leading to a considered conclusion as to how all aspects of the case should be resolved. But, unlike a judgment, the Opinion does not decide the case.[48]

The Advocate General, unlike the judges, can, of course, offer alternative solutions to the legal problem. A provision of Community law might be interpreted in

[42] Fennelly (n 36 above) 11. [43] Court of Justice Rules of Procedure (n 12 above), Art 59.
[44] Ibid, Art 61. [45] Ibid, Art 60.
[46] J Bengoetxea, N MacCormick and LM Soriano, 'Integration and Integrity in the Legal Reasoning of the European Court of Justice' in G de Burca and J Weiler, *The European Court of Justice* (2001).
[47] Ibid, 44. [48] F Jacobs, (n 26 above) at 17–18.

different ways depending on the reasoning and the approach taken. Some Advocates General have used their Opinions to demonstrate how alternative reasoning can lead to quite different results, or to advise the Court of inconsistencies that have arisen as a result of the Court's own case-law. The key issue is, however, that the function of the Opinion at this stage in the proceedings is to assist the Court. The best way in which the Advocate General can assist the Court is by suggesting a solution (or solutions) based on strong legal reasoning.

At this stage in proceedings, the primary audience to whom the Advocate General expresses his Opinion comprises the judges who are hearing the case.[49] In other words, the primary audience is a legal audience. The Advocate General will have shared his thinking with the Reporting Judge some weeks before the formal reading of the Opinion in court by sending him a copy of it.[50] If the Advocate General is to assist the Court, he must provide in this Opinion convincing arguments on which the Court may subsequently rely on to justify the binding decision that it will make. This function was recognized by the former President of the Court, Robert Lecourt, in his valedictory address to former Advocate General, Karl Roemer, on the latter's retirement. He discussed the role played by the Advocate General in the following terms: 'Insérer entre le débat judiciaire et le deliberé du juge une étape personelle d'étude, de réflexion, de conception et de dialectique, *apte à faciliter la décision*, et, par-delà, à éclairer la doctrine'.[51] Given that the European Court of Justice is the supreme court of Europe, the process of justification is crucial to any public acceptance of its role. The Court itself must convince a wide audience of the soundness of its decision-making to legitimate its role and to create the conditions in which its judgments are accepted by the parties, by the Member States on which its existence depends, and also by the citizens of Europe.

As will be seen in the studies of individual Advocates General in this book, different Advocates General have different styles, reflecting their backgrounds in one legal tradition or another and reflecting different professional experience. It is not to be expected that an Advocate General coming from a common law tradition and with a professional background in academics and human rights would approach the task of writing an Opinion in the same way as an Advocate General coming from a civil law tradition and with a professional background in the French judicial system. They may use different forms of argumentation, rely more heavily on economic, social or political arguments, take more account of precedent, favour

[49] On legal audiences, see LV Prott, *The Latent Power of Culture and the International Judge* (1979). See also Bengoetxea, who quotes Eric Stein on legal audiences. The literature suggests that legal audiences (as distinct from the public) carry out a form of control. Bengoetxea states, for example, that 'the European Court of Justice will try to present its judgment as an assertion of normative order and a definition in terms of legal doctrine'; J Bengoetxea (n 46 above) 126.

[50] Fennelly (n 36 above) at 13.

[51] R Lecourt, 'Allocution prononcée par Monsieur Le President Robert Lecourt lors de l'audience solonelle du 9 octobre 1973 à l'occasion du départ de Monsieur l'avocat general K.Roemer' (1973).

brevity over exhaustive argument, and so on. The key point about the Opinion is that it is written to convince the audience, the Court.

Stage 3: The Deliberations

After hearing the Opinion of the Advocate General, the judges proceed to deliberations. As has been noted, deliberations are secret and the judges are sworn to uphold this secrecy. The Advocate General is excluded from this stage of proceedings as are all other persons, including interpreters. It is impossible, therefore, to discover the process by which a decision is reached. However, there is some evidence of the influential role that the Advocate General's Opinion has played in the process of deliberation. Judge Edward is, as ever, helpful in giving some insight into the process,[52] telling us that shortly after the Advocate General has given his Opinion, the Reporting Judge will circulate a note to the other judges setting out his proposals for how the case should be handled. He will state whether he agrees or disagrees, and to what extent, with the Advocate General and then he will draft his judgment accordingly.[53] Any judge who disagrees with the approach suggested by the Reporting Judge would normally be expected to circulate a note setting out his disagreement. Where there is clear disagreement within the Court, the President will list the case for discussion.

The Advocate General's Opinion appears to be the starting point for deliberations. Further anecdotal evidence of the importance of the Opinion is provided by Fennelly, who recalls a question put by the Queen of the Netherlands to a former judge as to how the judges' deliberations proceeded. The judge apparently replied, 'Your Majesty, the first question which we ask ourselves is the following: are we going to follow the Opinion of the Advocate General?'.[54] In the often quoted words of former President Lecourt addressing former Advocate General Roemer, the deliberations take place 'en l'absence de votre personne, mais non dans le silence de votre voix'. Nonetheless it is the judges alone who must reach the final binding decision with all the consequences for the parties concerned and, in many cases, for the Member States and the European Union itself.

Article 300(6) EC procedure

The two stage procedure described above is not followed when the Court is asked to give an Opinion on the compatibility with the Treaty of proposed international agreements. Article 300(6) EC provides that 'the European Parliament, the

[52] Edward (n 20 above) at 555.

[53] Of course the Reporting Judge may also have some form of draft judgment, at least in outline at this stage. Judges who are familiar with practice in the *Conseil d'Etat* almost certainly will have drafted a preliminary judgment by this stage. He is unlikely to be starting afresh. It may also be the case that the Reporting Judge may borrow sections of the Opinion to form the basis of the draft judgment.

[54] Fennelly (n 36 above) at 19.

Council, the Commission or a Member State may obtain the opinion of the Court of Justice as to whether an agreement envisaged is compatible with the provisions of this Treaty. Where the opinion of the Court is adverse, the agreement may enter into force only in accordance with Article 48 of the Treaty on European Union'. This means that where the opinion of the Court is adverse, the Community may only ratify the agreement following an amendment to the Treaty itself. The procedure aims to bring a degree of certainty into the relations between the Community and third states. Quoting Opinion 1/75, Lenaerts and Van Nuffel state that 'the prior opinion of the Court is intended to avoid complications arising as a result of a finding made in judicial proceedings that an international agreement which is binding on the Community is incompatible with the provisions of the EC Treaty'. This would otherwise give rise to 'serious difficulties' and 'adverse consequences for all interested parties, including third countries'.[55]

The Rules of Procedure of the Court of Justice provide that such an opinion may deal with questions of compatibility of a proposed agreement with the EC Treaty and also the question of competence of the Community or any Community institution to enter into an agreement.[56] Such is the sensitivity of such opinions, that the Rules of Procedure provide that the procedure takes place in closed session. Once a request for an opinion has been lodged, the President allocates the case to a Reporting Judge. From then on, the procedure differs in all respects from other procedures before the Court. One key difference is that all the Advocates General are involved in this procedure rather than just one. The Court hears the Advocates General together in closed session rather than in open court and, thereafter, once the Advocates General have withdrawn, deliberates to arrive at a reasoned opinion. Although the opinion of the Court is published, the advice given to the Court by the Advocates General is not made available in any form whatsoever. No minutes of the closed session proceedings are taken and there is no written record of any of the deliberations. It is therefore impossible to determine what kind of advice is given by the Advocates General to the Court.

It is possible to see how these procedures work in practice by examining the well-known Opinion 1/76.[57] The procedure began with a request from the Commission in September 1976 as to whether the draft agreement establishing a European laying-up fund for inland waterways was compatible with the Treaty. The request for an opinion was served on the Council and the Member States. Written observations were received from the Council and on behalf of the governments of Denmark and the UK. In a subsequent written communication, the Commission submitted additional observations. In January 1977 the Advocates General were heard in the Deliberation Room and the Opinion of the Court was given on

[55] K Lenaerts and P Van Nuffel, *Constitutional Law of the European Union* (2nd edn, 2005) 895. See also P Eeckhout, *External Relations of the European Union: Legal and Constitutional Foundations* (2005) 228–32.

[56] Art 107.

[57] Opinion 1/76 Draft Agreement establishing a European laying-up fund for inland waterway vessels [1977] ECR 741.

26th April, 1977. There was no element of an oral procedure and all arguments were exchanged in the written dossier.

It is entirely possible that the four Advocates General who were involved in Opinion 1/76 Warner, Reischl, Mayras, and Caportorti presented a joint opinion to the judges in the Deliberation Room. It is equally possible that each was heard separately in turn. Certainly there was likely to be discussion, questions and arguments. Nowadays, when an opinion is sought under Article 300(6) EC, the First Advocate General requests one of the Advocates General to draft an Opinion. All the Advocates General meet together prior to the meeting with the judges to discuss the draft opinion. An Advocate General might work with leading specialists in the area in drawing up this draft.[58] Therefore, before their meeting with the judges, the Advocates General have attempted to work through the legal issues that are likely to arise. The Advocates General then meet with the judges and the lead Advocate General presents the opinion and a discussion follows. The Advocates General withdraw and the judges continue their deliberations.

The joint deliberation between the Advocates General and the judges, which takes place in the Deliberation Room, could be described as a form of 'preliminary deliberation'. All deliberations by the judges are in camera, regardless of the form of procedure before the Court. In the procedure under Article 300(6) EC, the Advocates General are, in effect, being brought into the deliberations and this is one explanation as to why the advice that they give to the Court is confidential to the judges. This is also an explanation as to why no record of the meeting is kept since no public record of judicial deliberations is made. There are thus procedural explanations for the confidentiality of the views of the Advocates General. However there are also political sensitivities which explain why these procedures have been chosen. These sensitivities are on the part of both the Community institutions and/or the Member States, who would not wish their negotiating position to be undermined by open discussions but also sensitivities of third states who are involved in negotiations of treaties. Typically such negotiations are not conducted in open fora, particularly where there are possible legal complications that require to be explored prior to agreement on a text.

Article 103 Euratom procedure

The procedure for the involvement of the Court under the Euratom Treaty differs in several respects from that under the Treaty Establishing the European Communities. Whereas under the Treaty Establishing the European Community the Court is asked to examine the compatibility of a proposed agreement between the Community and a third state or third states, under the Euratom Treaty the

[58] We are grateful to Francis Jacobs for discussing his experience of the Art 300(6) procedure with us. It was in discussion with Francis Jacobs that we arrived at the term 'preliminary deliberation'.

Court is requested to rule on the compatibility of a proposed agreement between one of the Member States and a third state. Article 330(6) EC is therefore a procedure involving questions of constitutionality relating to the extent and degree of Community competence whereas Article 103 Euratom relates to the extent to which Member States are constrained in exercising their own powers to enter into international agreements in matters covered by the Euratom Treaty: it is a supervisory procedure.

The Euratom Treaty requires the Member States to inform the Commission of any proposed agreement with a third state or an international organization where that agreement falls within the material scope of the Euratom Treaty.[59] If, in the view of the Commission, there are provisions in the proposed agreement that might impede the application of the Euratom Treaty, it must inform the Member State concerned within one month. The Member State must either comply with the Commission's proposals or submit an application to the Court for a Ruling on the compatibility of the offending clauses. Thus the procedure under Article 103 Euratom can be seen as a form of appeal against the Commission's decision on compatibility. According to MacLeod et al. this means that the task of the Court is much narrower than its task under Article 300(6) EC and a literal reading of Article 103(3) EURATOM would suggest that its jurisdiction is limited to a 'consideration of those clauses in respect of which the Member State has been unable to satisfy the concerns of the Commission'.[60] However they equally point out that, in Ruling 1/78, the Court itself appears to have equated its jurisdiction under Article 103(3) with its parallel jurisdiction under the EC Treaty.[61] In Ruling 1/78 the Court stated that Article 103(3) EURATOM is to be given a broad interpretation and the Court's 'examination must take account of all the relevant rules of the Treaty whether they concern questions of substance, jurisdiction or of procedure'.[62] It has to be said, however, that the particular issues arising in that case meant that the Court was confronted with complex questions requiring analysis of major parts of the Euratom Treaty.

There are further differences in the Rules of Procedure between Article 330(6) EC and Article 103(3) EURATOM. Once the Member State has lodged its application, the Commission has 10 days to submit its observations. A Reporting Judge is appointed and a single Advocate General. Both the Member States and the Commission have the right to present oral arguments to the Court. The Court gives its Ruling in closed session after hearing the Advocate General. As is the case with the procedure under Article 330(6) EC the Opinion of the Advocate General is not published and he presents that Opinion in the Deliberation Room. This part of the procedure is comparable to the preliminary deliberation stage discussed above.

[59] The procedure is discussed in I MacLeod, ID Hendry and S Hyett, *The External Relations of the European Communities* (1996) 114–15.

[60] Ibid, 115.

[61] Ruling 1/78 Re Draft Convention of the International Atomic Energy Agency on the Physical Protection of Nuclear Materials, Facilities and Transports [1978] ECR 2151.

[62] Ibid, 2167.

Only one Ruling has been given under the supervisory jurisdiction of the Court provided for by Article 103(3) Euratom, and Advocate General Capotorti is the only Advocate General ever to have participated in these proceedings. It is all the more intriguing that we cannot assess his role, as the only participant, in the procedure.

A different approach—The Court of First Instance

The increasing workload of the European Court of Justice led to calls, from the 1970s onwards, for the establishment of a tribunal to take over certain types of cases from the Court. The Commission, for example, proposed that a new tribunal might deal with staff cases. It was not until the Single European Act 1986 that these proposals began to take concrete shape. The Single European Act inserted what is now Article 225 into the Treaty.[63] Article 225 provides that the Court of First Instance is attached to the Court of Justice and hears such classes of action as determined by the Council at the request of the Court of Justice. Appeal on points of law may be made to the European Court of Justice. Unlike the Court of Justice, the composition of the Court of First Instance is not determined by Treaty rules. Rather, the Council determines, at the request of the Court of Justice, the composition of the Court of First Instance.

The Council's Decision to establish the Court of First Instance specified that there are 15, later increased to 25,[64] judges who sit in chambers of three or five. Any of the judges 'may be called upon to perform the task of an Advocate General'.[65] The task of such an Advocate General, like his counterpart in the Court of Justice, is to make reasoned submissions in open court to assist the Court of First Instance in the performance of its task. A judge takes on the role of Advocate General in cases defined in the Rules of Procedure of the Court of First Instance. An Advocate General is to be appointed when the Court of First Instance sits in plenary session.[66] Alternatively, a chamber may be assisted by an Advocate General 'if it is considered that the legal difficulty or factual complexity of the case so requires'. The decision to appoint an Advocate General in a particular case is taken by the Court of First Instance sitting in plenary session at the request of the relevant chamber.[67]

It is very rare for the Court of First Instance to sit in plenary session. Normally a case is assigned to a chamber and this can be a chamber of one. A Reporting Judge is appointed for every case. As in the Court of Justice there is a written and oral procedure. In those rare cases where a judge is designated as Advocate General he is heard on procedural matters, such as the decision to join cases[68] or the decision

[63] Formerly Art 168a EC.
[64] EC Treaty, Protocol on the Statute of the Court of Justice, Title IV, Art 48.
[65] Ibid, Art 2(3). [66] Ibid, Art 17. [67] Ibid, Art 19. [68] Ibid, Art 50.

to instigate measures of inquiry.[69] He is also consulted on the action recommended by the Reporting Judge in the latter's preliminary report.[70] In the course of the oral procedure, the Advocate General is entitled to ask questions.[71] The oral stage in the procedure tends to be more substantial than in the Court of Justice indicating 'a greater emphasis on reviewing evidence'.[72] The delivery of the Advocate General's Opinion, whether delivered in writing or orally, brings the oral stage to a close.[73] The judge appointed as Advocate General is not entitled to participate in the decision on the case.[74]

Several plausible reasons have been advocated as to why it would be unwise to have replicated the role of Advocate General in the Court of First Instance. Schermers and Waelbroeck argue that the fact that decisions of the Court of First Instance can be appealed to the European Court of Justice reduces the need for an Opinion of an Advocate General.[75] They also point to a further disadvantage, in that 'the parties would almost always appeal to the Court of Justice whenever the Court of First Instance diverged from the Opinion of the Advocate General': the Advocate General's Opinion would provide the basis of the appeal. In fact, the Court of First Instance very rarely appoints an Advocate General to a case. By 1996, the power to appoint an Advocate General had been used in only 16 cases, 4% of the total and it was seen then as 'likely that the power will be exercised sparingly, if at all'.[76] Of the 19 cases where an Advocate General had been appointed, as identified by Plender prior to 1994, three had been cases heard in plenary session where the appointment of an Advocate General is compulsory, while 14 of the remaining 16 concerned a polypropylene cartel.[77]

Gardner suggests that the decision to appoint an Advocate General would only be taken where a case involved 'substantial factual investigation'. The jurisdiction of the Court of First Instance lies, in part, precisely in those cases where complex factual situations require close investigation; competition, anti-dumping, and so on. The heart of decision-making in these cases consists more of getting the facts right before the application of the relevant Community rule than in the more creative work of the European Court of Justice in developing and maintaining the Community legal order. In the more factually-based cases the assistance of an Advocate General based on the model of the Advocate General in the European Court of Justice is not required. He has other 'judge-like' skills that are not presently so much in demand in the Court of First Instance as they are in the European Court of Justice.

[69] Ibid, Art 49. [70] Ibid, Art 52. [71] Ibid, Art 58.

[72] JP Gardner (ed), *The Role and Future of the European Court of Justice* (1996) 34.

[73] For a discussion of one of the cases where a Judge was designated to act as Advocate General see R Greaves, 'Judge Edward Acting As Advocate General' in M Hoskins and W Robinson (eds), *A True European: Essays for David Edwards* (2003) 91.

[74] Rules of Procedure of the Court of First Instance, Art 2.

[75] HG Schermers and DF Waelbroeck, *Judicial Protection in the European Union* (6th edn, 2001) 754.

[76] JP Gardner (ed), *The Role and Future of the European Court of Justice* (1996) 31.

[77] Plender (n 9 above) at 855.

3

The Advocate General and human rights standards

Introduction

Chapter 2 concerned the role of the Advocate General in the context of proceedings before the European Court of Justice. The submissions of the Advocate General in cases before the European Court of Justice have become a well established, if not always fully understood, part of the proceedings of the Court. Yet more than 50 years after the establishment of the Court, the Advocate General has come under some scrutiny. In the context of the case-law of the European Court of Human Rights as to the nature of fairness in trial procedures, a question has arisen as to whether the failure to accord parties the right to reply to submissions of the Advocate General might constitute a violation of Article 6(1) of the European Convention on Human Rights.[1]

It is ironic that the Advocate General and his role in proceedings before the European Court of Justice might come under fire on human rights grounds given that successive Advocates General have argued forcibly and convincingly that human rights form part of the general principles of European law that the Court is obliged to uphold. Yet as early as 1982, parties to proceedings have objected to their inability to reply to the Opinion of the Advocate General in cases in which they are a party. In *Alvarez v Parliament*, the European Parliament sought an Order to have the oral procedure re-opened on the ground that the Advocate General had argued that a report on a probationary member of staff should be annulled although the applicant had not himself put forward such an argument. The Court rejected this approach arguing that to 'grant such a request would be tantamount to enabling the parties to discuss the Advocate General's Opinion'. Furthermore, the Court argued, 'the Parliament had an opportunity of answering a question on that issue put by the Advocate General'.[2]

[1] Art 6(1) of the European Convention on Human Rights begins: 'In the determination of his civil rights and obligations or of any criminal charge against him, everyone is entitled to a fair and public hearing within a reasonable time by an independent and impartial tribunal established by law'.

[2] Case 206/81 *Alvarez v European Parliament* [1982] ECR 3369, para 9.

The almost throwaway line from the Court in *Alavarez* demonstrates that in 1982 it could be taken for granted that the role of the Advocate General and his place in the procedures of the Court were unassailable. However, since 1982 the European Court of Human Rights has been asked to consider the role of law officers of one kind or another in light of Article 6 of the European Convention on Human Rights. In particular, there were significant developments during the 1990s in the case-law of the European Court of Human Rights about the nature of a fair trial. The right to equality of arms and the right to adversarial proceedings have been used as arguments that aspects of national procedures fall foul of human rights standards.

The case-law of the European Court of Human Rights

There is now considerable jurisprudence from the European Court of Human Rights on the right to a fair trial although it appears that there are no absolute rules as to what constitutes a fair trial under the European Convention of Human Rights. The concept of 'fairness' is said to be 'overarching and all pervading'[3] in that Article 6 of the European Convention introduces an 'overriding requirement that the proceedings should be fair'.[4] The suspicion that proceedings before the Court of Justice may not be fair, and that the fault for this lies at the feet of the Advocate General, arises from two key and interlocking elements of this overriding conception of fairness. Both are procedural: (1) fairness requires 'equality of arms'. This is taken to mean 'that each party must be afforded a reasonable opportunity to present his case—including his evidence—under conditions that do not place him at a substantial disadvantage vis-à-vis his opponent'.[5] The principle of equality of arms is part of the second element of the conception of fairness (2) the right to an adversarial process including disclosure of evidence. This is taken to include 'the opportunity for the parties to have knowledge of and comment on the observations filed or evidence adduced by the other party'.[6]

In a series of cases from the early 1990s onwards, the European Court of Human Rights has examined the role and function of various officers of the courts from a variety of contracting parties to the European Convention on Human Rights and has, from time to time, held that their involvement in proceedings might infringe Article 6. The Court acknowledges that this is an area where there has been 'considerable evolution' in its case-law with increasing 'importance attached to appearances and to the increased sensitivity of the public to the fair

[3] Lord Reed and J Murdoch, *A Guide to Human Rights Law in Scotland* (2001) 302.

[4] C Ovey and R White, *Jacobs & White: The European Convention on Human Rights* (4th edn, 2006) 155.

[5] Quoted both in Reed and Murdoch and Ovey and White. See also *Komanický v Slovakia*, App. No. 32106/96, judgment of 4 June 2002.

[6] *Komanický*.

administration of justice'.[7] Important in this regard is the issue of whether the particular court officer in question can be seen as 'opponent or ally' in proceedings. In none of these cases has the Court suggested that the officer of the court in question actually lacks objectivity or that, in the case under consideration, any perceived lack of objectivity has led to bias in the judgments of the national court. What matters is overall fairness and this includes appearances and public sensitivity.

Key principles have been elaborated by the European Court of Human Rights. Of relevance to the discussion relating to the Advocate General in the European Court of Justice are three key issues:

- the concept of opponent or ally as it can be applied to an officer of the court;
- the importance of the right to reply to submissions made to the court by such an officer, a right which is variously described in the case-law as being the doctrine of appearances or the need to respond to increased public sensitivity to the fair administration of justice, both part of the doctrine of equality of arms and forming part of the right to adversarial proceedings;
- the necessary safeguards in proceedings to ensure a fair trial.

From a comparative perspective it is interesting to note the wide variety of officers of the court that have been challenged before the European Court of Human Rights. None of these court officers has a function which exactly parallels another, nor is there any direct equivalent of the Advocate General of the European Court of Justice. Nonetheless the Court of Human Rights applies a broadly similar analysis in all of these cases.

Borgers v Belgium concerned criminal proceedings in the Belgian Court of Cassation. At the relevant time, the department of the *Procureur Général* at the Court of Cassation carried out 'with full independence, the duties of adviser to the Court'.[8] The report of the case makes clear that this advice might extend to recommending to the Court that an appeal might be dismissed or allowed. Only in exceptional circumstances and in a limited number of cases defined by law could the department assume the role of a party in the case. The case in point was not such a case. In *Borgers*, therefore, the *Avocat Général*, a member of the department of the *Procureur Général*, participated in the proceedings as an adviser to the Court. He made his submissions in open court and then immediately participated in the deliberations of the Court after the hearing. Unable to comment on the *Avocat Général*'s submissions, Mr Borgers argued before the Court of Human Rights that his right to a fair trial and the principle of equality of arms had been infringed. He argued that the *Avocat Général* should in this context be seen as his opponent and the breach of the principle of equality at arms was aggravated by the

[7] *Borgers v Belgium*, Series A No. 214-B, App. No. 12005/86, judgment of 30 October 1991, (1993) 15 EHRR 92, para 24.

[8] *Borgers*, para 16. *Borgers* overturned the earlier case of *Delcourt* on the question of the right to respond to the submissions of the *Commissaire du Gouvernement*. See *Delcourt v Belgium*, Series A No. 11, judgment of 17 January 1970 (1970).

fact that this opponent then participated in the Court's decision on his case. The rules of the Court at the time permitted the *Avocat Général* to participate in the deliberations of the Court but not to vote.

The Court of Human Rights on this point held that there had been a violation of the Convention. The Court argued that when the *Avocat Général* recommended that Borgers' appeal should not be allowed he became, 'objectively speaking', Borgers' opponent. Not to allow Borgers to reply to the submissions, the content of which he was unaware due to the fact that they had not been communicated to him, was an unjustifiable restriction of the rights of the defence. The Court of Human Rights stated that the inequality of arms was indeed aggravated by the participation of the *Avocat Général* in the deliberations since such participation 'afforded the *Avocat Général* an additional opportunity to promote, without fear of contradiction by the applicant, his submissions to the effect that the appeal should be dismissed'.[9]

The *Avocat Général* in the Belgian system is not functionally comparable to the Advocate General in the European Court of Justice. The latter is not part of a Ministry of Justice but is a member of the Court. The Advocate General in the European Court of Justice does not attend deliberations. It is not possible, therefore, merely to transpose the principles of this case to the situation of the Advocate General. A key question does, however, arise from *Borgers*, and that is whether the Advocate General could ever be perceived as an ally or opponent of one of the parties in a case before the European Court of Justice. If the Advocate General could be seen in this way, does the fact that the parties are not afforded the opportunity to comment on his opinion breach the principle of equality of arms?

In a second case brought against Belgium, challenging the role of the department of the *Procureur du Roi, Vermeulen*, this issue of opponent or ally was further explored.[10] *Borgers* involved criminal proceedings whereas *Vermeulen* involved civil proceedings originating in the Furnes Commercial Court and ending in the Court of Cassation. The questions for the European Court of Human Rights were the same. Vermeulen had not had the opportunity to reply to the *Avocat Général*'s submissions in his case and the *Avocat Général* had participated in the deliberations of the court. It was noted in this case that these practices had been discontinued in criminal proceedings but not for civil cases.

Vermeulen argued that the same principles applied in his case as in *Borgers*. The Belgian Government argued against this approach, although it conceded that in criminal cases the *Avocat Général* could have been mistaken, particularly by an 'uninformed accused', for an opponent or an ally.[11] In civil cases, however, such a misunderstanding was not possible, as there the role of the *Avocat Général* was confined to discussing issues raised by the appellant, and his function was

[9] *Borgers*, para 28.

[10] *Vermeulen v Belgium* [GC] App. No. 19075/91, judgment of 20 February 1996, (1996) ECHR 1996-I.

[11] Ibid, para 28.

'to advise the court neutrally and objectively as an amicus curiae'.[12] He was not a party to the proceedings and, accordingly, the equality of arms principle did not apply.

The Court of Human Rights rejected all these arguments. Despite the fact that the Court was emphatic that the department of the *Procureur Général* acted at all times 'with the strictest objectivity', the fact was that the *Avocat Général* was 'intended to advise and accordingly influence the Court of Cassation'. Given what was at stake for Vermeulen, the Court held that the impossibility for him to reply to the submissions of the *Avocat Général* was an infringement of his right to adversarial proceedings. In a key passage, the Court held that 'that right means in principle the opportunity for the parties to a criminal or civil trial to have knowledge of and comment on all evidence adduced or observations filed, *even by an independent member of the national legal service*, with a view to influencing the court's decision' (emphasis added).[13] This fact in itself is a breach of Article 6(1). As in *Borgers*, the Court added that the breach was aggravated by the involvement of the *Avocat Général* in the deliberations of the court. In the deliberations, he was afforded the opportunity 'if only to outward appearances, an additional opportunity to bolster his submissions in private'.[14]

The right to adversarial proceedings does therefore mean that parties to a dispute, whether of a criminal or civil nature, have the right to comment on all evidence or observations filed. That includes observations intended to advise the Court since such advice might influence it. Does that include advice given to a court by a member of the court itself? What would be the position of an Advocate General in the European Court of Justice? The significance of these cases for proceedings in cases before the European Court of Justice and in courts other than the Belgian Court of Cassation was not lost on some of the judges of the European Court of Human Rights. In both these cases there were powerful dissenting voices. Judge Martens in *Borgers* reviewed some of the comparative literature before warning that 'a further ground of circumspection is that the Court's decisions may have far-reaching consequences for other national legal systems'.[15]

It was in the case of *Van Orshoven v Belgium*[16] that there were strong hints (and fears) that the logic of the case-law of the European Court of Human Rights might be applied to the Advocate General in the European Court of Justice. A rather alarmed Judge Storme warned that the direction that was being taken by the Court of Human Rights in that case would lead to a situation where the parties 'would have a right to make observations on the opinion of the representative of the Belgian *Conseil d'Etat* and on the submissions of the Advocate General at

[12] Ibid, para 28.
[13] Ibid, para 33. [14] Ibid.
[15] *Borgers*, dissenting opinion of Judge Martens, Pt IV, para 4.3.
[16] *Van Orshoven v Belgium*, App. No. 20122/92, judgment of 25 June 1997, (1997) Reports 1997-III.

the Court of Justice in Luxembourg'.[17] Judge Pettiti hoped that 'the Court will no doubt have an opportunity to refine its case-law when dealing with similar proceedings whilst remaining alert to its international impact (particularly with respect to Advocates General at the Court of Justice of the European Communities)'.[18]

The cause for alarm in *Van Orshoven* was the apparent focus by the Court of Human Rights on the formal aspect of the right to adversarial proceedings. This case concerned proceedings in the Court of Cassation on appeal from a tribunal involving the disciplining of medical practitioners. In this case the parties were clearly defined, the representative of the department of the *Procureur Général* could not be confused with the parties, and the proceedings related to a clarification of the law. Nonetheless the European Court of Human Rights reiterated its approach in *Borgers* and in *Vermeulen* to the effect that the very fact that the applicant was unable to reply to the submissions of the *Avocat Général* was sufficient to find a breach of the applicant's rights—because the right to adversarial proceedings means having the opportunity to comment on all evidence adduced and observations made.

In these Belgian cases, which all refer to the department of the *Procureur Général*, a key issue is the existence of a department of government from which the authority of the submissions of the *Avocat Général* derive. The Advocate General in the European Court of Justice does not derive his authority from any external source. The authority of the Advocate General derives from his position as a member of the European Court of Justice. It is possible on these grounds to distinguish these cases from that of the Advocate General at the Court of Justice.

When we examine the case in France the situation is more complex. The involvement of an officer of the court in proceedings is also a feature of French judicial proceedings and a number of cases have come before the European Court of Human Rights challenging the fairness of proceedings where law officers have been involved. One such case came before the European Court of Human Rights in 1998, *Reinhardt and Slimane- Kaïd v France*.[19] This case concerned proceedings before the Criminal Division of the Court of Cassation, which is composed of a 'president, the divisional presidents, the Judges, the auxiliary Judges, Principal State Counsel, the Principal Advocate General, the Advocates General and a divisional registrar'.[20] In criminal cases, the function of the Principal State Counsel's office, which incorporates the work of the Advocates General, is to ensure that the law is correctly applied. Except when State Counsel is instructed by the Minister of Justice to lodge an appeal for the purposes of clarifying the law, he receives no instructions regarding the performance of his duties. In the instant case, therefore,

[17] Ibid, dissenting opinion of Judge Storme.

[18] Ibid, dissenting opinion of Judge Pettiti.

[19] *Reinhardt & Slimane-Kaïd v France, No. 3*, App. No. 45130/98, judgment of 6 April 2004, (2004) Reports 1998-II, 640, (1999) 28 EHRR 59.

[20] The organization of the Court of Cassation is explained in para 70 of this judgment.

the office of Principal State Counsel was acting independently of the Ministry and, as described above, the office does not form part of that Ministry.

Typically, proceedings before the Court of Cassation are written and only where there is a request from the parties' lawyers will an oral hearing be held. Once a case is filed, the president assigns it to a Reporting Judge who draws up a written report in which he reviews the arguments of the parties, sets out the arguments and makes a recommendation as to the disposal of the case. At this stage he prepares a draft judgment which provides the basis for deliberations. This report and all related documents are sent to the Advocate General assigned to the case, and the parties' lawyers are informed of the recommendation. In practice, at this stage additional pleadings may be lodged by the parties, although in principle such pleadings should be declared inadmissible. The Advocate General in these proceedings therefore has the opportunity to read the draft prepared by the Reporting Judge before he gives his opinion, which can either be in writing or may be delivered orally. This procedure compares to that before the European Court of Justice where the Advocate General may see several drafts of the Reporting Judge's report, although in formal terms it is not sent to him for his consideration. In the Court of Cassation, the Advocate General has two options; he may agree with the Reporting Judge or he may disagree. As the Court of Human Rights states, his role is 'maieutic'.[21] The Advocate General becomes involved a few days before the date is set for the hearing of the case. A preparatory meeting is held between the president and senior judges of the division and the duty Advocate General, and this is where the Advocate General makes his submissions. After this meeting the Advocate General customarily informs the parties' lawyers 'of the tenor of his submissions'.[22] The President and the senior judge provide a reasoned opinion on the basis of the views of the Reporting Judge's report and the submissions of the Advocate General, and this Opinion plus the submissions of the Advocate General are then relayed back to the Reporting Judge. Thus, even before the hearing commences, a view has been formed as to the outcome of the case.

At the hearing, the Reporting Judge is first to read out his report but does not state his recommendations. If there are to be oral submissions they follow, first the appellant and then the respondent. 'The Advocate General is the last to address the Court; he makes submissions that are confined to legal issues and may concern the consideration of a ground of appeal raised by the court of its own motion'.[23] Crucially, where oral submissions are made, it is customary to allow the parties' lawyers to reply to the Advocate General's submissions orally or by way of a note introduced to the court in deliberations. Deliberations are held in private and the Advocate General normally attends, although he does not become involved in the discussion. It seems that it is for practical reasons that he remains in the same

[21] Defined in Collins Dictionary as being a Socratic mode of enquiry serving to bring out a person's latent ideas into clearer consciousness.

[22] *Reinhardt & Slimane-Kaïd*, para 78.

[23] Ibid, para 79.

room as the judges due to the volume of cases. In difficult cases, he leaves the room, showing in public the fact that it is the judges who will make the final decision without influence from the Advocate General. Once again, we see here a difference in the proceedings. In the European Court of Justice, the Advocate General closes the oral proceedings; parties may not make further submissions and the Advocate General never participates in deliberations.

Amongst other bases of the appeal, the appellants argued in this case that there had been a breach of the adversarial principle in that they had not been provided with the report of the Reporting Judge whereas the Advocate General had. Furthermore, as society's representative in the case, the Advocate General was effectively their opponent and, as such, they ought to have been given the opportunity to reply to his submissions. Acknowledging that where oral submissions were made in the Court of Cassation there was in practice a limited right of reply, the appellants pointed out that normally proceedings were written and proceedings tended to be 'focused' on the written submissions.

The European Court of Human Rights looked at the proceedings as a whole in order to determine whether they were fair. It held that, given its importance in the context of the proceedings, an imbalance had been created by the failure to provide the appellants with the report of the Reporting Judge, considering that this was provided for the Advocate General. The Court pointed out that the Advocate General is not a member of the Court hearing the appeal but does advise the judges on the solution of the case and 'through the authority of his office, [he] may influence their decision in a way that is either favourable or runs counter to the case put forward by the appellants'.[24] The Court went on to say that the fact that the Advocate General's submissions were not submitted to the parties was also 'questionable'. Taken together, these factors led to a violation of Article 6, paragraph 1 of the Convention.[25]

Procedures in France's supreme administrative Court, the *Conseil d'Etat*, were the issue in the case of *Kress v France*, decided in 2001.[26] The role of the *Commissaire du Gouvernement* was questioned in the context of the ongoing debate about the nature of fairness in trial processes. The Court of Human Rights describes the institution of the *Commissaire du Gouvernement* as being 'one of the most distinctive features of French administrative justice, in particular because Government commissioners rapidly established themselves as *judicial officers totally independent of the parties*'.[27] The role of *Commissaire du Gouvernement* has

[24] Ibid, para 105.

[25] The European Court of Human Rights reiterated this position in *Meftah and ors v France* where it added that where procedures were essentially written the rules set out *Reinhardt & Slimane-Kaïd* should be followed. See *Meftah and ors v France*, [GC] App. Nos. 32911/96, 35237/97, 34595/97, judgment of 26 July 2002, (2002) ECHR 2002-VII. The Court has subsequently followed this approach in several further cases.

[26] *Kress v France*, [GC] App. No. 39594/98, ECHR 2001-VI.

[27] *Kress*, para 41, emphasis added.

been compared to that of the Advocate General in the European Court of Justice although there are differences in the role played by each in the context of the actual proceedings. In fact, in *Kress*, the Court of Human Rights noted that the function of the Advocate General at the European Court of Justice was modelled on the role of the *Commissaire du Gouvernement*, citing the Order of the Court of Justice in *Emesa*.[28]

Procedure in the *Conseil d'Etat* begins with the Reporting Judge drawing up a draft decision based on the papers in the file.[29] The draft decision, accompanied by a memorandum outlining the legal arguments in the case including questions of both substance and procedure, are forwarded to a reviser, who is the president of the section or one of the other judges. The function of the reviser is to take a view as to how the case should be decided. In case of disagreement, the reviser may draft an alternative decision. The draft decision is considered at a preparatory session of the section at which the *Commissaire du Gouvernement* is present but, unlike the judges, he does not vote on the draft. After the decision has been adopted by the section, the file is forwarded to the *Commissaire du Gouvernement*, who then has the opportunity to prepare his submissions, and may also ask for a new preparatory session to be convened or for the case to be transferred to a differently constituted court. The submissions of the *Commissaire du Gouvernement* are generally oral and they are not shared with the parties, the Reporting Judge or members of the bench.

Before the hearing, the *Commissaire du Gouvernement* will share the tenor of his submissions with the parties. At the hearing, the Reporting Judge sets out the issues. The parties, if they wish, can present oral arguments and the *Commissaire du Gouvernement* is the last to speak. He sets out the case, the relevant law and finally submits that the application be dismissed or allowed. The stated purpose of this procedure is to assist the Court in its deliberations. Parties to the case do not have the right to reply to these submissions but they may prepare a memorandum for the deliberations which will then be read out by the Reporting Judge before debate on the case begins. The *Commissaire du Gouvernement* attends the deliberations where, although he may not vote, he may answer any questions which are put to him.

In her submissions, Kress complained that the type of procedures outlined above offended against the principle of equality of arms. In her case she had not had his submissions communicated to her in advance and she had been denied the opportunity to reply to him at the hearing or to be the last to speak. Furthermore, given that the *Commissaire du Gouvernement* had submitted in public that her appeal should be dismissed and then went on to attend the private deliberations of the Court, this cast doubt about the impartiality of the Court. She argued that, objectively, the *Commissaire du Gouvernement* must be perceived as either an ally or opponent in a particular case because of this very fact that he could express an

[28] Case C-17/98 *Emesa Sugar (Free Zone) NV v Aruba*, Order of the Court of 4 February 2000 (discussed below).

[29] *Kress*, para 40ff.

opinion in public and then participate, even without voting, in the deliberations. In her case, she argued, he was, objectively speaking, an opponent. She argued that the possibility of submitting a Memorandum for the deliberations did not sufficiently ensure that the adversarial principle was respected.

The French government argued that the principles that had been developed by the European Court of Human Rights to that date in cases involving criminal and civil proceedings should not be applied to a system of administrative courts. The European Court of Human Rights rejected this argument. It also rejected more instrumental arguments that the system of administrative courts had worked well for a century or more and that no-one had questioned the impartiality or integrity of the *Commissaire du Gouvernement* in the past. The Convention, according to the Court, was a living instrument and had to be interpreted in the context of contemporary views of fairness. It seems, therefore, that whatever the nature of proceedings, the Court of Human Rights is willing to apply the principles of the Convention and, where relevant, its own case-law to judge the impartiality and fairness of proceedings. What matters is the part played in the proceedings by the law officer and the content and effects of his submissions.

The Court acknowledged that the submissions of the *Commissaire du Gouvernement* were made available to the parties to the dispute and to the bench for the first time at the public hearing. The appellant could not argue therefore that there had been a breach of the principle of equality of arms. In particular, she could not derive the right to have the submissions of the *Commissaire du Gouvernement* disclosed to her prior to the hearing where such information was not disclosed to other parties. This is a significant statement insofar as a potential challenge to the Advocate General in the European Court of Justice is concerned, since the Advocate General makes his submissions in open court at the end of the oral proceedings. He does not disclose the content of his submissions to the parties, to the Reporting Judge (although he may do so informally) or to members of the bench prior to this. The principle of equality of arms would not therefore require him to circulate his submissions in advance of the oral procedure.

However, there is a second limb to the argument in relation to the fairness of a trial. The Court stated that the concept of a fair trial 'also means in principle the opportunity for the parties to a trial to have knowledge of and comment on all evidence adduced or observations filed, even by an independent member of the national legal service, with a view to influencing the Court's decision'.[30] This is a summary of the previous case-law.[31]

[30] *Kress*, para 74.

[31] See *Bulut v Austria* concerning criminal procedure; *Bulut v Austria*, App. No. 17358/90, judgment of 22 February 1996, Reports 1996-II, 346, (1997) 24 EHRR 84 The appellant complained about the practice whereby the Advocate General submitted observations (*croquis*) to the Supreme Court which were not made available to the defence. The Court held that 'each party must be afforded a reasonable opportunity to present his case under conditions that do not place him at a disadvantage vis-à-vis his opponent (para 47). The Court stated that this was because of 'appearances'

Proceedings in the *Conseil d'Etat*, unlike proceedings in the European Court of Justice, do provide an opportunity for the parties to respond to the submissions of the *Commissaire du Gouvernement*. Three safeguards exist which the Court believed were sufficient guarantee of the right to adversarial proceedings in the procedures before the *Conseil d'Etat*. The first is the opportunity available to lawyers to ask the *Commissaire du Gouvernement* before the hearing to indicate the general tenor of his submissions. The second is the possibility to present to the Court a Memorandum for the deliberations. This was stated by the Court to be 'vital' since it helps to ensure compliance with the adversarial principle. The third safeguard is the possibility open to the presiding judge to adjourn a case if the *Commissaire du Gouvernement* raised a ground not raised by the parties giving the parties the opportunity to present arguments on the point raised.

Unlike the Advocate General at the European Court of Justice, the *Commissaire du Gouvernement* at the *Conseil d'Etat* attends the deliberations of the judges. Although not directly relevant to our discussion of the role of the Advocate General it is interesting to examine why the European Court of Human Rights decided that such attendance constitutes a violation of Article 6. In this respect the Court shifted the burden of the argument away from the principle of equality of arms towards a doctrine of appearances. The doctrine of appearances arises from an increased public sensitivity to the fair administration of justice. Here the Court of Human Rights held that in recommending whether an appeal should be allowed or dismissed, the *Commissaire du Gouvernement* becomes, objectively speaking, and if only to outward appearances, an ally or opponent of one of the parties regardless of the acknowledged objectivity of the office. He might then be perceived as being able to bolster his arguments in private in favour of one party or the other. There is no guarantee in the French system that this cannot occur. The Court of Human Rights found support for this view in the fact that the Advocate General at the European Court did not attend deliberations and thereby maintained the doctrine of appearances in this regard.[32]

and 'the increased sensitivity to the fair administration of justice. See *Apeh Üldözötteinek Szovetsége and ors v Hungary* regarding commercial proceedings and the intervention of the Public Prosecutor's Office and the Attorney General's Office in non-contentious proceedings; *Apeh Ülodözötteineh Szövetsége and ors v Hungary*, App. No. 32367/96, judgment of 5 February. 2000, (2002) 34 EHRR 34. This approach has been maintained subsequently. In *Göç v Turkey*, the European Court of Human Rights considered the position of the Principal Public Prosecutor (ppp) in the Turkish criminal system; *Göç v Turkey*, [GC] App. No. 36590/97, judgment of 11 July 2002, (2002) ECHR 2002-V, 133. In cases of appeal from a Court of First Instance, the PPP submits an opinion on the case to the Court of Cassation. The opinion is not binding on the Court for whose benefit it is written. The parties are not given the opportunity to comment on the opinion. The Court of Human Rights held that 'the right to adversarial proceedings means in principle the opportunity for the parties to a civil or criminal trial to have knowledge of and comment on all evidence adduced or observations files, even by an independent member of the national legal service, such as the PPP in the instant case, with a view to influencing the court's decision'.

[32] One year after the European Court of Human Rights had given its judgment in the case of *Kress*, the Court was asked again to examine the procedure before the *Conseil d'Etat* in *Fretté v France*,

From the case-law of the European Court of Human Rights it is possible to derive certain key principles about fairness in court proceedings insofar as these principles relate to officers charged with advising the court. These principles appear to apply not only to members of a ministry of justice but also to members of the court themselves. The most directly comparable institution to the Advocate General in the European Court of Justice is the *Commissaire du Gouvernement* in the French *Conseil d'Etat*. It is clear that the function of the *Commissaire du Gouvernement* is subject to an overall test of fairness.

The test that is applied by the Court of Human Rights is whether the officer in question can influence the court in a particular case. If so, then the case-law relating to the right to adversarial proceedings and equality of arms comes into play. The nature of the proceedings is not relevant in determining whether these principles apply. The Court of Human Rights has been asked to investigate criminal and civil proceedings, administrative procedures and contentious and non-contentious proceedings. In all these circumstances the Court has looked to the overall fairness of the procedure in the light of Article 6(1) of the European Convention on Human Rights.

The European Court of Human Rights is concerned with the overall fairness of proceedings. The Court seeks to ensure that there is equality of arms between the parties. Neither party should be placed at a substantial disadvantage. Can the Advocate General be seen to side with one party or the other when he gives his Opinion on the case? If so, does he become an opponent or an ally in the case? Does this mean that the principle of equality of arms is violated? Should the doctrine of appearances apply to his position particularly in the light of public sensitivity to fairness of legal processes? Equality of arms is closely connected with the right to adversarial proceedings. The Court has defined this right on numerous occasions. Essentially it means the 'opportunity for the parties to a civil or criminal trial to have knowledge and comment on all evidence adduced or observations filed even by an independent member of the national legal service'.[33] In light of

App. No. 36515/97, judgment of 26 February 2002, (2004) 38 EHRR 21, ECHR 2002-I, 345. This case related to an application by a homosexual man to adopt a child. Fretté had not exercised his right to appoint a member of the Bar to argue his case before the *Conseil d'Etat*. He had attempted to enquire about the date of the hearing of his case but was unfamiliar with the procedure. He argued that he was unable to attend the hearing of his case because he had not been notified of the date. The French government argued that the dates of hearings were posted in the *Conseil'd'Etat* and that appellants could visit the Court to ascertain the date when their case might be heard. Fretté had been unable to hear the submissions of the *Commissaire du Gouvernement* because he had not known of the date of the hearing. He was therefore unable to respond to the submissions. Neither was he able, because he was not represented by a lawyer, to ascertain the tenor the submissions of the *Commissaire du Gouvernement*. In these circumstances the Court of Human Rights held that the applicant had been denied a fair trial.

[33] *Vermeulen v Belgium* [GC] App. No. 19075/91, judgment of 20 February 1996, (1996) ECHR 1996-I, para 33.

this, should the parties to a case have the right to respond to the Opinion of the Advocate General? What should be the safeguards applicable to ensure that Article 6(1) is not violated?

The Advocate General and the Court of Human Rights

The single occasion on which the European Court of Human Rights has had reason to examine the question of the Advocate General in the proceedings of the European Court of Justice has been in the case of *Emesa Sugar*.[34] Emesa brought its action against the Netherlands which had, in compliance with a Decision of the Council of the European Union, imposed import duties on sugar from an overseas country and territory (OCT). A series of cases originating in the Netherlands had led to the reference to the European Court of Justice for a preliminary ruling in which the Advocate General, according to Emesa, issued an Opinion which adversely affected its case. Emesa therefore argued before the ECJ that it should have the right of reply. The European Court of Justice rejected this claim.[35]

Emesa's complaint before the European Court of Human Rights was that it had been deprived of a fair hearing before the Court of Justice as it had not been allowed to respond to the Opinion of the Advocate General. Given that the case at this stage concerned the admissibility of the action rather than the merits of the case, the Court of Human Rights did not engage with the central arguments. It held the case to be incompatible *ratione materiae* since the case did not involve a dispute about 'civil rights and obligations' and concerned matters within the realm of taxation which fall outside the scope of the concept of civil rights and obligations. Thus the Court did not rule on the merits of the dispute.

The approach of the European Court of Justice to date

The concept of opponent or ally

In *Borgers*, the European Court of Human Rights examined the circumstances under which an officer of the court could be perceived as an opponent or ally of one of the parties to a dispute. The violation of the Convention occurred at the point where the *Avocat Général* expressed an opinion that ran counter to the interests of one of the parties and that party was not given the opportunity to reply. At that point he became, objectively speaking, the opponent of the party to the dispute and, by definition, the ally of the other party.

[34] *Emesa Sugar v Netherlands*, App. No. 62023/00, decision as to admissibility of 13 January 2005.
[35] Case C-17/98 *Emesa Sugar (Free Zone) NV v Aruba* [2000] ECR 1-655.

In *Emesa*, a preliminary reference procedure, the applicant sought leave to submit written observations on the Opinion of the Advocate General.[36] Neither the Statute of the Court of Justice nor the Rules of Procedure of the Court provide for this possibility. Emesa relied on the case-law of the Court of Human Rights and, in particular, on *Vermeulen* where the Court of Human Rights held that there had been a breach of Article 6(1) where parties were not given the opportunity to respond to observations 'even by an independent member of the national legal service'.

The Court of Justice ruled that the context in which the Advocate General operates can be distinguished from law officers in other courts.[37] This being the case, and having regard to 'both the organic and functional link between the Advocate General and the Court' the Court held that the reasoning of the Court of Human Rights could not be transposed to its own proceedings. In its reasoning the Court recalled the status of the Advocate General in the Treaties. The Advocate General is a member of the Court and his status is equivalent to that of a judge in terms of immunity and the grounds on which he may be removed from office. His independence and impartiality are guaranteed by the Treaty and by the Statute of the Court. Moreover no Advocate General is subordinate to another and neither is he subject to any external authority. Crucially, argued the European Court of Justice, the Advocates General 'are not entrusted with the defence of any particular interest.' The Court went on to state that the Opinion of the Advocate General 'does not form part of the proceedings between the parties' but is an 'individual reasoned opinion, expressed in open court, of a member of the Court of Justice itself'. Without using the language of the Court of Human Rights, the Court of Justice rejected implicitly any argument that the Advocate General could be seen as the ally or opponent in any particular case.

However, it is difficult to completely distinguish the offices of the Advocate General in the Court of Justice and the *Commissaire du Gouvernement* in the French *Conseil d'Etat*. The *Commissaire du Gouvernement* is a judicial officer, a member of the *Conseil d'Etat*, and totally independent of the parties. Like the Advocate General, the *Commissaire du Gouvernement* is the last to speak. His submission is intended to assist the *Conseil d'Etat* in its deliberations. These factors suggest that the Advocate General should be subject to the same analysis as that applied by the Court of Human Rights in *Kress*. Indeed in *Kress*, the Court of Human Rights drew on the *Emesa* Order as part of its reasoning and drew attention to the fact that the office of Advocate General was modelled on that of the *Commissaire du Gouvernement*.

There is certainly a perception in some instances that the Advocate General can be seen by one of the parties to a dispute as their opponent. A good example is the case of *Kaba*.[38] The UK Immigration Adjudicator referred questions to the Court

[36] Ibid.

[37] Case C-17/98 *Emesa Sugar (Free Zone) NV v Aruba*, Order of the Court of 4 February 2000.

[38] Case C-356/98 *Kaba v Secretary of State for the Home Department* [2000] ECR I-2623.

regarding the interpretation of the rules relating to the right of a spouse of a migrant worker to apply to obtain leave to remain indefinitely in the UK. At the relevant time, UK law provided two sets of conditions relating to spouses. Spouses of EU nationals were required to have remained in the UK for four years before they could apply to obtain indefinite leave to remain. Spouses of persons who were 'settled' in the UK required a residence period of 12 months before they could apply for such leave. The Immigration Adjudicator essentially asked the European Court of Justice if this constituted discrimination prohibited by law.

It is not necessary to discuss the technicalities of the law in this area but it is crucial to note aspects of the procedure. The hearing before the Court was held on 15 June 1999. The Advocate General delivered his Opinion on 30 September 1999. The English version of the Opinion of the Advocate General was sent to Kaba on 27 January 2000. By fax of 3 February 2000, Kaba informed the Court of his doubts as to the accuracy of certain factual issues on which the Advocate General had based his Opinion. He argued that these constituted exceptional grounds justifying re-opening of the proceedings and stated that further observations would be lodged. On 16 March 2000, Kaba submitted further observations where he stated in conclusion:

> The points raised above are demonstrated by the documents already submitted to the Court. However, if the Court considers that it is necessary to re-open the oral procedure to ensure that it fully understands the critical facts and corrects any erroneous conclusions reached by the Advocate General, Mr Kaba's representatives would offer the Court every assistance.[39]

On 31 March, the Registrar informed Kaba that the Rules of Procedure made no provision for submission of observations after the oral procedure had been concluded and his observations were returned to him and not accepted as part of the Court file. On 11 April 2000, the Court gave judgment and held that there was no issue of discrimination based on Community law in the case.

At this stage it is worth recalling some of the language used by the Court of Human Rights in its case-law regarding the right to adversarial proceedings. The Court of Human Rights insisted that Vermeulen be awarded a right of reply 'given what was at stake' for the individual concerned. In *Kaba*, what was at stake was his right to remain in the UK. Kaba was a Yugoslav national who had earlier applied for asylum in the UK and had his appeal rejected. His situation in the UK was dependent on his French wife remaining in the UK. A great deal was at stake in his case. The ruling given by the European Court of Justice was crucial to his case before the Immigration Adjudicator.

When proceedings were resumed before the Immigration Adjudicator in the UK, Kaba argued that the Court's ruling was based on a misunderstanding of the facts found in the first order for reference and of the relevant national law.

[39] Ibid.

He argued that the Court might have been influenced by the Advocate General and he argued that the Advocate General had reappraised the facts in the case. Significantly, the Immigration Adjudicator agreed with Kaba on this point. The Immigration Adjudicator also stated that there were errors in the Opinion of the Advocate General. In these circumstances she was unsure whether the proceedings before the European Court of Justice had been conducted in accordance with Article 6(1). She stated that the proceedings before the European Court were an integral part of proceedings before her and therefore she would be responsible for any infringement of the European Convention by virtue of the UK Human Rights Act 1998.

The Adjudicator made a second reference to the European Court of Justice. She asked the Court to identify the mechanisms available to the 'referring court or the parties to the proceedings (before the referring court and the European Court of Justice) to ensure that the totality of the proceedings comply with the obligations under Article 6 ECHR and therefore to ensure that no liability for breach of Article 6 ECHR arises either under the domestic human rights statute or before the European Court of Human Rights'.[40] She also asked whether the procedure followed in this case was in compliance with Article 6 and, if not, would that affect the validity of the first judgment of the European Court of Justice. In addition she asked a second question about the interpretation of Community law in relation to the rights of spouses.

The European Court of Justice gave its judgment in this case in March 2003. It had been presented with an opportunity to revise its Order in *Emesa* in the light of the new case-law of the European Court had it so wished. The Immigration Adjudicator had put her finger on the exact doubts about whether the role of the Advocate General in proceedings before the Court of Justice did, or did not, infringe the right to an adversarial trial. These doubts had been raised by academic commentators. For example, Schermers and Waelbroeck consider that 'it is not certain that the parties should not be granted such a right [the right to comment on the Opinion of the Advocate General] in order to comply with Article 6 of the European Convention on Human Rights'.[41] In addition, comments had been made by judges in the Court of Human Rights itself and now a domestic tribunal was raising similar questions. Here was the opportunity for the Court to engage with the issues arising from the case-law of the Court of Human Rights. It declined to do so. It reversed the order of questions put to it by the Immigration Adjudicator and answered the questions regarding the Community law provisions on the rights of spouses. In doing so, it reiterated its ruling in the first *Kaba* case. Then, given that it had answered these questions it held that 'it is unnecessary to reply to the first question'.

[40] Case C-466/00 *Kaba v Secretary of State for the Home Department* [2003] ECR I-2219, para 29. Also known as *Kaba 2*.

[41] HG Schermers and DF Waelbroeck, *Judicial Protection in the European Union* (6th edn, 2001) 668.

The right to reply

It seems that in *Emesa* the Court set itself against a right of reply out of very practical considerations. It stated 'given the special constraints inherent in the Community judicial procedure, connected in particular with its language regime, to confer on the parties the right to submit observations in response to the Opinion of the Advocate General, with a corresponding right for the other parties (and, in preliminary ruling proceedings, which constitute the majority of cases brought before the Court, all the Member States, the Commission and other institutions concerned) to reply to these observations, would cause serious difficulties and considerably extend the length of the procedure'. Thus the European Court of Justice rejected the right of reply on pragmatic rather than principled grounds.

Necessary safeguards

In *Kress*, the Court of Human Rights approved three particular aspects of the procedures within the *Conseil d'Etat* which, taken together, ensured the fairness of the proceedings: the opportunity available to lawyers to discover the tenor of the Opinion of the *Commissaire du Gouvernement* prior to the hearing, the possibility of presenting the Court with a memorandum prior to its deliberations and the possibility open to the Court to adjourn a case if the *Commissaire du Gouvernement* introduces a ground not raised by the parties. Of these, the European Court of Human Rights classified the second as a vital safeguard.

In proceedings before the European Court of Justice, lawyers are unable to approach the Advocate General to seek the tenor of his submissions prior to the hearing. As *Kaba* demonstrated, neither can parties to a dispute present a memorandum for the deliberations even where the judge in the national court acknowledges that there are factual legal errors in the submissions of the Advocate General. The first two of the essential safeguards, including the vital safeguard are therefore missing in proceedings before the European Court of Justice.

The third safeguard is in place and the Court of Justice in *Emesa* relied on this safeguard to justify the fairness of its proceedings. The possibility exists for the Court of Justice to reopen the oral procedure 'if it considers that it lacks sufficient information, or that the case must be dealt with on the basis of an argument which has not been debated by the parties'. The Court may do this on its own motion, on a proposal from the Advocate General or at the request of the parties. In *Emesa*, the Court provided examples of where it had reopened the procedure. In practice, the Court of Justice is reluctant to reopen the oral procedure. For example, in the period between delivering its Opinion in *Emesa* in February 2000 and up to April 2004, the European Court of Justice was requested by the parties on at least six occasions to reopen the proceedings because of procedural issues relating to the Advocate General. In all these cases it declined to do so.[42]

[42] The Court does occasionally reopen the oral procedure when the Advocate General raises matters which have not been discussed by the parties. See, for example, Case C-304/02 *Commission v France*,

In *Vick*, Deutsche Telecom argued for the reopening of the oral proceedings since the Advocate General had read the operative part of his Opinion at a sitting of the Fifth Chamber whereas the it was the Sixth Chamber that was to give judgment on the case.[43] The Court replied to this argument that the judges of the Sixth Chamber were apprised of the Opinion of the Advocate General through the deposit of the Opinion with the Registry. The deposit of the Opinion at the Registry and a reading of the operative part of the Opinion were sufficient to make the Opinion public. Deutsche Telecom also wished to submit observations on the Opinion of the Advocate General in the light of an order made by the German Federal Constitutional Court in the period following the close of the oral proceedings. Deutsche Telecom argued that a refusal to accept that the oral proceedings may exceptionally be reopened to allow parties 'to draw attention to any manifest errors or omissions in the account of the facts or the findings of law, or indeed to reply to the Advocate General's Opinion' might be a breach of Article 6(1) of the European Convention on Human Rights. The Court did not engage with the jurisprudence of the European Court of Human Rights but repeated the wording of its Order in *Emesa* that the Court may order the reopening of proceedings if the Court considers 'that it lacks sufficient information, or that the case must be dealt with on the basis of an argument which has not been debated by the parties'. It held that this is in deference to the right to adversarial proceedings. In this case Court found nothing in Deutsche Telecom's application to indicate that it would be useful or necessary to reopen the proceedings and rejected the request.

In *Wouters*, the Court was asked to reopen the oral proceedings on the ground that the Advocate General had raised an issue in his Opinion which had not been expressly raised by the national court.[44] The European Court of Justice declined to do so on the ground that it was in possession of all the necessary facts for it to answer the questions raised by the national court and those facts were the subject of argument presented to it at the hearing. In *Hirschfeldt*, Mr Hirschfeldt requested a reopening of the oral procedure to allow him to respond to the Opinion of the Advocate General which, according to him, contained a number of contradictions.[45] The Court declined to do so since it had all the information that it needed to determine the appeal. In *Schilling*, Mr and Mrs Schilling requested the Court to reopen either the written or oral proceedings insofar as it intended to base its judgment on a point raised by the Advocate General in his Opinion and which had not been the subject of discussion by the parties.[46] The Court found no reason to reopen the procedure and rejected the request. In *Alabaster*, the United Kingdom Government requested the Court to reopen the

Order of the Court of 16 June 2004. However this case could nor raise a human rights issue since a Member State could not claim to be a victim of a violation of Art 6.

[43] Case C-234/96 *Deutsche Telekom Advocate General v Agnes Vick* [2000] ECR I-799.

[44] Case C- 309/99 *Wouters v Algemene Raad van de Nederlandse Orde van Advocaten* [2002] ECR I-1577, para 43.

[45] Case C-184/01 *Peter Hirschfeldt v European Environment Agency* [2002] ECR I-10173.

[46] Case C-209/01 *Schilling v Finanzampt* [2003] ECR I-13389.

proceedings claiming that the Advocate General gave his views on a question which had not been expressly referred by the national court.[47] The Court held that it had all the necessary details necessary for it to answer the questions referred and that those matters were addressed in the arguments presented to it at the hearing. The Court again declined to reopen the proceedings. Finally, in *Kvaerner Warnow Werft GmbH*, KWW asked the Court to reopen proceedings arguing that if the Court were to follow the Opinion of the Advocate General it would be forced to depart from the principle laid down in its earlier case-law that an interpretation by the Court of First Instance constitutes an assessment of fact and not a question of law and cannot therefore be the subject of appeal.[48] The Court declined to reopen the oral proceedings on the basis that it had before it all the necessary elements to allow it to deal with the questions raised in the case and that those elements had been discussed before it. Thus, although the possibility does exist for the reopening of proceedings the Court seems reluctant to follow this course of action.

It would appear that of the three procedural safeguards deemed by the European Court of Human Rights to be essential, two are absent and the third, in practice, leaves a great deal of discretion to the Court itself. It can therefore be argued that existing procedural safeguards are insufficient to ensure the degree of fairness of procedures required by Article 6.

Concluding observations

Not all cases which come before the European Court of Justice require the Court to determine the civil rights and obligations of individuals and the Court itself is never directly concerned with criminal proceedings. It could be argued therefore that Article 6(1) of the European Convention on Human Rights is not relevant. However, in increasing numbers of cases, the European Court of Justice is required to determine an individual's civil rights and obligations and the Court is indirectly asked to give preliminary references in cases where the Member States have implemented Community law and provided criminal sanctions for breaches of it. Article 6(1) is therefore of clear relevance to the European Court of Justice.

It is clear from the discussion of the cases above that there is unease on the part of some parties to proceedings before the European Court of Justice about the position of the Advocate General. This arises from a desire to have the opportunity to respond to the submissions of the Advocate General for fear that he might influence the Court to make a ruling which adversely affects their interests. In

[47] Case C-147/02 *M.K. Alabaster v Woolwich plc and Secretary of State for Social Security* [2004] ECR I-3101.

[48] Case C-181/02-P *Commission v Kvaerner Warnow Werft GmbH* [2004] ECR I-5703.

these cases, the European Court of Justice has admitted the importance of Article 6 and has held that:

> it is in deference to Article 6 of the European Convention of Human Rights and to the very purpose of every individual's right to adversarial proceedings and to a fair hearing within the meaning of that provision that the Court may of its own motion, on a proposal from the Advocate General or at the request of the parties, order that the oral procedure be reopened, in accordance with Article 61 of its Rules of Procedure, if it considers that it lacks sufficient information, or that the case must be dealt with on the basis of an argument which has not been debated between the parties.[49]

The European Court of Human Rights has tended to rely on a number of principles in its case-law, one of which is the doctrine of appearances. The Court, in the Belgian and French cases discussed above, accepts that the officer under scrutiny acts at all times with the strictest objectivity. Nonetheless where the function of the officer in question is to advise and accordingly influence the court in favour of, and therefore against the interests, of one of the parties his position becomes suspect. In *Reinhardt & Slimane-Kaïd* the Court of Human Rights spoke of the possibility that the Principal State Counsel might influence the Court through the authority of his office in a way that might be unfavourable to the interests of one of the parties. Thus, whilst it is true that the Advocate General is not entrusted with the defence of any particular interest this does not mean that parties to a case should not have the right of reply if his submission to the court might influence it to decide a case in a way that is prejudicial to them.

For the moment, the European Court of Justice appears to have set itself against a full consideration of the human rights aspects of its procedures insofar as they concern the function of the Advocate General. There is no doubt that there are some good and sound practical reasons for wanting to deny parties the right to comment on the submissions of the Advocate General. The volume of additional work that would be entailed by amending the procedures is a deterrent to the Court. However, practical reasons should not stand in the way of the application of human rights principles.

Given the direction of recent amendments to the judicial architecture of the European Union, it seems clear that for reasons of practicality rather than principle, the Advocate General will be involved in a lower percentage of cases than the founding fathers of the Court envisaged. Increasing devolution of the jurisdiction of the workload of the Court of Justice to the Court of First Instance and the creation of Judicial Panels means that there are numerous cases where the Advocate General will not be heard. In addition, the implementation of the amendments introduced by the Treaty of Nice (2001) mean that the Advocate General will be involved in cases only where an important point of law is in issue. In these circumstances it is essential that any suspicion that the procedures in the European Court

[49] *Vick*, n 43 above.

of Justice are unfair can be rebutted. Otherwise the credibility of the Court itself is called into question. The doctrine of appearances requires, at least, that the Court re-examine its own procedures.

There is at least an arguable case that the parties to a dispute should have the right to respond in some way to the submissions of the Advocate General. Trends in the case-law of the Court of Human Rights indicate that current procedures may not survive a human rights challenge. If such a challenge is successful, although this is by no means certain, then the procedures in the Court of Justice would have to be amended. The Court of Human Rights has provided indications of the kind of procedural safeguards that are needed to ensure fairness of proceedings. For example, providing an opportunity for the parties to a dispute to submit a memorandum for the deliberations of the Court would be a strong indication that the proceedings were indeed fair. Such a procedure would not entail a total reopening of the proceedings and some limitations might be imposed. For example, it might not be necessary to allow all parties who intervene in the case to have the right to submit a memorandum but only those who are affected directly by its outcome. In a preliminary reference procedure, for example, the parties to the initial dispute have the most at stake in the totality of the proceedings and they might be accorded the right to submit a memorandum.

Without some reform of proceedings, there is likely to be a growing number of cases which challenge the present arrangements and, failing to address the issue, the Court of Justice risks losing credibility. Confidence in the Court and in the function of the Advocate General will decline and the Court will continue to be confronted with requests to reopen the oral proceedings. Before the Court suffers a human rights challenge it is time to consider appropriate reforms in its procedures to ensure that such a challenge need not be brought.

Part II

Selected Advocates General and specific areas of Community law

4

The first Advocate General, Maurice Lagrange*

Introductory background

Maurice Lagrange was appointed Advocate General in 1953 and retired in 1964. He delivered over 60 Opinions in a period of 10 years, covering a wide range of issues.[1] The first Opinions exclusively concerned the European Coal and Steel Treaty (ECSC Treaty), whilst the remainder covered all the three Treaties.[2] The idea of having 'advisers' to assist the judges of the Court of Justice of the European Communities (European Court of Justice) in reaching a consensus judgment originated with the French delegation when negotiating the ECSC Treaty, which created the first of the three European Communities.[3] Maurice Lagrange, a member of the French delegation, is generally regarded as the founder of the office of Advocate General.[4] He was the first appointed Advocate General and took his experience as a former *Commissaire du Gouvernement* in the French *Conseil d'Etat*, with him.

This chapter focuses mainly on the Opinions delivered by Advocate General Lagrange on the admissibility of direct actions before the European Court of Justice brought by undertakings and on the scope of new procedures introduced by the EC Treaty which have played a significant role in creating and sustaining a uniform Community legal order (Article 226 action and Article 234 preliminary ruling).

*This chapter is an extended version of a paper entitled 'A Study of Selected Opinions delivered by Advocate General Lagrange' in (2003–04) 6 Cambridge Yearbook of European Legal Studies 83–103.

1 Approximately 36 on ECSC Treaty, 11 on EC Treaty and 16 on staff matters.

2 The European Coal and Steel Treaty (ECSC Treaty); the European Atomic Treaty (Euratom); and the European Economic Community Treaty (EEC Treaty), which has been renamed the European Community Treaty (EC Treaty). Throughout this chapter reference will be made to the European Community Treaty (EC Treaty) and to the current numbering of its Articles, even though, in the relevant period, the correct title was the EEC Treaty and the numbering of its provisions was different.

3 When the text of the European Coal and Steel Treaty was finalized, reference to the Advocate General was only made in the Protocol on the Statute of the Court of Justice. It was not until the 1965 Merger Treaty, when the institutions of the three Communities were merged, that reference to the Advocate General was inserted into the ECSC Treaty itself in the form of Art 32a.

4 Funeral oration for Maurice Lagrange delivered by Lord Mackenzie Stuart on 3 October 1986.

The Opinions in context

Although Lagrange delivered almost half of his Opinions in matters concerning the interpretation and application of the ECSC Treaty this chapter concentrates primarily on the Opinions he delivered in respect of the European Economic Community Treaty.[5] There are two reasons for this emphasis. First, the EC Treaty is of wider application, establishing a common market based on the four fundamental economic freedoms (goods, workers, establishment/services and capital) and common policies in other areas. Second, a new legal order—independent from national and international law—has been created and established mainly on the basis of the EC Treaty. This is the legal order we have today. The ECSC Treaty was specific to the coal and steel market and expired at the end of 2002.

The creation of a legal system

Right from the beginning Lagrange chose the comparative method and recourse to relevant literature as the tools to determine what principles and rules of law should be incorporated into the Community's legal order. As far as his methodology was concerned the Opinions were primarily based on an analysis of comparable situations in the national legal systems of the Member States,[6] and, where relevant, he also referred to international law. He examined the relevant laws of the Member States, and studied the national solutions to similar legal problems in order to extract common principles which could be applied, by analogy, to the interpretation of the Community's Treaties. For example, in his third Opinion, a Joined Opinion delivered in the first two cases brought by associations of undertakings,[7] Lagrange found that the concept of 'misuse of powers' was a common legal principle which underlines the control of the administration by the national courts. Administrative acts are to be performed within the limits of the law.[8] The function of the court is to determine whether those limits have been observed. In the same Opinion he also considered relevant literature as support for his own conclusion.[9]

[5] See n 1 above. Cases concerning disputes between the Institutions and their staff have been excluded.

[6] Sometimes Lagrange even referred to national law of non-Member States. For example, in Case 18/60 *Louis Worms v HA* [1962] ECR 195 he cited Swiss case-law, at 209.

[7] Cases 3/54 *Associazone Industrie Siderurgiche Italiane (ASSIDER) v HA* [1954–56] ECR 63 and 4/54 *Industrie Siderurgiche Associate (ISA) v HA* [1954–56] ECR 91 respectively at 73 of the Opinion. See also Cases 2/57 and 15/57 *Compagnie des Hauts Fourneaux de Chasse v HA* [1957–58] ECR 199 and 211, 235 et seq.

[8] Cases 3/54 and 4/54 at 85 of the Opinion.

[9] Ibid, 86. See also, for example, Cases 17/57 *De Gezamenlijke Steenkolenmijnen in Limburg v HA* [1959] ECR 1, 11; 23/59 *Acciaieria Ferriera di Roma (F.E.R.A.M.) v HA* [1959] ECR 245, 254.

In the first case where an applicant sought an interpretation of an earlier judgment,[10] Lagrange sought inspiration from international law, namely from a judgment of the Permanent Court of International Justice,[11] to define the conditions of admissibility.

In his first Opinion,[12] Lagrange's main task was to advise the Court as to what methods of interpretation to use in order to interpret Article 60(2)(a) ECSC.[13] Was the requirement in the Article to make the price lists and conditions of sale public a strict duty? The High Authority (HA) had issued several decisions[14] including Decision 2/54 in which Article 1 permitted undertakings to make a mean variation upwards or downwards of actual market prices and published prices without a prior publication of amendments to the price lists having been made. Lagrange considered that the literal meaning of the subsection was inconclusive and the interpretation of the subsection in context of Article 60 as a whole was also unhelpful. He therefore went on to interpret the subsection in the context of the Treaty as a whole. There is an immediate recognition that this Community Treaty is different from all other international Treaties. This teleological approach was defended as follows:

> Therefore it is necessary to go further; the question in dispute must be examined in relation to the Treaty in its entirety. Such an approach is always legitimate; it is particularly necessary in the case of this Treaty of 18 April 1951 because all its parts are interconnected. In particular, all the provisions of Title III represent only the implementation of the principles laid down in Title I, from which Title III must never be dissociated.[15]

He believed the drafting of Article 60(2)(a) to be loose and looked beyond the words at the objective of the Treaty as a whole. The European Court of Justice, however, reached a different interpretation and did not follow the advice of the Advocate General as to the meaning of Article 60(2).[16] The Court concluded that the duty expressed in the Treaty provision was a 'strict rule of law' and must be fulfilled in its entirety.[17] Thus Article 1 of Decision 2/54 was declared invalid.

Although, in the first case brought before the European Court of Justice, the Court reached a different conclusion from the Advocate General, the approach chosen by Lagrange, the so-called teleological interpretation method, has been one which the European Court of Justice has often adopted in its rulings.

[10] Case 5/55 *Assider v HA* [1954–56] ECR 135.

[11] Judgment of 16 December 1927 in the *Case Concerning the Factory at Chorzów*, PCIJ Rep Series A, No.13.

[12] Case 1/54 *France v HA* [1954–56] ECR 1, 18.

[13] Art 60(2)(a) provides that 'the price lists and conditions of sale applied by undertakings within the common market must be made public to the extent and in the manner prescribed by the Commission after consulting the Consultative Committee'.

[14] Decisions 1/54 and 2/54 [1952–58] OJ Spec Ed 14 respectively 15. Decision 3/54 JO of 13 January 1954, 219.

[15] Case 1/54 *France v HA* [1954–56] ECR 1, 26.

[16] Examples of other cases where the Court did not follow Lagrange's Opinion include: Case 1/55 [1954–56] ECR 135; Cases 20-23/58 [1959] ECR 75, 99, 107 and 117; Case 15/59 [1960] ECR 1; Cases 36-40/59 [1960] ECR 423; Case 8/55 [1954–56] ECR 245 (in part); Case 1/59 [1959] ECR 199.

[17] Case 1/54 *France v HA* [1954–56] ECR 1, 10.

Advocate General Lagrange was aware of the reaction outside the European Court of Justice to his Opinions. For example, in Cases 8/55 and 9/55, he took the opportunity to reply to one such criticism and defended the reliance he had placed on documents relating to the national ratification procedures of the ECSC Treaty when seeking to interpret the relevant Treaty provision in Cases 3/54 and 4/54. Lagrange underlined the fact that there were hardly any preparatory documents to assist with the interpretation of the ECSC Treaty. Therefore, the grounds stated by individual Member States during the national ratification procedures had greater importance, particularly as attempts had been made to coordinate such statements.[18]

As to the preferred method of interpretation to be applied to the ECSC Treaty, Lagrange first considered the wording of the provision in order to establish the common intention of the parties who signed this international contractual document, and then to apply general principles of law.

Another matter which is striking about these first Opinions is the prominence of procedural issues in the development of the Community's legal order. The first significant matter Advocate General Lagrange had to express a view on was whether it was possible for a party, in one single action, to bring annulment proceedings against more than one HA decision.[19] Given the connection between the decisions themselves and the fact that they were issued by the same institution, he perceived no valid reason which required them to be separate actions.

Role and style

Lagrange perceived his role very clearly. In his first Opinion he started by referring to Article 11 of the Protocol on the Statute of the Court of Justice which outlines the duty of the Advocate General. In his own words, this duty 'is to ensure that in the interpretation and application of the Treaty, and of rules laid down for the implementation thereof, the law is observed'.[20]

Although Lagrange was the product of a civil law system, he adopted a common lawyer's approach to case-law. In his Opinions he often drew the Court's attention to its own limited case law in order to promote consistency and fulfil one of the roles of the Advocate General, namely to protect the coherence of the Community's legal system. He also warned the Court, for example, in the *De Geus v Bosch*[21] case, where he informed the Court of the consequences of delivering a ruling before the conclusion of national proceedings on the appeal against a referral to the European Court of Justice. Similarly, in the *Costa v ENEL*[22] case he warned the Court of the danger of Article 234 rulings going too far and, in the guise of interpretation, resulting in the European Court of Justice actually performing the

18 Joined Opinion in Cases 8/55 and 9/55 [1954–56] ECR 245, 271.

19 Case 1/54 *France v HA* [1954–56] ECR 1.

20 Ibid, 18. The duty of the Advocate General is now enshrined in Art 222 EC.

21 Case 13/61 [1962] ECR 45.

22 Case 6/64 [1964] ECR 585.

function of the national court. The significance of this approach lies in the fact that Lagrange regarded his role primarily as an adviser to the judges, offering solutions but also warning the Court of possible consequences. In discharging the role he gave great importance to the consistent and coherent development of the Community legal order and, in particular, to the creation of Community legal principles compatible with the national legal orders.

The style Lagrange adopted was rather academic, identifying principles which the Court was advised to adopt as Community law principles and thus to build up the embryonic legal system which had been created by the EC Treaty.[23] Lagrange's approach was fundamentally to identify matters of principle upon which a ruling from the European Court of Justice was necessary. In the *De Geus* case he urged, as a matter of principle, that the Court must deliver an 'abstract interpretation'. In the *Wagner*[24] case he urged the Court not to wait for the European Assembly's decision on whether or not they were prepared to waive the immunity of two of their members, because the meaning of 'duration of sessions' was a matter for the Court to decide, not the Assembly. Similarly, in the *Da Costa en Schaake*[25] case Lagrange pressed the European Court of Justice to rule on the relationship between the Court and the national court of last instance as a matter of principle.

As to the style of the Opinions themselves, Lagrange described the facts of the cases briefly. In the *Costa v ENEL* case, for example, Lagrange states '[t]he facts are known to you' and then summarizes them in one paragraph.[26] The Opinions however were written in a discursive manner contrasting vividly with the short and laconic judgments of the Court.

The Opinions were a product of the time: face-to-face delivery encouraged a dialogue with the Court which is inconceivable today when merely the operative part of the Opinion is read out in open court. It is evident from the tone of the Opinions that Advocate General Lagrange engaged in a dialogue with the Court, sometimes with subtle humour,[27] which can only be imagined in a situation when the Opinions were read in full in open court. For example in the *Costa v ENEL* case he began the Opinion thus:

> The preliminary question upon which you have to give a ruling under Article 177 [Article 234] of the EEC Treaty does not, for once, come from a Netherlands court, but from an Italian one, and it is no longer a question of social security or of Regulation No 3, but

[23] See, for example, Opinion delivered in Cases 3 and 4/54 on 'misuse of powers' ground for allowing organizations to challenge general acts of the High Authority directly before the European Court of Justice and Lagrange's approach to the interpretation of the scope of Art 234 EC.

[24] Case 101/63 *M. Albert Wagner v MM Jean Fohrmann and Antoine Krier* [1964] ECR 195.

[25] Joined Cases 28, 29 and 30/62 *Da Costa en Schaake NV, Jacob Meijer NV, Hoechst-Holland NV v Netherlands Inland Revenue Administration* [1963] ECR 31.

[26] In Cases 1/57 and 14/57 Lagrange expressly dispenses with the facts 'which were admirably set out in the report of the Juge-Rapporteur, were the subject of detailed consideration in the pleadings, and will be fresh in your minds'. [1957–58] ECR 105, 116.

[27] For example: Cases 17 and 20/61 [1962] ECR 357, 349 where Lagrange stated 'The applicant companies are really rather engaging in these cases in a sort of rear-guard action showing in this

rather of a certain number of provisions of the Treaty itself, in respect of which your interpretation is requested in circumstances that are such as to bring in issue the constitutional relations between the European Economic Community and its Member States. This highlights the importance of the judgment you are called upon to pronounce in this case.[28]

This conversional style was again evident in *Commission v Italy* where Lagrange states 'you know the two opposing arguments'.[29] Diplomatic and flattering language was also used by Lagrange. For example, in his second Opinion, he apologizes for his failure to address the Court in the language of the case, Italian. Since the case was almost identical to the one already considered by the Court, Lagrange apologizes to the Italian Government for a brief Opinion but reassures the applicant that 'this does not imply that I have studied the questions raised only on the occasion of the first action. I have read with the same attention all the statements submitted in the two cases'.[30] Lagrange maintained this style throughout his period in office. For example, in *Costa v ENEL* which was one of his last Opinions, having given a detailed analysis of the relationship between national laws, including national constitutions, and Community law he concluded with the following words:

I feel bound to add that, if I have considered it necessary to present such observations, it was solely to clarify the issues, and to allow everyone to accept his responsibilities. I do not for a moment, however, consider that Italy, which has always been in the forefront amongst the promoters of the European idea, the country of the conference of Messina and the Treaty of Rome, cannot find a constitutional means of allowing the Community to live in full accordance with the rules created under its common charter.[31]

Direct actions brought by undertakings

An important element of the Community Treaties was the establishment of a court, the European Court of Justice, and the agreement of the contracting parties, the Member States, to refer any matter of validity or interpretation of the Treaties exclusively to that Court. The Treaties grant direct access to the European Court of Justice not only to the Member States, but also to organizations and natural and

respect a skill which the inherent difficulty of this kind of warfare makes particularly praiseworthy'; Case 36/62 [1963] ECR 289, 299 where Lagrange stated 'the applicant recalls at length—one might even say, with nostalgia—the argument developed in its first application'. In this case the applicant, SNUPAT, has brought several actions against the HA concerning the administration of the equalization scheme.

[28] See Case 6/64 *Costa v ENEL* [1964] ECR 585, 600. Other examples: Cases 16-18/59 [1960] ECR 17, 27, where, at the beginning of the Opinion, Lagrange states 'I think I can omit even a summary history of the joint marketing organizations of the Ruhr which we all are beginning to know quite well'; Cases 3-18/58 and 25-26/58 and 19/58 [1960] ECR 173, 201, where Lagrange states 'It is possible that the Court may share such a point of view. I can only say that the Court's Advocate-General certainly does not'. Case 66/63 [1964] ECR 533, 552, where he states 'It would, I think, be an insult to the Court to relate, even summarily the history of the joint-selling organization for Ruhr coal'.

[29] Case 7/61 [1961] ECR 317.

[30] Case 2/54 *Italian Republic v HA* [1954–56] ECR 37, 57.

[31] Case 6/64 *Costa v ENEL* [1964] ECR 585, 606.

legal persons under specific conditions set out in each of the respective Treaties. This novel element was put into practice pretty quickly. The first two cases were brought before the European Court of Justice by two Member States (France and Italy) [32] but the next two cases were brought by two organizations seeking annulment of the very same acts of the HA.[33]

As stated above, one of the most interesting and unusual features of the Community's legal order is the *locus standi* granted by the Community Treaties to organizations or natural and legal persons to challenge individual and general acts directly before the European Court of Justice. The international legal order under which the Community Treaties were negotiated and signed does not normally grant the right of non-States to enforce rights conferred on them by such treaties. The ECSC Treaty however permitted, in Article 33, that 'undertakings or associations' be permitted to institute proceedings against certain acts concerning them and, more significantly, against general acts 'which they consider to involve a misuse of powers affecting them'. The wording chosen in the equivalent provision under the EC Treaty, Article 230, is different. As far as general acts are concerned 'any natural and legal person' may institute such proceedings against a general act only when the latter is 'of direct and individual concern' to them.

Admissibility of actions: *locus standi* of undertakings under Article 33 ECSC Treaty

In this initial period in the creation of the Community's legal order most of the applications to the European Court of Justice were for annulment of HA decisions concerning the administration of an equalization scheme set up by the HA to regulate prices for ferrous scrap. Often a single Opinion was delivered for several cases which were brought by different parties since the legal issues raised in these cases were common to them all.[34]

As stated earlier, the first two ECSC Treaty cases brought by undertakings (Cases 3 and 4/54) challenged the same HA decisions which had been challenged by France and Italy. The two organizations were seeking annulment of a general act of the HA, therefore whether the action was admissible was dependent on whether the organizations concerned could show that there had been misuse of powers by the HA affecting them (Article 33 ECSC).[35] 'Misuse of powers' was a concept with two functions under Article 33 since it was both a condition of

[32] Cases 1/54 *France v HA* [1954–56] ECR 1 and 2/54 *Italy v HA* [1954–56] ECR 37.

[33] Cases 3/54 *ASSIDER v HA* [1954–56] ECR 63 and 4/54 *ISA v HA* [1954–56] ECR 91.

[34] For example, Cases 8/57 to 13/57 [1956–57] ECR 265 et seq. where Belgian, German and French organizations, as well as three individual French undertakings, sought annulment of the HA's Decision 2/57; Cases 3-18, 25-26/58 [1960] ECR 173 and Case 19/58 [1960] ECR 225.

[35] Similar issues were raised in Case 8/55 *Federation Charbonniere de Belgique v HA* [1954–56] ECR 245 and Case 9/55 *Société des Charbannages de Beeringen and others v HA* [1954–56] ECR 311 brought by three individual undertakings against the same general decision of the High Authority.

admissibility for challenges against general acts and one of the four grounds for annulment listed in the Article. In a single Opinion, Lagrange identified this dual function and then proceeded to determine the meaning of 'misuse of powers' by carrying out a comparative analysis of national laws. He found that the legal principles which underline control of the administration in the Member States are all the same. He then examined the wording of Article 33 itself concluding that the authors of the Treaty were concerned with a situation where a decision of the HA, individually affecting an organization, was disguised as a general act. They perceived such a situation as being a misuse of power per se thus enabling the organization concerned to challenge the act which, on the face of it, appeared to be general in application. Thus, in order for the action to be admissible in these circumstances the substantive issue of misuse of powers should have to be considered first. Since the applicants in these cases failed to show that the challenged measure was in fact adopted to harm the Italian industry which they represented, Lagrange concluded that the action was inadmissible. The European Court of Justice, however, admitted the action declaring it was enough to allege 'formally' (with reasons) misuse of powers. Nevertheless, following its earlier judgment in Cases 1/54 and 2/54, the Court dismissed the action as unfounded.[36]

In the next group of cases raising issues of admissibility of organizations, Case 8/55 *Fédération Charbonnière de Belgique v HA*[37] and Case 9/55 brought by three individual undertakings,[38] Advocate General Lagrange's approach was consistent with the one he had expressed in his first Opinion on this matter.[39] He emphasized the concept of 'legal interest' and rejected a narrow and rigid interpretation of Article 33. However, where the organization challenged a general HA decision, it had to show that the misuse of powers had affected it. He concluded that the action was admissible on all points as regards Case 8/55 but the application in Case 9/55 was admissible only as regards the decision which deprived the three individual undertakings of equalization or reduced equalization. The European Court of Justice took the opportunity in these cases to clarify the meaning of Article 33 ECSC. The Court confirmed its earlier ruling in Cases 3/54 and 4/54

[36] Having failed in their action, ASSIDER brought another action (Case 5/55 *ASSIDER v HA* [1954–56] ECR 135) requesting an interpretation from the European Court of Justice of the judgment delivered in *Italy v HA* (Case 2/54 [1954–56] ECR 37) to which it had not been a party. This raised a procedural issue as to whether an applicant in these circumstances had *locus standi*. Both the Court and the Advocate General concluded that ASSIDER had established the necessary 'interest' within the meaning of Art 37 of the Statute of the Court which provides for an application for interpretation of judgments. Given that there were a number of applications made against the same HA decision, and in one of those applications the decision had been annulled, then the applicants in the other cases had an 'interest' in an interpretation of the judgment. The Advocate General concluded that the applicant had failed however to demonstrate another condition of Art 37 namely that 'the meaning or scope of a judgment is in doubt'. The Court expressly agreed with the Advocate General but was willing to quote the relevant paragraphs of the earlier judgment which defined the scope of that judgment.

[37] [1954–56] ECR 245.

[38] [1954–56] ECR 311.

[39] Joined Opinion on Cases 3/54 *ASSIDER v HA* and 4/54 *ISA v HA* [1954–56] ECR 63, 174.

that it was sufficient for organizations to claim formally misuse of powers. The Court went on to state that:

as against the general decision, therefore, the applicant may rely only on the submission of misuse of powers affecting it. As regards the individual decision, since the parties are agreed that it may be so described, the applicant may rely on all submissions set out in the first paragraph of Article 33.[40]

Advocate General Lagrange was also prepared to consider issues of standing not raised by the defendants. For example, in Joined Cases 17 and 20/61,[41] he examined whether a parent company is a properly qualified entity to take proceedings against the HA, concluding that it was so qualified. The question was particularly interesting in this case as the HA had argued for a different concept of undertaking when applying the equalization scheme!

Admissibility of actions: *locus standi* of undertakings under Article 230 EEC Treaty

Lagrange also delivered the first ever Opinion on the admissibility of Article 230 actions brought by non-privileged applicants. The cases, *Confédération nationale des producteurs de fruits et légumes and ors v Council*[42] and *Fédération nationale de la boucherie en gros et du commerce en gros des viandes and others v Council*,[43] were brought by associations of producers and wholesalers who wished to challenge the validity of Council regulations applying certain rules to the production of and trade in agricultural products. Since the same issues on admissibility were raised in all the cases, Lagrange decided to deliver one single Opinion.

Although questions of admissibility and of substance are often dealt with together, Lagrange viewed this case differently since the issue of principle, involving interpretation of the Treaty as to the extent of judicial control of the 'executive', was a matter of public interest to be settled 'clearly, once and for all, independently of the actual case before the Court'.[44] The advice was indeed followed by the Court.

Having compared the provisions in the EC Treaty with the corresponding ones in the ECSC Treaty he concluded that the EC Treaty was more liberal as to the definition of non-privileged applicants; however, the EC Treaty was stricter with regard to the conditions that non-privileged applicants must fulfil before instituting proceedings challenging decisions addressed to others or against general measures.[45] The Court concurred with his advice.

40 Case 8/55 *Fédération Charbonnière de Belgique v HA* [1954–56] ECR 245, 258.

41 *Klöckner-Werke AG and Hoesch AG v HA* [1962] ECR 357, 349.

42 Joined Cases 16 and 17/62 [1962] ECR 471.

43 Joined Cases 19 to 22/62 [1962] ECR 491.

44 Joined Cases 16 and 17/62 *Confédération nationale des producteurs de fruits et légumes and ors v Council* [1962] ECR 471, 482.

45 Under Art 33 ECSC only undertakings and their associations (rather than 'any natural or legal person' under Art 230 EC) may have direct access to the European Court of Justice. However, these non-privileged applicants may challenge individual decisions addressed to others provided that they

Given the current debate on the *locus standi* of individuals before the European Court of Justice,[46] some *obiter dicta* passages in Lagrange's Opinion are of particular interest:

Let me limit myself to observing, although strictly this is superfluous, that it will be of no avail to follow the applicant associations in their efforts to compare their interests or the sphere of interests that they represent with the provisions of the regulations interfering with their interests. These efforts might be upheld in a legal system other than that which has been established by the Treaty and particularly if the Treaty has been limited to requiring as in the internal law of those Member States which allow applications for annulment against regulations, proof of an *interest*, or even of a direct interest, before an application can be admissible.[47]

The Court too has never admitted that this concept of interest was itself capable of affecting the legal character of the measure in question; it is for that reason that the Court has not followed the suggestion to introduce an element of *relativity* into the concept of an individual decision, and has kept instead to the orthodox concept of a regulation, to which it seems to have assimilated that of a general decision.[48]

In this Treaty, in short, there is no place for a body of case law governing the concept of an interest, because from all the evidence its authors intended themselves to determine the conditions governing the admissibility of proceedings by persons other than those I have called 'privileged persons,' and that has been done in terms so precise as to leave hardly any room for interpretation.[49]

Such is the system that the jurist, for his part, might find unsatisfactory, but which the Court is bound to apply. This is not the place to justify the system. One might observe only that it is coherent and that serious arguments can be put forward to justify it.[50]

Lagrange then proceeded to consider the arguments against the system established by the EC Treaty and, in support of the status quo, concluded with the following words: 'I beg to be excused for this incursion into the political arena. I have undertaken it only to show that we are presented here, by the authors of the Treaty, with a considered device which it cannot be for the Court to correct'.[51]

'*concern* them' and challenge general measures 'which they consider to involve a misuse of powers *affecting* them'. Under Art 230 EC natural or legal persons may only challenge a decision addressed to others or a general measure if they can demonstrate that the measure concerned is 'of *direct* and *individual* concern' to them.

[46] See among others, A Ward, 'Judicial architecture at the cross-roads: private parties and challenge to EC measures post-*Jégo Quéré*' (2001) 4 Cambridge Yearbook of European Legal Studies 412; A Albors-Llorens, 'Standing of private parties to challenge Community measures: has the European Court missed the boat?' (2003) 62 CLJ 72.

[47] Joined Cases 16 and 17/62 *Confédération nationale des producteurs de fruits et légumes and ors v Council* [1962] ECR 471, 485.

[48] Ibid, 486.

[49] Ibid.

[50] Ibid, 486.

[51] Ibid, 487. These quotes from Lagrange's Opinion vividly illustrate that from an early stage in the development of the Community legal order the limitations on the *locus standi* of non-privileged applicants under Art 230 EC were found to be unsatisfactory. Nevertheless, Lagrange succinctly examined the reasons for such limitations and concluded that the expressed will of the authors of the Treaty should prevail. This is very much the same conclusion that the European Court of Justice reached in Case C-50/00 *Unión de Pequeños Agricultores v Council (UPA)* [2002] ECR I-6677, 40 years later. The Opinion of Advocate General Jacobs in *UPA*, and the support it received from jurists (see, for example, n 46 above) is a clear indication that this matter is not yet settled.

Admissibility and other issues raised in the context of ECSC Treaty cases

Although Lagrange interpreted Article 33 strictly in respect of *locus standi* of undertakings, he had a much more generous approach to other issues of admissibility and substance.[52] In respect of admissibility issues, this is clearly demonstrated in the Joined Opinions he delivered in Cases 2/57 and 15/57[53] and subsequently. The applicant in Case 15/57 sought annulment of a HA decision seeking recovery of sums due as equalization levy. The applicant relied on the provisions of Article 36 ECSC which expressly provided for the 'objection of illegality' in the case of appeals against decisions imposing fines or periodical penalty payments. Thus the applicant alleged the illegality of the general decision upon which the decision for recovery of the levy was based.

Advocate General Lagrange had no difficulty in advising the European Court of Justice that the plea of illegality of the general decision should be admissible. Furthermore, he argued that it should be unconditionally admissible meaning that the applicant could rely on all grounds of illegality listed in Article 33 ECSC and not simply on the 'misuse of powers' ground. The latter would have been the only allowable ground for annulment of the general decision had the undertakings sought to annul the contended decision soon after it had been adopted. In reaching this conclusion Lagrange relied mainly on the wording of Article 33 itself. The Article clearly provided that where undertakings challenge decisions which are individual in character they may rely on all grounds of annulment listed in Article 33 paragraph 1. Lagrange stated: 'I cannot see why a review of the legality of a basic decision should be confined to a single ground of misuse of powers once it is accepted that the objection of illegality may be raised in support of proceedings against a decision in an individual case'.[54] The European Court of Justice agreed with the Advocate General's conclusions.

A large number of cases concerning the concept of 'own resources scrap' within the meaning of Decision 2/57 raised interesting legal issues for the Advocate General and the Court.[55] The applications for annulment raised the question as to whether letters from the HA addressed to an agency entrusted with the implementation of the equalization systems were to be considered 'decisions' and therefore reviewable. The first cases concerned four German undertakings.[56] The issue

[52] See for example Case 1/59 *Macchiorlati Dalmas & Figli v HA* [1959] ECR 199, 211 where Lagrange proposed a reduction of the fine (not followed by the Court) because 'the infringement is a first offence . . . and should be regarded as a token penalty'.

[53] Case 15/57 *Compagnie des Hauts Fourneaux de Chasse v HA* [1957–58] ECR 199 and 211, 233.

[54] Ibid, 235.

[55] By successive decisions taken since 1954 the HA had established a system of equalization of prices requiring contributions to be paid by ECSC iron and steel undertakings as the basis of their consumption of 'bought scrap'. Their own resources scrap however was excluded from the levy. The criterion adopted by the HA to define scrap subject to the equalization levy was the amount of scrap purchased by the undertaken consuming it.

[56] Cases 20-23/58 [1959] ECR 75, 99, 107 and 117.

of admissibility centred on whether a letter from the HA contained a decision.[57] The agency in charge of implementing the equalization system for ferrous scrap sought a clarification from the HA as to the meaning of the concept 'own resources scrap' within the meaning of Decision 2/57. Certain undertakings consuming scrap from their own resources benefited from an exemption and, therefore, from making a financial contribution. The HA replied and the letter was published. The German undertakings sought annulment of this letter. Lagrange had no hesitation in reaching the conclusion that the letter was indeed a decision (within the meaning of Article 14 ECSC) against which action could be brought. He reviewed the requirements of the basic general Decision 2/57 and concluded that, in the absence of unanimity of the delegated body, the HA had an obligation to take a decision and therefore to exercise a power. Furthermore, he considered that the decision was individual in character and concerned each of the four undertakings. Thus he was persuaded to allow the undertakings to rely on all the grounds for annulment listed in Article 33 ECSC and not simply on a misuse of powers.[58]

The generous approach of the Advocate General contrasts with the more conservative one of the European Court of Justice which reached the opposite conclusion. In a shorter than normal judgment, the Court dismissed the application as inadmissible. The expressed wording of the letter indicated that the HA had no intention of adopting a decision but was reaffirming principles which followed logically from Decision 2/57. The Court classified the letter as an internal document intended to direct the activity of the body whose services came under its authority.

The next set of cases (Cases 32 and 33/58), raising similar issues as to the nature of various letters, concerned two French undertakings seeking annulment of letters addressed to them and issued, not by the HA but, by the agencies to whom the HA had delegated the implementation of the equalization systems.[59] Were

[57] See also joined Cases 1/57 and 14/57 *Société des usines à tubes de la Sarre v HA* [1957–58] ECR 105 where the admissibility of the cases depended on whether letters written to the applicants by the HA in response to the investment proposal submitted by the applicant were reviewable acts of the HA. Both the Advocate General and the Court concluded that one of the letters was an opinion within the meaning of the fourth paragraph of Art 54 ECSC. Lagrange considered at length whether such an opinion was a reviewable act—'a question of principle'. He focused on the text of the Article which distinguished three categories of acts, one of which was an 'opinion' with no binding effect. Since the fifth paragraph provided that an *adverse* opinion delivered on investments 'shall have the force of a decision', the non-adverse opinions challenged in these cases were not reviewable. Another example raising the question whether a letter from the HA was in fact a reviewable decision is Case 14/59 *Société des fonderies de Pont-à-Mousson v HA* [1959] ECR 215.

[58] cf Case 17/57 *De Gezamenlijke Steenkolenmijnen in Limburg v HA* [1959] ECR 1, at 10–13 where Lagrange reached a different conclusion as to the nature of a HA letter. In this Opinion Lagrange undertakes an in depth analysis relying on literature, French national cases and distinguished earlier European Court of Justice rulings.

[59] Joined Cases 32/58 and 33/58 *SNUPAT v HA* [1959] ECR 127 and Case 42/58 *SAFE v HA* [1959] ECR 183.

these letters reviewable acts of the HA? Since the judgment in the earlier group of cases had not been delivered before Lagrange delivered his Opinion, he had no chance to take into account the judgment of the European Court of Justice. As Lagrange had concluded that the HA letter on 'own resources scrap' was a reviewable decision, he naturally continued to follow the same conclusion in respect of this specific letter. The European Court of Justice judgment, although not favourable to the applicants, nevertheless contained an important finding. The Court stated that, although the exemption of own resources scrap was a legitimate exemption, the assimilation of group scrap to 'own resources' was incompatible with the ECSC Treaty.[60] Thus ferrous scrap known as 'group scrap' was to be regarded as bought scrap and subject to a levy. The consequence of this ruling was another two applications from SNUPAT (Cases 42 and 49/59) seeking various remedies for alleged inaction by the HA upon the Court's ruling of illegality of group scrap (ie failure to withdraw the exemptions granted to undertakings prior to the Court's judgment in Cases 32 and 33/58). Finally, we have consensus between Lagrange and the Court. In Case 42/59, a letter from the Market Division of the HA was held not to be a decision and the application was declared inadmissible.[61] In the second application, Case 49/59, new points were raised. In this application SNUPAT sought a declaration that the HA had failed to act by not revoking the group scrap exemption that it had granted to two undertakings following the European Court of Justice's judgment confirming the incompatibility with the ECSC Treaty of the group scrap own resources exemption. Both the Advocate General and the Court concluded that the application was admissible and the implied decision not to revoke was annulled. Lagrange, in his Opinion in Case 49/59, accepted expressly the Court's ruling in the earlier case (Cases 20-23/58) where, contrary to his own conclusion, the Court ruled that the HA's letter on the concept of own resources scrap was not a reviewable decision. He provided a succinct resume of the Court's rulings to date as to when and under what conditions undertakings may challenge acts of the HA or acts of agencies to whom the HA has delegated the implementation of the equalization systems.[62] This kind of analysis of the existing case-law is extremely helpful in mapping out the development of Community law as to the nature of a reviewable decision. Furthermore, Lagrange was discharging an important function of the Advocate General, namely to give coherence to the Court's case-law.[63]

In his Opinion Lagrange also considered another delicate issue—namely the effects of a judgment of annulment. This is the first case where an annulment of a

[60] The term 'group scrap' was used to describe ferrous scrap produced by an undertaking and consumed by another in the same group of undertakings.

[61] Joined Cases 42 and 49/59 *SNUPAT v HA* [1961] ECR 53. [62] Ibid, 93–94.

[63] For another example see Case 30/59 *De Gezamenlijke Steenkolenmijnen in Limburg v HA* [1961] ECR 1, 37–38 where Lagrange sets out the development in the case-law of the Court in respect of the conditions which organizations and undertakings have to meet in order to challenge HA general decisions.

decision is proposed. Should such an annulment have legal effects only on the applicant or should it have a more general consequence? Should the annulment have retroactive consequences? Although accepting that normally such annulments should be confined to the applicant, Lagrange concluded that in this case the annulment should apply generally. The matter concerned the equalization system which was of interest to all participating undertakings. The Advocate General stated: 'Any other solution would disregard the principle of equality and unity which is at the basis of the equalization machinery established as between competing undertakings in their common interest'.[64]

On the principle of retroactivity, Lagrange was of the view that a period of limitation was appropriate in terms of several years rather than months but this was initially up to the HA to decide.[65]

Applicants sometimes combined an action for annulment (Article 33 ECSC) with an action for failure to act (Article 35 ECSC). In Case 17/57 [66] a Dutch association of undertakings sought annulment of an alleged decision contained in letters written by the HA to the German Government and also alleged that the HA had failed to act, in breach of Article 35 ECSC. Both the Court and the Advocate General found the application inadmissible in respect of both actions but with different reasoning. The European Court of Justice ruled the failure-to-act plea inadmissible on procedural grounds since the plea was introduced in the Reply which was too late in the proceedings. Lagrange, however, taking a less strict approach, did consider the admissibility of the plea. He found that the request from the applicants to the HA was a sort of notification that could lead to a failure-to-act action if the HA did not respond. As Lagrange stated, the object of the Article 35 procedure was, in that particular case, to protect the general rule requiring preliminary administrative action. Once the HA took action, that act could then be challenged under Article 33 but not under Article 35 ECSC.

The ECSC Treaty also provided, in Article 40, for undertakings to bring direct actions against the HA for wrongful acts or omissions. Such actions brought against administrative organs are difficult to prove since it is not every wrongful

[64] Joined Cases 42 and 49/59 *SNUPAT v HA* [1961] ECR 53, 96.

[65] This matter of the retroactive effect of a withdrawal of an exemption was mentioned by the European Court of Justice in its judgment but the Court simply stated this was a matter for the HA to exercise its discretion once it considered all the relevant factors. However, the issue was brought back to the European Court of Justice in Case 14/61 *Koninklijke Nederlandsche Hoogovens en Staalfabrieken N.V. v HA* [1962] Spec Ed 253. The applicants challenged the failure of the HA, upon the Court's ruling (SNUPAT judgment) in respect of the illegality of the group own resources exemptions, to withdraw the group scrap exemptions it had granted to two other undertakings. Both the Advocate General and the Court reached the conclusion that the action was unfounded. In his Opinion Lagrange gave much thought to the question of what the limits were on the Court's powers to review, so far as the legality of the decision not to withdraw the exemptions are concerned. In his view the legal control exercised by the Court should be carried out in the normal conditions of an application for annulment of a decision. The Court should look at the evidence to decide whether it justified the decision in law.

[66] Case 17/57 *De Gezamenlijke Steenkolenmijnen in Limburg v HA* [1959] ECR 1.

act or omission which results in a successful damage claim. Lagrange delivered important Opinions in applications alleging wrongful act or omission by the HA. Together with the European Court of Justice's judgments, these Opinions laid the foundations for future development of this cause of action.

The first non-staff case where an applicant sought pecuniary reparation from the HA was *FERAM*.[67] The applicant, however, was unable to prove that the HA had failed in the exercise of its supervisory functions by not checking the veracity of information supplied by an official in a Dutch Ministry. The Dutch official had signed fraudulent declarations concerning consumption of ferrous scrap. In this case, and in several others that followed relying on the same facts,[68] the Advocate General and the Court dismissed the actions as unfounded. However, in Cases 33/59 and 46-47/59,[69] Lagrange was prepared to be more generous to the applicants. As to the liability of the HA, Lagrange relied on an earlier ruling of the Court, where the Court had ruled that the HA was liable for the wrongful acts or omissions committed by the equalization agencies[70] to whom they had delegated an administrative task. He reasoned that since the equalization agencies were administrative organs, they had failed in their duty to check the information supplied. Thus Lagrange concluded that the HA was responsible for that wrongful act of the agencies and should compensate the applicants. Lagrange, therefore, advised the Court to refer the matter back to the HA to fix the compensation due. The Court, however, observed that the applicants' pleadings relied only on the failure of the HA to check the information received from the Dutch official. The judgment, therefore, was confined to that allegation which had already been dismissed in the *FERAM* case. The European Court of Justice merely repeated, almost word for word, the ruling it had delivered in the *FERAM* case.

Failures of Member States to fulfil their Treaty obligations: Article 226 EC Treaty

Member States' failures to meet their Treaty obligations are dealt with differently depending on whether the matter concerned the ECSC Treaty or the EC Treaty. Under the ECSC Treaty such failures were assigned to the executive, the High Authority, and only the decision of the High Authority was subject to judicial review under Article 33 ECSC. The EC Treaty, on the other hand, confers on the European Court of Justice sole responsibility, upon an application by the Commission (Article 226 action) or by another Member State (Article 227 action), to decide whether a Member State has failed to fulfil a Treaty obligation.

[67] Case 23/59 *Acciaieria Ferriera di Roma (F.E.R.A.M.) v HA* [1959] ECR 245.

[68] Joined Cases 14, 16, 17, 20, 24, 26 and 27/60 and 1/61 [1961] ECR 161 and Case 18/60 [1962] ECR 195.

[69] [1962] ECR 411.

[70] Joined Cases 19 and 21/60 and 2 and 3/61 *Société Fives Lille Cail and ors v HA* [1961] ECR 281 (AG Roemer).

Advocate General Lagrange delivered Opinions in only two Article 226 actions but they were significant in laying down the foundations for future development.

Both cases alleged that Italy was in breach of 'standstill' obligations laid down in the EC Treaty provisions concerning the free movement of goods.[71] In *Commission v Italy*,[72] the European Court of Justice, for the first time, was asked to rule on a number of questions concerning the scope of this type of action which concerns the investigation of the failures of Member States to fulfil their EC Treaty obligations. This was a new cause of action and Lagrange immediately perceived that it conferred on the European Court of Justice a very important responsibility since the objectives of the EC Treaty are so dependent on the conduct of the Member States.

Two issues were identified in this first case for the Court to rule upon: one in respect of admissibility; the other a matter of substance but with an impact on admissibility, namely, whether the Commission's application was devoid of purpose since the alleged breach was no longer in existence. Should the case proceed even if the Member State was now meeting its Treaty obligations?

Although acknowledging that the issue of admissibility should normally be considered first, Lagrange asked the Court's permission to deal with the question of lack of purpose first. The reason given was that 'its solution depends essentially on the interpretation of Article 169 [Article 226] and Article 171 [Article 228] of the Treaty and that interpretation governs in part the consideration of the objections of inadmissibility entered by the defendant'.[73]

He proceeded to examine the wording of Article 226 in order to express a view as to whether a lack of purpose would defeat the action. He concluded that '[t]he Court had no other duty than to say whether or not the Italian Government complied with the Commission's opinion'.[74] He did not accept the argument that the action was devoid of purpose since the action was to establish the breach which could not be remedied by compliance at a later date. He stressed the point by stating '[a]ny other solution would appear to me not only contradictory to the wording of Article 171 [Art. 228], but apt to deprive the procedure for the establishment of failures of States to fulfil their obligations of a large part of its effectiveness'.[75]

The European Court of Justice's judgment followed the order of issues chosen by Lagrange and accepted his interpretation of Article 226 by ruling that: 'if the Member State does not comply with the opinion within the prescribed period, there is no question that the Commission has the right to obtain the Court's judgment on that Member State's failure to fulfil the obligations flowing from the Treaty'.[76]

As to the issue of admissibility, one of the arguments of the Italian Government was particularly interesting, namely that the document from the Commission was not a 'reasoned opinion' within the meaning of Article 226 because it did not

[71] Case 7/61 *Commission v Italy* [1961] ECR 317 and Case 10/61 *Commission v Italy* [1962] ECR 1. These standstill provisions required Member States to refrain from introducing between themselves any quantitative restrictions (Case 7/61) or new customs duties (Case 10/61) before such measures were abolished completely.

[72] Case 7/61 [1961] ECR 317.

[73] Ibid, 333.

[74] Ibid.

[75] Ibid, 335.

[76] Ibid, 326.

examine the arguments set out by the Italian Government alleging a serious crisis and the necessity for the provisional measures taken by the Government. Lagrange concluded that:

> [N]o formalism must be demanded of this document, since, as I have said the reasoned opinion is not an administrative act subject to review by the Court of its legality. There can be no question here of "inadequacy of reasons" producing a defect of form. The reasoned opinion is intended solely to convey the Commission's point of view in order to enlighten the Government concerned and, should the need arise, the Court. If the opinion contains an inadequate statement of the reasons on which it is based, the consequence is merely the risk that the Court may not be able to find that there has been a failure to fulfil obligations and may for that reason have to dismiss the action, but that is a question of substance and not of form.[77]

The European Court of Justice was, as usual, much briefer than the Advocate General. The Court's view of this ground for inadmissibility was simply that a 'reasoned opinion' is sufficient where it contains 'a coherent statement of the reasons which led the Commission to believe that the State in question has failed to fulfil an obligation under the Treaty'.[78] Here the Court clearly followed the Advocate General's thinking on the matter.

Opinions delivered in preliminary rulings under Article 234 EC Treaty

This was an innovative procedure which is generally recognized as the single most significant mechanism in the EC Treaty for ensuring the uniformity of Community law and the respect for the rule of law in the Community. The Article 234 preliminary ruling procedure has also transformed national courts into Community courts giving the Community a ready-made judicature.

The scope of Article 234—preliminary ruling procedure

The importance of the Article 234 procedure was understood straight away by Lagrange. In *De Geus v Bosch,* the first case referred to the European Court of Justice under this procedure,[79] Lagrange stated that the procedure is 'designed to play a central part in the application of the Treaty,' that 'Article 177 [234] is also in part a matter of constitutional law' and that 'the procedure is one which is largely governed by considerations of public policy; it operates without the active participation of the parties and does not affect their property or legal relations'.[80]

[77] Ibid, 336. [78] Ibid, 327.

[79] Case 13/61 [1962] ECR 45. Being the first case on Art 234 and raising issues of EC competition law which were of importance to all Member States, there were a number of interveners, namely the Commission and the Governments of Germany, France, Belgium and The Netherlands.

[80] Ibid, 56, 60, and 61.

Advocate General Lagrange adopted a style in his Opinion which, to a large extent, is still followed today. He extracted from the national court's reference a number of precise questions which, in his view, the European Court of Justice was required to answer in order to decide its competence in delivering the interpretation sought by the national court.

In the *De Geus v Bosch* case, Lagrange identified the following two key issues as to the scope of the preliminary ruling procedure: first, whether a preliminary ruling can be given at the request of a national court when an appeal against the national court's decision to refer has been lodged; second, whether the European Court of Justice can refuse the request where the national court's questions require the application of the Treaty to the facts of the case rather than the interpretation of a Treaty provision. These are issues which, even though the European Court of Justice provides written guidance to national judges, still arise today and are likely to arise each time there is an enlargement of the European Union.

How did Lagrange progress with the questions he identified? The first question raised a very important procedural matter, namely the effect on national proceedings of a decision by a national court to seek a preliminary ruling from the European Court of Justice. As the EC Treaty itself had nothing to say on the matter, Lagrange resorted to Article 23 (ex Article 20) of the Protocol on the Statute of the Court of Justice of the EC (the Statute). Article 23 states that the referring court is required to suspend 'its proceedings' but does the phrase include the suspension of all proceedings in the national legal system? Lagrange proceeded from the assumption that: 'in the absence of clear words it would be unreasonable to suppose that the authors of the Treaty intended to change such an important rule and one which relates to the internal working of the national judicial system'.[81] In reaching that conclusion he clearly considered that national procedural rules are protected from interference from Community law. He proceeded to examine the general principles contained in the national law of the Member States where a system of preliminary rulings are 'well established' and concluded that the suspension of proceedings relates only to the referring court.

Lagrange, however, did warn the European Court of Justice of the risk of following his conclusion, namely that the national appeal results in the referral decision of the lower national court being quashed or annulled with consequences for the European Court of Justice. He told the Court that if a referral decision is quashed before the Court delivers its ruling, then the European Court of Justice should abstain. He admitted the risk would be greater where the European Court of Justice delivers its ruling before the national appeal court quashed the decision to refer. This would result in the European Court of Justice's ruling having no effect on the main action. Nevertheless, having warned the Court, Lagrange proceeded to advise the Court that:

> [t]his is a risk, however, which ought in my opinion to be taken, particularly in a case like the present one when the principles underlying the interpretation which is sought from

[81] Ibid, 59.

this Court are of an importance which far exceeds the interests of the parties to the action, whose rights are moreover quite adequately safeguarded by the national procedure and by the jurisdiction of national courts.[82]

Was the Court persuaded by the Advocate General? It is very difficult to be certain. The European Court of Justice judgments are often short, straightforward and with little elaboration. In this case the Court relied solely on the wording of Article 234 which: 'makes the jurisdiction of this Court dependent solely on the existence of a request for a preliminary ruling within the meaning of Article 177 [Art 234]. And it does so without requiring this Court to discover whether the decision of the national Judges has acquired the force of *res judicata* under the national law'.[83]

These words suggest that the Court did not find it necessary to look at Article 20 of the Statute nor to consider the repercussions within the national legal order of a later national appeal court decision which would conflict with the ruling. In fact the Court took the opportunity to emphasize the distinctiveness of the Community legal order. The Court expressly quashed the *res judicata* argument raised by the intervening French Government by indicating that such an argument 'rests on a failure to appreciate that the municipal law of any Member State, whose courts request a preliminary ruling from this Court, and Community law constitute two separate and distinct legal orders'.[84] The emphasis on the 'two separate and distinct legal orders' was not one made in the Opinion. This certainly suggests independent thinking by the judges.[85]

The European Court of Justice's practice of not commenting on matters raised *solely* by the Advocate General, for example, Article 20 of the Protocol on the Statute of the Court of Justice in *De Geus v Bosch*, is repeated in the *Unger*[86] case where the European Court of Justice omits to comment on a novel point raised by the Advocate General in his Opinion. Lagrange considered of his own motion the admissibility of a reference where the national court did not formulate the questions but deferred to its President to do so. He urged the Court to accept the reference and reply to the questions. The European Court of Justice did not mention the 'unusual nature of the procedure employed' by the national court to bring the matter before the Court. A likely explanation is that the European Court of Justice did not feel the need to refer to it since admissibility was not one of the issues raised by the parties. Obviously it accepted the advice of the Advocate General as it proceeded to deal with the matters of substance!

The second issue raised in *De Geus v Bosch* concerned the need to rephrase the questions from the national court to ensure that the reference fell within the scope of Article 234. Lagrange had no hesitation in concluding that the European Court

[82] Ibid, 61. [83] Ibid, 49–50. [84] Ibid, 50.

[85] It should also be noted that this reference to 'two separate and distinct legal orders' was made by the European Court of Justice in *De Geus v Bosch*, a full 10 months before the ruling in the *Van Gend en Loos* case (Case 26/62 [1963] ECR 1) which is always cited as the authority for this statement.

[86] Case 75/63 *Unger v Bestuur der Bedrijfsvereniging voor Detailhandel en Ambachten* [1964] ECR 177.

of Justice could examine the judgment contained in the reference in order to 'extract from it what is within the Court's competence, namely, a question of the *abstract* interpretation of the Treaty, and which, emerging from the case in hand, underlines the request'.[87]

The European Court of Justice gave a brief ruling on its competence to deal with the request from the national court, which arguably asked the European Court of Justice to apply, as opposed to interpret, the Treaty. By implication the Court agreed with the reasoning of Advocate General Lagrange as to its competence to reformulate the question asked by the national court. The Court recalled that: 'the Treaty neither expressly nor by implication prescribes a particular form in which a national court must present its request for a preliminary ruling . . . The direct form in which the request in the present case has been drawn up enables this Court to abstract from it without difficulty the questions of interpretation which it contains'.[88]

As already mentioned, in the Opinion he delivered in *Unger*, Lagrange considered the admissibility of a reference where the national court did not formulate the questions but referred to its President to do so. Urging the Court to accept the reference he warned the European Court of Justice that 'if it refused to do so, the Court would risk criticism for interfering in the functioning of national justice'.[89] He went on to remind the Court in a manner more familiar to common law than civil law that:

> according to your case-law, the Court is not concerned in judging the considerations upon which the national court has based the formulation of its questions nor the importance attached to it within the framework of the dispute before it. This Court is judge only of its own jurisdiction and should reply to the questions posed in so far as they come within the scope of the first paragraph of Article 177 [Art 234].[90]

As to the type of answer the Court should give, Lagrange was clear it must be an abstract interpretation. He stated that: 'it must not be forgotten that the procedure under Article 177 [Art 234] always functions within the framework of a dispute and that the substantive aspects of the litigation often contribute usefully to clarify the problem of abstract interpretation because an example helps to support a theory'.[91]

In another preliminary ruling, in *Wagner*,[92] another aspect of admissibility was raised and considered by the Advocate General and by the Court. In this case the national court referred *the parties* to the European Court of Justice (the plaintiff had raised doubts on the validity of the reference) rather than make a reference

[87] Case 13/61 *De Geus v Bosch* [1962] ECR 45, 63. [88] Ibid, 50.
[89] Case 75/63 *Unger v Bestuur der Bedrijfsvereniging voor Detailhandel en Ambachten* [1964] ECR 177, 189. [90] Ibid.
[91] Ibid. [92] Case 101/63 *Wagner* [1964] ECR 195.

itself. Both the Advocate General and the European Court of Justice were satisfied that the requirements of Article 234 were met, and the reference was therefore admissible, since the request and the file were transmitted to the Registrar of the European Court of Justice directly by the Chief Registrar of the national court. However another issue of jurisdiction was also raised. The judgment of the national court did not mention the provisions for which it sought an interpretation nor indicated the nature of the difficulties of interpretation which it faced. Advocate General Lagrange proposed that the Court look beyond the questions to the national grounds of judgment to determine that the national court sought a clarification as to the meaning of 'duration of the sessions' of the European Assembly (now the European Parliament) under, *inter alia*, Article 196 of the EC Treaty. As he pointed out, the Court 'has never hesitated to make the necessary effort to extract from the questions posed by the court of reference those which relate to its own interpretative jurisdiction. This effort does not appear very great in this case so far as the Treaties are concerned'.[93]

Another matter of concern in this case was whether the European Court of Justice should wait for a response from the European Assembly to a request to waive the immunity of two of its members before issuing a ruling. Lagrange was of the view that a ruling should be given since the Court was considering questions of principle, namely the meaning of 'duration of the sessions' of the European Assembly, which should be 'settled *beforehand* by the Court'.[94]

Finally, in *Costa v ENEL*,[95] the issue was raised by the intervening Italian Government that the application for a preliminary ruling was 'absolutely inadmissible' since the national court not only asked a question of interpretation of the Treaty but also asked whether the Italian law was in conformity with the Treaty. The latter question according to the Italian Government was a matter for a direct action under Articles 226 and/or 227, and they contended that in the dispute before the national court, the latter had to apply merely the national law of Italy and therefore there was no need for an interpretation of the Treaty.

Lagrange identified two preliminary issues in respect of the admissibility of the reference which needed to be considered: first, the usual problem as to whether the reference really related to the interpretation of the Treaty and second, the question of 'absolute inadmissibility'.

As far as the first issue is concerned, the Advocate General was satisfied that the national court had shown how the Italian law nationalizing the electricity industry might constitute an infringement of the Treaty. Lagrange encouraged the Court to assist the 'national court to give a decision within the limits of its

[93] Ibid, 204.

[94] Ibid, 206. Both the Advocate General and the Court reached the same conclusion as to the scope of Art 234, but on the question of substance, namely whether the European Assembly was 'in session' during an adjournment, they reached different conclusions!

[95] Case 6/64 [1964] ECR 585.

jurisdiction, whilst remaining within the sphere of your own'. However he also warned the Court that:

[W]hat must be avoided—and this is a danger which becomes apparent as cases under Article 177 [Art 234] multiply—is that this Court, under the guise of interpretation, might more or less substitute itself for the national court which, let us not forget, retains jurisdiction to apply the Treaty and the regulations of the Community which have been incorporated into national law by ratification. Finding clear-cut division between application and interpretation is indeed one of the most delicate problems posed by Article 177 [Art 234], all the more so because this dividing line corresponds to that of the jurisdiction of the Community Court and the national courts, a problem which no court has had the task of resolving in the case of conflict. It is apparent that a conflict between the Court of Justice and the highest national courts could be of such a nature as seriously to prejudice the system of judicial review instituted by the Treaty, which rests upon a necessary, and frequently even organic, cooperation between the two jurisdictions.[96]

The European Court of Justice again followed the Advocate General's reasoning stating:

the Court has power to extract from a question imperfectly formulated by the national court those questions which alone pertain to the interpretation of the Treaty. Consequently a decision should be given by the Court not upon the validity of an Italian law in relation to the Treaty, but only upon the interpretation of the above mentioned Articles in the context of the points of law stated by the Giudice Conciliatore.[97]

As far as the second preliminary issue was concerned, the 'absolute inadmissibility' ground, Lagrange understood fully the 'constitutional difficulties' and analyzed the arguments thoroughly. The European Court of Justice was reminded of its case law where it had resisted the temptation to consider the reasons that may have led the national court to refer the question of interpretation to the Court. The Court needed merely to satisfy itself that a question of interpretation of the Treaty or validity of Community law had been raised. He then went on to reconsider this position. Should this be applied without any reservation or limitation?

[F]or instance even in cases where a preliminary question is manifestly unrelated to the main action: should the Court in such cases consider itself bound to give an abstract interpretation of the Treaty which, in these circumstances would then appear to be purely theoretical exercise unconnected with the solution of a dispute, when such interpretation might have a bearing upon questions of great importance or be such as to create serious conflicts with national courts? One may be allowed to have some doubts in this connexion. It is for this reason, and with a view to eliminating any possible misunderstanding and with the precise hope of avoiding such a conflict, that I feel that I should deal as clearly as possible with the objections of the Italian Government.[98]

Advocate General Lagrange went on to do precisely that. The core of the problem: 'is that of the *coexistence of two opposing legal rules* (as a hypothesis) *which both*

[96] Ibid, 601. [97] Ibid, 593. [98] Ibid, 602.

apply to the domestic system, one deriving from the Treaty or the Community institutions, the other from the national legislature and institutions: which must predominate until such time as the conflict is resolved? This is the real problem'.[99]

How to deal with it? Lagrange resisted recourse to legal theory as to the nature of Community law and to political theory as to whether the Community is a 'Federal Europe' or 'the Europe of Countries' or whether it is a supranational or an international entity. His advice was to keep it simple and only consider the Treaty as it is: '[I]t creates its *own legal system* which, although distinct from the legal system of each of the Member States, by virtue of certain precise provisions of the Treaty, which bring about a *transfer of jurisdiction* to the Community institutions, partly replaces the internal legal system'.[100]

Here he was certainly drawing from the Court's ruling in the *De Geus* case that there are two distinct legal orders and from the ruling in the *Van Gend en Loos* case delivered 14 months earlier. He concluded that the transfer of jurisdiction or limitation 'of their sovereign rights', to use the actual words of the Court in the *Van Gend en Loos*[101] case, inevitably leads to a replacement of the national legal systems of the Member States.[102]

He then proceeded to examine how Community law is incorporated into the national legal systems. The analysis lead him to the conclusion that: '[t]herefore we cannot avoid the problem which results from the coexistence within each Member State of two systems of law, domestic and Community, each operating in its own sphere of competence, nor can we avoid the question what sanction should follow the encroachment by one into the sphere of competence reserved to the other'.[103]

After considering the sanction available where the encroachment is done by the Community institutions,[104] Lagrange considered the appropriate sanction where the encroachment is on the part of national authorities. He stated that: 'there must also be a sanction and this too must be available not only at the instance of the States but also in favour of individuals when the latter derive individual rights from the Treaty or Community regulations'.[105] The analysis and conclusion were driven by the need to ensure that the scope of Article 234 is wide enough to allow the national court to ask the European Court of Justice, as a question of interpretation, whether it should apply Community Law or a conflicting national law.

[99] Ibid, 602. [100] Ibid, 603. [101] Case 26/62 [1963] ECR 1, 12.

[102] Although *Costa v ENEL* is considered to be the first case establishing the fundamental principle of supremacy of Community law, this principle had already been considered in earlier cases in the context of the relationship of Community law with international agreements signed by the Member States. In Case 10/61 *Commission v Italy* [1962] ECR 1, which was decided before *Van Gend en Loos* (1963), the European Court of Justice ruled that '[I]n fact, in matters governed by the EEC Treaty, that Treaty takes precedence over agreements concluded between Member States before its entry into force, including agreements made within the framework of GATT', at 10.

[103] Case 6/64 *Costa v ENEL* [1964] ECR 585, 603.

[104] Proceedings may be brought before the European Court of Justice either directly by an Art 230 application for annulment or indirectly by relying on the plea of illegality as provided in Art 241.

[105] Case 6/64 *Costa v ENEL* [1964] ECR 585, 603–4.

It is clear from the Opinion that Lagrange was fully aware of the constitutional consequences for Member States, particularly where conflicting national law came into force after the incorporation of the Treaty in their national legal orders. As the Treaty was ratified by an ordinary law in the Member States, countries with a constitutional court (Germany and Italy) were likely to face difficulties of principle: 'It would seem therefore that the real question is whether the creation of such a legal system by a Treaty ratified by an ordinary law is compatible with the Constitution: and this is surely a problem which the national constitutional Court is alone competent to resolve'.[106]

Lagrange was fully aware of these undecided constitutional issues and expected the Court to have to face them in the future. How right he was! Two examples will be given to demonstrate his foresight. Lagrange pre-empted cases such as *Nold v Commission*[107] and *Internationale Handelsgesellschaft*[108] by identifying problems that would arise if the Community legal system did not offer guarantees similar to the fundamental rights enshrined in some national constitutions. His apprehension, that the ratification of the Treaties by an ordinary national law with no alteration to the Constitution of a Member State could cause problems in the future, was once again demonstrated to be realistic in the *Solange I*[109] case. Lagrange also anticipated *Foglia v Novello*[110] where the European Court of Justice delivered the first ruling rejecting a preliminary reference on the ground that there was no real dispute requiring an interpretation or a declaration of validity of Community law. Although Lagrange urged the European Court of Justice repeatedly to adopt a wide interpretation as to the scope of Article 234, he recognized the future likelihood of the Court having to consider what action to take where a preliminary question from a national court is manifestly unrelated to the main action.[111]

The effect of an earlier European Court of Justice ruling, particularly on the obligation of a court or tribunal of last instance to refer

In the *Da Costa en Schaake*[112] case Advocate General Lagrange had the opportunity to consider again the scope of Article 234. The case raised the same questions of interpretation as those raised in *Van Gend en Loos*[113] which had been decided two

[106] Ibid, 605. Cf the Opinion of Advocate General Roemer in *Van Gend en Loos* where he identified the problem but failed to provide a solution (Case 26/62 [1963] ECR 1, 23–24).

[107] Case 4/73 [1974] ECR 491 concerning the alleged violation of a property right and the right to pursue a business activity which is protected by the German Basic Law (Grundgesetz).

[108] Case 11/70 [1970] ECR 1125, 1134 where the Court reaffirmed the supremacy of Community law even in the face of 'fundamental rights as formulated by the constitution' of a Member State.

[109] [1974] 2 CMLR 540; however, in *Solange II* [1987] 3 CMLR 225, the German Federal Constitutional Court reversed its earlier position.

[110] Case 104/79 [1980] ECR 745.

[111] See C Barnard and E Sharpston, 'The changing face of Article 177 references' (1997) 34 CML Rev 1113 for an in-depth analysis of the European Court of Justice's response in later years to the problem foreseen by Lagrange.

[112] Joined Cases 28, 29 and 30/62 [1963] ECR 31.

[113] Case 26/62 [1963] ECR 1.

months earlier. This in itself raised two important issues: first, whether a preliminary ruling should have binding effect on all national courts when the same questions of interpretation were raised; second, what was the effect of the earlier judgment on the obligation imposed on national courts or tribunals of last instance to refer to the European Court of Justice every question of interpretation of EC Law pleaded before them–had the purpose of the reference been lost and should the European Court of Justice dismiss the case for lack of substance as urged by the Commission?

The European Court of Justice ruling was very brief: two pages. Lagrange on the other hand undertook a rigorous analysis of the two issues because '[A] matter of principle is involved here which is not without importance to the future application of Article 177 [Art 234] and the relationships between the Court of Justice and the national courts which flow from it'.[114] Once again he demonstrated complete understanding of the importance of the preliminary ruling procedure for the development of the Community's legal order.

To resolve the first issue on the binding effect of an European Court of Justice ruling on future cases, the Advocate General reviewed the principles common in the Member States which govern *res judicata* and the principles which govern the system of references for preliminary rulings.

As far as *res judicata* itself was concerned he found nothing in the Treaty to derogate from the principle that *res judicata* applies only to the case in question. The legal issue may have been the same in several cases but the subject matter was different and there was no identity of parties.

As to the principles which govern references for preliminary rulings, Lagrange quoted the Court itself in *Van Gend en Loos*:

> in order to confer jurisdiction on the Court in the present case, it is necessary only that the question raised should clearly be concerned with the interpretation of the Treaty. The considerations which may have led a national court or tribunal to its choice of questions as well as the relevance which it attributes to such questions in the context of a case before it, are excluded from review by the Court.[115]

Thus an earlier judgment does not have binding effect on future cases. Although he accepted the strength of the counter-argument that 'public policy' requires a unified interpretation of the Treaty, he had no hesitation in giving great importance to the *process* by which such *ratio legis* is affected. He stated that 'it is thus a collaboration between the Court of Justice and the national courts which ought to result, by way of case law, in that unity of interpretation which is so desirable: through decisions and not through regulations'.[116]

In his view:

> it is from the moral authority of its decisions, and not from the legal authority of *res judicata* that a jurisdiction like ours should derive its force. Clearly no one will expect that, having

[114] Joined Cases 28, 29 and 30/62 [1963] ECR 31, 40.
[115] Ibid at 41, quoting from Case 26/62 [1963] ECR 1, 11.
[116] Ibid, 42.

given a leading judgment, such as the judgment in case 26/62, the Court will depart from it in another action without strong reasons, but it should retain the legal right to do so.[117]

He considered that the rule that *res judicata* applies only to the particular case is a wise one because:

[re *res judicata* rule] . . . it obliges it [the European Court of Justice] increasingly to retain awareness of its responsibility, that is, to confront the realities of the situation with the legal rule in each action, which can lead it in appropriate cases to recognize its errors in the light of new facts, of new arguments or even of a spontaneous rethinking, or more frequently to alter its point of view *subtly* without changing it fundamentally, thus being party in the light of experience and the evolution of legal theories and economic, social or other phenomena, to what is called the evolution of case law.[118]

Thus, on the binding effect of the European Court of Justice's ruling, Lagrange concluded:

I do not think so. This would be, in effect, to recognize a jurisdiction of a truly constitutional nature in the Court. Although our court, in certain respects, plays the role of a constitutional court within the Communities, the Treaties have not given it all the prerogatives of a court of that nature. Above all, the Treaties themselves may only with prudence and only in part or under certain aspects be considered as true constitutions for each of the Communities which they institute. One should be aware of analogies which are stretched too far.[119]

The European Court of Justice merely stated that Article 234 'always allows a national court, if it considers it desirable, to refer questions of interpretation to the Court *again*'.[120]

As to the second issue, on the effect of an earlier ruling on the obligation imposed on a court of last instance to refer a question of interpretation of Community law, Advocate General Lagrange referred expressly to the *acte clair* doctrine as a demarcation rule between two jurisdictions. In his opinion the third paragraph of Article 234 imposes the obligation on courts of last instance where there is a question relative to the interpretation of the provision of Community law.[121] If the provision is perfectly clear there is no longer the need for interpretation but only for application: the latter belongs to the jurisdiction of the national court.

The European Court of Justice agreed with the Advocate General's interpretation stating that:

the authority of an interpretation under Article 177 [Art 234] already given by the Court may deprive the obligation of its purpose and thus empty it of its substance. Such is the case especially when the question raised is materially identical with a question which has already been the subject of a preliminary ruling in a similar case.[122]

117 Ibid. 118 Ibid, 42–43. 119 Ibid, 43. 120 Ibid, 38, emphasis added.

121 Ibid, 45. For an opposite view see Advocate General Capotorti's Opinion in Case 283/81 *CILFIT* [1982] ECR 3415, 3437.

122 Ibid.

This of course refers to the obligation imposed on a national court of last instance to refer a question of interpretation of Community law to the European Court of Justice. Therefore, although the *acte clair* doctrine as part of the Community's legal order is normally associated with the *CILFIT*[123] case, it was aired for the first time by Advocate General Lagrange in the *Da Costa en Schaake* case.

Concluding observations

Can the influence of the Opinions of Advocate General Lagrange be identified in the judgments or rulings of the European Court of Justice? This is of course the most difficult thing to demonstrate objectively. The European Court of Justice judgments did not normally acknowledge the Advocate General's Opinions[124] but the omission is not a significant factor since the Advocate General is viewed as a member of the Court and not as an advocate.[125] On the other hand, the fact that in most of the cases the European Court of Justice did not reach a different conclusion from the Advocate General is of some significance and supports the proposition that the Opinions carried weight with the judges.[126]

The analysis of the Opinions delivered by Lagrange demonstrate the importance of the issues which arose in the early cases on the scope of the Community Treaties provisions which enabled the European Court of Justice to play such a pivotal role in the development of the Community's legal order. This is probably the most interesting aspect of the research. Important constitutional issues as to the relationship between the European Court of Justice and national courts were raised right at the beginning and there is much evidence of Lagrange's complete understanding of the nature of the Community Treaties as being a different creature from other Treaties—raising issues of constitutional conflicts between the national and Community legal systems. Lagrange understood the dangers for the coherence of the Community legal order if the European Court of Justice became too involved in national constitutional issues. Lagrange foresaw that the incorporation of the EC Treaty (wider in scope than the ECSC Treaty) into the national legal systems by ordinary laws and not by amendments to the national Constitutions was likely to give rise to conflicts in the future. He therefore advised the European Court of

[123] Case 283/81 [1982] ECR 3415.

[124] It should be noted that in the first European Court of Justice judgment, Case 1/54 *France v HA* [1954–56] ECR 1, the European Court of Justice referred five times to the Opinion of Advocate General Lagrange at 9, 10, 11, 12 and 16. Other early cases where the Advocate General is expressly mentioned include Case 5/55 *ASSIDER v HA* [1955] ECR 135, 143, and Cases 1/57 and 14/57 [1957–58] 105, 112.

[125] See, for example, Case C-17/98 *Emesa Sugar (Free Zone) NV v Aruba* [2000] ECR I-665 where the Court stated that the Advocate General's Opinion 'constitutes the individual reasoned opinion, expressed in open court, of a Member of the Court of Justice itself' (p 672). The Court added that 'the Advocate General thus takes part, publicly and individually, in the process by which the Court reaches its judgment, and therefore in carrying out the judicial function entrusted to it'.

[126] Fewer than 10 Opinions of Lagrange were not followed by the Court.

Justice to distance itself from these difficulties by simply identifying the conflicts as issues for the national courts, not the European Court of Justice, to resolve.[127]

On the admissibility of actions brought by organizations or by individual undertakings, Lagrange's Opinions show a strict interpretation of the Treaties as far as the *locus standi* of these applicants was concerned. He was stricter than the Court in interpreting Article 33 ECSC. Lagrange's analysis of the conditions under which an organization or an individual undertaking should be allowed to challenge a general decision of the HA led him to the view that the applicant would have to succeed first in the substantive issue of proving that the HA had misused its powers before the action could be declared admissible. The Court, however, was more lenient and ruled that it was enough to allege *formally* (but with reasons) misuse of powers for admissibility to be established. The question of whether the general act should be annulled on the basis of misuse of power was to be judged subsequently as a matter of substance.[128]

Lagrange also delivered the first Opinion on the admissibility of an Article 230 action for annulment brought by natural and legal persons, the so-called non-privileged applicants.[129] The wording of this Article is different from Article 33 ECSC. Lagrange's analysis of the limitations imposed under Article 230 is striking for its clarity, precision and coherence. He realized that jurists might find the conditions which non-privileged applicants have to meet 'unsatisfactory' but, nevertheless, he accepted the evidence and the political reality that the authors of the EC Treaty had intended these limitations to govern the admissibility of proceedings brought by natural and legal persons

Lagrange's approach was however much more generous when considering admissibility issues other than those based on the *locus standi* of the applicants. He consistently sought to interpret provisions of the EC Treaty in a manner that enabled the Court to review the legality of acts adopted by the Community's administrative organs. He argued successfully not only for the plea 'objection of illegality' to be admissible against a general HA decision but, more significantly, he concluded that the plea should be unconditional. This meant that the applicant could challenge the general HA decision on all the grounds listed in Article 33 ECSC and not only on the ground of 'misuse of power' which would have been the situation if the applicant had sought annulment of the general decision in the first place.[130]

Similarly, his Opinions on applications where undertakings sought to review HA letters were more generous than the Court's rulings. Lagrange was more likely to conclude that the letters contained a reviewable decision.[131] He was ingenious in trying to find ways which would enable the Court to review administrative acts.

[127] In Cases 13/61 *De Geus v Bosch* [1962] ECR 45 and 6/64 *Costa v Enel* [1964] ECR 585.

[128] Cases 3/54 *ASSIDER v HA* [1954–56] ECR 63 and 4/54 *ISA v HA* [1954–56] ECR 91.

[129] Joined Cases 16 and 17/62 *Confédération nationale des producteurs de fruits et légumes and ors v Council* [1962] ECR 471.

[130] Case 15/57 *Compagnie des Hauts Fourneaux de Chasse v HA* [1957–58] ECR 211.

[131] Joined Opinion in Cases 20-23/58 [1959] ECR 75, 99, 107 and 117, and Joined Opinion in Joined Cases 32 and 33/58 *SNUPAT v HA* [1959] ECR 127.

Such an example can be found in Lagrange's failed attempt to persuade the Court to rule that general decisions could be general for some applicants and individual for others.[132] On the other hand, applicants found it difficult to persuade Lagrange and the Court that the HA had committed a wrongful act or omission within the meaning of Article 40 ECSC.

Why was Lagrange stricter on *locus standi* of undertakings and on the scope of Article 40 ECSC, and yet generous in finding a reviewable act whose validity could be challenged by undertakings? It is possible that, as a specialist in French administrative law, Lagrange saw his primary role to advise the European Court of Justice to take every opportunity to exercise its exclusive jurisdiction to review the validity of acts adopted by the Community's administrative organs. He clearly had a vision of a Community legal order, governed by the rule of law where the European Court of Justice acted as an administrative/ constitutional court. There is no evidence that he perceived natural and legal persons as having significant roles in creating and developing the Community's legal order.

The same focus can also be found in Lagrange's approach to the scope of Articles 226 and 234 EC. Lagrange's Opinions on the scope of Article 226 action is a clear example of his perceptive understanding of the importance of bringing Member States to account for their conduct.[133] He immediately recognized the opportunity that this cause of action gives the European Court of Justice to strengthen its role in the development of the Community's legal order. The Court is the sole judge of whether a Member State has failed to fulfil a Treaty obligation. The Member State cannot avoid a negative judgment of the Court by complying with the Commission's reasoned opinion once the period for meeting its obligations has expired. The fact that an alleged breach may no longer be in existence was not a good enough reason for Lagrange to be persuaded that the Member State should not be brought to account before the Court. Furthermore, on the issue of admissibility, he adopted the same generous approach which he pursued in the Opinions he delivered in the ECSC Treaty cases. He urged the European Court of Justice not to refuse to hear the case on grounds of inadmissibility. Lagrange successfully persuaded the Court that the Commission's reasoned opinion should not be more than a mere statement of the Commission's view and, therefore, any inadequacies as to the reasoning of that opinion, was a matter of substance, not of form.

Similarly, the Opinions he delivered on the interpretation of Article 234 support the contention that, for Lagrange, the key to the establishment of a strong legal order was to ensure that the European Court of Justice was at its centre. He understood fully the importance of the preliminary ruling procedure for the development of the European Community's legal order. He took every opportunity to advise the Court to adopt the widest possible meaning of its competence under

[132] Joined Opinion in Cases 8 and 9/55 [1954–56] ECR 245, 269.

[133] Case 7/61 *Commission v Italy* [1961] ECR 317 and Case 10/61 *Commission v Italy* [1962] ECR 1.

Article 234 in order to assist the national court and facilitate this relationship between the national courts and the European Court of Justice. It was considered irrelevant if the national court asked questions of application instead of interpretation or failed to ask a question at all. As long as the full facts of the case were available to the European Court of Justice, he foresaw no problem for the European Court of Justice to extract the questions within its competence that the national court should have asked. Similarly, there was no need to enquire as to the reasons that led the national court to seek a preliminary ruling from the European Court of Justice. It was sufficient if a question of interpretation of Community law could be identified by the European Court of Justice.

Advocate General Lagrange's Opinions provide fascinating evidence of his remarkable grasp of the significance of the unique nature of Community law created by the Treaties. Equally impressive is his perceptive identification of significant problems and conflicts that would arise as the Community's legal order matured. Lagrange correctly predicted that the solutions would have to be provided by both the European Court of Justice and the national courts.

5

Walter van Gerven and the principle of equal treatment of men and women

Walter van Gerven was Advocate General in the European Court of Justice for six years between 1988 and 1994. During that time he delivered Opinions in almost 200 cases. He was Advocate General in cases which have become household names in Community law such as *Marleasing* or *Keck and Mithouard*.[1] It might seem invidious, therefore, to narrow down this chapter to an examination of his contribution to the arguably narrow principle of equal treatment of men and women, yet this is certainly one area where it is acknowledged that van Gerven made a distinctive contribution to the law.[2]

Van Gerven delivered Opinions in 15 cases involving aspects of gender discrimination. His was the most significant analysis available to the Court on the very contentious issues arising in cases relating to occupational pension schemes. He was Advocate General in the seminal cases of *Barber*, *Ten Oever*, *Moroni*, *Colorall*, *Neath*, *Birds Eye Walls*, *Smith*, *Fisscher* and *Vroege*, and *Smith and Van den Akker*.[3] In these cases the Court was confronted with questions relating to: the definition of pay and the extension of equal pay principles to occupational pension schemes; the need to impose temporal limitations on its judgments and the difficulties surrounding the precise manner of delimiting such temporal limitations; the problem of uncertainties

[1] Case C-106/89 *Marleasing SA v La Comercial Internacional de Alimentacion SA* [1990] ECR I-4135 and Joined Cases C-267/91 and C-268/91 *Keck and Mithouard* [1993] ECR I-5789.

[2] T Tridimas 'The Role of the Advocate General in the Development of Community Law: Some Reflections' (1997) 3 CML Rev 1349.

[3] Cases C-262/88 *Douglas Hervey Barber v. Guardian Royal Exchange* [1990] ECR I-1889; C-109/91 *Gerardus Cornelis Ten Oever v Stichting Bedrijfspensioenfonds voor het Glazenwassers-en Schoonmaakbedrijf* [1993] ECR I-4897; C-110/91 *Michael Moroni v Collo GMBH* [1993] ECR I-00453; C-152/91 *David Neath v Hugh Steeper Ltd* [1993] ECR I-6935; C-200/91 *Coloroll Pension Trustees v James Richard Russell and ors* [1994] ECR I-04389; (van Gerven delivered a joint Opinion in the last four mentioned cases, see [1993] ECR I-4893); C-132/92 *Birds Eye Walls Ltd v Friedel M. Roberts* [1993] ECR I-5579; C-128/93 *Geetruida Catharina Fisscher v Voorhuis Hengelo BV and Stichting Bedrijfspensioenfonds voor de Detailhandel* [1994] ECR I-4583 and C-57/93 *Anna Adriaantje Vroege v NCIV Instituut voor Volkshuisvesting BV and Stichting Penioenfonds NCIV* [1994] ECR I-04541 (van Gerven delivered a Joint Opinion in these last two cases, see [1994] ECR I-04541); C-408/92 *Constance Christina Ellen Smith and ors v Advel Sytems Ltd* [1994] ECR I-4435 and C-28/93 *Van den Akker and ors v Stichting Shell Pensioenfonds* [1994] ECR I-4527 (van Gerven delivered a Joint Opinion in these last two cases, see [1994] ECR I-4435).

created by opposing understandings of key concepts between the Community Court and the Community legislature, and the difficulty in confronting entrenched views and practices that are inherently discriminatory but have persisted over time, such as the use of actuarial statistics in the calculation of pension contributions and benefits. It has been claimed that, in these cases, the Court of Justice 'has extended the concept of "pay" well into what was originally regarded as the area of social security'.[4] That these were contentious cases is witnessed by the fact that, following the Court's decision in *Barber*, the Member States believed it was necessary to insert a Protocol to the Treaty clarifying the meaning of Community law, and they were also obliged to amend their own secondary legislation in light of the decisions of the Court. Van Gerven was part of the process that pushed the boundaries of Article 141[5] to their limits. An analysis of this case-law reveals a process of the Advocate General working with the Court to achieve a radical interpretation of that Treaty Article. This chapter concentrates on these occupational pension cases.

Van Gerven took up his appointment in 1988. Prior to this date the Court had already confronted the occupational pension issue in a series of cases, and so van Gerven was placed in a situation where he had to try to draw some key threads together, as well as solve some novel problems. He was, in some senses, 'dropped' into a series of difficult legal questions in an area where the Court was feeling its own way on a case-by-case basis, and where it was difficult to discern clear principles from the existing case-law. In order to evaluate van Gerven's own contribution it is, therefore, necessary to explain what had gone before in the jurisprudence of the Court.

Van Gerven was also Advocate General in two cases relating to equal treatment in social security issues.[6] Neither of these cases is of fundamental importance in

[4] A McColgan, *Discrimination Law: Text, Cases and Materials* (2000) 534.

[5] Consolidated Version of the Treaty Establishing the European Community, Art 141 (formerly Art 119): Art 141 reads as follows:

1. Each Member State shall ensure that the principle of equal pay for male and female workers for equal work or work of equal value is applied.
2. For the purpose of this article, 'pay' means the ordinary basic or minimum wage or salary and any other consideration, whether in cash or in kind, which the worker receives directly or indirectly, in respect of his employment, from his employer.

   Equal pay without discrimination based on sex means:

(a) that pay for the same work at piece rates shall be calculated on the basis of the same unit of measurement;
(b) that pay for work at time rates shall be the same for the same job.

3. The Council, acting in accordance with the procedure referred to in Article 251, and after consulting the Economic and Social Committee, shall adopt measures to ensure the application of the principle of equal opportunities and equal treatment of men and women in matters of employment and occupation, including the principle of equal pay for equal work or work of equal value.

[6] Case C-9/91 *R v Secretary of State for Social Security, ex p Equal Opportunities Commission* [1992] ECR I-4297; Joined Cases C-63/91 and C-64/91 *Sonia Jackson and Patricia Cresswell v Chief Adjudication Officer* [1992] ECR I-4737.

our understanding of Community law as they deal with very specific questions relating to UK social security schemes currently no longer in force. The case of *Jackson and Cresswell*[7] concerned the interpretation of the material scope of Directive 79/7, and in particular whether the failure to take into account child-minding expenses when determining the amount of benefits payable under a (now) defunct benefits scheme previously operating in the UK. The litigation had been proceeding for five years before the issue came before the Court. In an Opinion of some 26 pages, Advocate General van Gerven explored every conceivable aspect of the issue before concluding that all the matters that had been referred to the Court of Justice were, in reality, matters for the national judge to decide. The Court ignored the Opinion of the Advocate General in its entirety before holding that Directive 79/7 did not apply to the case in question and neither did Directive 76/207, the Equal Treatment Directive. This case can be used to illustrate the point that, where the Court does not find the Opinion of the Advocate General to be helpful in providing a response to questions posed by the national court, it may opt to disregard the Opinion of the Advocate General in its entirety and such was the fate of van Gerven's Opinion in *Jackson and Cresswell*.[8]

The cases of *Foster* and *Marshall* raised principles of Community law as they were applicable to gender discrimination but, in reality, the principles extend far beyond that field.[9] *Marshall* will be discussed extensively in chapter 8—relating to the direct effect of Community law. Van Gerven was one of the Advocates General who advocated that the Court should recognize the horizontal direct effect of directives, and he did so in eloquent terms, but to no avail.

Background

Walter van Gerven came to the Court of Justice from a distinguished academic background. He was Professor of Law at Leuven and had written extensively, amongst other things, on European Community Law. He was also a practising advocate and had extensive business experience as President of the Belgian Banking Commission, and as a Director of several industrial and commercial companies.

Van Gerven's Opinions are characterized by their scholarship. His Opinions are lengthy, extensively referenced and present comparative legal analysis, as well as being extremely analytical of both the factual and the legal issues, and particularly detailed in respect of the variety of occupational pension schemes arising in the cases. He often offers the Court a variety of different solutions, drawing on his knowledge of international law, and German, UK and US precedents. He is always passionate about principles of equality and justice. His Opinions are still, by far, some of the best analyses of key principles of sex discrimination. On his

7 Ibid, *Jackson and Cresswell*.

8 Ibid.

9 C-188/89 *A Foster and ors v British Gas plc* [1990] ECR I-3313; C-271/91 *M.H. Marshall v Southampton and South West Hampshire Area Health Authority* [1993] ECR I-4367.

retirement from the Court, the (then) President paid tribute to his scholarship and depth of analysis, saying:

Your Opinions have always been so comprehensive as to leave no problem unaddressed. Often you have discovered aspects of a legal problem which had escaped the attention of counsel. Sometimes your Opinions have even resulted in a party requesting the reopening of the oral procedure. For the Judges your Opinions have been almost inexhaustible as a source of inspiration and a mine of legal information.[10]

Van Gerven did not see his role solely as assisting the Court, however. In an interview at the end of his period in office, he explained the role of the Advocate General in the following terms: 'I see myself as a bridge between the Court and the legal community. One tries to explain the case-law of the Court and make observations on it to help practitioners understand the reasoning of the Court and the system'.[11]

He saw the function of the Advocate General as linking the Court and the legal Community, by making the reasoning of the Court more transparent and, therefore, democratic. It is not surprising that his opinions read as if they were judgments in the House of Lords: they have an almost common law quality about them.[12] It seems that he was conscious of this and wrote:

Not only does the Advocate General play an indispensable role, in difficult cases, in showing the way in which he believes the Court should follow, but he also plays a role in clarifying the Court's case-law to the advantage of the legal community as a whole, and in making it more transparent and democratic as, after the judgment has been rendered, his Opinion will serve a similar purpose as a concurring or a dissenting Opinion.[13]

Article 141[14] and occupational pensions

Van Gerven was not the first Advocate General to be confronted with the question of whether contributions made to, and benefits payable from, occupational pension schemes could be defined as coming under the ambit of Article 141. Neither could it be said that he, or any other Advocate General, was responsible for first

[10] European Court of Justice, Annual Report (1994) 137.

[11] D Bentley, 'An Advocate for the European Court' (1994) 37 International Corporate Law 15 at 16.

[12] One of the themes of van Gerven's academic work has been the development of a common law for Europe in the sense of set of legal principles and institutions common to the legal systems of the Member States—see, for example, W van Gerven, 'The European Court of Justice's Case Law as a Means of Unification of Private Law', Fordham International Law Journal (1997) 680–98 (also published in: European Review of Private Law (1998) 293–307 and in A Hartkamp et al. (eds), *Towards a European Civil Code* (2nd edn, 1998) 91–104); W van Gerven, 'A Common Law for Europe: the Future meeting the Past?', European Review for Private Law (2001) 485–503; and W van Gerven, *Bringing (Private) Laws Closer to Each Other at the European Level* (2005).

[13] W van Gerven, 'The Role and Structure of the European Judiciary Now and in the Future' (1996) ELR 211, 222.

[14] At the time these cases were heard Art 119 EEC (now Art 141 as amended) read as follows: 'Each Member State shall during the the first stage ensure and subsequently maintain the application of the principle that men and women should receive equal pay for equal work. For the purpose of this

raising this question in the minds of the judges of the European Court of Justice. This was an issue of interpretation raised by parties to genuine disputes in the courts of some of the Member States. The Advocates General were, therefore, in the position of reacting to arguments of the parties, and their role was one of synthesizing and analysing the arguments being put forward, and of coming to a reasoned conclusion. In that sense their contribution has to be seen in the analytical and decision-making skills they displayed in the case law.

It was Advocate General Dutheillet de Lamothe in the first *Defrenne* case[15] who intially encountered the argument that Article 141 should be interpreted to include pension contributions. Ms Defrenne argued that the term 'pay' should be given a wide interpretation to include not just the salary paid to a worker but also the social salary. The latter concept would encompass such matters as paid holidays and retirement pensions.[16] She also argued that there was a link between the Belgian scheme for air crew employed by Sabena and the contract of employment for such staff. It was the contract of employment that determined the payment of the pension, and she argued that the fact that the pension scheme was established by Royal Decree did not affect the fact that the pension was paid because of the contract of employment. She further argued that the financing of the scheme was from contributions made by the employer and the employee and, taking these factors together, the pension should be seen as a form of deferred pay, or a benefit paid in cash which the employee receives indirectly from the employer. An occupational pension, following this line of argument, would clearly fall within the definition of pay in Article 141.

Ms Defrenne was opposed in her arguments by the European Commission. The Commission argued that a distinction should be drawn between a salary in active employment and a salary from non-active status (a reallocated salary). Only the former could be defined as pay within the meaning of Article 141. The latter must be considered as a social security benefit. The Commission relied on its interpretation of ILO Convention No. 100 in coming to this conclusion and also its own Recommendation to the Member States, issued in July 1960. In this Recommendation, the Commission had determined that Article 141 should not be read as to include occupational pensions. Occupational pensions, in the view of the Commission, were social security benefits.

In this case Advocate General Dutheillet de Lamothe was, therefore, faced with two opposing views as to the scope of Article 141. Given that this was the first case

Article, "pay" means the ordinary basic or minimum wage or salary and any other consideration, whether in cash or in kind, which the worker receives, directly or indirectly, in respect of his employment from his employer.

Equal pay without discrimination based on sex means:

(a) that pay for the same work at piece rates shall be calculated on the basis of the same unit of measurement;

(b) that pay for work at time rates shall be the same for the same job'.

15 Case 80/70 *Defrenne v Belgium* [1971] ECR 445.

16 Ibid at 448.

in which the European Court of Justice was asked to interpret Article 141, his approach would be important in assisting the judges as to how they should read it. He reminded the judges that Article 141 had both a social and an economic function; it has a social objective in that it pursues the principle of equality but also an economic objective as a means of avoiding social dumping. He drew the attention of the judges to the drafting of Article 141, contrasting the wording of current Article 141 (formerly Article 119) with that of former Articles 117[17] and 118,[18] which, he stated, fixed general objectives. By contrast, Article 141, far from setting general objectives, 'creates an obligation for the Member States'.[19] Although it was not raised in this case, he added that it seemed obvious to him that Article 141 has direct effect.

It was against this background, and taking into consideration the importance of Article 141 in the Treaty, that Dutheillet de Lamothe approached the question of whether occupational pension schemes were governed by the principle of equal pay. He steered the Court away from the controversial question of how to define an occupational pension, pointing out that there was no agreement in the Member States on this issue, and instead looked to the then current debate as to how the concept of a salary should be defined. The question was, should it cover all sums paid to a worker 'not only as consideration for, but also because of, the work' or should it only apply to the price of a service at the time it is performed?[20]

The approach the Court should take, he argued, was simply to interpret the words of the Treaty. The question, in his view, was whether a retirement pension constitutes consideration as provided by Article 141. The Advocate General distinguished two types of retirement schemes: general retirement pension schemes provided by the state and schemes which were applicable to only certain categories of workers. He had no difficulty in arguing that the former type of schemes were not covered by Article 141, as they constituted a form of social security, but retirement pension schemes paid to ex-employees because of their employment status were different.

He thus attempted to reclassify these schemes. Those which the employed person received directly from the employer, paid for by deductions from wages, clearly satisfied the conditions laid down in Article 141 because they are a form of consideration payable as a result of the employment relationship. He also believed that so-called supplemental schemes might be classified as consideration, as these schemes paid additional benefits to certain categories of workers in addition to the basic state pension. Despite the fact that some of these schemes are governed by law, they are also independent of the state scheme, and their management or organization is based on an occupational basis. He thought, however, that bringing such schemes into the ambit of Article 141 required 'more effort of interpretation'

[17] Current Art 136.

[18] Current Art 137, substantially amended from the original Art 118 by the Consolidated Version of the Treaty Establishing the European Community.

[19] Case 80/70 *Defrenne v Belgium* [1971] ECR 445 at 456.

[20] Ibid, 456.

than in the first case.[21] Nonetheless, in analysing the nature of these schemes, he did conclude that they were not excluded from the ambit of Article 141. He argued that such schemes were financed by a combination of contributions from employers and employees, and the mere fact that the employer was not solely responsible for their financing was not sufficient to exclude such schemes from the ambit of the article. The wording of Article 141 covers payment paid directly or indirectly, and Dutheillet de Lamothe believed that this wording was intended to cover such items as supplemental pensions. In these cases too he believed there was the necessary employment link.

A third category of schemes were those provided within the framework of special schemes of social security. These schemes are either paid from the general funds or linked to them, and they provide special advantages in relation to certain posts; he pointed to various special schemes for miners, railway workers and so on. In Belgium at the time of this case, such a special scheme operated in favour of air-crew employed by the (then) state run airline, Sabena, although in these cases Dutheillet de Lamothe confessed to having 'doubts and hesitation'.[22] He argued that there were similarities between such schemes and the supplemental schemes described above and that it was difficult to make a distinction between the schemes. There was certainly no difference in the beneficiaries. He also pointed to the fact that the scheme provided pensions for particular posts rather than for individuals. Most difficult for him, however, was that he did not wish to see some employees included or excluded from the ambit of Article 141 by the vagaries of the schemes established in the different Member States. In this respect he stated that the Belgian scheme was a special scheme of social security, whereas the French scheme for air crew was a supplemented scheme. If Article 141 was considered in isolation, taking into account both its economic and social objectives, then these factors would have been decisive.

However, Dutheillet de Lamothe agreed that Article 141 could not be read in isolation. Article 137 commits the Member States to cooperate to harmonize social security schemes but does not lay down a clearly defined objective in the way that Article 141 does. He then went on to state that it is difficult to separate special schemes from the general state social security schemes. The link between the employer and such special schemes is non-existent. He argued that it was the absence of this relationship which prevents the pension in question from coming within the ambit of Article 141, and thus his advice to the Court was:

> You should rule that within the meaning of Article 119 of the Treaty only the retirement pensions which employed persons who have occupied certain posts in the undertaking receive directly from the employer or indirectly from occupational or inter-occupational organisations, over and above the retirement pension to which the general social security entitles such employed persons, may be regarded as consideration which the worker receives, directly or indirectly, in respect of his employment from his employer. On the

[21] Ibid, 459. [22] Ibid, 460.

other hand pensions from the general scheme or the special schemes of social security cannot be regarded as having the same character.

The Court accepted the reasoning of the Advocate General, although its judgment was not detailed. The Court stated that, in principle, consideration in the form of social security benefit was not alien to the concept of equal pay but, nonetheless, retirement pensions 'directly governed by legislation without any element of agreement within the undertaking or the occupational branch concerned, which are obligatorily applicable to general categories of workers' could not fall within the definition of pay in Article 141. These schemes are matters of social policy and are not determined by the employment relationship, and therefore retirement pensions that form part of a social security scheme laid down by legislation are not eligible for consideration within the meaning of Article 141.

Dutheillet de Lamothe provided the framework in which all subsequent cases relating to occupational schemes over the next three decades would be analysed. His Opinion is detailed and he indicates in parts the additional background research he did to help him come to his conclusions. In particular, he drew on his research of the French schemes for retirement pensions to assist in clarifying the issues. His categorization of pension schemes, into those to be classified as consideration and those which were by their nature social security, drew the boundary between Articles 137 and 141. Given that this was the first case relating to the interpretation of Article 141 this was a crucial boundary. The Advocate General clearly flagged up the importance of Article 141 as a potential source of directly enforceable Community rights and drew into Article 141 those occupational pension schemes that arose from the employment relationship, and which were paid either directly by the employer or via some form of organization such as a trust fund.

The Court itself was less expansive and did not indicate which occupational schemes would fall within Article 141. Instead it laid down the factors which would lead to the exclusion of some schemes. Had the Court followed the reasoning of Dutheillet de Lamothe, three decades of case-law, one Directive and one Protocol to the Treaty would not have been necessary.

Dutheillet de Lamothe was clearly aware of the consequences both for the principle of equality and for the proper interpretation of Article 141 of the issues raised in this first *Defrenne* case. He speaks of his doubts and hesitation and of his searching of conscience to arrive at a proper interpretation of the Treaty. He recognizes the economic and social principles underlying Article 141, and sees the importance of equality, but also the limitations imposed by the Member States in negotiating the Treaty. In balancing these principles he sets out some clear parameters: he is unwilling to interpret Article 141 so expansively as to negate the importance of Article 137, but he does not impose an unreasonably tight definition of consideration on Article 141. A proper reading of his Opinion invites both the Commission and the Member States to consider carefully the boundary between occupational and state pensions schemes—an invitation which they failed to take up.

Some 10 years later, Advocate General Warner took a much more restrictive view of the scope of Article 141 than had Dutheillet de Lamothe.[23] In *Worringham*, the Court was asked to determine whether contracted-out pension schemes could be considered as pay. The system in place in the UK at the time of this case was based on a double system of pension income, in that the state scheme provided a basic level of pay that was the same for everyone, plus there was a variable earnings-related component. Pensions were funded by contributions from employers, employees and the state. Where an employer provided for an occupational scheme, its members could be contracted out of the variable earnings-related part of the state pension provided the scheme met certain requirements. Employers and employees thereafter paid reduced contributions to the state scheme.

In his Opinion, Advocate General Warner addressed the question of whether such contracted-out schemes could be deemed to fall within the ambit of Article 141, although the Court itself did not answer this question since it was not essential in order to provide an answer put to it by the English Court of Appeal. Referring to the Opinion of Dutheillet de Lamothe in the case of *Defrenne I*, Warner believed that contracted-out schemes would fall within the ambit of Article 141 as defined by the Advocate General in that case, except for the additional factors of the contracted-out scheme. That factor was the link to the state scheme. He argued that if Article 141 were held to cover contracted-out schemes this would mean that ever since Article 141 took effect that Member States would have been obliged to ensure that contracted-out schemes provided for equality for men and women, whereas the state scheme, for which the contracted-out scheme was a substitute, would not have been subject to such a requirement. That, he argued, would be 'an unbalanced result'.[24] A substitute scheme, he argued, was not the same as a supplementary scheme of the kind described by Dutheillet de Lamothe in the case of *Defrenne I*.

The Court, as noted, did not rule directly on the question but it did hold, in this case, that 'contributions to a retirement benefits scheme which is paid by an employer in the name of employees by means of an addition to the gross salary and which therefore helps to determine the amount of that salary constitutes pay'.[25]

Advocate General Darmon was the third Advocate General to be faced with the question of whether an occupational scheme could be defined as pay for the purposes of Article 141. In the case of *Bilka-Kaufhaus*, the question was important for part-time workers who were excluded from a pension scheme adopted after negotiation between the employer and the staff group in accordance with the framework established by German law.[26]

Some 15 years after the case of *Defrenne I*, Darmon recognized that the question of whether a retirement pension was to be regarded as pay within the meaning of Article 141 was still an open question. He based his own analysis on that of Dutheillet

[23] Case 69/80 *Worringham v Lloyds Bank* [1981] ECR 767. [24] Ibid, 806.
[25] Ibid, 768. [26] Case C-170/84 *Bilka-Kaufhaus GmbH v Weber von Hartz* [1986] ECR 1607.

de Lamothe. Specifically, he stated that, 'with that approach in mind, it must be possible to conclude that the retirement scheme at issue, governed essentially by agreement, does not fall outside the ambit of Article 119'. Once again, the initial analysis done by the Dutheillet de Lamothe in the case of *Defrenne I* was used to respond to the difficult question of the relationship between occupational pension schemes and the concept of pay. Darmon specifically based his reasoning on the link between the consideration, the employer, the employed person and the employment, thereby echoing Dutheillet de Lamothe. The scheme in question in the case of *Bilka-Kaufhaus*, according to Darmon, was a voluntary scheme that either topped up the statutory scheme or supplemented it, and that is incorporated into the contract of employment.

The Court echoed this analysis in its judgment, holding that the scheme in question was based on an agreement between the employer and the staff committee, and that it had the effect of supplementing social security benefits. It was the contractual nature of the scheme that persuaded the Court to determine that benefits paid to employees under the scheme constituted consideration within the meaning of Article 141.[27] In this case, therefore, the Court applied the reasoning of Dutheillet de Lamothe and Darmon. Perhaps more telling was that the Commission had clearly accepted that its own original arguments in the case of *Defrenne I* lacked validity. The Commission no longer argued for the restrictive interpretation of Article 141.

By the time van Gerven was faced with the question of whether occupational pension schemes came within the definition of pay for the purposes of Article 141, there had been extensive analysis by three Advocates General, with Dutheillet de Lamothe having first laid down the parameters for the analysis of the issue.

There had also been legislative developments which, rather than clarifying these issues had, in fact, confused them even further. Council Directive 76/207/EEC, the Equal Treatment Directive, was designed to implement the principle of equal treatment of men and women as regards access to employment, vocational training, promotion, and working conditions.[28] It excluded from its scope social security matters, as these were to be the subject of further legislation. Council Directive 79/7/EEC was designed to implement the principle of equal treatment of men and women in matters of social security falling within its material scope.[29] Specifically excluded were matters relating to occupational schemes, which were also to be the subject of future legislative provisions. Finally, Directive 86/378/EEC of 24 July 1986 was adopted to regulate occupational social security schemes.[30]

[27] Ibid, 1635.

[28] Council Directive 76/207/EEC of 9 February 1976 on the implementation of the principle of equal treatment for men and women as regards access to employment, vocational training and promotion, and working conditions [1976] OJ L39/40.

[29] Council Directive 79/7 EEC of 19 December 1978 on the progressive implementation of the principle of equal treatment for men and women in matters of social security [1979] OJ, L6/24.

[30] Council Directive 86/378/EEC of 24 July 1986 on the implementation of the principle of equal treatment for men and women in occupational social security schemes [1986] OJ L225/40.

That Directive purported to regulate occupational pension schemes and should have been implemented by 30 July 1989.

The judgment in *Bilka-Kaufhaus* was handed down on 13 May 1986, and this resulted in a palpable disagreement between the Community Court and the Community legislature as to how the principle of equal treatment in questions of occupational pensions should be put into effect. The Court had held that such matters were governed by the equal pay provisions of the Treaty, while the Community legislature and the Member States held to the view that occupational pensions, even those provided by virtue of the contract of employment, were not regulated by Article 141. The matter was of acute importance for, if occupational pension schemes were governed by Article 141, then pension funds that had failed to implement the principle of equal treatment could be faced with back payments potentially amounting to millions of pounds. This was the state of play when van Gerven was confronted with the question of whether contracted-out pension schemes came within the ambit of Article 141 in the case of *Barber*.

The scheme in question in *Barber* was a contracted-out occupational pension scheme, substituting for the earnings-related part of the state pension. It was authorized under the Social Security Pensions Act 1975. By virtue of its existence, employees covered by such a scheme made reduced contributions to the state scheme. The terms of the scheme provided for different normal retirement ages for men and women, 65 and 60 respectively, though because Barber had originally been a member of a scheme provided by his former employer which had been taken over by the Guardian Group, the retirement ages were 62 and 57. At age 62 Barber would have been immediately entitled to a pension, whereas a woman could obtain her pension at 57.

In fact, Barber was made redundant at the age of 52. Under the terms of the scheme, male members of the pension fund over the age of 55 who were made redundant were entitled to an immediate pension. Female members were so entitled after the age of 50. Others, including Barber, were entitled to lump sum payments calculated on the basis of years of service and a deferred pension payable at the normal retirement age, in this case 62 for men and 57 for women. In addition they received statutory redundancy pay.

The Employment Appeal Tribunal recognized that there was discrimination in this case but the Sex Discrimination Act of 1975 exempted provisions in relation to death or retirement from its ambit. Barber, therefore, had no remedy in UK sex discrimination law. The question was whether he had a remedy in European Community Law, as he had been dismissed by reason of redundancy on 31 December 1980, well before the date of implementation of Directive 86/378/EEC, the legislation which was to implement the principle of equal treatment in occupational pension schemes.

In this case, Barber's estate (Barber died before the litigation was complete) argued that the benefits payable under the severance scheme were pay because they formed part of the contractual arrangements between the employer and the employee. Any such set of terms and conditions which an employer provides in respect of employment constitute pay, and so private pensions are pay. The only issue in this case was that it was substitute for the state scheme. However, it would be inconsistent to argue that contracted-out schemes were not pay whereas other private pensions schemes that were not contracted out could be defined as pay.

Guardian Royal Exchange Assurance Group argued that, in the circumstances of the case, the alleged discrimination was in relation to the terms governing Barber's dismissal. This would not be a question of pay but of discrimination in working conditions. Guardian also argued that a contracted-out scheme was a substitute for a social security scheme, and therefore could not be pay for the purposes of Article 141.

This case raises some of the same issues highlighted in *Defrenne I*, *Worringham* and *Bilka-Kaufhaus*, and the arguments of the parties reflect this. That there was still confusion over the issue of whether occupational pension schemes fell within the ambit of Article 141 was clear not just from this case but also from the case of *Newstead*.[31] In *Newstead*, Darmon was asked to give his Opinion in a case involving the situation where an employer deducted payments from the pay of all employees to pay into a fund to provide a widows' pension. Even though no pension was provided for widowers, all employees, married or unmarried, were required to pay into the fund. A confirmed bachelor, Newstead, objected to such a deduction in pay which, he claimed, amounted to sex discrimination in pay.

In his first Opinion, Darmon argued that such a deduction was compatible with Community law as it then stood. He examined the case from the point of view of the obligation imposed on employees to pay into the fund. This, he argued, was a working condition. The Equal Treatment Directive, 76/207/EEC exempted from its scope 'provisions concerning survivors' benefits'. Thus, his argument ran, such deductions were an exception to the principle of equal treatment provided for in the Directive. At the time of the litigation the proposed Directive, which would regulate occupational pension schemes, seemed likely to be under discussion for some time.

In May 1986, the Court gave its decision in the case of *Bilka-Kaufhaus*. The Fifth Chamber, which had originally heard *Newstead*, now referred the case to the Full Court. Two new elements had come to light. The first, as mentioned, was the decision of the Court in *Bilka-Kaufhaus*, and the second was the publication of Directive 86/378 in July 1986 on the implementation of the principle of equal treatment for men and women in occupational social security schemes.

Darmon delivered his second Opinion in June 1987,[32] although it was clear that he did not believe that these additional factors altered his original position. He distinguished the facts of *Bilka-Kaufhaus* from those in *Newstead*. The case of *Bilka-Kaufhaus* concerned benefits paid to employees and, as such, and as held by Court, they constituted pay. Darmon contrasted that case with an obligation to

[31] Case C-192/85 *Newstead v Department of Transport and HM Treasury* [1987] ECR 4753.
[32] *Newstead*, second Opinion, 4775.

contribute to a scheme, the issue here being the effect on his pay, and argued that there was no discriminatory effect in this case. Given that Directive 86/378 specifically excluded survivors' benefits, he also rejected the need to revise his Opinion on this ground.

The Court followed the analysis by Darmon, and held that the disparity in pay was neither a benefit paid to workers nor a contribution made by an employer to a pension scheme on behalf of an employee. It did not, therefore, fall within the definition of a consideration within the meaning of Article 141. The contribution paid by employees is the equivalent to a contribution to a statutory social security scheme and therefore within the scope of Article 137.[33]

Van Gerven, therefore, when faced in the case of *Barber* with another reference from an English court on the boundaries of an occupational scheme, was also confronted with an array of potentially conflicting signals. The case law of the Court was far from clear, the legislative provisions were in the course of development, and there was potential conflict between Article 141 and the newly adopted Directive 86/378 on occupational social security schemes insofar as pension issues were concerned. He did, however, have the benefit of the analyses of previous Advocates General to assist him.

He first dealt with the question of redundancy payments. There were two issues here. The first was whether redundancy payments in excess of the statutory minimum were pay. Van Gerven applied the test set by Advocate General Velhoren van Themaat in the case of *Burton*,[34] that any consideration paid in respect of his employment fell within the definition of pay for the purposes of Article 141. The key test was whether there was 'an unseverable causal connection between pay and employment', and van Gerven argued that redundancy payments met this test. The causal connection was illustrated by the fact that the amount of redundancy pay was determined, in part, by the length of service.

Could this analysis, then, be applied to statutory redundancy payments where the employer did not determine the level of payment but where such a level was fixed by law? The UK argued that statutory redundancy pay could not be considered as consideration for the purposes of Article 141 but should be considered as a social security benefit. Van Gerven rejected this view, relying on the judgment of the Court in *Defrenne II*, where the Court had stated that Article 141 could be relied on 'as regards those types of discrimination arising directly from legislative provisions', to reach this conclusion. That, he argued, was the case here. The causal connection was the key. The employer was providing payment from his own funds by virtue of the employment relationship, albeit because he was required to do so by law. The Court applied the same test although it did not replicate the exact wording of the Advocate General. It looked at the employment relationship and held that redundancy payments were payments made because of

[33] Formerly Art 118 (n 18 above).

[34] Case 19/81 *Burton v British Railways Board* [1982] ECR I-554.

the existence of the employment relationship, even when such payments were required by law.

Van Gerven then turned to the question of whether benefits payable under an occupational pension scheme could be classed as pay. Examining the decision in *Defrenne I* where the Court excluded statutory pension schemes from the ambit of Article 141, he asked whether it was possible to infer an argument *a contrario* that payments of a contractual origin could come within Article 141. He argued that this was precisely the sense in which *Bilka-Kaufhaus* must be read, as this case concerned a contractual scheme established by contract and funded exclusively by the employer.

However, *Barber* concerned a contracted-out scheme. Warner in *Worringham* had taken the view that, as a substitute for a social security scheme, a contracted-out scheme fell outside the scope of Article 141. As noted above, the Court based its decision in that case on other arguments and did not address the issue. In *Newstead*, the Court had held that the disparity in that case was not in relation to benefits under a scheme 'which might be regarded a consideration'. Again, it did not directly address the issue although the UK believed that *Newstead* confirmed that contracted-out schemes could not be considered under Article 141.

Van Gerven argued that the UK was taking too general a conclusion from the case of *Newstead*. He distinguished *Newstead* and *Barber* on the facts. In the former case men and women received equal gross pay and a deduction was made from the salary of the men to pay for a widows' pension scheme. That was a statutory requirement to bring the scheme within the contracted-out framework. Van Gerven argued that this was a special scheme within the definition of the Court's judgment in *Defrenne I*. The contracted-out scheme in *Barber*, he argued, was akin to the scheme in *Bilka-Kaufhaus*. Pensions granted under this scheme were paid because of the terms of the scheme which were 'purely contractual in nature'. The scheme was financed by the employer's contributions and not from deductions in salary. These contributions were paid into a fund and thus the pension was paid indirectly to the employee as a result of the ending of the employment relationship.

The Court came to the same conclusion as the Advocate General and for much the same reasons. The Court went back to its own approach in *Defrenne I*, reiterating that Article 141 does not encompass retirement pensions 'directly governed by legislation without any element of agreement within the undertaking [which] . . . are compulsorily applicable to general categories of workers'.[35] Such schemes, normally co-financed by employers, employees and the state, constitute measures of social policy while, in contrast, contracted-out schemes are the result of an agreement between workers and employers. They are financed either exclusively by employers or jointly by workers and employers, but not by the state. They are,

[35] Case C-262/88 *Douglas Hervey Barber v Guardian Royal Exchange* [1990] ECR I-1889, para 22.

therefore, in the nature of consideration. They are not generally applicable to categories of workers but they derive from the employment relationship. They are governed by their own rules and not by the terms of legislation. The Court rejected the view that contracted-out schemes should be regarded as supplements of the state schemes since the benefits they confer are often wider than the state scheme. For all these reasons, the Court held, in specific terms, that a contracted-out scheme 'constitutes consideration paid by the employer to the worker in respect of his employment and consequently falls within the scope of Article 141 of the Treaty'.[36] In so holding, the Court followed the approach first laid down by Dutheillet de Lamothe and refined by van Gerven, and rejected the approach taken by Warner and reinforced by Darmon.

Van Gerven was not satisfied with proposing a solution to the questions posed by the English Court of Appeal in this case. He also took up the arguments put forward by the Commission which seemed to be concerned about the approach taken by the Court in *Bilka-Kaufhaus*. Was this a new departure? Did it conflict with earlier case-law of the Court on the delimitation of the boundary between the Equal Treatment Directive and Article 141? In particular, in this case, where the discriminatory treatment was not in the amount of benefits payable under a scheme but the conditions under which access to the benefits were regulated, did Article 141 extend so far as to outlaw discrimination in terms of access to a pension where differential ages applied between men and women? The Commission believed that it was the Court itself in *Burton* where that distinction had been drawn.

Burton concerned a voluntary scheme. Only staff aged 60–55 could access the scheme, men at 60 and women at 55. Mr Burton, who was 58 at the relevant time applied for voluntary severance, but his application was turned down. The Court held that the discrimination was not in the benefit but in the terms of access to the benefit. The former would be a question to be governed by Article 141, while the latter would be governed by the Equal Treatment Directive as a working condition.

The Commission believed that the case of *Bilka-Kaufahaus* also concerned the conditions of access to a pension scheme; in that case the full or part-time status of the employees. The Court had not, however, held that such conditions of access were matters of equal treatment but of equal pay.

Van Gerven provided alternative ways of analysing the case-law of the Court, even although this was not required, to assist the Court in providing a solution to the questions posed in the case of *Barber*. In that sense, he was going beyond his remit. In his own view the Commission's arguments raised what he termed 'an intermediate question' which required examination before the Court could examine whether the discrimination complained of in *Barber* was prohibited by Article 141.

The question was not, of course, purely academic or hypothetical. The Court had held that Article 141 had direct effect. It could therefore be relied on, as an Article of the Treaty, both against the state as an employer and as against a private

[36] Ibid, para 28.

sector employer or a private trust. The Equal Treatment Directive, as a directive, was not horizontally directly effective. From the point of view of Barber, therefore, a solution based on Article 141 was preferable.

Van Gerven offered three kinds of analysis. First, he argued that *Bilka-Kaufhaus* should not be seen as setting a precedent and that the scope of Article 141 should be confined to covering the amount of remuneration or benefit. This analysis was consistent with the approach taken by the Court in *Defrenne III*, where the Court had held Article 141 was limited to pay discrimination linked to precise factors and should not be extended to other aspects of discrimination. Van Gerven argued against this approach, in that this would be a restrictive view of the concept of pay and would also be an interpretation less consistent with the principle of equality. Van Gerven reminded the Court that it had itself repeatedly emphasized the importance of this principle.

His second level of analysis was to see *Bilka-Kaufhaus* as heralding an expansion of the interpretation of Article 141 whereby all working conditions having financial consequences could be brought within its scope. The advantage to this approach was that it would expand the scope of the principle of equality but, at the same time, its disadvantage was that it would blur the distinction between Article 141 and Articles 136 and 137. The Court itself had previously contrasted the wording of these Articles—the precision of the wording in Article 141 as against the programmatic approach in 136 and 137. A broad interpretation of 141 would therefore encroach onto areas reserved to the Member States.

His third approach, and the one that he favoured, was to try to reduce the case-law of the Court as well as *Bilka-Kaufhaus* to what he referred to as a 'common denominator'. He analysed *Burton* (and other relevant cases) from the point of view of age conditions or limits regarding the termination of employment, albeit that this had financial consequences. Such conditions or limits should be viewed as working conditions, ie the conditions governing the selection of those whose employment is to be terminated. These conditions are regulated under the terms of the Equal Treatment Directive. He contrasted that approach to the problem in the *Barber* case, as in this case the age condition was not being used to make decisions about terminating the employment relationship but to determine who had access to specific benefits. That, he argued, was a condition governing pay and was therefore within the scope of Article 141. He admitted that this approach brought 'working conditions (including conditions governing dismissal or other forms of redundancy) which directly govern access to that is to say the grant of, remuneration' within the scope of Article 141. This comparison, he argued, brought within the scope of Article 141 conditions governing pay in a broad sense but this approach did not excessively impinge on Articles 136 and 137. What he did not say (most probably because of deference to the Court) is that this approach makes sense of the apparently contradictory case-law of the Court itself.

This part of van Gerven's Opinion is an extremely sophisticated and fine-grained legal analysis which sought to reconcile: the case-law of the Court, the proper interpretation of Articles 136, 137 and 141, the competences of the Community and the inherent limitations on the extent of Community competences in the Treaty, the conflicting advice given to the Court in earlier Opinions of Advocates General, all within the framework of the principle of equality. It had to be done, because the courts of the Member States were confused as to the correct interpretation of the Treaty. The incremental legislative approach preferred by the Member States was creating confusion, particularly as the Member States developed a fondness of legislating for exceptions within exceptions. Thus, although this intermediate question was not strictly necessary to assist the Court in dealing with the questions posed in the *Barber* case, it was a way of clarifying a difficult and confused legal situation. As such, this Opinion could be compared to *doctrine* as it is understood within civilian systems of law.[37]

An alternative, and certainly less generous view, is that van Gerven was indulging his own academic interests in this Opinion. His Opinion in *Barber* could be read as an academic article and, since he raised issues that were not necessary to enable the Court to answer the questions put to it by the national court, he was not performing the task entrusted to the Advocate General in the Treaty, namely assisting the Court. However, the Treaty does not limit the kind of assistance that can be given by the Advocate General to the case in question, and the issues that van Gerven raised in *Barber* in relation to access to a pension scheme were later referred to the Court in a number of subsequent cases, including both those of *Fisscher* and *Vroege*, in which van Gerven was appointed Advocate General. The crucial question is therefore whether van Gerven's critical and timely analysis of the confused state of Community law, in the longer term, helped to establish the basic principles surrounding the limits of interpretation of Article 141. Van Gerven provided the reasoning for the Court to distinguish matters relating to pay and those relating to social security. He argued that redundancy payments should be seen as pay as against the arguments of the UK which saw them as social security benefits and therefore excluded from the ambit of Article 141. The Court agreed with van Gerven, and this has subsequently paved the way for the Court to hold that other matters lying on the boundary between social security and pay fall within the ambit of Article 141 such as sick pay[38] or, and perhaps even more radically, compensation for unfair dismissal.[39] Van Gerven also provided the reasoning for the Court to hold that contracted-out pension schemes fall within the ambit of Article 141.

As noted above, the Court had skirted around this issue for a number of years and, in the meantime, the Member States had sought to legislate to exclude this

[37] In the French system, for example, *doctrine* 'can be taken into account by the Judges when interpreting the law . . . academic writing is most influenctial when the case-law is not yet settled'. C Elliott, E Jeanpierre and C Vernon, *French Legal System* (2nd edn, 2006) 83.

[38] Case C-171/88 *Rinner-Kuhn v FWW Sezial-Gebaudereiningung GmbH & Co KG* [1989] ECR 2743.

[39] Case C-167/97 *R v Secretary of State for Employment, ex p Seymour-Smith and Perez* [1999] ECR I 623.

type of pension scheme from the ambit of the principle of equal treatment. In an overall context of prioritizing the equality principle as being a fundamental principle of Community law, van Gerven teased out for the Court the way in which the principle of equality could inform its decision and allow the Court to interpret Article 141 in a way that did not do violence to the text of the Treaty. As noted above, van Gerven was not coming to this issue cold and in his Opinion he built on the very firm foundations laid by Dutheillet de Lamothe. It would, therefore, be invidious to credit van Gerven with developing the entire framework of analysis; however, he could have taken the Court in an entirely different direction had he followed Warner in limiting the scope of Article 141. Warner, himself with the benefit of de Lamothe's Opinion before him, had come to a very different conclusion in holding that contracted-out schemes should be viewed as part of the state's scheme of social security.

Contracted-out pension schemes, it could be argued, are a feature of just one aspect of the myriad of pension schemes that operate within the Member States, and this is true. However, the decision of the Court in *Barber*, and van Gerven's analysis, which provided the Court with a framework of legal reasoning, allowed the Court in subsequent cases to bring most, if not all, types of occupational pension schemes within the ambit of Article 141 and hence the principle of equal treatment in pay. For example, in the case of *Beune*, a Dutch statutory pension scheme for civil servants was brought by the Court into the remit of Article 141.[40] The Court in *Beune* relying on *Barber*, held that 'benefits awarded under an occupational scheme which, partly or entirely, take the place of the benefits paid by a statutory social security scheme may fall within the scope of Article 119 [current Article 141]'. The Court has applied this reasoning in subsequent cases. Indeed, if *Defrenne I* were now to be heard by the Court, a different answer would be given.

Survivors' pensions and the scope of Article 119

A related but separate question was whether a survivor's pension, paid to the widow or widower of an employee who was a member of a pension scheme, came within the ambit of Article 141. This question was raised in both *Ten Oever* and *Coloroll*.[41] The Dutch government had argued against such an interpretation of Article 141. It argued that survivors' benefits were excluded from the ambit of Community sex discrimination law by virtue of Article 3(2) of Directive 79/7, which excludes survivors' benefits in matters of social security as well as Article 9(b) of Directive 86/378 which allows the Members States to defer implementation of the equal

[40] Case C-7/93 *Bestuur van het Algemeen Burgerlijk Pensioenfonds v G.A. Beune* [1994] ECR I-4471.

[41] Cases C-109/91 *Gerardus Cornells Ten Oever v Stichting Bedrijfspensioenfonds voor het Glazenwassers-en Schoonmaakbedrijf* [1993] ECR I-4897; C-200/91 *Coloroll Pension Trustees v James Richard Russell and ors* [1994] ECR I-04389.

treatment principle with regard to survivors' benefits until such time as a new directive on equal treatment in statutory social security schemes would be adopted. In further support of this view, the Dutch government referred to the (then) proposed directive on occupational social security, which deferred implementation of the principle of equal treatment in matters of occupational social security relating to survivors' pensions for some years. Finally, the Dutch government relied on *Newstead* to support its case.

Van Gerven concentrated on answering two questions. The first was the right of a survivor to claim a benefit where he or she was not the employee. Here he argued that the benefit under consideration was one deriving from the employment relationship and aid in respect of the employment of a deceased spouse. The second was whether the scheme in question was outside the scope of Article 141. Here he systematically went through the conditions laid down in the case of *Defrenne I* and showed that the scheme in question was the result of collective consultation, with the role of the state being to make the scheme compulsory for the whole industry. The scheme was funded by contributions from employees and employers without any contribution from the state and it was not a scheme applicable to all workers but to a limited category of workers employed by certain undertakings. As such, this was not a social security scheme but a matter of pay within the meaning of Article 141. From both these points it followed that survivors' pensions fell within the scope of Article 141. On the question of whether the survivor could rely on the direct effect of Article 141, a question raised in the case of *Coloroll*, van Gerven argued that not to allow a surviving spouse to do so would deprive Article 141 of its useful effect. Van Gerven also recommended that, in view of the uncertainty created by the legislation discussed above that the Court impose a temporal limitation on its judgment dating from the judgment of the Court in this case; however, the Court did not follow this advice.[42]

The Court followed the analysis of van Gerven on the scope of Article 141, repeating his formulation in relation to the nature of the scheme in question. It also accepted the point in relation to the survivor as the recipient of the benefit rather than the worker holding that 'entitlement to such a benefit is a consideration deriving from the survivor's spouse's membership of the scheme, the pension being vested in the survivor by reason of the employment relationship between the employer and the survivor's spouse and being paid to him or her by reason of the spouse's employment'.[43] In the case of *Coloroll*, echoing van Gerven, the Court also held that 'if a survivor were to be denied the possibility [of relying on Article 119], this would deprive Article 119 of all its effectiveness as far as survivors' pensions are concerned'.[44]

[42] The issue of temporal limitations is discussed below.

[43] Case C-57/93 *Anna Adnaantje Vroege v NCIV Institut voor Voikshuis vesting BV and Stichting Penioenfonds NCIV* [1994] ECR I-04541, para 13, repeated in Case C-200/91 *Coloroll Pension Trustees v James Richard Russell and ors* [1994] ECR I-04389, para 18 (n 3 above).

[44] *Coloroll*, ibid at para 19. Ex Art 119 is current Art 141 EC.

Access to occupational pension schemes

The cases of *Vroege* and *Fisscher* dealt with the issue highlighted by van Gerven in *Barber*—that of access to pension schemes. Can Article 141 be interpreted to include a right to join a pension scheme irrespective of sex as opposed to taking benefits from such a scheme? Van Gerven delivered a joint Opinion in respect of both these cases. He had already addressed this issue in his Opinion in *Barber*. In these two cases he did not repeat his arguments but based his advice solely on the judgment of the Court in the case of *Bilka-Kaufhaus*. That judgment made clear that the ambit of Article 141 extended to membership of an occupational pension scheme. Van Gerven also suggested an answer to a question that had not been put directly by the Court in these cases, namely: was exclusion of married women and part-time female employees contrary to the principle of equal treatment? He argued that the exclusion of married women was direct discrimination, and the exclusion of part-time workers might amount to indirect discrimination provided that it could be shown that a larger proportion of women were excluded from the scheme than men by virtue of their part-time status.

The Court followed this analysis. Relying on *Bilka-Kaufhaus* for the proposition that 'Article 141 covers not only entitlement to benefits paid by an occupational pension scheme but also the right to be a member of such a scheme',[45] the Court also agreed with the Advocate General that exclusion for married women was direct discrimination and prohibited by Article 141, and also that Article 141 is contravened only if the exclusion of part time workers affects a greater number of women than men and that the exclusion cannot be objectively justified.

Bridging pensions

From a conceptual point of view, one of the most interesting of the gender discrimination cases in which van Gerven was involved was *Birds Eye Walls*. At its heart this case did not concern so much the interpretation of the Treaty but an understanding of the concept of equality as it is understood in European Community law. The employer, Unilever, provided an occupational pension scheme with a retirement date of 65 for men and 60 for women which mirrored the (then) state pensionable age in the UK. In the case of ill-health retirement before the pensionable age, Unilever provided a bridging pension which was designed to place an employee in the position in which they would have been had they not had to retire. The bridging pension for women was reduced, in the years between her 60th and 65th birthdays by the amount she received in state pension. Since men did not receive a

[45] Case C-170/84 *Bilka-Kaufhaus Gmbh v Weber von Hartz* [1986] ECR 1607, para 15.

state pension during these years, the bridging pension paid by Unilever to a man was at a higher rate than to a woman. Overall, taking into consideration the bridging pension and the state pension, the actual income of a man and a woman under the terms of the scheme were the same.

All the parties to this dispute agreed that there was differential treatment between men and women. For Roberts, the applicant, who had raised the issue in the English courts, the difference in treatment amounted to direct sex discrimination and, as such, could not be justified since only indirect discrimination could be justified, and only then if there was an objective justification for the difference in treatment. Van Gerven chose to focus on this point. He argued that in the case-law of the Court it was not absolutely clear that direct discrimination could never be justified. Indeed, he urged the Court not to restrict the possibility of justification solely to indirect discrimination. In some cases the distinction between direct and indirect discrimination was blurred; for example, the differential treatment in this case could be seen as direct discrimination since the employer pays a lower rate to his female than to his male employees. Alternatively it might be seen as indirect discrimination since the difference in payment is based on an objective factor, namely the receipt by female employees of the state pension. In this particular case van Gerven was swayed by the arguments of the employer that their policy was justified. The aim of the scheme was to prevent women receiving a higher overall pension than men. The deductions made were intended to prevent any inequality arising as regards pension payments. Van Gerven reasoned that a scheme which has the object or effect of removing or preventing another inequality of treatment and leads to equal treatment in practice can be objectively justified. He argued, therefore, that the employer was not in breach of Article 141.

In its judgment on this point the Court did not rely on the arguments of the Advocate General at all. It took a completely different line of argument. The Court accepted that the bridging pension was pay, but it did not accept that there had been any discrimination on the grounds of sex, either direct or indirect. Instead the Court examined whether male and female ex-employees were in a comparable situation since 'the principle of equal treatment . . . presupposes that the men and the women to whom it applies are in identical situations'. Between the ages of 60 and 65 men and women were not in identical situations—she could draw her state pension whereas he could not. 'That difference as regards the objective premise, which necessarily entails that the amount of bridging pension is not the same for men and women, cannot be considered discriminatory'. Furthermore, 'the mechanism for calculating the bridging pension is neutral, which confirms the absence of any discrimination'.[46] The Court concluded that there had been no breach of Article 141.

The second part of the case concerned women who had opted to pay reduced contributions to the national insurance fund and who, therefore, received a

[46] Case C-132/92 *Birds Eye Walls Ltd v Friedel M. Roberts* [1993] ECR I-5579, paras 20 and 23.

reduced pension. Under Unilever's scheme, the bridging pension of such women was also reduced to the extent that the old-age pension itself was reduced. Roberts' pension was not in fact reduced as, although she had paid reduced contributions, she was a widow and the widows' pension was paid at the full rate. Given the importance of this question for other individuals in the scheme, van Gerven did not believe that it was purely a hypothetical question. He argued that it would be an unfair advantage for women who had opted to pay reduced contributions if they were able to claim the same overall retirement pension as others, male and female, who had paid the full rate of contributions. If this was to be the effect of Article 141 it would encourage women to pay the lower rate and would also introduce further inequality into the scheme. This was the case, *a fortiori*, where the woman could draw the full state pension (because she was a widow) after having paid reduced contributions. In its judgment the Court repeated these arguments almost word for word after having acknowledged the logic of van Gerven's reasoning.

The conditions for the imposition of temporal limitations on the judgments of the Court

The decision in the case of *Barber* settled the question of whether contracted-out and similar pension schemes fell within the ambit of Article 141. In the second *Defrenne* case, the Court had held that Article 141 could be relied on as from the date of that judgment in cases before the national courts. It was an unusual step for the Court to impose a limitation in time and the Court justified such a limitation in terms of legal certainty. The question of whether the Court should impose a temporal limitation arose again in the *Barber* case, again on the grounds of legal certainty. The Commission, in its submissions to the Court, raised the possibility of the Court restricting the effects of its judgment, suggesting that the Court should make it possible for individuals to rely on the judgment 'only in proceedings already pending before the national courts and in disputes concerning events occurring after the date of the Judgement'.[47] The UK, in its submissions, raised the serious financial consequences of the decision of the Court if it were to determine that benefits paid under contracted-out schemes did fall within the definition of consideration within the meaning of Article 141.

Van Gerven realized that there were serious implications were the Court to follow his advice that contracted-out schemes fell within the ambit of Article 141, as this might require the Court to impose a reservation in respect to the temporal effect of its decision. Given that the Council had specifically legislated to permit the adoption of different pensionable ages in Directive 86/378, he argued that this could be a ground, in accordance with the principle of legal certainty, for such a reservation. Having raised the issue, van Gerven immediately seemed to scotch

[47] Case C-262/88 *Douglas Hervey Barber v Guardian Royal Exchange* [1990] ECR I-1889, para 39.

the idea and, in a somewhat unconvincing passage, argued that there was in fact no need for such a limitation. This is because he believed that Article 9(1)(a) of Directive 86/378, which permitted the adoption of differential pensionable ages, was not relevant to the facts of this case. However, the question relating to legal certainty still remained, irrespective of Directive 86/378. It was far from clear, until the case of *Barber*, whether contracted-out pension schemes did fall within the scope of Article 141, and the interpretation offered by van Gerven itself was, in fact, quite radical. The issue of legal certainty should therefore have been addressed in the light of the implications of the potential judgment in *Barber* rather than in the light of the implications of Directive 86/378.

The Court disagreed with the Advocate General on this point. It held that the Member States and the parties concerned had been 'reasonably entitled to consider that Article 141 did not apply to pensions paid under contracted-out schemes'.[48] The Court came to this conclusion in view of the legislative history of provisions relating to equal treatment, which had been in existence since 1978. Directive 79/7 on equal treatment in social security authorized Member States to defer implementing the principle of equal treatment as regards determining the pensionable age and a similar exemption had been incorporated into Directive 86/378. 'Overriding considerations of legal certainty' led the Court to impose its famous reservation *rationae temporis* in this case:

> Overriding considerations of legal certainty preclude legal situations which have exhausted all their effects in the past from being called in question where that might upset retroactively the financial balance of many contracted-out pension schemes. It is appropriate, however, to provide for an exception in favour of individuals who have taken action in good time in order to safeguard their rights. Finally, it must be pointed out that no restriction on the effects of the aforesaid interpretation can be permitted as regards the acquisition of entitlement to a pension as from the date of this Judgment.
>
> It must therefore be held that the direct effect of Article 141 of the Treaty may not be relied upon in order to claim entitlement to a pension with effect from a date prior to this Judgment, except in the case of workers or those claiming under them who have before that date initiated legal proceedings or raised an equivalent claim under the applicable national law.[49]

Van Gerven was subsequently involved in four cases where the scope of this temporal limitation was in issue: *Ten Oever*, *Moroni*, *Neath* and *Coloroll*.[50] What exactly had the Court meant in its judgment in *Barber*? How was the judgment to be interpreted? It was clear that the national courts had some difficulty in divining the underlying meaning of the European Court of Justice. Van Gerven was

[48] Ibid, para 43. [49] Ibid, paras 43 and 44.

[50] Cases C-109/91 *Gerardus Cornelis Ten Oever v Stichting Bedrijfspensioen fonds voor net Glazenwassers-en Schoonmaakbedrijf* [1993] ECR I-4897; C-110/91 *Michael Moroni v Collo GMBH* [1993] ECR I-00453; C-152/91 *David Neath v Hugh Steeper Ltd* [1993] ECR I-6935; C-200/91 *Coloroll Pension Trustees v James Richard Russell and ors* [1994] ECR I-04389 (van Gerven delivered a joint opinion in these cases, see [1993] ECR I-4893)

assigned to all four cases and he gave a joined Opinion in April 1993. His Opinion, which runs to some 44 pages of the European Court Reports, dealt with the common thread running through these cases; what are the effects of the temporal limitation laid down in *Barber*? In addition, he dealt with the specific question raised in each case.

The facts of these cases illustrate the problem. Ten Oever was a widower. His wife had contributed to a pension scheme, funded by employers and employees. The pension scheme provided for a survivor's pension for the surviving widow of a member but did not provide, at the time of his wife's death, for a widower's pension. Ten Oever's wife died in October 1988. The rules of the pension scheme were amended in January 1989 to provide a widower's pension, but not with retroactive effect. Ten Oever, a widower, was not therefore entitled to a survivor's pension.

Moroni had been employed by the German firm, Collo, for 15 years from 1968 to 1983, and had joined Collo's pension scheme in 1968 upon taking up employment. Under the terms of the scheme he was entitled to a pension on reaching the age of 65 (for women the age would have been 60), provided that he had been employed by Collo for 10 years. In November 1990 he raised an action against Collo claiming that he should be entitled to a pension when he reached the age of 60 (he was then 42) but, more crucially, that his future entitlement should be calculated on the basis of his becoming entitled to a pension at the age of 60. In other words, the pension scheme should be immediately adjusted to provide for equal pension ages for men and women.

The situation in *Moroni* was made even further complicated by German law. An individual who contributed to a pension scheme for a certain length of time, but who left employment before the normal pensionable age under the company's scheme, acquired 'a right vested in interest to benefits'. At the age of 65, for a man, such a right vested in future benefits is transformed into an entitlement vested in possession of benefits. The size of pension is calculated on a ratio of actual time in employment as against service he would have completed had he worked until the normal retirement age of 65. A woman became entitled to benefits at the age of 60 and the ratio used to determine the level of pension was based on the number of years of her service and the years she would have worked until reaching the age of 60. A man could claim his pension entitlement before the age of 65 but he would then be subject to an actuarial deduction. A woman was not subject to any further reduction if she claimed her pension before the age of 60.

Neath was made redundant in June 1990, after the judgment in the case of *Barber* had been delivered. He was almost 55 years old and was a member of a contracted-out pension scheme. Women could retire on full pension at the age of 60 but men could only retire on full pension at the age of 65. Men and women were entitled to take early retirement under the scheme and the pension entitlement would then be calculated on the basis of the pension that the individual would have received, subject to a 6% per annum reduction for each year between the date of retirement and the normal retirement age—65 for men and 60 for women. The effect of this rule is substantially to reduce the amount of pension payable to men who retire early as compared to their female counterparts. Alternatively, men and women who retired early were entitled to commute their pensions into a lump sum, which was based on actuarial factors and could be paid into another pension scheme. The difference in actuarial factors worked to the disadvantage of Neath, since they were in part determined by the different pensionable ages of men and women. In Neath's case, the pension fund did not consider the use of male and female actuarial factors could amount to discrimination.

The *Colorall* case concerned pension schemes for the Colorall group of companies, which had collapsed in 1990. All the schemes were based on differential retirement ages of men and women with the result that different amounts of pension were payable to men and women having the same length of service and the same level of pension contributions. Where lump sum payments were chosen, such payments were based on actuarial assumptions of the different life expectancies of men and women. The Coloroll Trustees, in the light of the *Barber* case, were unclear as to what level of pension payments it should make to former employees of the Colorall Group.

All these cases raised the same question: what was the point in time at which the principle of equal pay should be applied? Pension schemes, by definition, are based on the principle of accrued benefits with payments into a scheme being made over 20, 30 or 40 years. Benefits are taken from the scheme at the point of retirement from the scheme and are then, typically, payable until the death of the individual concerned. That period might be lengthy or short. Van Gerven suggested that four possible interpretations could be inferred from the judgment in *Barber.*

The first interpretation would limit the application of the principle of equal treatment only to workers who became members of occupational schemes after the date of the *Barber* judgment. As van Gerven said, the effect of applying this interpretation would be to delay the application of the principle of equal pay for up to 40 years when its full effect was felt. His second interpretation would be to limit the principle of equal treatment to benefits payable in respect of periods of service after the date of the *Barber* judgment. A third interpretation would be to apply the principle of equal treatment to pensions which fall to be paid after the date of the *Barber* judgement. This would be irrespective of the length of service and the contributions made up to that point. A final, and by far the most far-reaching interpretation, was to apply the principle of equal treatment to all pension payments made after the date of the *Barber* judgment irrespective of the date of the periods of service accrued.

None of the intervening parties supported the first interpretation and neither did van Gerven. The Commission, in its submissions in the first of the three of the cases to come to Court, had supported the third interpretation but had shifted its position in favour of the second, and the fourth had only limited support.

The second was supported by most of the intervening parties, including those Member States who had intervened in the cases. It is not surprising that the Member States supported the second point of view: the Court had delivered its judgment in *Barber* in May 1990 and, concerned by the potential impact of the Court's decision on the financial sustainability of the pensions industry, the Member States had negotiated a Protocol to the Treaty during the IGC leading up to the signing of the Treaty on European Union (TEU) in February 1992. At the time van Gerven gave his Opinion—in April 1993, the Treaty was not yet in force but in the process of ratification.

The Protocol provides that 'benefits under occupational social security schemes shall not be considered as remuneration if and in so far as they are attributable to periods of employment prior to May 17 1990, except in the case of workers or those claiming under them who have before that date initiated legal proceedings or introduced an equivalent claim under the applicable national law'.[51] Thus the Member States had effectively legislated for the second interpretation. As van Gerven pointed out to the Court, from the moment the TEU came into effect, any decision of theirs contrary to this interpretation would be overruled. In light of that advice, it is perhaps surprising, therefore, that he engaged in a lengthy exposition of the law to date on temporal effect of judgments in European law as well as on the potential interpretation of the words of the Court in the case of *Barber*.

Van Gerven reminded the Court that their judgments in cases brought before them under the preliminary reference procedure was to clarify and define the meaning and scope of a rule as it ought to have been understood from the date of its coming into force. The rule as interpreted should therefore be applied, even to legal relationships existing before the Court gave its judgment. It is only exceptionally, therefore, that the Court may limit the effect of its interpretation. The Court had set the conditions for such a restriction in *Defrenne II* when it held that the general principle of legal certainty, combined with the serious effects that the judgment would have on pre-existing legal relationships, were sufficient conditions to restrict the effect of its judgment. Van Gerven went on to review subsequent case-law, reminding the Court that in the past it had taken into consideration the good faith or the legitimate expectation of the parties or the Member States, particularly where the Community institutions themselves had created an impression of validity by approving an act of secondary Community law (such as the Directive on occupational pensions in issue in *Barber*) or other circumstances. It was partly in view of the good faith of the market participants that the Court had limited the temporal effects of its decision in *Defrenne II*. In *Blaizot*,[52] the Court had accepted that its judgment would have serious repercussions on the financing

[51] Protocol Concerning Art 141 of the Treaty Establishing the European Community (No.17). Protocol added by the Treaty of Maastricht.

[52] Case 24/86 *Blaizot v Belgium* [1988] ECR 379.

of Universities and had imposed a limitation, while in *Legros*,[53] it had recognized the catastrophic financial repercussion of its judgment on the French overseas territories if its judgment had had retrospective effect.

Van Gerven based his interpretation of the *Barber* judgment on the distinction between the accrual of an occupational pension and its falling due. He believed that this distinction was implicit in *Barber*. In deciding that pension payments made under a contracted-out scheme constituted consideration within the meaning of Article 141, the Court recognized the concept of deferred pay. Van Gerven equates deferred pay with accrual. This interpretation is helpful for the Court, even if it was not what the Court intended in the *Barber* case, since it opens the way for the Court to interpret *Barber* in the same sense as the Protocol. In *Barber*, the Court had used the term 'the acquisition of entitlement to a pension as from the date of this judgment', and van Gerven reasoned that, since it is service and contributions which define entitlement (since benefits are accrued), the Court clearly had in mind periods of service after 17 May 1990.

Van Gerven also tried to give meaning to the phrase 'legal situations which have exhausted all their effects in the past may not be called into question', which the Court had used in its judgment in the case of *Barber*. He rejected the meaning ascribed to this phrase by some of the Coloroll Trustees, who had argued that it meant that the effects of an occupational pension are exhausted only once the pension has been paid in full to the retired employee. He agreed that this was the literal interpretation of the words but also that, if that was the meaning to be ascribed to the phrase, then the useful effect of the temporal limitation would vanish. Returning to his distinction between accrual and the falling due of the pension, van Gerven reasoned that what the Court had in view were situations where rights to a pension had been acquired by virtue of service prior to the date of the Court's judgment. Pension rights acquired prior to that date had exhausted their legal effects since the worker had definitely acquired pension rights on the basis of that service. On a more practical level, van Gerven argued that the reason why the Court had imposed a temporal limitation was precisely not to upset the financial balance of contracted out schemes and this interpretation was consistent with that aim. Legal certainty in this context means that the rules of Community law as they were understood at the time should govern the legal relationships existing at that time. Van Gerven was able to cite precedent for this approach from previous case-law of the Court. It also sits most easily with the good faith of employers and occupational schemes. For all these reason van Gerven advised the Court to choose the second interpretation.

In its judgment in *Ten Oever*, the Court relied on the arguments of van Gerven although it did not make specific reference to his Opinion. The Court explained that its ruling in *Barber* 'took account of the fact that it is a characteristic of this form of pay that there is a time-lag between the accrual of entitlement to the pension, which occurs gradually throughout the employee's working life, and its

[53] Case C-163/90 *Legros* [1992] ECR I-4625.

actual payment, which is deferred until a particular age'.[54] The Court also stated that it took into account the way that pension funds are financed by periodic contributions set against future amounts to be paid, and explained that 'it must be made clear that equality of treatment in the matter of occupational pensions may be claimed only in relation to benefits payable in respect of periods of employment subsequent to 17 May 1990', except for those individuals who had already initiated legal action before that date.[55] The Court repeated this formulation in *Moroni*,[56] *Coloroll*[57] and *Neath*.[58] Where the Advocate General had taken several pages to reason out the possible interpretations for the Court, it took just three short paragraphs to reach its conclusion. In this case it is clear that the Court accepted the argumentation of the Advocate General, summarized in two sentences, to allow it to reach a conclusion that was perfectly acceptable in terms of legal reasoning but also in line with the Protocol that would, irrespective of its own decision in these cases, govern the application of the principle of equal treatment in respect of occupational pensions in the future.

There is however, an irony in the case of *Ten Oever*. Perhaps because van Gerven had failed to argue the point fully in relation to a possible temporal limitation in *Barber*, he picked up this theme again in *Ten Oever*. As noted above, this case dealt with survivor's pensions and it was the first time that the Court had held that this type of pension fell within the ambit of Article 141. Van Gerven suggested to the Court that in the light of the principle of legal certainly it should impose a temporal limitation in the case of survivors' pensions; however, the Court rejected this argument and held that the temporal limitation in *Barber* applied equally to that in *Ten Oever*. It was not going to impose a new temporal limitation each time an additional scheme was deemed to come within the ambit of Article 141!

Ten Oever seemed to have settled the question of the temporal limitations in terms of contributions to and benefits from occupational schemes, but it did not seem to have answered all the questions in the minds of the courts of the Member States. Van Gerven was Advocate General in two further cases that came before the Court relating to the right to join an occupational pension scheme, *Fisscher* and *Vroege*.[59] The national courts wished to know whether the temporal limitation in *Barber*, and in the Protocol attached to the TEU, was applicable to the right to join a pension scheme—did such a right date from 17 May 1990? The pensions funds in these cases, as well as the UK and Belgian governments, argued

[54] Case C-109/91 *Gerardus Cornelis Ten Oever v Stichting Bedrijfspensioenfonds voor net Glazenwassers-en Schoonmaakbedrijf* [1993] ECR I-4897, para 17.

[55] Ibid at para 18.

[56] Case C-110/91 *Michael Moroni v Collo GMBH* [1993] ECR I-00453, para 33.

[57] Case C-200/91 *Coloroll Pension Trustees v James Richard Russell and ors* [1994] ECR I-04389, para 48.

[58] Case C-152/91 *David Neath v Hugh Steeper Ltd* [1993] ECR I-6935, para 16.

[59] Cases C-128/93 *Geetruida Catharina Fisscher v voorhuis Hengelo BV and Stichting Bedrijfspensioenfonds voor de Detailhandel* [1994] ECR I-4583 and C-57/93 *Anna Adriaantje Vroege v NCIV Institut voor Volkshuisvesting BV and Stichting Pensioenfonds NCIV* [1994] ECR I-04541.

that the *Barber* limitation should apply as, prior to that case, it had not been clear that occupational pension schemes were governed by Article 141. By contrast, the parties and the Commission argued that the Court had settled the issue of the right to join a pension scheme in the earlier case of *Bilka-Kaufhaus* and the Court had not imposed a temporal limitation in that case.

Relying on *Bilka-Kaufhaus*, van Gerven argued that, as far as membership of an occupational scheme was concerned, there was no ambiguity in Community law. *Bilka-Kaufhaus* had brought exclusion from membership of a pension scheme within the ambit of Article 141 and the Court had not imposed a temporal limitation in that case. Therefore the temporal limitation in *Barber* did not apply.

Neither, he argued, did the *Barber* Protocol apply. The purpose of the Protocol was to clarify the judgment of the Court and not to amend it. He sought an explanation of the Court's ruling in *Ten Oever* to the effect that the *Barber* limitation applied to that case also, and found only one explanation. Both the *Barber* judgment and the *Barber* Protocol must apply to the question of *pensionable* ages and 'to the matters in relation to which until the *Barber* judgment the parties concerned were reasonably entitled to consider, having regard to the exceptions provided for in Directive 86/378, that derogations from the principle of equal treatment continued to be permitted'.[60]

The Court followed this reasoning. Paraphrasing van Gerven, the Court held 'the *Barber* judgment concerns only those kinds of discrimination which employers and pension schemes could reasonably have considered to be permissible owing to the transitional derogations for which Community law provided and which were capable of being applied to occupational pensions'.[61] The Court also stated, as van Gerven had argued, that it had been clear since *Bilka-Kaufhaus* that a breach of the rule of equal treatment, through not recognizing the right to join a pension scheme, is caught by Article 141.

In subsequent cases, the Court of Justice has maintained this case-law as it applies to the right to join a contracted-out occupational pension scheme. For example, in *Magorrian*, the Court held that a part-time worker who had suffered indirect discrimination because of a refusal to allow her membership of an occupational pension scheme, was entitled to have periods of service dating from 8 April 1976 taken into account, for the purpose of calculating additional benefits.[62] More recently the Court has rejected an argument that the temporal limitation in either *Bilka* or in *Barber* can be used to require a national judge to set aside more favourable national provisions than those provided under Community law.[63]

[60] Ibid, *Vroege* at para 25. [61] Ibid, para 27.

[62] Case C-246/96 *Magorrian & Cunningham v Eastern Health & Social Service Board and Department of Health and Social Services* [1997] ECR I-7153.

[63] Cases C-50/96 *Deutsche Telekom v Schröder* [2000] ECR I-743; C-234 and 235/96 *Deutsche Telekom v Vick and Conze* [2000] ECR I-799; C-270/97 and 271/97 *Deutsche Post v Sievers and Schrage* [2000] ECR I-929.

Post *Barber*—levelling up or levelling down?

In the wake of the decision in the *Barber* case, the trustees and administrators of countless occupational pension schemes found that they had to revise their schemes to eliminate any discriminatory provisions. The question of whether the terms of schemes could be levelled down in order to achieve equality was raised in *Coloroll* and in *Smith* and *Van den Akker*;[64] for example, where women were entitled to receive their pension at an earlier age than men, should the scheme be adjusted to her level or his?

Van Gerven admitted that this was a 'delicate' question. In *Coloroll*, a number of defendants had argued that the social aim underlying the treaty was intended to raise the standard of living of workers, thus levelling up was required to achieve equality. In *Defrenne II* the Court had seemed to indicate that the only way to satisfy a claim that a woman had received less pay than a male would be to set aside the lower pay rate. Van Gerven distinguished *Defrenne II*, arguing that it was a claim for past compensation, whereas in the cases relating to occupational pension schemes discrimination was to be eliminated in the future. He argued that, where past discrimination had occurred (past discrimination being defined in terms of periods of service between the decision of the Court in *Barber* and the measures taken to equalise pension schemes) levelling up was the correct solution. Quoting the Court, he argued that this must be the case since the higher level of benefits was the 'only valid frame of reference'. However, he argued that Community law did not preclude a reduction in benefits as a means of equalizing the conditions between men and women. Otherwise the Community would be interfering unnecessarily into a policy area which is a matter for the Member States.

These issues were explored more fully in *Smith* and *Van den Akker*.[65] In both these cases, the schemes were amended so as to raise the pensionable age for women, and in such a way that many women were in danger of losing a considerable part of their pensions. In these cases van Gerven argued that the key question was whether the raising of the pensionable age for female employees was compatible with Article 141, particularly as, in the *Smith* case, this was disadvantageous for women. Referring back to *Coloroll*, he distinguished three different periods of time. Between 17 May 1990 and the date chosen by pension schemes to equalize pensionable ages, it is necessary to increase the level of benefits to bring those benefits up to the level of the advantaged sex. Here the only valid frame of reference was the more beneficial provisions. However, this did not mean that the advantageous conditions must be applied in respect of periods of service prior to 17 May 1990, since up to that date, in effect, Community law on equal treatment did not apply to occupational pension schemes. Once equalization had been achieved, van Gerven advised that Community law does not preclude a lowering of benefits

[64] See n 3 above. [65] Ibid.

provided that such benefits are equal for men and women. Otherwise Community law would be interfering too far into the organization of pension schemes.

The Court agreed with this analysis, holding that once the Court has found discrimination to exist, and where measures have not been taken to rectify that situation, the only proper way to comply with Article 141 is to 'grant to the persons in the disadvantaged class the same advantages as those enjoyed by the persons in the favoured class'.[66] Prior to 17 May 1990, employers and trustees are not required to ensure equal treatment as far as those benefits are concerned. For periods of service after equalization has been achieved, the Court held that 'Article 141 does not preclude measures which achieve equal treatment by reducing the advantages of the persons previously favoured. Article 141 merely requires that men and women should receive the same pay for the same work without imposing any specified level of pay'.[67]

The use of actuarial calculation factors differing according to sex—is this contrary to Article 141?

Prior to the case of *Neath*, the question of whether actuarial calculation factors differing according to sex could be used to determine contributions paid to and benefits paid from occupational pension schemes without infringing Article 141 had not been raised in the case-law of the Court. In the schemes in question actuarial assumptions based on the different life expectancies of men and women were used, amongst other things, to determine the level of contributions paid by the employer into the scheme. Most of the intervening Member States and the pension funds insisted that such factors were objective and essential in order to calculate the liabilities of the pension scheme. Opposed to them was the Commission, which argued that the right to equal pay was an individual right and entitlements should not be determined according to the membership of a particular group. The Commission based its argument on the approach taken by the US Supreme Court, which had held that such discrimination was incompatible with the Civil Rights Act. The original proposal for a directive on occupational pension schemes proposed by the Commission would have prohibited the use of such factors. However, Directive 86/378 permitted pension schemes to take account of different actuarial calculation factors in several respects.

Van Gerven sided with the Commission on this important aspect of the law. He admitted that women tended to live longer than men but was not convinced that this fact constituted a relevant objective difference that would justify disregarding the aspiration in Article 141 of treating workers as individuals and not as members

[66] Cases C-408/92 *Constance Christina Ellen Smith and ors v Advel Systems Ltd* [1994] ECR I-4435 and C-28/93 *Van den Akker and ors v Stichting Shell Pensioenfonds* [1994] ECR I-4527, para 17 of Joint Opinion

[67] Ibid, para 21.

of a particular gender group. He stated that not a single state scheme made use of such actuarial factors. Pointing out that there was nothing to prevent actuaries from using whatever factors they believed relevant in order to ensure the financial balance of the scheme, he insisted that this did not mean that the contributions and benefits should not be the same irrespective of sex. If the Court were to accept this analysis, he further argued that it should impose a temporal limitation as from the date of its judgment in view of overriding reasons of legal certainty.

The Court did not follow its Advocate General on this point. Instead it looked to the manner in which final salary pension schemes were funded. Both employees and employers contribute to such schemes but while all employees contribute a fixed percentage of their salary, the employers' contribution varies over time depending on a number of factors, of which the longer life expectancy of female employees is only one. The result is that, when acquired rights are transferred from one scheme to another or when an employee opts to convert part of his pension into capital, male employees are entitled to lower payments. For the Court the key question here was not so much whether this constituted discrimination, but whether such transfer benefits and lump-sum options actually constitute pay within the meaning of Article 141. The Court distinguished the commitment to make certain payments to an employee from the arrangements for funding of such commitments. In the case of a defined benefit occupational scheme, the Court held that the concept of pay applies only to the employer's commitment to pay, at a given moment in time, a 'periodic pension for which the determining criteria are already known at the time the commitment is made'.[68] The funding arrangements chosen to secure this commitment fell outside the scope of Article 141. Payments made into the fund by the employer do not constitute pay at all since their purpose is to cover the cost of the promised pensions. Therefore, the Court held, the inequality of an employer's contributions paid under funded defined-benefits schemes is not struck at by Article 141. The Court then extended this principle to include the transfer of benefits and lump sum options, since these were both linked to the funding arrangements of the scheme. The Court therefore advised the national court that the use of actuarial factors differing according to sex does not fall within the scope of Article 141.[69]

Concluding observations

It is well understood that the Treaty provisions are written in very general terms and that there is scope for a variety of possible interpretations. In the cases concerning Article 141 and the boundary between that Article, which relates to equal

[68] Case C-152/91 *David Neath v Hugh Steeper Ltd* [1993] ECR I-6935, para 30.

[69] This continued to be a controversial area of Community law. It has been partially resolved by Council Directive 2004/113/EC of 13 December 2004 implementing the principle of equal treatment

pay, and other provisions of the Treaty relating to social security, the Court eventually gave an expansive interpretation in favour of Article 141. In so doing, the Court brought into the ambit of Community law aspects of national law and policy which, it is at least arguable, were reserved to the Member States by virtue of the wording of Article 136 and 137. In giving his Opinion in *Defrenne*, Dutheillet de Lamothe spoke of his doubts and reservations in advising the Court on the correct boundary. He recognized that there was no 'right' interpretation of the Treaty.

It is a truism to state that the European Court of Justice continually faces such problems of interpretation. Its task is to interpret the Treaty and to explain or justify its reasoning in any particular case. It must seek coherence in the European legal order in that it must make sense of the whole body of Community legal rules, but it must also display integrity in its decisions in the sense of ensuring that they are underlined by principles which can be broadly accepted and understood by the citizens of Europe.[70] The Court must justify its decisions in the sense of providing sufficient reasons for them. Justification has both an internal aspect, in that any decision of the Court must be justified 'in law', and an external aspect, in that decisions must be justified ethically, politically and ideologically.

When van Gerven confronted the problem of defining the boundary between the concept of pay and the concept of social security in the cases discussed above, he was faced with the task of assisting the court to come to decisions that could be justified in law and justified externally. Both tasks were equally difficult. The case-law of the Court to date had seemed confused and contradictory, and while the internal logic of a case such as *Newstead* could be discerned, it did not sit well with other cases such as *Defrenne II* or *Bilka-Kaufhaus*. Justification in law for the outcome in *Barber* was therefore crucial and, whilst *Barber* succeeded in settling the boundary question, it raised further difficulties because of the decision to impose a temporal limitation, which led to the need for further clarification, explanation and justification. This was because the Court had expressed the temporal limitation in terms that were far from specific and needed further interpretation. Van Gerven's task was, therefore, to guide the Court in such a way as to make some sense out of the previous case-law, and to suggest lines of argument that could provide sufficiently acceptable reasons for the Court to determine, once and for all, the boundary between Articles 136 and 137, and Article 141.

In doing so, van Gerven was also confronted with the requirement of external justification. Neither the Commission nor the Member States initially accepted the interpretation of Article 141 that was eventually settled by the Court of Justice.

between men and women in the access to and supply of goods and services. OJ 2004 L373/37. This Directive outlaws the use of actuarial statistics in new insurance and financial services contracts as from 21 December 2007 with Member States being allowed an additional two years for full implementation of this rule.

[70] These arguments are based on the chapter by J Bengoetxea, N MacCormick amd LM Soriano, 'Integration and Integrity in the Legal Reasoning of the European Court of Justice' in G de Burca and J Weiler (eds), *The European Court of Justice* (2001) 43.

This is evidenced not only by their interventions in the cases but also in the secondary legislation (which of course was subsequently radically amended) that they adopted to exclude from the ambit of Article 141 provisions relating to pensions. In his Opinions van Gerven sought an ethical justification for his interpretation which he found in the principle of equal treatment. He reminded the Court time and again of their own statement that the principle of equality is one of the foundational values of the European Community, while relating the cases before him to analogous cases where the principle of equal treatment was used to justify a particular decision.

It can be argued that van Gerven's approach to an understanding of the principle of equality was limited to one of seeing equality in formal rather than substantive terms. The totality of the cases in relation to occupational pensions resulted in a solution that he described in two of the cases as being 'delicate'. This notion of 'delicacy' was in reference to the fact that, having achieved equality, the position for women was seriously disadvantaged and men's position was not improved. Most of these cases were brought by men, presumably to improve their situation *vis-à-vis* women (if not then they were just downright curmudgeonly). However, the result was to allow a levelling down of benefits for women, with no improvement for men except in that narrow window between the date of the decision in *Barber* and the date on which their pension scheme was equalized. In the UK, for example, the state pensionable age (which was, admittedly, not in issue in these cases) has been increased for women, as have most occupational pension schemes. Barbara Castle was the Minister responsible for the legislation introducing a different pensionable age for men and women as a compensatory device designed to recognize the double burden of work taken on by women who had family or other caring responsibilities.[71] Hers was a substantive view of equality which sought to recognize the difference between the burdens imposed by society on working women and working men. Van Gerven's approach was a formal or symmetrical equality perspective that ignored these differences. Equal misery won the day for most workers, apart from those who had been excluded from schemes on account of their marital or part-time status. These workers, mostly women, did gain from the case-law but that was reliant on the decision of the Court in *Bilka-Kaufhaus* rather than in the cases in which van Gerven was involved.

It is van Gerven's attachment to the principle of equal treatment that perhaps explains the difference between his Opinion in *Birds Eye Walls* and the decision of the Court. In that case, van Gerven analysed the difference in treatment on the assumption that *all* differences must be seen as discrimination. He argues strongly that such discrimination, whether direct or indirect, could potentially be justified, but nonetheless any difference in treatment where one sex appears to be advantaged over the other is, in law, discrimination. The Court rejected this view. Its starting point was to recognize that the principle of equal treatment could only be

[71] B Castle, *Fighting All The Way* (1993).

applied to individuals who were in the same or comparable positions. Where there was no such comparison, then the principle of equal treatment simply did not apply. Although in *Birds Eye Walls* the Court applied that reasoning to the benefit of men, it has subsequently used the same line of reasoning in cases where the benefit was in favour of women.[72]

Van Gerven therefore assisted the Court in developing justifications, in terms of sufficiently acceptable reasons, for the radical view it took of Article 141. He provided the detailed reasoning that is otherwise lacking in these cases. In comparison with the depth of reasoning displayed by van Gerven, the reasoning of the Court is muted and thin. The Court often used a 'shorthand version' of the carefully worked reasoning of the Advocate General to support its decision. Reading these cases without the benefit of the Advocate General's Opinion, would not convince an audience of their integrity and coherence. In some passages, van Gerven suggests to the Court an interpretation that makes sense of the previous case-law but that did not make sense to others at the time that the decision was made. It is not quite that he offers a line of reasoning that covers the embarrassment of the Court, but at least a line of argument that allows a subsequent Court to make sense of preceding judgments. In this he is assisting the Court but, as he himself has stated, his intention was to assist the wider audience of practitioners and academics to appreciate the meaning of the ambiguous words of the Court's judgments. Perhaps his background in the world of business and finance meant that he appreciated the need for certainty and a lack of ambiguity in these cases. How precisely were trustees to apportion risks and benefits in a new situation when, compared with their previous comfort zone of national law, they were now faced with revising their procedures and financial arrangements without warning? Perhaps this is also why, when the Court decided that benefits payable to survivors were also within the ambit of Article 141, he suggested that additional temporal limitations should apply.

As noted in the discussion of the cases, sometimes the Court accepted the reasoning of the Advocate General in whole or in part or sometimes not at all. His own estimate of the persuasiveness of the Advocate General is summed up in the following quotation:

> Overall in about 70% or 80% of cases the Court follows the Advocate-General's opinion. But there's a difference between decisions in chambers and decisions taken in plenary session. Normally, cases where the law is sufficiently clear for a decision to be reached simply by applying it are allocated to the Court in chambers. In about 90% of these cases the opinion of the Advocate-General will be followed by the Court. But in the full Court there is less likelihood of the Advocate-General's opinion being followed. The cases are less straightforward and there are 13 Judges sitting; so opinions are more likely to diverge.[73]

[72] Case C-218/98 *Abdoulaye v Renault SA* [2001] ICR 527.

[73] W van Gerven, 'The Role and Structure of the European Judiciary Now and in the Future, (1996) ELR 211,222.

All of the cases discussed at length in this chapter were decided in the full Court, and it not surprising, therefore, that there were divergences between the Advocate General on the one part and the judges sitting in their deliberations on the other. Nonetheless, the Court agreed with van Gerven on several key points: the inclusion of redundancy payments, contracted-out pension schemes and survivors' pensions within the ambit of Article 141, the precise delimitation of the temporal limitation in *Barber*, and the absence of a requirement in Community law to level up schemes following the introduction of equalization rules. However, van Gerven was building on the legacy of Dutheillet de Lamothe and Darmon and, in his meticulous and scholarly approach, acknowledged that legacy. His particular genius was to build on and develop Community law.

Van Gerven consciously wrote his Opinions in the style of a dissenting or concurring judgment in a common law court, although of course at the time of his writing and delivering his Opinion he could not know the outcome of the case. However, this understanding of his role explains his approach and style. He addresses all of the issues raised by the parties in a systematic fashion, responding to the arguments in a systematic and structured way. He does not avoid difficult questions and engages fully with the arguments of the parties, the Commission and any interveners. He does not dismiss arguments out of hand but weighs each argument with a respect due to the lawyers before the Court. Where he does raise an issue that has not been raised by one of the parties, he recognizes that, if the Court were to wish to pick up that argument, the case should be re-opened to allow the parties time to respond to his novel point.[74] In this he shows his understanding of the need for equality of arms.

At the same time van Gerven remains the academic lawyer too. His Opinions could equally be read as essays on Community law. They are extensively researched in terms of the case-law of the Court, the relevant Community and national legislation and the work of other Advocates General. He shows himself aware of academic commentary on the Court and footnotes his Opinions with care, sometimes drawing on academic analysis to point to the possible interpretations or misinterpretations of the decisions of the Court. He did this, for example, in relation to the four possible interpretations that could be given for the words of the Court in *Barber* setting out the temporal limitation.

It could be asked whether, in providing such lengthy, detailed and closely argued Opinions, the Advocate General does assist the Court. Would perhaps a better approach be to provide straightforward advice to the Court, possibly setting out alternatives, but always providing a succinct and focused response? Given that whereas the Advocate General is likely to be faced with some 60 files per year and a judge five or six times that number, it might be thought that there may be a preference for the short and focused Opinions. However, in cases where there are

[74] Case C-262/88 Douglas Hervey Barber v Guardian Royal Exchange [1990] ECR I-1889. On the importance of this principle see chapter 3.

difficult factual and legal issues then the Advocate General must do what he can to assist the Court. This is all the more the case where the impact of the case will affect such a large number of Community citizens and impose substantial financial obligations on employers, employees and trust funds. Here the Court needs to be able to justify its decisions not just internally but also externally. Advocate General van Gerven played a major role in developing those justifications in the cases discussed in this chapter.

6

Advocate General Jacobs and intellectual property law

Contextual background

Francis Jacobs took up his appointment as Advocate General in 1988, at a time when the European Project had just been restarted with the adoption of the Single European Act and the establishment of the Court of First Instance. The Single European Act provided the Community with further legal bases for action and reformed the Community's legislative process in order to achieve the objectives of the internal market[1] by the end of 1992. The establishment of the Court of First Instance introduced an appeal structure within the European Community's judicial architecture.

Advocate General Jacobs retired in December 2005, having been a member of the European Court of Justice for 17 years, the second longest holder of the office.[2] During those 17 years he delivered over 500 Opinions. Given his long period in office it is not surprising that he delivered Opinions on most areas of Community competence. In the first few years of his mandate, the vast majority of his Opinions were delivered in the areas of agriculture, staff regulations, taxation and social security. In this period he also delivered Opinions in important cases such as in *Alpine Investments*[3] (freedom to provide services) and *Leclerc-Siplec*[4] (free movement of goods and services). As far as intellectual property rights cases are concerned, during this early period in office Jacobs delivered a single Opinion in two cases, *Tournier*[5] and *Lucazeau*[6] (copyright royalties and collecting societies), another in *Phil Collins*[7]

[1] The expression 'internal market' is the term used post 1988 for the 'common market'. The expression 'single European market' is also used, primarily by politicians.

[2] Advocate General Karl Roemer was Advocate General from February 1953 to October 1973.

[3] Case C-384/93 *Alpine Investments BV v Minister van Finacien* [1995] ECR I-1141.

[4] Case C-412/93 *Société d'Importation Edouard Leclerc-Siplec v TF1 Publicité SA and M6 Publicité SA* [1995] ECR I-179.

[5] Case 395/87 *Ministère public v Jean-Louis Tournier* [1989] ECR 2521.

[6] Joined Cases 110/88, 241/88 and 242/88 *François Lucazeau and ors v Société des Auteurs, Compositeurs et Editeurs de Musique (SACEM)* [1989] ECR 2811.

[7] Joined Cases C-92/92 and C-326/92 *Phil Collins v Imtrat Handelsgesellschaft mbH and Patricia Im-und-Export Verwaltungsgesellschaft mbH* and *Leif Emanuel Karul v EMI Electrola GmbH* [1993] ECR I-5145.

(copyright and discrimination on grounds of nationality) and he delivered the Opinion in the *HAG II*[8] (free movement of goods) case where for the first time the European Court of Justice expressly overruled itself.

Prior to Jacobs's appointment as Advocate General, the European Court of Justice had delivered relatively few rulings on intellectual property rights. These judgments were primarily concerned with the application of EC Treaty provisions on free movement of goods (Articles 28–30 EC) and competition (Articles 81 and 82 EC)[9] on the exercise of national intellectual property rights.

Soon after his arrival at the Court the European Community, in pursuit of achieving an internal market by the end of 1992, adopted Directive 89/104 (Trade Mark Directive)[10] which harmonized national trade mark law and Regulation 40/94 (Community Trade Mark Regulation)[11] which created the first intellectual property right conferred directly by Community Law (Community Trade Mark).[12] The Trade Mark Regulation provided for the establishment of the Office for the Harmonisation of the Internal Market (OHIM) with powers to take decisions on the grant of registration. The decisions of OHIM may be appealed to the Court of First Instance and a further appeal to the European Court of Justice is possible but only on points of law.

From 1993 onwards referrals from national courts seeking a preliminary ruling on the interpretation of various provisions of the Trade Mark Directive began to be lodged at the European Court of Justice. In a period of 10 years, from December 1995 to the end of 2005, Jacobs delivered over 20 Opinions[13] on the interpretation

[8] Case C-10/89 *SA CNL-SUCAL NV v HAG GF AG* [1990] ECR I-3711.

[9] Cases 56 and 58/64 *Consten and Grundig v Commission* [1966] ECR 299; Case 40/70 *Sirena v Eda* [1971] ECR 69; Case 78/70 *Deutsche Grammophon v Metro* [1971] ECR 487; Case 127/73 *BRT v SABAM & FONIOR* [1974] ECR 313; Case 192/73 *Van Zuylen v HAG* [1974] ECR 731; Case 15/74 *Centrafarm v Sterling* [1974] ECR 1147; Case 16/74 *Centrafarm v Winthorpe* [1974] ECR 1183; Case 51/75 *EMI Records v CBS United Kingdom* [1976] ECR 811; Case 119/75 *Terrapin v Terranova* [1976] ECR 1038; Case 102/77 *Hoffmann-La Roche v Centrafarm* [1978] ECR 1139; Case 3/78 *Centrafarm v American Home Products Corp* [1978] ECR 1823; Case 62/79 *Coditel v Cine Vog Films* (Coditel I) [1980] ECR 881; Cases 55 and 57/80 *Merck-Vertrieb-Membran v GEMA* [1981] ECR 147; Case 187/80 *Merck v Stephar* [1981] ECR 2063; Case 1/81 *Pfizer v Eurim-Pharm* [1981] ECR 2913; Case 144/81 *Keurkoop v Nancy Kean Gifts* [1982] ECR 2853; Case 7/82 *GVL v Commission* [1983] ECR 483; Case 35/83 *BAT v Commission* [1985] ECR 363; Case 243/83 *Binon v AMP* [1985] ECR 2015; Case 19/84 *Pharmon v Hoechst* [1985] ECR 2281; Case 158/86 *Warner Brothers v Christiansen* [1988] ECR 2605; Case 35/87 *Thelford v Fiamma* [1988] ECR 3585; Case 53/87 *CICRA v Renault* [1988] ECR 6039; Case 341/87 *EMI Electrola v Patricia* [1989] ECR 79.

[10] Directive 89/104 on the approximation of the laws of the Member States relating to trade marks [1989] OJ L40/1.

[11] Regulation 40/94 on the Community trade mark [1994] OJ L11/1.

[12] Another Community property right has also been created by Regulation 6/2002 [2002] OJ L3/1, namely the Community registered design right. Directive 98/71 [1998] OJ L289/28 had already been adopted on the legal protection of design.

[13] Most of these Opinions were delivered between December 1995 and November 2001, a period of six years. The first non-Jacobs Opinion on the interpretation of the Trade Mark Directive was delivered at the end of 2001 by Advocate General Ruiz-Jarabo Colomer in Case C-273/00 *Sieckmann* [2002] ECR I-11737. Since then Jacobs delivered Opinions on the interpretation of the Trade Mark Directive in the following preliminary references: *LTJ Diffusion* (C-291/00 [2003] ECR I-2799),

of provisions of the Trade Mark Directive.[14] An interesting feature of the Trade Mark Directive referrals where Jacobs delivered the Opinion is that, with one exception,[15] the Reporting Judge was always Gulmann;[16] this partnership is remarkable and worthy of further study but this is, regretfully, beyond the scope of this book.[17]

In addition, Jacobs also delivered Opinions in the first appeals from the Court of First Instance on the interpretation of Regulation 40/94[18] (Community Trade Mark Regulation).[19] This chapter examines the Opinions delivered by Jacobs where issues involving the rights of owners of intellectual property were raised. In particular, the analysis will demonstrate his contribution to the development of a Community trade mark law.

The chapter will be structured as follows: first, a brief résumé of the case law on intellectual property rights prior to the appointment of Jacobs will be given by way of background; consideration will be given to the Opinions he delivered on

Davidoff II (C-292/00 [2003] ECR I-389), *Aventis* (C-433/00 [2002] ECR I-7761), *Adidas* (C-408/01 [2003] ECR I-12537), *Class International* (C-405/03 [2005] ECR I-8735), *Medion* (Case C-120/04 [2005] ECR I-8551) and *Matratzen Concord* (C-421/04 [2005] ECR I-2303).

[14] Since January 2002 it has been Ruiz-Jarabo Colomer who can be singled out as the person who has delivered most of the Opinions in preliminary rulings on the interpretation of the Trade Mark Directive; up to December 2005, Ruiz-Jarabo Colomer delivered Opinions in the following cases: *Koninklijke* (C-363/99 [2004] ECR I-1619), *Ricordi* (C-360/00 [2002] ECR I-5089), *Arsenal* (C-206/01 [2002] ECR I-10273), *Ansul* (C-40/01 [2003] ECR I-2439), *Linde Winward* (C53–55/01 [2003] ECR I-3161), *Shield Mark* (C-283/01 [2003] ECR I-14313), *Telefon & Buch* (C-326/01 [2004] ECR I-1371), *Nichols plc* (C-404/02 [2004] ECR I-8499) and *Novartis* (C-207/03 and 252/03 [2005] ECR I-3209). Opinions were also delivered by Advocates General Stick-Hackl, Léger, Tizzano and Kokott.

[15] *LTJ Diffusion* where the Reporting Judge was Macken.

[16] Gulmann was an Advocate General before being appointed judge in the European Court of Justice. As Advocate General he delivered Opinions in two important intellectual property rulings: Cases C-242/91P *Radio Telefis Eirann (RTE) and Independent Television Publications (ITP) v Commission (Magill)* [1995] ECR I-743 and C-9/93 *IHT Internationale Heiztechnik GmbH and Uwe Dansinger v Ideal-Standard GmbH and Wabco Standard GmbH* [1994] ECR I-2789. Gulmann retired from the European Court of Justice at the same time as Jacobs, at the end of 2005. In January 2006, on the occasion of the formal European court of Justice farewell to Jacobs and Gulmann, the President of the European Court of Justice specifically praised their contribution to the development of the Community's trade mark case-law.

[17] A similar 'partnership' appears to have existed between Ruiz-Jarabo Colomer and Judge Macken. See the following preliminary references: *Konenkleg, Arsenal, Linde Windward, Shield Mark*, above n 14. Ruiz-Jarabo Colomer was also the Advocate General in approximately half of all the appeals from the Court of First Instance on the Trade Mark Regulation decided by the end of 2005 *Proctor & Gamble* (Cases C-383/99P [2001] ECR I-6251; C-468 to 474/01P [2004] ECR I-5141); and C-107/03P [2004] (unpublished)), *Henkel* (C-456 to 57/01P [2004] ECR I-5089), *Mag Instrument* (C-136/02P [2004] ECR I-9165) and *Vedial* (C-106/03P [2004] ECR I-9573).

[18] Regulation 40/94 on the Community trade mark [1994] OJ L11/1. The Opinions in these appeals were delivered in a relative short period of just over a year (March 2003 to June 2004) in the following cases: *Proctor & Gamble* (C-383/99P [2001] ECR I-6251), *Christina Kik* (C-361/01P [2003] ECR I-8283), *DOUBLEMINT* (C-191/01P [2003] ECR I-12447), *Zapf Creation* (C-498/01P [2004] ECR I-11349), *Streamserve* (C-150/02P [2004] ECR I-1461), *SatellitenFernsehen* (C- 329/02P [2004] ECR I-8317), *Glaverbel* (C-455/02P [2004] ECR I-10549).

[19] These Opinions on appeals from the Court of First Instance were delivered after 2001 as it took a number of years for these appeals to work themselves through the various stages of the appeals process.

the relationship between the EC Treaty rules on competition and free movement and the exercise of intellectual property rights; this will be followed by an examination of the Opinions he delivered in cases where interpretation questions were raised in respect of the Trade Mark Directive and the Trade Mark Regulation: in this section the Opinions will be grouped on specific issues irrespective of the manner in which these cases reached the European Court of Justice;[20] finally some observations will be made by way of conclusion.

Intellectual property rights and the EC Treaty rules: pre-1988 rulings

In a series of seminal cases the European Court of Justice delivered important judgments on the relationship between national intellectual property rights and the application of the EC Treaty. First, the Court ruled in *Consten & Grundig v Commission*[21] that the existence of an intellectual property right was a matter for national law whilst the exercise of those national intellectual property rights were subject to the EC Treaty rules. Thus the EC Treaty rules on free movement of goods and on competition apply to the manner in which intellectual property owners exercise their rights. Second, in the *Centrafarm v Stirling* and *Centrafarm v Winthrop*[22] cases the Court identified the specific subject matter of a patent and of a trade mark respectively as the core of the existence of the right which is protected by national law. The European Court of Justice also formulated the doctrine of exhaustion of rights as the solution to the conflict between national rights which protect owners of intellectual property rights from parallel imports and the EC Treaty rules on free movement of goods which seek to remove all obstacles to the free movement of goods.[23] The exhaustion of rights doctrine states that once goods or services protected by intellectual property rights are placed on the market[24] by the owner or with the owner's consent, the goods and services in question are free to circulate anywhere in the Community.[25] These cases clarified the extent

[20] These cases have come before the European Court of Justice either as appeals from the Court of First Instance judgments or by way of an Art 234 EC referral from a national court. Where the European Court of Justice hears appeals from the Court of First Instance, the Court will be concerned with matters relating to the Trade Mark Regulation. Preliminary rulings will raise issues of interpretation of the Trade Mark Directive.

[21] Joined Cases 56 and 58/64 [1966] ECR 299.

[22] Case 15/74 [1974] ECR 1147 and Case 16/74 [1974] ECR 1183.

[23] See for example Joined Cases 55 and 57/80 *Musik-Vertrieb-Membran v GEMA* [1981] ECR 147 (re copyright).

[24] Originally the 'common market', but now it applies to the EEA market which consists of the 25 EU Member States plus Iceland, Liechenstein and Norway.

[25] However the European Court of Justice has also ruled that the doctrine does not extend to goods placed on the market outside the European Economic Area. See Case C-355/96 *Silhoutte International Schmied GmbH & Co KG v Hartlauer Handelsgesellschaft GmbH* [1998] ECR I-4799. See below for a discussion of this case.

of the expressed derogation in favour of intellectual property rights conferred by Article 30 EC. The central focus of these rulings was on the *consent* of the owner to the first marketing of the protected product or service. The European Court of Justice delivered a number of rulings before the meaning of 'consent' was clarified.[26]

As far as the EC competition rules are concerned the relevant EC Treaty articles are Articles 81 and 82. Article 81 prohibits agreements or similar arrangements between undertakings which have as their object or their effect the restriction or distortion of competition and affect trade between Member States. Thus a licensing agreement, whereby the owner of an intellectual property right (the licensor) permits another undertaking (the licensee) to use the property right but under specified restrictive conditions, is likely to be caught by the prohibition. This was established by the European Court of Justice in a number of cases.[27] However the licensing of such rights is considered an important market activity which assists with the achievement of one of the main objectives of the EC Treaty, namely the integration of national markets. By licensing intellectual property rights across national frontiers, goods and services penetrate foreign markets more easily and to the benefit of the consumer as far as choice and eventually the price are concerned.

In order to achieve a balance between encouraging the licensing of intellectual property rights and ensuring that the EC competition rules are not infringed, the Community has adopted legislative measures. The current relevant measure is the Transfer of Technology Block Exemption Regulation.[28]

The owner of intellectual property rights may also infringe Article 82 EC Treaty where the owner is in a dominant position within a substantial part of the common market and the rights are used in a manner which is considered to be abusive. The leading case on Article 82 in the context of intellectual property rights is the *Magill*[29] case where the European Court of Justice ruled that in certain circumstances the refusal to license an intellectual property right is an abuse within the meaning of Article 82.

[26] See Case 19/84 *Pharmon v Hoechst* [1985] ECR 2281, where the European Court of Justice ruled that there was no consent to the marketing where the product was placed on the market under a compulsory licence. However in Case 187/80 *Merck v Stephar* [1981] ECR 2063, the European Court of Justice ruled that there had been consent where the owner first marketed a pharmaceutical product in a Member State where, at the time, no protection was available for pharmaceutical products or processes. This ruling was confirmed in Joined Cases C-267/95 and C-268/95 *Merck & Co Inc v Primecrown Ltd* and *Beecham Group plc v Europharm* [1996] ECR I-6285.

[27] For example, Case 258/78 *L.C. Nungesser and Kurt Eisele v Commission* [1982] ECR 2015.

[28] Regulation 772/2004 on the application of Art 81(3) of the Treaty to categories of technology transfer agreements [2004] OJ L123/11.

[29] Case C-242/91P *Radio Telefis Eirann (RTE) & Independent Television Publications Ltd (ITP) v Commission (Magill)* [1995] ECR I-743. The ruling was confirmed in Case C-418/01 *IMS Health GmbH & Co v NDC Health GmbH & Co* [2004] ECR I-5039.

Post-1988 developments on the relationship between the EC Treaty rules and the exercise of intellectual property rights

The cases under this section are grouped as follows: first, those where issues of compatibility of the EC Treaty competition rules (Articles 81 and 82) with the exercise of intellectual property rights have been referred to the European Court of Justice; second, where similar issues have been raised in the context of the EC Treaty provisions on the free movement of goods, and in particular in repackaging/re-labelling/re-branding disputes; and third, rulings determining the scope of the Community concept of exhaustion of intellectual property rights.

EC Treaty competition rules

Jacobs' first Opinion on an intellectual property matter was delivered in the *Tournier* and *Lucazeau* cases which concerned the practices of copyright management societies.[30] However, with one exception,[31] this is the only Opinion he delivered on the application of the EC Treaty competition rules to intellectual property rights.

These cases concerned SACEM, a copyright management society which manages copyright in musical works in France. The dispute before the national French courts concerned the refusal of discotheque operators to pay royalties to SACEM for the performance of protected musical works on their premises. In defence, the discotheque operators alleged that SACEM's market behaviour was anticompetitive and amounted to a breach of the EC Treaty competition rules (Articles 81 and 82). In particular, it was alleged that the 'reciprocal representation agreements' which existed between national copyright management societies were anti-competitive and in breach of Article 81(1) EC since they prevented direct access to foreign repertoires. These agreements between national copyright management societies provide for reciprocal arrangements so that each society, within the territory for which they are responsible, is able to grant the necessary licences for any public performance of the copyright musical works owned by members of the other societies.

[30] Case 395/87 *Ministère public v Jean-Louis Tournier* [1989] ECR 2521 and Joined Cases 110/88, 241/88 and 242/88 *François Lucazeau and ors v Société des Auteurs, Compositeurs et Editeurs de Musique (SACEM)* [1989] ECR 2811. Copyright management societies (also known as copyright collecting societies) are organizations whose membership consists of authors, composers and publishers. The members assign to the society to which they belong their exclusive rights to the exploitation of the intellectual property they own. The society in turn grants licences to users and distributes the royalties to the owners of the respective intellectual property.

[31] Although Jacobs delivered an Opinion in Case C-53/03 *Syfait and ors v GlaxoSmithKline plc and ors* [2005] ECR I-4609, no judgment on the substance was delivered as the European Court of Justice dismissed the referral as inadmissible. In the Opinion, Jacobs considered the application of Art 82 EC to a refusal to supply trade marked pharmaceutical products by an undertaking in a dominant position.

In addition, an abuse of a dominant position contrary to Article 82 EC was also alleged given that SACEM refused to license anything other than its whole repertoire. The operators had to obtain a global licence and pay royalties for the whole repertoire even though they were only interested in parts of the repertoire namely Anglo-American dance music. They contended the royalties were excessively high and an abuse of the society's dominant position.

Although Jacobs and the Court were in broad agreement concluding that there could be a breach of Articles 81 and 82 EC in these cases, there was a noticeable difference in emphasis and approach. Jacobs concluded that the refusal of the copyright management societies to license directly the use of their national repertoires to music users in each other's national territories was directly linked to the existence of a network of reciprocal representation agreements. The refusal was a logical consequence of the existence of these agreements and therefore there was no need to establish the existence of a concerted practice. The European Court of Justice, however, ruled that these agreements were not in themselves restrictive of competition so it had to consider the possibility of the existence of a concerted practice, which, of course, was a matter for the national referring court to determine on the evidence. The Court stated that Article 81(1) EC prohibited a concerted practice which enabled each society to refuse to grant direct access to its repertoire to users established in another Member State. It was for the national court to decide whether there was sufficient evidence of a concerted practice.

Jacobs also concluded that the reciprocal representation agreements were capable of restricting competition and given that they had been notified to the Commission he urged the latter to come to a decision since the Commission was in a better position than the national courts to examine the market on a Community-wide basis. Nevertheless, until the Commission took a decision, the national court would have to evaluate the evidence 'having regard to the special characteristics of the market for the management of performing rights'.[32]

As far as Article 82 EC was concerned Jacobs and the Court reached the same conclusion that existence of an abuse would be established if the level of the royalty could not be justified (European Court of Justice wording) or it was found to be disproportionate (Jacobs' wording). Although the different wording does not affect the nature and scope of the provisions, it does provide some evidence that the Court does not simply adopt the Advocate General's reasoning even when it agrees with the substance.

Parallel imports: EC Treaty free movement of goods rules and repackaged/re-labelled/re-branded products

As already demonstrated the doctrine of exhaustion of intellectual property rights played an important role in the reconciliation between the EC Treaty's provisions

[32] Para 41 of the Joined Opinion in Case 395/87 *Tournier* [1989] ECR 2521 and Joined Cases 110/88, 241/88 and 242/88 *Lucazeau* [1989] ECR 2811.

on the free movement of goods and the expressed derogation to that freedom in favour of the protection of intellectual property rights set out in Article 30.[33]

Some of the major problems concerned the repackaging of trade-marked pharmaceutical products which was undertaken by the parallel importer before placing the goods on the market. Jacobs delivered the Opinions in all the repackaging/re-labelling cases heard by the European Court of Justice during his period in office including, in particular, the Joined Opinion in the three 1996 cases, *Bristol-Myers Squibb/Eurim-Pharm/MPA Pharma*,[34] and the Joined Opinion in the 2002 cases of *Merck/Boehringer*.[35]

All these cases, which were heard by a Full Court, clarified the meaning and extent of the Article 30 EC derogation whereby owners of trade-marked products are able to oppose the repackaging of their products when imported from one Member State to another.[36] In the Joined Opinion he delivered in the 1996 pharmaceutical

[33] Although not considered in this chapter the following two cases raised important questions as to the extent to which the free movement of goods rules prevail over national laws precluding the importation of trade marked goods placed on the market of another Member State on the grounds of unfair competition and/or consumer protection. In Case C-313/94 *Fratelli Graffione SNC v Ditta Fransa* [1996] ECR I-6039 (AG: Jacobs, RJ: Gulmann) the European Court of Justice ruled that a sufficiently serious risk of misleading consumers (but not on the grounds of unfair competition) could override the requirements of the EC Treaty rules on free movement of goods. Earlier in Case C-315/92 *Clinique* [1994] ECR I-317 (AG: Gulmann, RJ: Grévisse) the European Court of Justice stated that the clinical and medical connotations of the word 'Clinique' was not sufficient to make the word so misleading as to justify the prohibition of its use in the circumstances of the case. In addition to the fact that the Advocate General in *Clinique* was the Reporting Judge in *Fratelli Graffione*, an interesting aspect of this case is that the Court concluded that 'Clinique' products could not be prevented from being imported into Germany whilst the Advocate General concluded that the free movement of goods provisions did not preclude a national measure impeding the free movement of goods on the grounds of consumer protection, but the national court would have to ensure that the prohibition was imperative for consumer protection and that it was proportionate to the objective pursued. Thus the Advocate General totally respected the division of competences under Art 234 EC.

[34] Joined Cases C-427/93 *Bristol-Myers Squibb v Paranova A/S*, C-429/93 *C.H. Boehringer Sohn, Boehringer Ingelheim KG abd Boehringer Ingelheim A/S v Paranova A/S* and C-436/93 *Bayer Aktiengesellschaft and Bayer Danmark A/S v Paranova A/S* [1996] ECR I-3457; Joined Cases C71–73 to C 73/94 *Eurim-Pharm Arzneimittel GmbH v Beiersdorf AG, Boehringer Ingelheim KG and Farmitalia Carlo Erba GmbH* [1976] ECR I-3603; and Case C-232/94 *MPA Pharma GmbH v Rhone-Poulenc Pharma GmbH* [1996] ECR I-3671. The cases are referred to in this chapter collectively as '*Bristol-Myers Squibb*'.

[35] Cases C-443/99 *Merck, Sharp & Dohme GmbH v Paranova Pharmazeutika Handels GmbH* [2002] ECR I-3703 and C-143/00 *Boehringer Ingelheim KG, Boehringer Ingelheim Pharma KG, Glaxo Group Ltd, The Wellcome Foundation Ltd, SmithKline Beecham plc, Beecham Group plc, SmithKline & French Laboratories Ltd and Eli Lilly and Co v Swingward Ltd and Dowelhurst Ltd* [2002] ECR I-3759. The other repackaging cases are C-349/95 *Frits Loendersloot, trading as F. Loendersloot Internationale Expeditie v George Ballantine & Son Ltd* [1997] ECR I-6227; C-379/97 *Pharmacia & Upjohn SA v Paranova A/S* [1999] ECR I-6927; and C-433/00 *Aventis Pharma Deutschland GmbH v Kohlpharma GmbH and MTK Pharma Vertriebs-GmbH* [2002] ECR I-7761.

[36] With the exception of one case, C-349/95 *Loendersloot v Ballantine* [1997] ECR I-6227, all the repackaging/re-labelling cases concerned pharmaceutical products. In a recent case, C-53/03 *Syfait v GlaxoSmithKline plc and ors* [2005] ECR I-4609, Advocate General Jacobs urged the European Court of Justice, in the context of Art 82 EC, to rule that the pharmaceutical products market is *suis generis*, given the fact that in some Member States the governments control the market price of these products and that in all Member States authorizations are required before a pharmaceutical product is placed on the market. As early as his Opinion in *Bristol-Myers Squibb* in 1995, Jacobs had already identified

repackaging cases, Advocate General Jacobs undertook an in-depth analysis of the Court's case-law and of the submissions of the parties and interveners.[37]

Prior to the *Bristol-Myers Squibb* judgment, the law on repackaging of trade-marked goods had been set out by the European Court of Justice in *Hoffmann-La Roche* and *American Home Products Corp.*[38] *Hoffmann-La Roche* concerned repackaging when the original trade mark was removed and reaffixed to the new packaging, whilst in *American Home Products* not only were the goods repackaged but the original trade mark was substituted for the trade mark used by the manufacturer when selling the identical product in the Member State of importation (re-branding).

In *Hoffmann-La Roche* the European Court of Justice confirmed that the essential function of a trade mark is to guarantee the origin of the trade-marked product to the consumer without any possibility of confusion to distinguish that product from products which have a different origin. Thus the Court ruled that the manufacturer of the imported trade-marked product was entitled to oppose the repackaging. However, Article 30 EC provides that this derogation to the fundamental freedom of movement of goods, will not apply where the exercise of the intellectual property right is a 'disguised restriction on trade between Member States'. Thus, in the *Hoffmann-La Roche* case, the Court stated further that the trade mark owner's opposition to repackaging is a 'disguised restriction' where the following four conditions prevail: first, if it is established that the trade mark owner's use of the trade mark contributes to the artificial partitioning of the markets between Member States; second, if it is shown that the repackaging cannot adversely affect the original condition of the product; third, if prior notice is given to the trade mark owner of the repackaging; and fourthly, if it is stated on the newly repackaged product by whom it has been repackaged.[39]

In the *American Home Products* case the European Court of Justice ruled on the situation where the repackaging was accompanied by the affixing of the trade

pharmaceutical products as a 'special market' (para 66 of the Opinion). In July 2001, in the Opinion he delivered in the *Merck* and *Boehringer* cases, Jacobs stated, in the context of the pharmaceutical market, that there were 'certain features not shared by the market in many other goods' (at para 99 of the Opinion in *Merck* and *Boehringer*) and that 'the market in pharmaceutical products has a number of features which distinguish it in important respects from the markets in many other products. In particular, prices are as a general rule set or affected by national regulators and do not reflect the normal play of supply and demand: wholesale and retail suppliers of pharmaceutical products cannot freely adjust prices in a given national market in order to increase sales' (para 112 of the Opinion in *Merck* and *Boehringer*). These price differences which resulted from divergent national regulations had already been recognized by the European Court of Justice in *Bristol-Myers Squibb* (para 46 of the judgment).

[37] The Opinion consisted of 130 paragraphs and included a contents page!

[38] Cases 102/77 *Hoffmann-La Roche & Co AG v Centrafarm* [1978] ECR 1139 and 3/78 *Centrafarm v American Home Products Corp* [1978] ECR 1823. Jacobs provided an excellent summary in paras 40–48 of his Opinion in *Bristol-Myers Squibb*. He quotes extensively from these rulings (paras 7–12 of *Hoffmann-La Roche* and paras 19–23 of *American Home Products*) as well as from Case 1/81 *Pfizer v Eurim-Pharm* [1981] ECR 2913 (paras 10–12).

[39] These requirements may be sometimes referred to collectively in the text as 'the *Hoffmann-La Roche* conditions'.

mark used by the manufacturer of the product in the imported territory (re-branding of the product by replacing one trade mark with another in the same ownership). The Court confirmed that the right granted to the owner of a trade mark to prohibit any unauthorized affixing of his mark to his product come within the specific subject-matter of the trade mark.[40] However, the Court also held that such a prohibition would constitute a disguised restriction on trade between Member States if it were established that the practice of using different trade marks for the same product had been adopted by the owner of those trade marks for the purpose of artificially partitioning the markets.[41]

Although the *Hoffmann-La Roche* judgment was helpful in interpreting the Article 30 EC derogation in the context of repackaging, national courts felt the need to seek further clarification of the above conditions in order to deliver their own judgments in national litigation. Thus a number of important clarifications, such as the meaning of a 'disguised restriction', were referred to the European Court of Justice with Jacobs delivering the Opinions. These Opinions and European Court of Justice rulings have been analysed with the objective of explaining the development of the case-law and also to study the correlation in reasoning between Jacobs and the Court.

'Disguised restriction'

The *Bristol-Myers Squibb/Eurim-Pharm/MPA Pharma* cases concerned the repackaging of imported pharmaceutical products in new external packaging. The packaging displayed the respective trade marks of the manufacturers and contained a statement naming the manufacturers of the product. Other alterations to the packaging were also carried out by the importers but none interfered with the content of the products.

The main questions raised in these cases concerned the first condition of *Hoffmann-La Roche*, namely whether the use of the trade mark right by the owner contributed to the artificial partitioning of the market between Member States. There was therefore a need to review the meaning of the concept of a 'disguised restriction' in the context of 'artificially' partitioning of the market. In Jacobs's view the concept of a 'disguised restriction' was to be understood as an element in the assessment of whether the trade mark owner has a justification within the meaning of the first sentence of Article 30 EC to oppose the repackaging.

The key question was therefore whether the importer had to show that the trade mark owner had deliberately (that is a subjective test) used his rights to divide up the market. Was it an objective or a subjective test? The doubt arose because in the *Hoffmann-La Roche* judgment the European Court of Justice used the word 'artificial' in expressing the scope of the first condition. Jacobs admitted that the 'wording is not without ambiguity'.[42] In the *American Home Products* case

[40] Paras 13, 14 and 17 of the ruling in *American Home Products*.
[41] Ibid, paras 22 and 23 of the ruling.
[42] Para 83 of the Opinion in *Bristol-Myers Squibb*.

(a repackaging and re-branding case), a judgment which had immediately followed the one delivered in the *Hoffmann-La Roche* case, the Court had made it explicit that the importer was not entitled to substitute the trade mark unless the use of the different marks by the owner was intentional, ie a subjective test.[43] In the *Bristol-Myers Squibb* case, Jacobs distinguished the *American Home Products* case on the facts since it did not involve re-branding[44] and applied an objective test.[45]

In his opinion, the first and last sentences of Article 30 EC should be read as a whole. Thus the artificiality to which the Court referred in the first condition of the *Hoffmann-La Roche* judgment was an element in the assessment of whether the trade mark owner was able to justify opposition to the repackaging. If the trade mark owner was unable to justify opposition, then a 'disguised restriction' would have been established.[46] The Court reached the same conclusion stating that 'there is no objective difference between reaffixing a trade mark after repackaging and replacing the original trade mark by another which is capable of justifying the condition of artificial partitioning being applied differently in each of those cases'.[47]

Nevertheless, the Court and Jacobs took different starting points in their reasoning. The Court confirmed that the trade mark owner has the right to oppose repackaging unless the situation is such that the opposition can be demonstrated to be a 'disguised restriction' on trade between Member States. Jacobs, on the other hand, focused on the essential function of the trade mark which is to guarantee the origin of the product. Thus his analysis led him to the conclusion that if the repackaging does not impair the ability of the trade mark function, then there are no grounds for opposing parallel repackaged imports.[48] The justification therefore must be found in establishing that the essential function of the trade mark has been affected by the repackaging process. He stated that for the Article 30 EC derogation to apply it is 'not whether the parallel importer affixes the trade mark or merely allows the original mark to remain visible but whether he interfered with the goods in such a way that it is no longer possible to be certain that their original condition has been affected'.[49]

The significance of the difference in approach between Jacobs and the Court is one for the national court, namely as to where does the burden of proof lie. The Court placed it on the defendant whilst Jacobs placed it on the trade mark owner.

In other aspects of the reasoning the Advocate General and the Court reached similar conclusions as, for example, on the relevance of national rules on the

[43] Case 3/78 [1978] ECR 1823, paras 21–23 of the judgment.

[44] Para 84 of the Opinion.

[45] However, two years later, after the judgment in the *Bristol-Myers Squibb* case, in the Opinion he delivered in *Upjohn* (C-379/97 *Pharmacia & Upjohn SA v Paranova A/S* [1999] ECR I-6927), he readily accepted the European Court of Justice's approach that the two situations should be treated in the same manner. Jacobs stated that given the 'body of coherent and clearly articulated principles hinging on objective factors' were set out in the *Bristol-Myers Squibb* judgment, this objective criteria should be applied equally to all cases of repackaging or re-branding (para 35 of the Opinion).

[46] Para 82 of the Opinion in *Bristol-Myers Squibb*.

[47] Ibid, para 37 of the judgment.

[48] Ibid, paras 67 and 78 of the Opinion.

[49] Ibid, paras 68 and 81 of the Opinion.

marketing of pharmaceutical products which affect the natural conditions of the market. The Court held that the trade mark owner cannot oppose the repackaging of the product in new external packaging when the size of the packet used by the owner in the Member State where the importer purchased the product cannot be marketed in the Member State of importation:

by reason, in particular, of a rule authorizing packaging only of a certain size or a national practice to the same effect, sickness insurance rules making the reimbursement of medical expenses depend on the size of the packaging or well-established medical prescription practices based, inter alia, on standard sizes recommended by professional groups and sickness insurance institutions.[50]

Jacobs expressly stated that it is not 'the function of trade marks to redress distortions caused by divergent legislation on prices'.[51]

The Court followed Jacobs's conclusion on the meaning of the phrase 'artificial partitioning of the market' and clarified that the concept 'does not imply a burden on the importer to show that the trade mark owner deliberately sought to partition the markets'.[52] Unfortunately, the Court also expressly stated that the rights of the owner of a trade-marked product to oppose the marketing of repackaged products under the trade mark should be limited only in so far as the repackaging undertaken by the importer was 'necessary'.[53] This condition that the repackaging needs to have been 'necessary' was not proposed by Jacobs in his Opinion. Whether this refinement of the requirement originated with the Court, the Reporting Judge or elsewhere cannot be determined.

Inevitably, the use of the word 'necessary' in the ruling led to a need for further referrals, that is, those in the *Loendersloot*, *Upjohn* and *Merck* and *Boehringer* cases where the European Court of Justice was asked to determine whether the word 'necessary' was to be interpreted objectively or subjectively. The definitive Opinion and ruling on this issue is to be found in the *Merck* and *Boehringer* cases but nothing new was added to what had already been determined in the cases of *Loendersloot* and *Upjohn*.

In the *Loendersloot*[54] case, the problem concerned the re-labelling of whisky bottles not pharmaceutical products. However, similar questions were raised as to the meaning of the word 'necessary' in the first condition of *Hoffmann-La Roche*. Both the Advocate General and the Court concluded that the test to be applied is an objective one. Thus in the *Loendersloot* case the national court was instructed to

[50] Ibid, para 53 of the judgment. The wording in the quote was not taken from the Jacobs Opinion but is now a standard statement (with stylistic improvements) in all relevant subsequent rulings, as for example in Case C-443/99 *Merck* [2002] ECR I-3703, para 26 of the judgment.

[51] Para 74 of the Opinion. Given his Opinion in Case C-53/03 *Syfait v GlaxoSmithKline plc and ors* [2005] ECR I-4609 it is submitted that he may well have changed his position, at least in the context of the application of Art 82 EC to the pharmaceutical industry.

[52] Para 57 of the judgment in *Bristol-Myers Squibb*.

[53] Ibid, para 56 of the judgment and in the operative part of the judgment.

[54] C-349/95 *Loendersloot v George Ballantine & Son Ltd* [1997] ECR I-6227.

assess whether the re-labelling was necessary to protect the sources of supply of the parallel trade and to enable the products to be marketed on the various markets of the Member States for which they were intended.[55]

In the *Upjohn*[56] case, the facts were similar to the *American Home Products* case since the dispute before the national court concerned re-branding of repackaged products by substituting marks owned by the manufacturer of the products in question. Thus in the *Upjohn* case the European Court of Justice clarified the judgment in the *American Home Products* case and stated that the test is to determine whether it was objectively necessary to reaffix or replace the trade mark after repackaging in order to enable the product in question to be marketed by the importer in the importing Member State.[57] The national court therefore was advised to consider the evidence as to whether the owner's opposition hinders effective access to the relevant markets.

It was also made clear by the Advocate General and the Court that the condition of necessity is not met when the replacement of the mark is solely explained by the importer's attempt to secure a commercial advantage.[58] Thus the test for the national court to apply is objective (*Loendersloot*) and centred on a finding that the opposition to repackaging/re-labelling or affixing a different trade mark would hinder 'effective access' (*Upjohn*) to the market in the importing Member State.[59] Where does this expression originate? In *Bristol-Myers Squibb* reference is made to the 'impossibility' of marketing the product in the Member State of importation. The first time the expression 'effective access' was used seems to have been in the context of repackaging and traced to Jacobs' Opinion in the *Upjohn*[60] case.

An interesting aspect of the Jacobs' Opinion in *Upjohn* is that, when justifying his reasons for concluding that a requirement of intention is not desirable, he addressed the concerns expressed by Advocate General Capotorti in the earlier case of *Pfizer*.[61] Capotorti had concluded that the requirement of intention was necessary as he expressed the fear that otherwise the owner of the parallel trade marks would never be in a position to oppose lawfully the replacement of the trade marks. Jacobs submitted that the problem had been resolved in the *Bristol-Myers Squibb* case, since in the latter case he considered that the European Court

[55] Ibid, para 38 of the judgment.

[56] C-379/97 *Pharmacia & Upjohn SA v Paranova A/S* [1999] ECR I-6927.

[57] Ibid, para 39 of the judgment.

[58] Ibid, para 44 of the judgment. Jacobs was less firm and unwilling to lay down a rule that 'purely commercial reasons' would never fall within the concept of necessary. See para 54 of the Opinion.

[59] Ibid, para 43 of the judgment (but not the operative part). See also para 52 of the Opinion and paras 25 and 54 of the reasoning in *Merck* and *Boehringer* respectively. Finally, the phrase found its way into the operative part of the ruling in *Merck* and *Boehringer*. This was also reiterated in Case C-433/00 *Aventis Pharma Deutschland GmbH v Kohlpharma GmbH & MTK Pharma Vertriebs-GmbH* [2002] I-7761 at para 26, where the European Court of Justice applied exactly the same test in the context of pharmaceutical products being marketed under central marketing authorizations in accordance with Regulation 2309/93 [1993] OJ L214/1 on procedures for marketing these products in the Community.

[60] Para 54 of the Opinion in Case C-379/97 *Upjohn* [1999] ECR I-6927.

[61] Case 1/81 *Pfizer v Eurim-Pharm* [1981] ECR 2913.

of Justice had recognized the right of the owner to oppose where it was justified by the need to protect the essential function of the trade mark. In addition, the *Bristol-Myers Squibb* judgment had expressly recognized the right to oppose where the repackaging (or replacement of the trade mark) would damage the reputation of the mark or of the owner.[62]

The judgment in the *Upjohn* case redefined the one delivered in the *American Home Products* case to bring the case-law on re-branding into line with that on reaffixing of a trade mark to a repackaged product. In the case of *Upjohn* Jacobs advised the Court to apply the case law on reaffixing of a trade mark to a repackaged product to a situation where there is re-branding.

Hoffmann-La Roche conditions

Another important development in the judgment in the *Bristol-Myers Squibb* case relates to the fact that even if the conditions of *Hoffmann-La Roche* were satisfied, 'there remains the possibility that the reputation of the trade mark, and thus of its owner, may nevertheless suffer from an inappropriate presentation of the repackaged product. In such a case the trade mark owner has a legitimate interest related to the specific subject-matter of the trade mark right in being able to oppose the marketing of the product'.[63]

Thus in the *Bristol-Myers Squibb* case, a further condition was added to the list in the *Hoffmann-La Roche* case, namely the quality and the manner in which the repackaging is carried out by the importer must not be likely to damage the reputation of the trade mark and of its owner.[64] This was a significant addition to the conditions of *Hoffmann-La Roche*. There is no evidence from the Opinion to suggest that the Court was adopting a proposal from the Advocate General. Indeed, Jacobs, when he applied the principles he had elaborated in the first part of his Opinion to the facts of *Bristol-Myers Squibb*, did raise the possibility that shoddy repackaging could affect the reputation of the trade mark and, consequently, damage the legitimate interests of the trade mark owner.[65] Unlike the Court, which expressly added this condition to the other four *Hoffmann-La Roche* conditions, Jacobs did not seem to give this requirement the same degree of importance. On the other hand, Jacobs, in his Opinion, when referring to the factual situation in one of the three cases, stated '[T]he importance of presentation may vary depending on the type of goods. For luxury goods such as perfume and jewellery an attractive presentation may be more important than for more functional goods such as pharmaceuticals'.[66] The impression given is that Jacobs considered this not as a requirement but simply as another element to be considered in deciding whether the *Hoffmann-La Roche* conditions had been met.

[62] Para 45 of the Opinion in *Upjohn*.

[63] Para 75 of the judgment in *Bristol-Myers Squibb*.

[64] Ibid, para 79 of the judgment lists the five conditions.

[65] Para 109 (last sentence) of the Opinion. The possibility of damage to the reputation of the mark was also mentioned earlier, para 89.

[66] Joined Cases C-71 to 73/94 *Eurim-Pharm*, at para 117 of the Opinion in *Bristol-Myers Squibb*.

This conclusion is further supported by Jacobs expressing recognition in the *Loendersloot* case of the additional requirement laid down by the Court, where he stated that 'although the requirement that the original condition of the product must not be affected refers to the condition of the product inside the packaging, the Court made the point that inappropriate presentation of the repackaged product, in particular defective, poor quality or untidy packaging, could damage the reputation of the trade mark'.[67]

However, another refinement of the conditions set out in *Hoffmann-La Roche* can be traced to Jacobs' Opinion in the *Bristol-Myers Squibb* case. Although the *Hoffmann-La Roche* conditions required prior notice to be given to the trade mark owner, Jacobs proposed that the owner should also be provided with a specimen of the repackaged product.[68] This was indeed adopted by the Court, not as an automatic requirement but as an obligation to do so if requested by the trade mark owner.[69] In the later case of *Boehringer*[70] the national court asked the European Court of Justice to rule on the appropriate length of time that the parallel importer has to give the trade mark owner before placing the repackaged or re-branded product on the market. Both the Advocate General and the Court agreed that it needed to be a 'reasonable time'.[71] The Court went on to state that 15 working days,[72] although purely indicative, was appropriate in the factual circumstances of this case. There was also agreement between the Advocate General and the Court that if the notice was not given then the repackaging or re-branding would automatically be an infringement.[73]

Free movement of goods and exhaustion of intellectual property rights

As far as the free movement of goods rules are concerned, Jacobs delivered Opinions in several cases referred to the European Court of Justice by national courts. The first Opinion he delivered on the so-called 'inherent' conflict between the national rights of trade mark owners and the EC Treaty rules on free movement of goods was in March 1990 in the *HAG II*[74] case. As already mentioned

[67] Para 6 of the Opinion in *Loendersloot*. Further evidence of Jacobs' reluctance to agree with the Court in *Bristol-Myers Squibb* that the damage to the reputation of a trade mark as an additional requirement to be added to those listed in *Hoffmann-La Roche* can be illustrated by his statement in the last sentence of para 28 of the same Opinion where he stated, '[i]t may be noted that even the last requirement, concerning the reputation of the trade mark, could to some extent be regarded as related to the guarantee of origin which is the essential function of the trade mark, since inappropriate presentation of the repackaged product could certainly cause confusion in the minds of consumers about the origin of the product'.

[68] Para 87 of the Opinion in *Bristol-Myers Squibb*.

[69] Ibid, para 79 of the judgment and also included in the operative part of the ruling.

[70] Case C-143/00 *Boehringer* [2002] ECR I-3759.

[71] Ibid, para 66 of the judgment and para 134 of the Opinion.

[72] Ibid, para 67 of the judgment. Jacobs had proposed three or four weeks (para 134 of the Opinion) which is equivalent to 15 working days.

[73] Ibid, paras 63 and 64 of the judgment and para 136 of the Opinion.

[74] Case C-10/89 *SA CNL-SUCAL NV v HAG GF AG* [1990] ECR I-3711.

above, the European Court of Justice expressly overturned its earlier judgment in the *HAG I*[75] case. The European Court of Justice in the *HAG I* case had adopted the common origin doctrine which provides that where similar or identical trade marks were originally owned by the same natural or legal person, but later become the property of two different owners in different Member States, neither of the current owners can keep each other's trade marked goods, if they had been lawfully placed on the market in a Member State, out of each other's territories. Thus the EC Treaty rules on free movement of goods prevail over national owned trade mark rights. This judgment was heavily criticized by commentators.[76] Unfortunately it took 20 years before a similar case was referred to the European Court of Justice, enabling the Court to reconsider its earlier judgment.

The common origin doctrine

Jacobs' Opinion in the *HAG II* case is remarkable for the forthright manner in which he demolished the reasoning of the European Court of Justice in the *HAG I*[77] case. He set out several arguments as to why the reasoning of the Court was flawed. He considered the principal fault of the reasoning in the *HAG I* case as the failure of the European Court of Justice to explain why the mere fact that trade marks have a common origin is relevant in the absence of any market-sharing agreement. Jacobs directly attacked the correctness of the doctrine of common origin, finding no rational basis for it and challenged the Court to find a justification for this doctrine in the EC Treaty. In fairness to the European Court of Justice, Jacobs acknowledged that 20 years earlier there was a negative attitude towards the value of trade marks. He quoted from the Opinion of Advocate General Dutheillet de Lamothe in *Sirena v Eda*[78] which considered the interests protected by patents to be much more important than those protected by trade marks. However, he was also critical of the Court's logic in trying to legitimize the doctrine of common origin two years later, in *Terrapin v Terranova*.[79] According to Jacobs the Court misunderstood the meaning of 'origin' in the context of the essential function of a trade mark. The essential function of a trade mark is to guarantee to consumers that the product has the same origin, meaning commercial origin of the goods themselves and not to the historical origin of the trade mark.[80] By the time *Terrapin v Terranova* was decided the Court had already recognized in *Centrafarm v Winthrop*[81] that trade marks have two functions,

[75] Case 192/73 *Van Zuylen v HAG* [1974] ECR 731.

[76] For example, FA Mann, 'Industrial Property and the EEC Treaty' (1975) 24 ICLQ 31; WR Cornish, 'Trade Marks, Customer Confusion and the Common Market' (1975) 38 MLR 329.

[77] Interestingly, as an academic, Jacobs published an article, 'Industrial Property and the EEC Treaty: A Reply' (1975) 24 ICLQ 643, responding to FA Mann's criticism of this ruling, cited above, and in defence of the European Court of Justice's ruling in *HAG I*.

[78] Case 40/70 [1971] ECR 69, 88 which was repeated by the European Court of Justice in its judgment in this case, para 7.

[79] Case 119/75 [1976] ECR 1039.

[80] Para 24 of the Opinion in Case C-10/89 *HAG II* [1990] ECR I-3711.

[81] Case 16/74 [1974] ECR 1183.

namely the protection of the owner's goodwill, and also to protect the consumer from confusion or deception as to the origin of the goods. Thus Jacobs implied that the Court should have reasoned more logically in *Terrapin v Terranova* rather than to confirm the position they had taken in *HAG I.* He concluded that the doctrine of common origin 'is not a legitimate creature of Community law'[82] and reminded the Court that the case-law since the *HAG I* case on free movement of goods and the exercise of intellectual property rights had developed and was centred on the notion of 'consent'. Thus the continuation of a doctrine of common origin was not reconcilable with the notion of consent where the property had been expropriated by the State.

The European Court of Justice in the *HAG II* case abandoned the doctrine of common origin stating right at the beginning of the judgment that 'it should be stated at the outset that the Court believes it necessary to reconsider the interpretation given in that judgment [*HAG I*] in the light of the case-law which has developed with regard to the relationship between industrial and commercial property and the general rules of the treaty, particularly in the sphere of the free movement of goods'.[83] What is less clear is whether this reversal would have happened irrespective of the Opinion. For example, the Reporting Judge in the case was René Joliet who was an expert in intellectual property rights and, as a former academic,[84] was fully aware of the massive amount of criticism that had been poured on the European Court of Justice's judgments in the cases of *HAG I* and *Terrapin v Terranova.* Nevertheless, Jacobs' Opinion is a coherent, authoritative and robust demolition of the European Court of Justice's reasoning in two cases.[85]

Post-adoption of the Trade Mark Directive

As already stated above, the adoption of Directive 89/104 on the approximation of the laws of the Member States relating to trade marks was an important legislative measure in the aim to complete the internal market programme by the end of 1992.[86] The European Court of Justice first commented on the effect of the Directive on prior case-law in the *Bristol-Myers Squibb*[87] case. The period for

[82] Para 26 of the Opinion in *HAG II.*

[83] Ibid, para 10 of the judgment.

[84] eg R Joliet and D Keeling, 'Trade mark law and the free movement of goods: The Overruling of the Judgment in HAG I' (1991) 22 International Review of Industrial Property and Copyright 303.

[85] Interestingly, Jacobs criticized the Court for lack of justification for adopting the doctrine of common origin in the *HAG I* judgment and specifically mentioned the fact that the Court's ruling was set out only in 10 short paragraphs. In *HAG II,* even though the European Court of Justice expressly overturned a 20-year-old doctrine, the Court dealt with this whole matter also in 10 paragraphs! This contrasts dramatically with Jacobs' Opinion in *HAG II* which covered 65 paragraphs.

[86] The date for implementation of Directive 89/104 was extended to 31 December 1992 by a Council Decision.

[87] In some of the referrals no mention of the Directive had been made by the national court in the order for reference. Jacobs, nevertheless, considered the effect of the provisions of the Directive on earlier case-law. The Court also followed suit. See, for example, Case C-352/95 *Phytheron International SA v Jean Bourdon SA* [1997] ECR I-1729, para 17 of the Opinion and paras 18 and 19 of the judgment; and *Loendersloot,* paras 21 to 23 of the Opinion and paras 17 and 18 of the judgment.

implementation of the Directive had not yet expired and some of the Member States on whose territory the disputes had arisen had not yet implemented the Directive. How would the Court determine the effect, in particular, of Article 7 of the Directive, on the prior European Court of Justice case-law on repackaging (*Hoffmann-La Roche*, *American Home Products* and *Pfizer-Eurim Pharm*)?

Article 7(1), on the exhaustion of rights principle, is framed in terms corresponding to those used by the European Court of Justice in its case-law interpreting Articles 28–30 EC. Article 7(2) defines the circumstances in which a trade mark owner may oppose the further marketing of his product.

Jacobs undertook an examination of the effect of the adoption of the Directive in respect of the EC Treaty provisions in the *Bristol-Myers Squibb* case. In one paragraph he gave a textbook analysis of the normal effect of legislation on prior case-law but, given that the provisions of the Treaty cannot be disregarded entirely, he concluded that the Directive must be interpreted in the light of the Treaty provisions. If there is a conflict, the Treaty provisions must prevail as a primary source of law. The Court followed the Opinion and concluded that the issue in question was to be assessed on the basis of the combined provisions of national trade mark laws and Article 7 of the Directive, interpreted in the light of Article 30 of the EC Treaty.[88] The European Court of Justice also confirmed that Article 7(2) permits the owner of a trade mark to oppose the repackaging of his product, where there is a legitimate reason for so doing. In particular, this would be the situation where the condition of the products has been changed or impaired since they were put on the market. Thus the Court confirmed that the case-law on Article 30 EC must be taken as the basis for determining whether under Article 7(2) a trade mark owner may oppose the marketing of repackaged products to which the trade mark has been reaffixed.[89]

The extension of the principle of exhaustion of rights doctrine

As far as the extent of the scope of the principle of exhaustion of rights set down in Article 7(1) of the Trade Mark Directive is concerned, the significant judgment is the one delivered in the *Silhouette*[90] case where Jacobs delivered the Opinion. Article 7(1) states that '[T]he trade mark shall not entitle the proprietor to prohibit its use in relation to goods which have been put on the market in the Community under that trade mark by the proprietor or with his consent'.

In the *Bristol-Myers Squibb* case it was confirmed that Article 7 of the Trade Mark Directive 'comprehensively regulates the question of the exhaustion of trade mark rights for products traded in the Community'.[91] In a subsequent case, *Pytheron*,[92] Jacobs referred to the judgment in the *Bristol-Myers Squibb* case with

[88] Para 54 of the Opinion and para 28 of the *Bristol-Myers Squibb* judgment.

[89] Ibid, para 41 of the judgment.

[90] Case C-355/96 *Silhouette International Schmied GmbH & Co KG v Hartlauer Handelsgesellschaft mbH* [1998] ECR I-4799.

[91] Para 26 of the judgment in *Bristol-Myers Squibb*.

[92] Case C-352/95 *Phytheron International SA v Jean Bourdon SA* [1997] ECR I-1729 (Fifth Chamber).

approval in the context of a dispute where there were no legitimate reasons for the trade mark owner to oppose the importation of goods from Germany. As far as intra-Community exhaustion was concerned he stated that the 'principle of exhaustion of trade marks rights has now been enshrined in Article 7'.[93]

In the *Silhouette* referral the national court sought clarification as to whether the principle of international exhaustion of intellectual property rights was governed also by Article 7(1). The goods in question had been placed on the market outside the Community with instructions to the purchaser not to export the goods to other countries. The goods, however, were imported into the Community and the trade mark owner wished to prevent their importation.

The *Silhouette* case is another case where Jacobs and the Court were very much of the same view and applied the same reasoning. For example, the Court ruled that 'Articles 5 to 7 of the Directive must be construed as embodying a complete harmonization of the rules relating to the rights conferred by a trade mark'.[94] This was also the view of Jacobs who concluded that 'Article 7(1) spells out the circumstances in which the trade-mark rights are exhausted; it is naturally read as doing so exhaustively'.[95] The Opinion, of course, has a wider context. Jacobs, for example, conceded that the adoption of the principle of international exhaustion would be favourable to consumers and promote competition. However, in his view, the European Court of Justice's case-law on trade marks was developed 'in the context of the Community, not the world market'.[96] In addition, applying a literal interpretation to Article 7(1), he concluded that Article 7(1) provides for exhaustion only where the goods are placed on the market in the Community.[97]

Another example of the similarity of reasoning and expression is to be found in the reasons given for not allowing Member States a free choice. Jacobs argued that international exhaustion is a matter which directly affected the functioning of the internal market and went on to state that '[I]f some Member States practise international exhaustion while others do not, there will be barriers to trade within the internal market which it is precisely the object of the Directive to remove'.[98]

The European Court of Justice reached exactly the same conclusion and expressed it in substantially identical wording. The Court stated that:

> [it is] is the only interpretation which is fully capable of ensuring that the purpose of the Directive is achieved, namely to safeguard the functioning of the internal market. A situation in which Member states could provide for international exhaustion while others provided for community exhaustion only would inevitably give rise to barriers to the free movement of goods and the freedom to provide services.[99]

The development of the Community's doctrine of exhaustion of rights has been primarily based on the existence or absence of 'consent' on the part of the trade

[93] Para 17 of the Opinion in *Pytheron*.
[94] Para 25 of the judgment in *Silhouette*.
[95] Ibid, para 33 of the Opinion.
[96] Ibid, para 49 of the Opinion.
[97] Ibid, para 30 of the Opinion.
[98] Ibid, para 41 of the Opinion.
[99] Ibid, para 27 of the judgment.

mark owner.[100] The *Silhouette* judgment was limited to the scope of Article 7(1) within the context of the specific questions referred by the national court. The judgment therefore gave insufficient guidance as to the application of Article 7(1) in different factual circumstances. Further referrals were necessary to establish the extent of the scope of Article 7(1).[101] Two such significant judgments are *Davidoff* and *Levi*[102] on the meaning of 'consent' and *Van Doren + Q*[103] on the burden of proof. The judgments were delivered by a Full Court with Gulmann as the Reporting Judge and Advocate General Stix-Hackl delivering the Opinions. Is there any evidence of the impact of Jacobs' Opinions on Stix-Hackl's own Opinions delivered in these two later cases? Indeed references to Jacobs' Opinions are to be found in the Opinion delivered in *Davidoff* and *Levi* but not in the Opinion delivered in *Van Doren*. This is not surprising given the nature of the questions referred by the national courts to the European Court of Justice.[104]

The issue in the *Davidoff* and *Levi* cases was the determination of the circumstances in which the owner of a trade mark may be considered to have consented to the importation and marketing of goods placed on the market outside the EEA.[105] Can consent be implied? Is the presence or absence of consent to be determined

[100] In Case 78/70 *Deutsche Grammophon* [1971] ECR 487, Advocate General Roemer had proposed a criterion of dependency to reconcile the free movement of goods rules with the rights of intellectual property owners. Thus he concluded that a trade mark owner exhausted his rights where the goods were placed in the territory of another Member State by the trade mark owner or an undertaking dependent on the owner. The European Court of Justice however replaced the criterion of dependency by one of consent.

[101] One such reference where Jacobs was the Advocate General was in Case C-173/98 *Sebago Inc. and Ancienne Maison Dubois & Fils SA v G-B Unic SA* [1998] ECR I-4103 (Fifth Chamber). The issue in the case was whether the Community law principle of exhaustion of trade mark rights relates to individual goods or whole product lines. This case followed soon after the *Silhouette* ruling so it was dealt with easily: both Jacobs and the Court concluded that Art 7(1) must be read in conjunction with Art 7(2) which clearly is concerned with further commercialization of the goods. Thus the exhaustion principle concerns individual products following the first marketing and not other sales of the same type of goods (para 22 of the Opinion and para 20 of the ruling for the similar conclusion of the Court). Both the Advocate General and the Court cited case C-337/95 *Dior Parfums, Christian Dior v Evora* [1997] ECR I-6013 and Case C-63/97 *BMW v Deenick* [1999] ECR I-905 as authority for the proposition that the exhaustion relates to the right of resale (paras 23 and 24 of the Opinion and paras 20 and 21 of the judgment).

[102] Joined Cases C-414/99 to C-416/99 *Zino Davidoff SA v A&G Imports Ltd* and *Levi Strauss & Co and ors v Tesco Stores Ltd and ors* [2001] ECR I-8691.

[103] Case C-244/00 *Van Doren + Q GmbH v Lifestyle Sports & Sportswear Handelsgesellschaft mbH and Michael Orth* [2003] ECR I-3051.

[104] In *Van Doren*, unlike the situation in *Davidoff*, the geographical market where the goods had been placed for the first time was disputed. The main question referred to the European Court of Justice was whether national law governed the burden of proof which in this case would have to be discharged by the defendant according to German procedural rules. This imposed a heavy burden on the defendant who would have to disclose the identity of the supplier. As a matter of procedural law, the burden of proof would normally be left for the national procedural rules. In *Davidoff*, the European Court of Justice stated that it was for the party alleging consent to prove it, not for the trade mark owner to demonstrate its absence. Would the same rule be applied to this situation? This was a totally novel point and had not been considered by Jacobs in his earlier Opinions.

[105] *Davidoff* and *Levi* concerned toiletries and jeans placed on the market in Singapore and the US respectively.

by reference to Community or national law? Both the Advocate General and the Court concluded that Community law governs this matter. Moreover, the European Court of Justice ruled that, given the serious effect of extinguishing the exclusive rights of the trade mark owner, consent must be so expressed that an intention to renounce the rights is 'unequivocally demonstrated'.[106]

In analysing Stix-Hackl's Opinion there is evidence that Jacobs' earlier Opinions were of some significance.[107] For example, there are direct references to his Opinions in the *Silhouette*, *Bristol-Myers Squibb* and *Loendersloot*[108] cases. Stix-Hackl referred to Jacobs's Opinion in the *Silhouette* case for confirmation of the conclusion that the exhaustion under Article 7(1) of the Trade Marks Directive is a derogation from the rights conferred on the trade mark owner by Article 5(1) of the Directive. The European Court of Justice has also stated that Articles 5 to 7 of the Directive 'embody a complete harmonization'.[109] Thus Stix-Hackl concluded that 'consent' must be a Community law concept for the sake of legal certainty. In the *Silhouette* case, Jacobs did not have an opportunity to express a view on this issue but it is reasonable to assume he would also have reached a similar conclusion. This case law historical analysis also supported the conclusion Stix-Hackl reached that consent within the framework of the Community's exhaustion of rights theory relates not to the intention of the trade mark owner but to the question as to whether the marketing of the trade marked goods on the market within the EEA can be attributed to the trade mark owner. This is an issue of responsibility and accountability for the marketing and not an expression of intent to transfer the trade marked goods.[110]

The references to Jacobs' Opinions in the *Bristol-Myers Squibb* and *Loendersloot* cases were made in the context of what constitutes the subject-matter and/or essential function of a trade mark. Stix-Hackl cites Jacobs in the *Loendersloot* case for authority that removal of batch code numbers affixed in compliance with a statutory obligation may be relevant for the purpose of a trade mark right only if this removal would have a disproportionate adverse effect on the specific subject-matter of the trade mark right.[111] Thus the removal of identification numbers cannot be opposed merely by virtue of trade mark rights. The Court, however,

[106] Para 45 of the judgment in *Davidoff* and *Levi*.

[107] In carrying out an historical review of the European Court of Justice's case law on the meaning of 'consent', Stix-Hackl, para 71 of her Opinion, also cites Advocate General Roemer in Case 78/70 *Deutsche Grammophon* [1971] ECR 487 who proposed a criterion of dependency to determine whether the free movement of goods rules prevailed over the exclusive right of the intellectual property owner. Thus according to this test goods were subject to the free movement of goods rules if placed on the market by the owner of the intellectual property right or an undertaking dependent on the owner. The European Court of Justice, however, replaced the criterion of 'dependency' by one of 'consent'.

[108] Paras 37, 86 and 119 respectively of the Opinion in *Davidoff* and *Levi*.

[109] For example paras 25 and 29 of *Silhouette*.

[110] See paras 68 to 74 of the Opinion in *Davidoff* and *Levi*.

[111] Paras 119 and 120 of the Opinion in *Davidoff* and *Levi*, referring to para 43 of Jacobs' Opinion in *Loendersloot*.

confirmed that compliance with legislative obligations cannot constitute an artificial partitioning of markets. However, in *Davidoff* and *Levi*, there was no such obligation and the issue for the European Court of Justice was purely to rule on whether there would be damage to the reputation of the trade marked goods by the removal of the batch numbers as these numbers are an important means of recalling defective goods.[112]

EC trade mark case law[113]

The Trade Mark Directive was followed soon after with the adoption of Regulation 40/94 creating the Community trade mark. In both measures the relative grounds[114] for refusing to register a trade mark (Article 4 of the Directive and Article 8 of the Regulation) have the same wording and are substantially identical to the grounds for infringement (Article 5 of the Directive and Article 9 of the Regulation) which are in themselves identical.[115] The referrals from the national courts during this period were primarily seeking an interpretation of various terms/concepts to be found in Articles 4 and 5 of the Trade Mark Directive such as the meaning of 'likelihood of confusion', 'similarity' between goods or services, as well as the extent of the protection of trade marks with a reputation (Article 5(2)). In the vast majority of these preliminary rulings the Advocate General was Jacobs.

In addition, appeals to the European Court of Justice from the Court of First Instance on matters concerning the meaning of the provisions of the Trade Mark Regulation began to be decided from 2001 onwards. Unsurprisingly, Jacobs was chosen as the Advocate General in these early appeals.

112 The Court, paras 53 to 58, stated that silence is not enough to imply consent. Consent must be expressed positively. The factors taken into account in finding implied consent must unequivocally demonstrate that the trade mark owner renounced an intention to enforce his exclusive rights. The burden of proof is on the trader alleging consent.

113 All the cases were heard by a Full Court unless specified otherwise. Since the restructuring of the European Court of Justice to accommodate the 2004 enlargement, similar judgments are delivered by the Grand Chamber.

114 Absolute grounds for refusal to register a mark are set out in Art 3 of the Directive and in Art 7 of the Regulation.

115 Advocate General Jacobs took the opportunity, even when not pertinent to the issues raised by the national court, to remind the European Court of Justice that the judgment it was going to deliver on the provisions of the Directive applied equally to the corresponding and substantially identical provisions in the Regulation. See, for example, para 27 of the Opinion in *Sabel*; para 43 of Opinion in *Canon*; para 22 of the Opinion in *General Motors*; paras 21 to 28 of the Opinion in *LTJ Diffusion*; para 9 of the Opinion in *Davidoff v Gofkid*. Recently, at paras 27 et seq. of the Opinion Jacobs delivered in *Medion*, he cites judgments from the Court of First Instance on similar issues raised in the context of the Trade Mark Regulation. Another example of this approach can be found in paras 55 to 62 of the Opinion Jacobs delivered in *Silhouette*. In interpreting the scope of Art 7(1) of the Directive in the context of international exhaustion of trade mark rights, Jacobs also considered Art 13 of the Trade Mark Regulation which is a virtually identical provision.

Preliminary rulings on the interpretation of the provisions of the Trade Mark Directive

From 1997 to the end of 2005, significant judgments (eg *Sabel*,[116] *Canon*,[117] *Lloyd*,[118] *Marca Mode*,[119] *General Motors*,[120] *LTJ Diffusion*,[121] *Davidoff v Gofkid*[122] and *Medion*[123]) were delivered by the European Court of Justice on the interpretation of certain provisions of the Directive. As already noted above, in all these cases Jacobs was the Advocate General,[124] and often with Judge Gulmann as the Reporting Judge.[125] With the notable exception of the judgment in *Davidoff v Gofkid*,[126] Jacobs' interpretations of the various provisions of the Directive were substantially followed by the European Court of Justice. There is also no evidence that the reasoning of the Opinions and of the rulings were significantly different in any important aspect.

The first cases before the European Court of Justice raising questions of interpretation of the provisions in the Trade Mark Directive were preliminary references from German courts (*Sabel v Puma*, *Canon* and *LTJ Diffusion*). The national courts sought an interpretation of Article 4(1)(b) (*Sabel v Puma* and *Canon*) which sets out one of the grounds for refusal of registration of a trade mark and of Article 5(1)(b) (*LTJ Diffusion*) whose wording is substantially identical to Article 4(1)(b) but refers to grounds for infringement.[127] The last Opinion delivered by Advocate General Jacobs on the concept of likelihood of confusion was in June 2005 in the *Medion*[128] case where he listed the principles laid down by the European Court of Justice in various rulings. These principles are as follows.

First, likelihood of confusion is to be established by a global evaluation taking into account all factors relevant to the circumstances of the individual fact situation.[129] Second, this evaluation is to be carried out by the national court in assessing the evidence.[130] Third, similarity between the marks is necessary but not sufficient in

[116] Case C-251/95 *Sabel BV v Puma AG* [1997] ECR I-6191.

[117] Case C-39/97 *Canon Kabushiki Kaisha v Metro-Goldwyn-Mayer Inc* [1998] ECR I-5507.

[118] Case C-342/97 *Lloyd Schuhfabrik Meyer & Co GmbH v Klijsen Handel BV* [1999] ECR I-3819.

[119] Case C-425/98 *Marca Mode CV v Adidas AG and Adidas Benelux BV* [2000] ECR I-4861 (Sixth Chamber).

[120] Case C-375/97 *General Motors Corp v Yplon SA* [1999] ECR I-5421.

[121] Case C-291/00 *LTJ Diffusion SA v Sadas Vertbaudet SA* [2003] ECR I-2799.

[122] Case C-292/00 *Davidoff & Cie SA and Zino Davidoff SA v Gofkid Ltd* [2003] ECR I-389.

[123] Case C-120/04 *Medion AG v Thomson* [2005] ECR I-8551 (Second Chamber).

[124] Other referrals on the interpretation of the provisions of the Directive where Jacobs was the Advocate General include Case C-2/00 *Michael Hölterhoff v Ulrich Freiesleben* [2002] ECR I-4187 on the interpretation of the phrase 'using in the course of trade'.

[125] The exception is *LTJ Diffusion* where the Reporting Judge was Macken.

[126] Case C-292/00 [2003] ECR I-389.

[127] Confirmed by the European Court of Justice in Case C-425/98 *Marca Mode* [2000] ECR I-4861, paras 26–28, that the European Court of Justice's interpretation of Art 4(1)(b) must accordingly apply to Art 5(1)(b).

[128] Case C-120/04 *Medion AG v Thomson* [2005] ECR I-8551.

[129] Para 22 of the ruling in Case C-251/95 *Sabel* [1997] ECR I-6191.

[130] Para 39 of the ruling in Case C-425/98 *Marca Mode CV v Adidas AG and Adidas Benelux BV* [2000] ECR I-4861.

itself for a finding of likelihood of confusion. Other factors need also to be taken into account.[131]

In providing guidance to national courts the European Court of Justice has confirmed that there is a clear interdependence between the various factors and, in particular, between the similarity of the mark and the similarity of the goods or services covered. For example, a lesser degree of similarity between the goods or services may be affected by a greater degree of similarity between the marks, and vice versa.[132] Furthermore, the more distinctive the earlier mark, whether per se or because of its reputation, the greater the likelihood of confusion.[133]

In addition, it is for the national court to determine the distinctive character of the mark by an overall assessment of the greater or lesser capacity of the mark to identify the goods or services for which it has been registered as coming from a particular undertaking, and thus to distinguish those goods or services from those of other undertakings.[134]

Finally, when the national court is determining the likelihood of confusion 'on the part of the public,' the perception of the mark in the mind of the average consumer plays a decisive role in the global appreciation of the concept. The average consumer perceives the mark as a whole and does not analyse its various details.[135] It is unlikely that the consumer will have the opportunity of seeing both marks at the same time. The perception of the consumer will also differ depending on the category of the goods or services.[136]

How much of the above principles were initiated by Jacobs in the Opinions he delivered? Are these principles traceable to his reasoning? The most significant Opinion Jacobs delivered on these matters was in *Sabel*, the first case to be referred to the European Court of Justice seeking interpretation of Article 4(1)(b).

The concept of 'likelihood of confusion'

Article 4(1)(b) states that a mark will be refused registration:

> if because of its identity with, or similarity to, the earlier trade mark and the identity or similarity of the goods or services covered by the trade marks, there exists a likelihood of confusion on the part of the public, which includes the likelihood of association with the earlier trade mark.

The central question from the national court was whether the expression 'likelihood of association' was an alternative to the concept of 'likelihood of confusion'.

[131] The European Court of Justice has given guidance in its case-law to a number of factors which the national court must take into account when carrying out the assessment. These are mainly listed in Recital 10 of the Directive.

[132] Para 17 of the judgment in Case C-39/97 *Canon Kabushiki Kaisha v Metro-Goldwyn-Mayer Inc* [1998] ECR I-5507.

[133] Para 24 of the judgment in *Sabel.*

[134] Para 22 and listing of the relevant factors in para 23 of Case C-342/97 *Lloyd Schuhfabrik Meyer & Co GmbH v Klijsen Handel BV* [1999] ECR I-3819.

[135] Para 23 of the judgment in *Sabel.*

[136] Para 26 of the judgment in *Lloyd.*

The historical background to the wording of this provision is relevant to the understanding of the problem facing the Court. The provisions of the Directive were based on the Benelux trade mark law. However there had been disagreement amongst the Member States as to whether mere likelihood of association with an earlier registered trade mark was a sufficient reason for refusing to register a trade mark. This was the position in the Benelux system but strongly opposed by other Member States such as the UK since it gave too broad a protection to the owner of the earlier registered trade mark. The wording of Article 4(1)(b) was therefore a compromise solution leaving the European Court of Justice, rather than the legislators, to sort out the problems that could arise. It is thus not surprising that the first referrals from national courts were on this issue.

Jacobs' Opinion is interesting as a good example of a common law approach to the interpretation of a legislative provision. First, he undertook an extensive analysis of the relevant Benelux law which protected the trade mark owner where there was no confusion as to origin[137]: but mere likelihood of association would be enough to permit the owner of the earlier mark to object. Then, he reviewed the history of the drafting of the Directive as well as the corresponding provisions in the Trade Mark Regulation.[138] He concluded that to embrace the concept of non-origin association would depart from the case-law on Articles 28 to 30 EC.[139] This of course is not surprising given Jacobs's totally consistent approach in his Opinions in the repackaging cases that the essential function of the trade mark is a guarantee of origin. According to Jacobs, it is that fact alone which justifies the derogation from the fundamental principle of the free movement of goods enshrined in the EC Treaty. He found further support for this reasoning in Recital 10 of the Directive with which the European Court of Justice also concurred.[140] The European Court of Justice followed Jacobs' interpretation of the concept of 'likelihood of confusion' and ruled that likelihood of association alone is not enough to establish likelihood of confusion but that it serves to define the scope of the concept of likelihood of confusion.[141] In order to determine whether a likelihood of confusion arises, a global assessment must be undertaken taking into account all the relevant factors.[142] As to the determination of whether the consumer is likely to be confused, the European Court of Justice followed Jacobs' similar approach accepting that the consumer looks at marks as a whole. The national

[137] Paras 35 to 41 of the Opinion in Case C-251/95 *Sabel* [1997] ECR I-6191.

[138] Ibid, paras 42 to 55 of the Opinion. This approach of reviewing the legislative history of secondary legislation was also applied in *Silhouette* in order to determine whether Art 7(1) of the Trade Mark Directive imposed international exhaustion of trade mark rights (at para 32 of the Opinion).

[139] Para 46 of the Opinion in *Sabel*, where he stated 'in the absence of clear wording to that effect, the Community legislature cannot be assumed to have intended to embrace such a concept', referring to the concept of non-origin association.

[140] Ibid, para 45 of the Opinion and para 19 of the judgment.

[141] Ibid, para 18 of the judgment. One may be forgiven for speculating that the fact that the Reporting Judge, Gulmann, was not from the Benelux countries was not unhelpful.

[142] Ibid, para 22 of the judgment.

court must therefore consider the evidence of the overall impression the marks make on the consumer rather than focus on the similarity of design.[143]

Both the Advocate General and the European Court of Justice concluded that conceptual similarity between marks could give rise to likelihood of confusion.[144] Jacobs, however, was more specific, stating it would be difficult to establish likelihood of confusion on the basis of conceptual similarity alone in circumstances where the earlier mark was not well known.[145]

Distinctiveness of the earlier mark as an element in establishing 'similarity' between the goods or the services

In *Canon* the Court stated that the distinctiveness of the earlier mark is an important factor where there is a lesser degree of similarity between the goods or services in question but the marks are very similar.[146] Indeed both the Advocate General and the Court rejected the notion of a purely objective test to establish similarity in this context.[147] Both stressed the need to find evidence of similarity between the goods or services even where one of the marks is identical to another with a highly distinctive character.[148] This is so because Article 4(1)(b) of the Directive requires the goods to be similar, whilst Article 4(4)(a) specifically concerns the situation where the goods or services are not identical or similar but the earlier mark has a high reputation.

However, in deciding that distinctiveness of the trade mark, due to its high reputation, was a relevant factor in establishing similarity of the goods or services, the Court undermined the logical underpinning of Article 4(1) and Article 5. It is clear from the wording of Article 4(1)(b) (and Article 5(1)(b)) and the case-law of the European Court of Justice up to the ruling in *Davidoff v Gofkid*,[149] that where the goods or services in question are similar, there is a requirement of likelihood of confusion being established before the trade mark owner is entitled to oppose the registration of another identical or similar mark. However, no such confusion needs to be proven when the earlier mark has a high reputation and the goods or services are dissimilar (Article 4(4)(a) and Article 5(2)).

Marks with reputation

The direct consequence of the ruling in *Canon* was that the reputation of a trade mark became an important factor in establishing rights not only under Article 4(4)(a) (or Article 5(2)) but also under Article 4(1)(b) (or Article 5(1)(b)) of the Directive.

143 Ibid, para 59 of the Opinion and para 23 of the judgment.
144 Ibid, para 62 of the Opinion and para 24 of the judgment.
145 Ibid, para 62 of the Opinion.
146 Para 19 of the judgment in Case C-39/97 *Canon* [1998] ECR I-5507.
147 Ibid, para 42 of the Opinion and para 22 of the judgment.
148 Ibid, para 44 of the Opinion.
149 Confirmed in *Marca Mode* at para 41 of the judgment, where the European Court of Justice rejected expressly the notion that where a trade mark has a reputation, likelihood of confusion may always be inferred if a similar mark is used for similar products.

Since Article 4(4)(a) does not require likelihood of confusion to be proven,[150] owners of trade marks which are distinctive due to their high reputation naturally prefer to argue that the goods or services are dissimilar and rely on Article 4(4)(a) rather than Article 4(1)(b) to claim their rights to oppose registration of a new mark or to take infringement action under Article 5(2). Considering all the hurdles that have to be met to show that there is a likelihood of confusion, this alternative approach is attractive.

The ruling, although perfectly reasonable in the context of *Canon*, has ultimately led the Sixth Chamber of the European Court of Justice in *Davidoff v Gofkid* to widen the scope of Article 5(2),[151] and consequently Article 4(4)(a),[152] as covering the situation where the goods or services are similar but the mark's reputation is high. In such a situation the owner is *mutatis mutandis* to be treated in the same manner as if the goods or services in question were dissimilar.[153]

Marca Mode was the first case to raise directly the question as to whether the owner of a distinctive mark by virtue of having a reputation is also required to prove the likelihood of confusion when infringement proceedings are brought under Article 5(1)(b). Both the Advocate General and the European Court of Justice were firm in their conclusion that it remained necessary in these circumstances to establish a likelihood of confusion.[154] It was reiterated that the reputation of the mark in these circumstances is an element making the mark distinctive. This distinctiveness will then be a factor for the national court when determining whether the goods or services in question are similar. Jacobs' conclusion was based on reasons of principle, in particular, stressing a position which he had made clear in *Sabel* and had consistently advocated in all subsequent relevant cases, namely, that a broad interpretation of the concept of likelihood of confusion would hinder the internal market project.[155] In *Marca Mode* he stressed that the concept itself is not novel to the Directive but merely reflects established case-law on Articles 28 to 30 EC.[156] He reminded the Court that where the earlier mark is distinctive by way of reputation (or otherwise), the rulings in *Canon* and *Lloyd* provide the weight to be given to this element when assessing whether there is a likelihood of confusion under Article 4(1)(b) or Article 5(1)(b).[157]

[150] First stated in *Sabel*, para 20 of the judgment and para 48 of the Opinion and referred to by Jacobs, para 26 of his Opinion in Case C-375/97 *General Motors* [1999] ECR I-5421.

[151] One earlier ruling on Art 5(2) was delivered in Case C-375/97 *General Motors* [1999] ECR I-5421. The national court sought guidance as to how to determine whether the mark has a reputation. The ruling is not relevant to the matters in issue in *Davidoff v Gofkid*.

[152] Confirmed by the European Court of Justice at para 17 of the judgment in *Davidoff v Gofkid*.

[153] It should be noted that Art 5(2) only applies where the trade mark owner can also prove that the use by the third party of the sign is 'without due cause' and 'takes unfair advantage of, or is detrimental to, the distinctive character or the repute of the trade mark'.

[154] Para 42 of the Opinion and paras 33 and 34 of the judgment in *Marca Mode*.

[155] Jacobs has consistently argued against too much protection being given to the owner of the earlier trade mark. See, for example, his Opinions, paras 50 to 51 of *Sabel* and para 20 (last sentence) of *Lloyd* as well as para 45 of *Davidoff v Gofkid*.

[156] See, for example, para 57 of the Opinion in *Davidoff v Gofkid*.

[157] Para 44 of the Opinion in *Marca Mode*.

However in *Davidoff v Gofkid*, Jacobs lost the argument and the European Court of Justice ruled that Article 5(2) applied equally to situations where the goods or services were identical or similar. Article 5(2) states:

the proprietor shall be entitled to prevent all third parties not having his consent from using in the course of trade any sign which is identical with, or similar to, the trade mark in relation to goods or services which are not similar to those for which the trade mark is registered, where the latter has a reputation in the Member State and where use of that sign without due cause takes unfair advantage of, or is detrimental to, the distinctive character or the repute of that trade mark.

The European Court of Justice preferred however to focus on the fact that the Directive provides specific protection against impairment of the distinctive character or repute of the marks.[158] The Court expressly rejected a literal interpretation of Article 5(2). Instead it chose to interpret the provision 'in the light of the overall scheme and objectives of the system of which it is part'.[159] The Court therefore was not prepared to accept the otherwise inevitable conclusion that a mark with a high reputation was better protected when the goods or services were dissimilar than when they were identical or similar.[160]

Jacobs recognized the attractiveness of this analysis but concluded that was not what the legislature had intended. Although he conceded that passages from earlier case-law could be cited in support of such an interpretation, he considered that the wording of Article 5(2) was clear. There is no qualification in the wording.[161] Furthermore, the drafting history of the Directive supported a literal interpretation. Finally, Jacobs identified no real gap in the protection of such marks.[162] He viewed the protection of Article 5(2) (and, of course, Article 4(4)(a)) for marks which 'enjoy a reputation in themselves rather than those which function only as a guarantee of origin'.[163] Thus he concluded that '[m]arks having a reputation thus do not enjoy a separate and independent system of protection but rather the same general protection as is afforded to all marks, together with a specific, supplementary and optional protection'.[164] In his view Article 5(2) is dependent on different criteria as it applies to a specific situation. It is not likelihood of confusion which needs to be established under Article 5(2) but that the use of the competing mark is without due cause and would take unfair advantage of, or be detrimental to, the distinctive character or repute of the protected mark.

Jacobs' reasoning in the *Davidoff v Gofkid* case was completely consistent with the interpretation methods he applied in earlier cases. He preferred a literal interpretation of the provisions and he stated that 'the wording of the Directive is clear and there is no compelling reason to interpret it in a manner contrary to its clear meaning'.[165]

[158] Para 21 of the judgment in *Davidoff v Gofkid*.
[159] Ibid, para 24 of the judgment.
[160] Ibid, para 25 of the judgment.
[161] Ibid, paras 32 and 33 of the Opinion.
[162] Ibid, paras 42 and 43, as well as the last sentence in para 47 of the Opinion.
[163] Ibid, para 46 of the Opinion.
[164] Ibid, para 46, last sentence of the Opinion.
[165] Ibid, para 53 of the Opinion.

The judgment in the *Davidoff v Gofkid* case is surprising for two reasons. First, the fact that the Advocate General in the case was Jacobs whose earlier Opinions in this area of Community law had always been followed by the Court. Second, the Court itself had referred to the difference between Articles 4(1)(b) and Article 5(2) on several earlier occasions.[166] Even though the case was heard by a Chamber rather than a Full Court, the Reporting Judge was, once again, Gulmann. Although one can only speculate, given the earlier statements of the Court in cases where Gulmann was also the Reporting Judge, one might be forgiven for suggesting that the composition of the Chamber was a relevant factor on this occasion. The matter will remain uncertain until a definitive ruling from a Full Court is delivered.

In answer to a question raised earlier as to the degree of influence that Jacobs may have had in these cases, the only conclusion that may be reached with confidence is that the Court agreed with Jacobs' interpretation of the concept of 'likelihood of confusion' but not with the narrow interpretation he urged the Court to adopt in respect of marks with a reputation under Article 5(2) of the Trade Mark Directive.

Appeals from the Court of First Instance on the interpretation of the provisions of the Trade Mark Regulation

Given the significant experience of Jacobs in this new field of Community law, it is not surprising that he was the Advocate General in the first appeals[167] from judgments of the Court of First Instance in disputes between trade mark applicants and the Office for Harmonisation in the Internal Market (OHIM) on the meaning of certain provisions of the Trade Mark Regulation.[168] The significant first Opinions were delivered in the *BABY-DRY* and *DOUBLEMINT*[169] cases which

[166] Paras 20 and 21 of the judgment in *Sabel*. See also Jacobs' strong views at para 48 of the Opinion in *Sabel*; and further at para 22 of the judgment in *Canon* and Jacobs' own statement at para 50 of his Opinion; para 23 of the judgment in *General Motors*.

[167] Jacobs also advised the European Court of Justice in the first appeals dealt with by an Order. Under Art 119 of the Rules of Procedure, where an appeal is clearly unfounded, the Court may at any time, acting on a report from the Reporting Judge, and after hearing the Advocate General, by reasoned Order dismiss the appeal. The first such Orders were issued in the following appeals: Cases C-150/02P *Streamserve Inc v Office for Harmonisation in the Internal Market (Trade Marks and Designs)* [2004] ECR I-1461; C-445/02P *Glaverbel SA v Office for Harmonisation in the Internal Market (Trade Marks and Designs) (OHIM)* [2004] ECR I-6267; and C-498/01P *Office for Harmonisation in the Internal Market (Trade Marks and Designs) (OHIM) v Zapf Creation AG* [2004] ECR I-11349 where the Advocate General was Jacobs.

[168] In almost all of these first few appeals, including where the appeal was dismissed by Order (see notes passim) the Reporting Judge was Puissochet. The exceptions are Rosas in Case C-361/01P *Christina Kik v Office for Harmonisation in the Internal Market (Trade Marks and Designs) (OHIM)* [2003] ECR I-8283 (Full Court but not on a substantive law point) and Gulmann in Case C-445/02P *Glaverbel SA* [2004] ECR I-10549 (Fifth Chamber) which was dismissed by Order.

[169] Cases 383/99P *Procter & Gamble Company v Office for Harmonisation in the Internal Market (Trade Marks and Designs)* [2001] ECR I-6251 and C-191/01P *Office for Harmonisation in the Internal Market (Trade Marks and Designs) (OHIM) v Wm Wrigley Jr. Company* [2003] ECR I-12447.

were heard by a Full Court[170] and concerned the scope of the absolute grounds for refusal to register a mark which are set out in Article 7 of the Community Trade Mark Regulation.[171]

In both these cases the OHIM had refused to register the marks 'BABY-DRY' and 'DOUBLEMINT' based on the absolute grounds of refusal set out in Articles 7(1)(b) and (1)(c) of the Trade Mark Regulation which permits a refusal on the grounds that the mark is 'devoid of any distinctive character' (Article 7(1)(b)) or the mark consists 'exclusively' of descriptive or geographical language (Article 7(1)(c)). Both refusals were upheld by the First Board of Appeal at OHIM resulting in appeals to the Court of First Instance to annul the decisions of the Board. In the case of *BABY-DRY* the Court of First Instance upheld the refusal by OHIM to register under Article 7(1)(b) and (1)(c) (ie the Court agreed that the mark was exclusively descriptive and devoid of distinctive character) but annulled the decision of the Board of Appeal on the ground that the Board had been wrong to have concluded that the plea based under Article 7(3) was inadmissible.[172] In the *DOUBLEMINT* case the Court of First Instance annulled the decision of the Board of Appeal, dismissing an appeal against the refusal to register the word 'DOUBLEMINT'. The Court of First Instance considered the mark not to be exclusively descriptive. The judgments of the Court of First Instance were appealed to the European Court of Justice.[173]

The European Court of Justice annulled the Court of First Instance judgment in the *BABY-DRY* case on the ground that the Court had erred in holding that the mark had been refused correctly on the basis of Article 7(1)(c). In the *DOUBLEMINT* case the European Court of Justice also annulled the Court of First Instance judgment on the basis that the Court had erred by applying the wrong test in applying Article 7(1)(c). The test is not based on whether the mark was 'exclusively descriptive' but on whether the mark was capable of being used by other economic operators to designate a characteristic of their goods or services. Although there was a period of eighteen months between the Court of First Instance judgments, the Opinion and judgment of the European Court of Justice in *BABY-DRY* was delivered after the Court of First Instance judgment in the *DOUBLEMINT* case. Thus, when Jacobs delivered his Opinion in the *BABY-DRY* case he was aware of the Court of First Instance judgment in the *DOUBLEMINT* case delivered just over two months earlier and expressly referred to it.[174] The Court

[170] The European Court of Justice judgment in Case C-361/01P *Christina Kik v Office for Harmonisation in the Internal Market (Trade Marks and Designs)* [2003] ECR I-8283 was delivered by a Full Court before the *DOUBLEMINT* judgment but it concerned procedural rules governing the languages at OHIM. With the exception of *BABY-DRY* and *DOUBLEMINT*, Court of First Instance appeals in trade mark cases are normally decided by Chambers of the European Court of Justice.

[171] The equivalent provision in the Trade Mark Directive is Art 4.

[172] Art 7(3) allows a mark which lacks a distinctive character to be registered if it has become 'distinctive' by use.

[173] The Court of First Instance judgment was delivered before the Opinion and judgment had been delivered on the *BABY-DRY* appeal.

[174] Para 95 of the Opinion in *BABY-DRY*.

of First Instance on the other hand, did not have the benefit of the Opinion or the judgment of the European Court of Justice in the *BABY-DRY* case when they decided the *DOUBLEMINT* case. Yet the Court of First Instance took a different position on the meaning of the phrase 'not exclusively descriptive' in Article 7(1)(c). The result was that the Court of First Instance considered the mark 'BABY-DRY' to be exclusively descriptive and the mark 'DOUBLEMINT' to be *not* exclusively descriptive! Both Jacobs and the European Court of Justice took opposing positions to the Court of First Instance. Furthermore, in between the European Court of Justice judgment in the *BABY-DRY* case in 2001 and the European Court of Justice judgment in the *DOUBLEMINT* case in 2003 (almost exactly two years later), there had been an explosion of criticism of the European Court of Justice *BABY-DRY* judgment both in academic literature and in practitioner circles.[175] Furthermore, the Opinion in the *DOUBLEMINT* case is particularly striking as Jacobs directly responded to the criticisms which had been expressed of the *BABY-DRY* judgment and urged the European Court of Justice to clarify and reconcile its case-law which was duly done.

Why did the *BABY-DRY* judgment cause so much controversy? Both Advocate General Jacobs and the European Court of Justice concluded in the *BABY-DRY* case that the Court of First Instance had been wrong in its interpretation of Articles 7(1)(b) and (1)(c) since descriptiveness of words should be determined not by examining each word individually but by an assessment of the words as a whole. Article 7(1)(c) excludes registration for marks which are 'exclusively' descriptive, therefore any *perceptible* difference between the combination of the words or terms used may confer distinctiveness. In the particular case, both the Advocate General and the Court concluded that the juxtaposition of the words 'BABY-DRY' was different from normal use and sufficient to confer distinctiveness. However, the common conclusion was reached by different approaches. Jacobs's view was that the Board of Appeal failed to consider whether the consumer would regard this mark not as descriptive of a product but as a guarantee that the product was produced or manufactured by a particular undertaking.[176] The guarantee of origin function of a trade mark has always been central to his analysis in formulating his conclusions. It is submitted, however, that the Court was perhaps influenced primarily by the French and Benelux trade mark law which excludes a mark *only if* it is exclusively descriptive. The Reporting Judge was Puissochet, a French trained lawyer, and likely to approach the interpretation of the provision from his own national legal training.

Other differences in approach to the interpretation of Article 7(1)(c) can tentatively be identified. In the *Windsurfing Chiemsee*[177] case protection was being sought

[175] eg I Kilbey, 'Baby-Dry: A Victory for the Ephemera of Advertising?' (2002) European Intellectual Property Review 493.

[176] Paras 95 and 96 of the Opinion.

[177] Joined Cases C-108/97 and C-109/97 *Windsurfing Chiemsee Produktions- und Vertriebs GmbH (WSC) v Boots- und Segelzubehör Walter Huber and Franz Attenberger* [1999] ECR I-2779 (Gulmann was the Reporting Judge and Cosmas the Advocate General).

of a geographical name which has a status of its own. The Court, in interpreting the equivalent provision under the Trade Mark Directive (Article 3(1)(c)), stated that the aim of the provision was one of public interest. Jacobs, however, in the *BABY-DRY* case, adopted a different approach to the interpretation of this provision. In his Opinion he sought to determine the difference between a mark being incapable of distinguishing two sets of goods and a mark being devoid of any distinctive character.[178] For that reason Jacobs does not view Article 7(1)(c) in terms of a public interest in preventing an ordinary descriptive word being monopolised by the owner of a registered mark but simply as a provision 'to avoid the registration of descriptive brand names for which no protection could be available'[179] because it could not distinguish the two sets of goods. Jacobs commented that it was highly unlikely that a reasonable person who had never encountered the name BABY-DRY would automatically associate it with babies' nappies. Jacobs argued for a broad approach to Article 7(1)(c) and cites precedent from OHIM itself and the Court of First Instance judgment which had been recently delivered in the *DOUBLEMINT* Case![180]

However, almost exactly two years later the Opinion of Jacobs in the *DOUBLEMINT* case suggested a change of approach, likely to have been brought about by the critical manner in which the Opinion and the European Court of Justice's judgment in the *BABY-DRY* case had been received. He strongly stressed that the academic community had misunderstood the European Court of Justice judgment and gave a meticulous detailed analysis to set the record straight.

Concluding observations

It is evident from the discussion above that Jacobs became the 'specialist' Advocate General in the field of EC trade mark law. By the time trade mark law cases came before the, raising matters of interpretation in respect of the Court Community's trade mark legislation, there was a good pool of Advocates General (nine at one time) to whom cases could have been allocated. Thus one may be forgiven for reaching the conclusion that, contrary to what is often asserted, the allocation of the cases to Advocates General is not simply an exercise in balancing the workload between them.[181]

What is much more difficult is to determine with confidence the degree of influence Jacobs may have had on the European Court of Justice judges and other Advocates General, and to reach a conclusion as to the extent of the contribution of Jacobs' Opinions to the development of EC intellectual property law.

178 Interesting discussion in paras 64–74 of the Opinion.

179 Para 78 of the Opinion in *BABY-DRY*.

180 Paras 92 to 96 of the Opinion.

181 For example, K Mortelmans, 'The Court Under the Influence of its Advocates General: An Analysis of the Case Law on the Functioning of the Internal Market' (2005) Yearbook of European Law 127, 132 where he cites L Neville Brown and T Kennedy, *Brown and Jacobs The Court of Justice of the EC* (5th edn, 2000) 65.

The influence of the Opinions on the judgments

There are two major obstacles in trying to assess Jacobs' influence on the European Court of Justice judgments. The first major obstacle is the practice of the European Court of Justice of not commenting on the Opinions of the Advocates General.[182] On rare occasions when the Court did refer to Jacobs' Opinion it was only in respect of matters of relatively minor importance.[183] Generally, the references to Jacobs' Opinions in the judgments are no more than a token gesture![184] Nevertheless, the fact remains that, in all the cases on the interpretation of the Trade Mark Directive, only once did the Court not follow Jacobs' conclusions. Where the European Court of Justice departed from the conclusion reached by Jacobs in *Davidoff v Gofkid*,[185] the Court made no effort to engage with the Jacobs' reasoning or conclusions.

The second major obstacle to the assessment of the influence that Jacobs's Opinions may have had on the judgments of the Court is that, in most cases examined,[186] the Reporting Judge, that is the Judge responsible for drafting the judgment, was Judge Gulmann. Before he became an European Court of Justice Judge he was an Advocate General and he delivered Opinions in difficult intellectual property law cases such as the *IDS* and *Magill*[187] cases. In all the cases, except the *Davidoff v Gofkid*[188] case already noted above, the Court did not disagree with Jacobs's conclusion. Thus it is reasonable to assume that these two members of the European Court of Justice, Gulmann and Jacobs, held similar views as to the interpretation of Community law in the field of intellectual property law. It is inconceivable that the President of the Court would appoint Gulmann as Reporting Judge in all these trade mark cases, unless there was also broad agreement amongst the judges with his draft judgments. As to the reason why the Court did not agree with Jacobs in the *Davidoff v Gofkid* case, one can merely speculate. The case was

[182] This may be explained by the position of the Advocate General as a member of the Court. See chs 1 and 2.

[183] For example, in the Joined Cases C-427/93 *Bristol-Myers Squibb v Paranova A/S*, C-429/93 *C.H. Boehringer Sohn, Boehringer Ingelheim KG abd Boehringer Ingelheim A/S v Paranova A/S* and C-436/93 *Bayer Aktiengesellschaft and Bayer Danmark A/S v Paranova A/S* [1996] ECR I-3457 where at paras 71 and 72 of the judgment, the European Court of Justice referred to Jacobs's conclusion (para 128 of the Opinion) on the duty of national court. Another example may be found in Case C-342/97 *Lloyd Schuhfabrik Meyer & Co GmbH v Klijsen Handel BV* [1999] ECR I-3819 at para 11 of the judgment referring to paras 8 to 13 of the Opinion where the division of functions between the European Court of Justice and the national court is addressed. Jacobs urged the Court 'to be particularly rigorous in observing the proper division of functions between itself and the national courts' (para 11).

[184] In Case C-349/95 *Loendersloot v Ballantine* [1997] ECR I-6227, for example, a reference is made to the Opinion at para 16 of the judgment but on a point of no significance. It reads almost as if the Court is simply recording that the Opinion has been read!

[185] Case C-292/00 *Davidoff & Cie SA and Zino Davidoff SA v Gofkid Ltd* [2003] ECR I-389.

[186] The exception was Case C-291/00 *LTJ Diffusion SA v Sadas Vertbaudet SA* [2003] ECR I-2799.

[187] Case 9/93 *IHT Internationale Heiztechnik GmbH & Uwe Danzinger v Ideal-Standard GmbH and Wabco Standard GmbH ('Ideal Standard')* [1994] ECR I-2789 and Case C-242/91P *Radio Telefis Eirann (RTE) and Independent Television Publications (ITP) v Commission ('Magill')* [1995] ECR I-743.

[188] Case C-292/00 *Davidoff & Cie SA and Zino Davidoff SA v Gofkid Ltd* [2003] ECR I-389.

decided in a Chamber of five judges: it may be that the Reporting Judge has more influence in a larger court than in a smaller one; it may also be that on this occasion the Reporting Judge simply disagreed with the strict literal interpretation applied by Jacobs.

Although it is impossible from the Opinions and judgments examined in this chapter to determine with certainty the influence that Jacobs' Opinions may have had on the Court, some observations will be noted below.

Observations on the approach to issues

An observation that can be made without reservation is that the Jacobs' Opinions, particularly in the repackaging cases, are more pro-active than the Court's judgments. For example, Jacobs addressed fundamental issues such as what is the function of an intellectual property right before addressing the specific legal questions which had been raised in the case. Thus, an intellectual property lawyer will immediately empathize with the Jacobs approach since it is one that such a lawyer would recognize. Jacobs approached the questions raised in each case from an intellectual property law rather than from an EC law point of view. Moreover, once Jacobs focused on the guarantee of origin as the primary function of a trade mark under EC law, he defended that conclusion rigorously in subsequent Opinions,[189] demonstrating full awareness of other views which were in the public domain. Moreover, he participated in the debate contending that a quality function is inherent in the concept of the guarantee of origin function.

Although in most cases Jacobs and the European Court of Justice reached the same conclusion on the consequences, the reasoning on specific issues was not always identical. For example, in the cases of *Tournier* and *Lucazeau*[190] Jacobs concluded that the refusal to license the intellectual property right was a direct consequence of the network of reciprocal representation agreements that operated in this market. The European Court of Justice, however, ruled that the agreements in themselves were not restrictive of competition so it was for the national court to decide whether there was evidence of a concerted practice.[191]

Jacobs' approach tended always to come from a market perspective whilst the European Court of Justice took the owner of the trade mark rights as the starting point. An illustrative example can be given in the context of identifying a 'disguised restriction' to trade between Member States in the repackaging cases. In the *Bristol-Myers Squibb*[192] case Jacobs argued that once the goods are marketed, the trade mark owner has no right to prevent parallel imports by opposing the repackaging

[189] For example in Case C-337/95 *Parfums Christian Dior SA and Parfums Christian Dior BV v Evora BV* [1997] ECR I-6013, paras 41 and 42 of the Opinion.

[190] Case 395/87 *Ministère public v Jean-Louis Tournier* [1989] ECR 2521 and Joined Cases 110/88, 241/88 and 242/88 *François Lucazeau and ors v Société des Auteurs, Compositeurs et Editeurs de Musique (SACEM)* [1989] ECR 2811.

[191] See text above at p 132 *BABY-DRY* is another example of a case where a different approach to interpretation can be identified even though there was an agreed conclusion p 156 above.

[192] Joined Cases C-427/93, C-429/93 and C-436/93 [1996] ECR I-3457.

of the goods in question. The owner is only able to prevent the repackaging if the essential function of the trade mark is endangered. He then proceeds to examine the *Hoffmann-La Roche* conditions to establish whether the function has been endangered by the repackaging. The European Court of Justice, however, reached a similar outcome but started from the positive right of the trade mark owner to prevent interference with the trade-marked product by way of repackaging or re-labelling. If the *Hoffmann-La Roche* conditions apply, then the right of the trade mark owner will be a 'disguised restriction' on trade between Member States if allowed to be exercised.[193]

Methods of interpretation

The approach to interpretation also showed some differences. Jacobs adopted a common-law approach to the interpretation of secondary legislation, applying a strict literal interpretation to the text. An example of this can be found in the Opinion he delivered in the *Davidoff v Gofkid* case where he interpreted Article 5(2) of the Trade Mark Directive strictly. The Court chose a more radical approach in interpreting the provision and decided that, irrespective of the unambiguous wording, it would be anomalous not to require the owner of a trade mark with a reputation to prove likelihood of confusion where the goods or services are dissimilar (as provided by Article 5(2) of the Trade Mark Directive) but to require such proof where the goods or services were similar (Article 5(1) of the Trade Mark Directive). The Court therefore ruled that Article 5(2) should be interpreted 'in the light of the overall scheme and objectives of the system of which it is a part'. The Court applied a teleological method of interpretation and ruled that where the situation concerns a mark with a reputation there is no need for the owner to proved likelihood of confusion.[194]

Examples in favour and against the proposition that Jacobs' Opinions had influence on the Court

Examples can be found in the Opinions and judgments which support a view that Jacobs' Opinions influenced the Court. However the evidence is inconclusive as it is evenly balanced by examples which support an opposite view.

An illustrative example in favour of the existence of some influence on the Court can be found in the *Bristol-Myers Squibb* judgment where the Court partially accepted[195] a suggestion which Jacobs had proposed in his Opinion. Jacobs had proposed that the *Hoffmann-La Roche's* conditions be refined so that where repackaging of goods takes place, one of the conditions that the re-packager must fulfil is to supply the owner of the trade-marked goods with a specimen of the repackaged goods. The Court, however, stated that such a specimen should be supplied 'on demand' from the trade mark owner. Unlike Jacobs' suggestion the Court placed the burden on the trade-mark owner to make the request.

[193] See text above, p 135, 'Disguised restriction'.

[194] Case C-292/00 *Davidoff & Cie SA and Zino Davidoff SA v Gofkid Ltd* [2003] ECR I-389, para 24 of the judgment.

[195] Para 79 of the judgment and n 69 and text above.

Furthermore, in this same judgment (*Bristol-Myers Squibb*) the Court added a further condition to the *Hoffmann-La Roche* criteria, namely that the quality and the manner in which the repackaging is carried out by the importer must not be likely to damage the reputation of the trade mark and of its owner. There is no evidence that this significant addition to the *Hoffmann-La Roche* conditions originated with Jacobs. In fact, although Jacobs referred in his Opinion to the possibility of shabby packaging affecting the reputation of the mark, he did not advise the Court that it should be added as a further requirement.[196] On the other hand, the mere mentioning of this possible harm to the reputation of the mark may have prompted the Court!

Occasionally, there is also a similarity of wording in both the Opinion and the judgment which may suggest a more firm acceptance of Jacobs' conclusions. For example, in the *Upjohn* judgment[197] the expression 'effective access' is used by the European Court of Justice which is identical to Jacobs' own choice of wording.[198] Another example is to be found in the *Silhouette* judgment[199] where the wording is identical to that of the Opinion in respect of the reasons for not allowing Member States a choice as to whether to adopt international exhaustion of trade mark rights.[200]

Finally the judgment in the *HAG II*[201] case has to be considered in the context of this discussion. This was the first judgment where the European Court of Justice expressly overruled an earlier judgment. Indeed the Opinion Jacobs delivered in the *HAG II* case was strongly worded and no doubt it was welcomed by the Court. However, given other factors, such as the overwhelming criticism of the *HAG I* judgment and a better understanding of the commercial value of trade marks, it is unlikely that the overruling of the earlier judgment can be directly attributed to Jacobs.

The degree of influence of Jacobs' Opinions on the Opinions of other Advocates General

What about the influence of the Jacobs' Opinions on the other Advocates General? Advocates General rarely comment or refer to Opinions of their colleagues, but

[196] See n 66 and text above.

[197] C-379/97 *Pharmacia & Upjohn SA v Paranova A/S* [1999] ECR I-6927.

[198] Ibid, para 43 of the ruling and para 54 of the Opinion. Also, in *General Motors*, paras 35 and 36 of the Opinion, Jacobs carries out a comparison of the various language texts of the Directive in respect of the word 'reputation'. The wording used by Jacobs is duplicated in paras 20 to 22 of the judgment. Similarly the factors listed for the assessment of a reputation which Jacobs sets out in para 41 of the Opinion is adopted substantially by the European Court of Justice, para 27 of the judgment. Cf *Tournier* and *Lucazeau*, in the context of the application of Art 82 EC to the level of royalty that was being demanded by the intellectual property owner, where Jacobs found the level to be 'disproportionate' whilst the European Court of Justice similarly concluded that the level could not be 'justified'.

[199] Case C-355/96 *Silhouette International Schmied GmbH & Co. KG v Hartlauer Handelsgesellschaft mbH* [1998] ECR I 4799.

[200] See n 98 and above text.

[201] Case C-10/89 *HAG II* [1990] ECR I-3711, see p 140–142.

examples can be found where such references have been made.[202] More recently, Advocates General Stix-Hackl and Ruiz-Jarabo Colomer, in particular, have referred to Opinions delivered by Jacobs when considering similar legal questions in cases raising issues involving EC intellectual property law. For example, in the *Davidoff*[203] and *Van Doren*[204] cases, Stix-Hackl[205] was clearly influenced by Jacobs' earlier Opinions.

The Opinion of Advocate General Ruiz-Jarabo Colomer in the *Arsenal*[206] case is striking as to the number of references he makes to Jacobs' Opinions in the cases of *Holterhoff*, *LTJ Diffusion* and *Davidoff v Gofkid*. For example, Ruiz-Jarabo Colomer relied[207] on Jacobs' similar views expressed in the Opinion he delivered in the *Holterhoff*[208] case to support his own view that under Article 5(1) of the Trade Mark Directive the owner may object to the use of his mark by a third party in the course of trade to distinguish identical or similar goods since this would be the use of the trade mark as such. He also referred with approval to Jacobs' Opinions in the *LTJ Diffusion*[209] and in *Davidoff v Gofkid*[210] cases. Although in the latter case Ruiz-Jarabo Colomer referred to the Opinion with approval where, in respect of Article 5(2), Jacobs had stated the aim of the provision is to safeguard the right of the owner of the distinctive sign to preserve goodwill by protecting the sign against unfair competition,[211] he did not agree with Jacobs' conclusion in respect of the latter's view that Article 5(2) applies only when the goods are *not* similar and so where the goods are similar a mark, even with a high reputation, can only be protected if there is the likelihood of confusion.[212]

Contribution to the development of EC intellectual property law

Jacobs delivered a number of Opinions on the interpretation of EC Treaty provisions on the exercise of intellectual property rights but his more marked contribution to the development of EC intellectual property law is, undoubtedly, to be

[202] K Mortelmans (n 181 above) at 164, mentions as a rare example Gulmann's Opinion in Case C-2/92 *Bostock* [1994] ECR I-955, para 31, where Gulmann quoted Jacobs' Opinion in Case C-168/91 *Christos Konstantinidis v Stadt Altensteig-Standesamt and Landratsamt Calw-Ordnungsamt* [1993] ECR I-1191 with disapproval, stating that Jacobs' views were 'too far reaching'.

[203] Joined cases C-414/99 to C-416/99 *Zino Davidoff SA v A&G Imports Ltd* and *Levi Strauss & Co and ors v Tesco Stores Ltd and ors* [2001] ECR I-8691.

[204] Case C-244/00 *Van Doren + Q. GmbH v Lifestyle Sports & Sportswear Handelgesellschaft GmbH & Michael Orth* [2003] ECR I-3051.

[205] In both cases the Reporting Judge was Gulmann.

[206] Case C-206/01 *Arsenal Football Club plc v Matthew Reed* [2002] ECR I-10273.

[207] At para 40 of Ruiz-Jarabo Colomer's Opinion.

[208] Case C-2/00 *Michael Holterhoff v Ulrich Freiesleben* [2002] ECR I-4187 at para 37 of Jacobs' Opinion.

[209] Paras 19 and 51 of Ruiz-Jarabo Colomer's Opinion where he cited para 35 et seq. of Jacobs' Opinion in Case C-291/00 *LTJ Diffusion SA v Sadas Vertbaudet SA* [2003] ECR I-2799.

[210] Para 22 of the Opinion referring to Case C-292/00 *Davidoff v Gofkid* at para 46 of Jacobs' Opinion. A further reference, at para 24 of Ruiz-Jarabo Colomer's Opinion, is made to para 66 of Jacobs' Opinion.

[211] Para 24 of Ruiz-Jarabo Colomer's Opinion referring to para 66 of Jacobs' Opinion in *Davidoff v Gofkid.*

[212] Para 33 of Ruiz-Jarabo Colomer's Opinion.

found in the Opinions he delivered on the interpretation of the Community's trade mark legislation.

EC Treaty provisions

Jacobs' contribution to the scope and nature of the EC Treaty provisions on the exercise of intellectual property rights has to be assessed in the context that, by the time he became Advocate General, the basic principles and concepts in this area of Community law had already been determined. Above, a summary has been provided of the various European Court of Justice judgments prior to his appointment which reconciled the EC Treaty provisions on the free movement of goods and competition rules with the national law of the Member States under which intellectual property rights are granted. Concepts such as the 'existence' and 'exercise' dichotomy, the 'specific-subject matter' of an intellectual property right and the 'exhaustion of rights' doctrine had already been created and defined by European Court of Justice case-law. Thus, Jacobs' contribution is principally on specific issues such as the repacking/re-branding of trade marked products, the meaning of the common origin doctrine, the scope of the Community's exhaustion of rights doctrine and the interpretation of provisions in the Community's trade mark legislation.

For example, the Opinions Jacobs delivered in the repackaging/re-branding cases[213] were mainly concerned with summarizing the Community legal framework and setting out the relevant European Court of Justice case-law in a coherent manner.[214] The best example of this is to be found in the Opinion he delivered in the *Upjohn*[215] case. The European Court of Justice judgments in the repackaging/re-branding cases (*Hoffmann La Roche, American Home Products, Bristol-Myers Squibb* and *Loendersloot*) were all preliminary references. This means that in each judgment the European Court of Justice ruled on narrow questions of Community law. The questions were formulated by the national courts and in the context of the factual situation of each individual case. Unsurprisingly in the circumstances, some confusion resulted from the European Court of Justice's judgments. For example, there was confusion as to whether the tests set out in the repackaging cases (*Hoffmann La-Roche* and *Bristol-Myers Squibb*) to establish whether Community law prevented trade mark owners from exercising their trade mark rights applied equally to re-branding situations. The judgments in the re-branding cases (*American Home Products* and *Loendersloot*) were not clear on this point. Jacobs'

[213] See p 132 et seq. above.

[214] eg paras 9 to 54 of the Opinion in Cases C-443/99 *Merck, Sharp & Dohme GmbH v Paranova Pharmazeutika Handels GmbH* [2002] ECR I-3703 and C-143/00 *Boehringer Ingelheim KG, Boehringer Ingelheim Pharma KG, Glaxo Group Ltd, The Wellcome Foundation Ltd, SmithKline Beecham plc, Beecham Group plc, SmithKline & French Laboratories Ltd and Eli Lilly and Co v Swingward Ltd and Dowelhurst Ltd* [2002] ECR I-3759 and paras 39–48 of the Opinion in *Bristol-Myers Squibb* where Jacobs provided an excellent, clear, and authoritative summary.

[215] C-379/97 *Pharmacia & Upjohn SA v Paranova A/S* [1999] ECR I-6927, paras 21–26 of the Opinion.

Opinion in *Upjohn* analysed in depth the relevant judgments and reconciled them, reaching the conclusion that the case-law supported an objective test to be applied in both situations.

Trade mark legislation

As far as the interpretation of the Trade Mark Directive was concerned there were two main questions of interpretation which determined the direction of the EC trade mark law. The first was resolved in the *Sabel* judgment[216] where the Court rejected the Benelux precedent as to the meaning of the expression 'likelihood of confusion including likelihood of association' in Article 4(1)(b) of the Trade Mark Directive. The Court adopted a common law position and ruled that likelihood of association was not an alternative criterion to likelihood of confusion. This judgment raises a pertinent question as to whether a different conclusion might have been reached by the Court if the Advocate General had not had his legal training in a common law system.

The second question was decided in the *Silhouette* judgment[217] where the Court rejected international exhaustion of rights as a principle of EC law. The basic question was whether the well-established principle of exhaustion of trade mark rights should apply when the goods are first marketed outside the EEA? In reality the Court was being asked to determine a question of policy not of law. The function of the Opinion in this case was to guide the Court to the best interests of the Community as a whole and not merely the consumer. Jacobs' strict literal interpretation was no doubt welcomed by a Court that perceives its role as protecting the internal market not furthering a free global market. Furthermore, given that the provision in the Trade Mark Directive was silent on the issue the matter had to be resolved by reference to the EC Treaty as a whole.

Given that there were already European Court of Justice judgments which demonstrated that concepts of Community law were created and developed for the achievement of the common market not a global free market,[218] the Court's judgment was not a surprise and therefore, once again, there is no evidence of direct influence of the Opinion.

[216] Case C-251/95 *SABEL BV v Puma AG* [1997] ECR I-6191.

[217] Case C-355/96 *Silhouette International Schmied GmbH & Co. KG v Hartlauer Handelsgesellschaft mbH* [1998] ECR I-4799.

[218] Case 51/75 *EMI Records Ltd v CBS UK Ltd* [1976] ECR 811 where the European Court of Justice ruled that the owner of a trade mark registered in all of the Member States could exercise his rights under the national laws of the Member States to prevent goods with the same trade mark from being imported into the Community from the USA. The European and the US registered trade marks had a common origin. This judgment was delivered less than two years after the judgment in *HAG I* which decided that where there was a common origin of two trade marks, the owners were unable to exercise their rights under national law. Another example is Case 270/80 *Polydor Ltd & RSO Records Inc v Harlequin Record Shops Ltd & Simons Records Ltd* [1982] ECR 329 where the European Court of Justice interpreted differently a provision in an Association Agreement with Portugal which was identical to Article 28 EC. The primary justification for the judgment was that the Association Agreement with Portugal had a different goal from the EC Treaty.

It is highly likely that the principles enunciated by the European Court of Justice in relation to packaging, exhaustion of rights and the interpretation of the provisions of the Trade Mark Directive are very much the product of the Jacobs/Gulmann partnership. It would, however, be unwise, without clearer evidence, to attempt to apportion credit to either individual. Not surprisingly, given that the views expressed in the Opinions, unlike the collegiate European Court of Justice judgment, are solely the views of an identified member of the Court, Jacobs' Opinions have had a greater impact outside the Court, particularly in academic circles. Thus, it would be churlish not to recognize the important contribution of Jacobs to a consistent and coherent development of the Community's legal order in the field of intellectual property rights.

7

Advocate General Jean-Pierre Warner and EC competition law

Introduction

Jean-Pierre Warner was appointed Advocate General in January 1973 on the occasion of the first enlargement of the European Economic Community (EEC) with the accession of Denmark, Ireland and the United Kingdom. Warner was the first Advocate General trained in a common law jurisdiction. He delivered over 200 Opinions during his eight years in office. Warner was at the European Court of Justice during the 1970s, a period noted for the Court's alleged activism[1] and for the stagnation of the EEC legislative process. He retired from the European Court of Justice in February 1981, a year after the accession of Greece.

In his obituary published in *The Times* on 23 February 2005, it was stated '[B]y patiently anglicizing some of the Court's procedures he laid the foundations of a bridge between the common law and the civil law traditions'. Indeed Warner was responsible for translating the European Court of Justice's rules of procedure into comprehensible English! However, his most visible contribution to the Court's procedure was in relation to oral hearings which became more useful by virtue of Warner's practice of questioning the submissions of the lawyers presenting the cases on behalf of the various parties and interveners.[2] This was probably inevitable, given that he came to the European Court of Justice straight from practice at the English Bar where there is an entrenched culture of dialogue between the advocates and the judges. In addition, although the practice of citing the European Court of Justice's judgments by Advocates General was not unknown by 1973, Warner, coming from a common law system where the doctrine of binding precedent was well established, had a significant influence in having

[1] H Rasmussen, *On Law and Policy in the European Court of Justice* (1986).

[2] eg Case 61/80 *Cooperatieve Stremsel-en Kleurselfabriek v Commission* [1981] ECR 851, where Warner stated that the parties during the oral procedure 'in answer to a question of mine, candidly accepted that the function of the fine was to act as a hindrance to resignation' (875) by the members from this co-operative which produced almost 100 per cent of the animal rennet and colouring agents for cheese in The Netherlands. This admission was useful as it confirmed to him that the Commission had been right in its conclusion that this obligation was an anti-competitive restriction.

earlier decisions of the Europen Court of Justice being treated as guiding principles by regularly citing them as authority for his own conclusions.

During his period in office he delivered most of his Opinions in those fields of Community law that defined the 1970s: namely, agriculture, migrant workers, staff cases, free movement of goods, and competition law. The Opinions on these five areas accounted for over 75 per cent of the total Opinions he delivered.

However, in this chapter only the Opinions he delivered in the area of competition law will be examined. EC competition law is rather special in the sense that it was created and developed without having to adjust to existing laws and practices in the Member States.[3] EC competition rules are laid down in the EC Treaty and supplemented by secondary legislation and judgments from the European Court of Justice and from the Court of First Instance. They have been interpreted and developed according to the general EC Treaty objective of establishing a common market.[4]

Procedural rules to implement the EC Treaty provisions dealing with anticompetitive agreements and conduct of undertakings (Articles 81 and 82 EC) were adopted in Regulation 17/62.[5] The Commission became the competition authority for the EC (then known as EEC) and was granted wide-ranging powers to enforce these rules. In particular, the Commission was empowered to take decisions to prohibit or exempt anticompetitive agreements and to prohibit abusive conduct of dominant undertakings as well as to impose substantial fines. These decisions directly affect private parties though they are subject to judicial review by the European Court of Justice. How would a common law practitioner view the processes by which the Commission reached these administrative decisions, some of which impose on private parties extensive fines or even prohibit their business activities?

By the time Warner arrived at the Court some significant European Court of Justice rulings on competition law had already been delivered[6] but EC competition law and practice was still at an embryonic stage. Indeed, very few cases had come before the Court challenging the powers and practices of the Commission as a competition authority. It is primarily the Opinions of Warner in cases where undertakings sought annulment of Commission competition decisions that will be examined in this chapter to identify his contribution to EC competition law and procedure.

This chapter will be structured as follows: first an introductory background will briefly summarize the state of play in 1973 as far as the EC competition rules and

[3] In 1973, Germany and the UK were the only Member States with national competition legislation (viz: Gesetz gegen Wettbewerbsbeschränkungen 1957 and the Restrictive Trade Practices Act 1956) regulating the market behaviour of natural and legal persons.

[4] In the earlier years in the history of the common market, the emphasis was on creating an integrated market but now the objective has shifted to achieving a competitive internal market.

[5] First regulation implementing Arts [81 and 82] of the Treaty [1959–62] OJ Spec Ed 87, replaced by Regulation 1/2003 [2003] OJ L1/1.

[6] For example, Joined Cases 56 and 58/64 *Établissements Consten S.à.R.L. and Grundig-Verkaufs-GmbH v Commission* [1966] ECR 299; Case, 56/65 *Société La Technique Minière v Maschinenbau*

procedure were concerned; this will be followed by an examination of the Opinions delivered by Warner which concerned the extent of the Commission's powers to adopt definitive and interim measures to terminate infringements and also the Opinions he delivered in cases which raised issues of procedural safeguards for the undertakings under investigation; and finally the Opinions delivered by Warner on issues of substance in respect of Articles 81 and 82 EC will be also be considered. The chapter will conclude with some observations.

Contextual background

The EC competition rules comprise rules concerning the behaviour of undertakings (Articles 81 and 82 EC)[7] as well as rules governing the behaviour of the Member States in granting State aids to their own undertakings (Articles 87 and 88 EC).[8] In practice, Articles 81 and 82 EC are normally referred to as 'the EC competition rules' whilst Articles 87 and 88 EC are known as 'the EC State aid rules'. Moreover, whilst secondary legislation was speedily adopted to confer on the Commission powers to implement the EC competition rules,[9] only lately has secondary legislation been adopted in respect of the enforcement of the State aid rules.[10]

The first procedural legislative measure, Regulation 17/62, conferred on the European Commission, as a competition authority, effective powers for investigating and adopting decisions prohibiting certain practices and conduct.[11] Powers were also granted to the Commission to impose fines up to 10 per cent of the annual turnover of the undertakings concerned.[12] In the same Regulation the Commission was also granted exclusive competence to exempt notified anti-competitive agreements or concerted practices from the prohibition of Article 81 EC Treaty.[13]

The European Court of Justice in *Consten and Grundig v Commission*[14] ruled that Article 81 EC applies to vertical agreements as well as horizontal agreements. One of the consequences of that ruling was that a large number of distribution agreements

Ulm GmbH [1966] ECR 234; and 41/69 *ACF Chemiefarma NV v Commission (Quinine cartel)* [1970] ECR 661.

[7] See for details: A Jones and B Sufrin, *EC Competition Law: Text, Cases and Materials* (2nd edn, 2004); M Furse, *Competition Law of the EC and UK* (4th edn, 2004); R Whish, *Competition Law* (5th edn, 2003); A Albors-Llorens, *EC Competition Law and Policy* (2002); R Lane, *EC Competition Law* (2000).

[8] See for details: C Quigley and A Collins, *EC State Aid Law and Policy* (2003) and A Biondi, P Eeckhout and J Flynn (eds), *The Law of State Aid in the EU* (2004).

[9] Regulation 17/62 [1959–62] OJ Spec Ed 87; Regulation 99/63 on the hearings provided for in Art 19(1) and (2) of Council Regulation No. 17 [1963–64] OJ Spec Ed 47; and Regulation 67/67 on the application of Art 81 (3) of the Treaty to certain categories of exclusive dealing agreements [1967] OJ Spec Ed 10.

[10] Regulation 659/1999 laying down detailed rules for the application of Art 88 of the EC Treaty [1999] OJ L83/1 and Regulation 794/2004, implementing Council Regulation (EC) No. 659/1999 laying down detailed rules for the application of Article 88 of the EC Treaty [2004] OJ L140/1.

[11] Arts 3, 11 and 14 of Reg 17/62.

[12] Ibid, Art 15.

[13] Ibid, Art 9(1). The Commission's exclusive competence ended with the adoption of Regulation 1/2003 [2003] OJ L1/1.

[14] Joined Cases 56 and 58/64 [1966] ECR 299.

were immediately notified to the Commission under the provisions of Regulation 17/62 seeking either a negative clearance or an exemption from the prohibition of Article 81(1).[15] Soon after this judgment the first block exemption regulation, Regulation 67/67[16] was adopted to reduce the Commission's administrative burden. The Regulation listed the forbidden, permissible and exempted typical clauses found in vertical agreements. If exclusive distribution and exclusive purchasing agreements were drafted within the terms of the block exemption regulation then they were automatically deemed to be exempted from prohibition and protected from fines. The block exemption regulations became particularly valuable once the European Court of Justice ruled in *BRT v SABAM*[17] that Articles 81(1) and (2) EC as well as Article 82 were directly applicable and therefore enforceable by private parties before national courts. Contracting parties felt safer if their distribution agreements were drafted in accordance with the terms set out in a block exemption regulation.

Meanwhile parties to whom the Commission addressed infringement decisions sought relief from the European Court of Justice by seeking annulment of the decision on the grounds listed in Article 230 EC.[18] Thus a number of challenges to Commission competition decisions came before the European Court of Justice during the 1970s, testing the extent of the powers of the Commission under Regulation 17/62. The examination that follows will focus first on the Opinions Warner delivered regarding the Commission's powers to adopt definitive and interim measures (*Commercial Solvents*,[19] *BMW Belgium*[20] and *Camera Care*[21]) and its powers during competition investigations (*Transocean Marine*,[22] *National Panasonic*[23] and *Distillers*[24]).

Commission's powers to adopt definitive and interim measures

The first relevant Warner Opinion in this area was the one he delivered in the *Commercial Solvents*[25] case where the power of the Commission to impose specific obligations on undertakings in order to remedy their anti-competitive behaviour

[15] For information on the application of Art 81(1) to vertical agreements, see A Jones and B Sufrin, *EC Competition Law* (2004), chap 9.

[16] [1967] OJ Spec Ed 10.

[17] Case 127/73 [1974] ECR 51.

[18] The grounds for annulment listed in Art 230 are: 'lack of competence, infringement of an essential procedural requirement, infringement of this Treaty or of any rule of law relating to its application, or misuse of powers'. The Single European Act 1986 created the Court of First Instance (in operation from October 1989) with competence to hear actions brought by undertakings seeking annulment of Commission competition decisions.

[19] Joined Cases 6 and 7/73 *Instituto Chemioterapico Italiano SpA and Commercial Solvents Corp v Commission* [1974] ECR 223.

[20] Joined Cases 32/78 and 36 to 82/78 *BMW Belgium v Commission* [1979] ECR 2435.

[21] Case 792/79R *Camera Care Ltd v Commission* [1980] ECR 119.

[22] Case 17/74 *Transocean Marine Paint Association v Commission* [1974] ECR 1063.

[23] Case 136/79 *National Panasonic (UK) Ltd v Commission* [1980] ECR 2033.

[24] Case 30/78 *Distillers Co Ltd v Commission* [1980] ECR 2229.

[25] Joined Cases 6 and 7/73 *Instituto Chemioterapico Italiano SpA and Commercial Solvents Corp v Commission* [1974] ECR 223.

was challenged.[26] The Commission concluded that the refusal of an Italian subsidiary of an American corporation, Commercial Solvents, to supply Zoja, an Italian undertaking, with the raw material for which it held a monopoly, was an abuse of their dominant position in the ethambutol market. In its decision the Commission not only ordered Commercial Solvents to supply Zoja with specified quantities of the raw material but also to submit proposals to the Commission for the on-going supply to Zoja. One of the central issues for the European Court of Justice to determine was whether the Commission had the power to impose specific obligations on the undertakings concerned.

The Commission's powers to put an end to infringements of the competition rules were then set out in Article 3 of Regulation 17/62[27] which provided as follows:

(1) Where the Commission, upon application or upon its own initiative, finds that there is infringement of Article [81] or Article [82] of the Treaty, it may by decision require the undertakings or associations of undertakings concerned to bring such infringements to an end.
(2) Without prejudice to the other provisions of this Regulation, the Commission may, before taking a decision under paragraph 1, address to the undertaking or associations of undertakings concerned recommendations for termination of the infringement.

The argument presented by Commercial Solvents was that the Commission had power only to take a decision ordering them to stop the infringement and not to dictate the manner in which that result should be achieved. In order to place the argument in context, it should be noted that the Commission's competition decisions, reviewed by the European Court of Justice before the judgment in the *Commercial Solvents* case, were concerned with the prohibition of Article 81(1) EC Treaty which applies to contractual arrangements or concerted practices. Most courts are reluctant to instruct parties on how to organize their contractual relationships so as to ensure that they are compatible with the law. Regulation 17/62 did not impose an obligation on the parties to notify restrictive agreements but merely offered incentives to do so.[28] In accordance with Article 9 of Regulation 17/62, notified agreements falling within the prohibition of Article 81(1) EC Treaty could be considered by the Commission for exemption under Article 81(3) EC Treaty. Furthermore, such agreements were protected from fines from the date of notification until the final Commission decision was taken. In dealing with infringements of Article 81(1) EC, the Commission has certain powers at its disposal such as imposing a fine or withdrawing the benefit of a block exemption regulation. Furthermore, if the arrangement was incompatible with the prohibition of Article 81(1), and had not been notified, Article 81(2) would apply and the

[26] This was also one of the first Opinions that Warner delivered in a case not concerned with agricultural or staff matters.

[27] The corresponding enhanced provision is now set out in Art 7(1) of Regulation 1/2003 [2003] L1/1.

[28] The notification procedure has now been abolished by Regulation 1/2003. The Commission, the national competition authorities and the national courts are now all empowered to apply the whole of Art 81 EC.

agreement would be declared void. Such solutions are not available for breaches of Article 82 EC Treaty.

In the *Commercial Solvents* case, Warner took a common sense approach and analysed Article 3 of Regulation 17/62 as a whole concluding that since Article 3(3) required specific recommendations it would be 'odd indeed if specific recommendations made under paragraph 3 could not be followed up, where necessary, with specific requirements imposed under paragraph 1'.[29] He also noted that, in his view, it would be unfair to the party concerned to be instructed to do something positive without specifying what that should be. He expressly relied on English case-law to support this interpretation[30] which was readily supported by the European Court of Justice.[31]

The European Court of Justice however did not agree with Warner's conclusion that the Commission had exercised its power improperly in not limiting the amount of raw material, which Commercial Solvents was required to supply to Zoja, to the amount they needed for intra-Community trade. Only 10 per cent of Zoja's sales were within the common market. During the proceedings the Commission had submitted that a significant decrease in Zoja's turnover would have a serious impact in its competitiveness. Warner acknowledged the argument but, given that the Commission had not provided the evidence in coming to its decision, he considered the Decision vitiated. The European Court of Justice, however, did not follow Warner on this point and concluded that there was sufficient reasoning in the decision, and that the Commission was justified in taking these necessary measures, given that Commercial Solvents' conduct was aimed at eliminating one of the principal competitors in the common market.

In the Opinion Warner gave a clear indication that he was concerned to ensure that the Commission, as a competition authority, acted promptly and fairly. He expressly criticized the fact that the Commission took over a year to investigate the case and to issue a Statement of Objections[32] but only gave the undertakings concerned 15 days to respond. He stated '[N]onetheless the contrast between the time taken by the Commission to perform its tasks and the time it allowed CSC and ICI to prepare their cases is glaring'.[33] He considered the 15 days 'patently unreasonable' and therefore had no hesitation in concluding that the Commission had adopted an improper procedure. In his view, the Commission should be penalized. He recommended to the Court that the Commission should be ordered to pay the applicants' costs and the fine should be annulled. The Court, however, was only prepared to halve the fine to take into account the Commission's delay in the investigation of the complaint.

29 Opinion in Joined Cases 6 and 7/73 [1974] ECR 223, 272.

30 *Morris v Redland Bricks Ltd* [1970] AC 652, cited ibid, 272.

31 Joined Cases 6 and 7/73 [1974] ECR 223, paras 45 and 46 of the judgment.

32 This is a stage in the Commission's investigation where the evidence against the undertaking under investigation is set out. The undertakings, to whom the Statement of Objections is addressed, have normally two months to reply.

33 Opinion in Joined Cases 6 and 7/73 [1974] ECR 223, 274.

The level of the fines was also a matter on which Warner had an opportunity to express his views when he delivered his Opinion in the *BMW Belgium* case.[34] This was the first case where the Commission imposed a fine not only on the dominant partner, the undertaking granting the dealership, but also on the dealers themselves. The Commission concluded that BMW Belgium's standard distribution agreement and subsequent circulars were incompatible with Article 81(1) EC.

As far as fines are concerned the Commission, upon a finding that an infringement of the competition rules has taken place, has been granted powers to fine the undertakings concerned up to 10 per cent of their annual turnover.[35] In calculating the fine the Commission is required to take into account the gravity and duration of the infringement. In an earlier case, *Miller International*, Warner had proposed a scale of levels of fines to reflect various degrees of the gravity of the infringement.[36] These ranged from an intentional infringement of the gravest kind to a negligent infringement of the most trivial kind.[37]

In the *BMW Belgium* case the point of law at issue was whether the level of fines imposed by the Commission was appropriate. BMW had drafted the circulars sent to their dealers which were found by the Commission to contain clauses incompatible with Article 81(1) EC. The circulars had also been signed by the Belgian Dealers' Advisory Committee which helped to strengthen the authority of the content of the circulars. The Commission considered that the level of the fines imposed reflected the fact that these parties had *intentionally* behaved in an anti-competitive manner.

On the question of what constitutes intentional infringement, Warner considered an earlier Opinion on the point cited by the parties. In the *General Motors* case Advocate General Mayras had discussed the meaning of intentional and negligent infringement.[38] Warner considered Mayras' Opinion not aimed at supplying an exhaustive definition of the two concepts as urged by the parties' submissions in the *BMW Belgium* case, but specific to the facts of the case that Mayras was examining. In this context Warner made the observation that '[a]t all events [Mayras'] Opinion has now been overtaken by the judgment of the Court in the *Miller International* case'.[39] Thus, Warner had no hesitation in transposing to the Community's legal order the common law practice that a later judgment overrules an earlier contrary one. There is no consideration in the Opinion as to whether this precedent may not be so appropriate for a developing new legal order.

[34] Joined Cases 32/78 and 36 to 82/78 *BMW Belgium v Commission* [1979] ECR 2435.

[35] Art 15(2) of Regulation 17/62 (now Art 23(2) of Regulation 1/2003).

[36] Case 19/77 *Miller International Schallplatten GmbH v Commission* [1978] ECR 131, 161. In this case the Commission found that a prohibition on the export of records, tapes and cassettes inserted by Miller International in an exclusive dealing agreement and in its terms and conditions of sale, constituted an infringement of Art 81(1) EC and imposed a fine.

[37] In its judgment in the *Miller International* case the European Court of Justice made no comment on Warner's proposed scale of fines.

[38] Case 26/75 *General Motors Continental NV v Commission* [1975] ECR 1367, 1388–90.

[39] Opinion in Joined Cases 32/78 and 36 to 82/78 *BMW Belgium v Commission* [1979] ECR 2435, 2494.

In the case of *Miller International* the applicant had claimed that it did not have the intention to infringe Article 81(1) EC Treaty by prohibiting exports. The European Court of Justice, however, stated that where undertakings accept obligations whose object is to restrict competition, they must be held to have intentionally committed an act prohibited by the Treaty. The parties cannot argue that they were unaware of the infringement. Intentional infringement therefore means intent to restrict competition, not an intention to infringe the EC competition rules.[40]

Warner accepted the judgment in the *Miller International* case as the correct authoritative precedent and concluded that the fines imposed on BMW Belgium and on the members of the Belgium Dealers' Advisory Committee, were appropriate. This conclusion was confirmed by the European Court of Justice.

Other interesting views expressed by Warner in the *BMW Belgium* case include his different opinion from Mayras in respect of the powers of the European Court of Justice. It was submitted, relying on Mayras' Opinion in the *General Motors* case, that where the Commission fined an undertaking on the basis of intentional infringement and the Court found the infringement to have been negligent rather than intentional, the latter's powers were confined to cancelling the fine. Mayras had expressed the view that the Court, in these circumstances, did not have competence to reduce the fine. Warner was of a different view and had no hesitation in concluding that the powers of the European Court of Justice under Article 17 of Regulation 17/62 were wide and enabled the Court to do whatever 'justice requires'.[41] This is not at all a surprising position for Warner to take given his training in a legal system where the courts have very wide powers and are expected to apply legal and equitable principles of justice. This experience may also account for Warner's view as expressed in the *Miller International* Opinion that the lack or wrong advice obtained from a legal practitioner should be a mitigating factor in determining the amount of fine to impose.[42] The European Court of Justice, however, rejected this conclusion.[43] Wrong legal advice was also pleaded as a mitigating factor in the *BMW Belgium* case giving Warner an opportunity to acknowledge the clear ruling of the European Court of Justice on this matter in the *Miller International* case.

[40] This has been confirmed by the European Court of Justice more recently in Cases T-305 to 307/94, T-313 to 316/94, T-318/94, T-325/94, T-328-329/94 and T-335/94 *Limburgse Vinyl Maatschappij NV v Commission (PVC Cartel II)* [1999] ECR II-931.

[41] Opinion in Joined Cases 32/78 and 36 to 82/78 *BMW Belgium v Commission* [1979] ECR 2435, 2494.

[42] Case 19/77 *Miller International Schallplatten GmbH v Commission* [1978] ECR 131, 162. Another interesting observation of Warner's in *Miller International* was that, contrary to the Commission's submission, he stated that traders in the Community ought not to be expected to be aware of the Commission's own decisions. He went on to state (at p 161) that '[d]ecisions are not law creating'. Indeed decisions are only binding on the undertakings to whom they are addressed. However, Regulation 1/2003, in Art 16, provides that national courts and national competition authorities, when applying Arts 81 and 82 EC to a particular situation which has already been the subject of a Commission decision, cannot take decisions contrary to that Commission decision.

[43] Ibid, para 18 of the judgment.

In the *BMW Belgium* case the Commission concluded that the 39 dealers had impliedly agreed to the restrictions by not objecting to their content on receipt of the circulars and, therefore, should be fined for infringing Article 81(1) EC . In a dealership agreement or network of agreements, it is the undertaking that grants the dealership which is normally the dominant partner. The dealers are often economically dependant on the distributor and accept the terms offered without complaint. On this issue, Warner considered that the Commission had already taken this factor into account by imposing on the dealers a much reduced fine. In addition he perceived the imposition of these fines as a deterrent for future dealers to empower them to oppose such pressures from the distributor. Future dealers would be in a stronger position when negotiating dealership agreements and ought to take responsibility for ensuring that anti-competitive obligations were removed from the agreement. This is perhaps an example of a statement more easily made by an Advocate General in an Opinion than by a court in judicial review proceedings. In judicial review actions the court's function is to assess whether the administrative bodies have exercised their powers properly, not to consider the wider consequences of the judgment.

The European Court of Justice in the *BMW Belgium* case agreed with Warner's conclusions but made no reference to either the *Miller International* judgment or to the plea that the fine should be reduced due to an alleged failure in the legal advice.[44]

The third and final Warner Opinion to be considered in this section is the one he delivered in the *Camera Care* case[45] on the power of the Commission to adopt interim measures. The European Court of Justice, contrary to Warner's advice, decided that the Commission had power under Article 3 of Regulation 17/62 to issue interim measures. This power is now expressly conferred on the Commission in Article 8(1) of Regulation 1/2003.[46]

Warner reached a different conclusion in his Opinion.[47] His reasoning was perfectly logical, adhering to a strict literal interpretation of the Treaty and secondary legislation. It was agreed by all the parties that there was no express power in the EC Treaty. Warner concluded also that there was no inherent power on the Commission as a competition authority, since that role was created by secondary legislation. Such bodies do not have inherent powers. He also rejected implied powers given that the EC Treaty expressly empowered the Council, under Article 87 (now Article 83) EC to adopt the measures necessary to implement the EC competition rules. Warner then analysed Article 3 of Regulation 17/62 and concluded

[44] It should be noted that Warner himself concluded that, on the evidence, the legal advice given did not support the applicant's case. The opposite was true!

[45] Case 792/79R *Camera Care Ltd v Commission* [1980] ECR 119.

[46] Art 8(1) provides that '[i]n cases of urgency due to the risk of serious and irreparable damage to competition, the Commission, acting on its own initiative may by decision, on the basis of a prima facie finding of infringement, order interim measures'. The only difference from the European Court of Justice's judgment in the *Camera Care* case is that Art 8(1) allows the Commission of its own initiative to act. This power has been used rarely by the Commission: its more normal practice has been to respond to requests from the parties and not to take the initiative, preferring to encourage the parties to offer undertakings (commitments in Regulation 1/2003 language).

[47] The Opinion was delivered on the same day as the oral hearing, an unimaginable possibility today!

that the wording of this article was clear and limited to a decision bringing the infringement to an end. He reasoned logically that there was a distinction between what the Commission was entitled to do after making a finding of infringement and what it could do before it reached that stage. It was evident to him that although the Commission could issue recommendations for terminating the infringement before adopting a final decision, Article 3 of Regulation 17/62 empowered the Commission to adopt a decision *only* after a number of procedural steps have been taken, namely the issue of a statement of objections, the oral hearing and a consultation with the Advisory Committee. Warner concluded that '[t]he crux, however, in my opinion, is that, under Article 3, no decision binding on the undertaking or undertakings concerned can be adopted before there is a finding of infringement'.[48] Although Warner admitted that he had heard attractive arguments for the Commission to have such a power he stated that, in his opinion, 'those arguments should be addressed to the Council, not this Court. This Court exists to say what the law is, not what it ought to be'.[49]

As already stated the European Court of Justice was much more radical in its approach to this issue. It did not involve itself in an interpretative exercise of Article 3 of Regulation 17/62 but stood back from the wording and considered that the primary objective of the legislation was to ensure decisions under Article 3(1) are effective. The Court therefore applied a teleological interpretative method and ruled that interim measures may be necessary and indispensable in order to ensure that effectiveness of a final decision.[50] The Court went on to list a number of conditions which must be adhered to if such an interim measure is to be judged lawful.[51] In practice the Commission has refrained from adopting interim measures, preferring to accept commitments from the undertakings concerned.

Warner's conclusion in this case is disappointing but understandable. He applied a strict literal interpretation to the wording of the legislative measure which granted the Commission the power to adopt decisions in competition investigations. Although this method of interpretation is quite commonly applied by courts to determine the scope of provisions in secondary legislation, on this occasion, the European Court of Justice preferred a more radical but pragmatic approach.

Procedural safeguards during the Commission's investigation

Warner's first Opinion in a matter concerning EC competition rules was in the *Transocean Marine* case.[52] The case arose out of an application by the Transocean Marine Paint Association for an extension of an Article 81(3) exemption granted

[48] Opinion in Case 792/79R *Camera Care Ltd v Commission* [1980] ECR 119, 136.
[49] Ibid, 137. [50] Ibid, para 18 of the judgment.
[51] These are that there must be urgency in order to avoid serious and irreparable harm to a party. In addition the interim measure must be temporary and of a conservatory nature and restricted to what is required in the given situation (para 19 of the judgment).
[52] Case 17/74 *Transocean Marine Paint Association v Commission* [1974] ECR 1063.

by the Commission some years earlier. The Commission issued a decision extending the exemption but it listed conditions, one of which had not been raised in the statement of objections nor during the oral hearing that had taken place before the decision was adopted. This meant that the parties had no opportunity to express their own views on this additional condition set out in the decision. The legal issue for the European Court of Justice was whether, as a matter of law, there was a duty on the Commission to have given an opportunity to the parties to comment before imposing the condition. It is clear from the tone of the Opinion that Warner was not impressed by the Commission's argument justifying their actions. He ironically stated that the arguments of the Commission 'amount to no more than saying that the Applicants ought to have divined what it had in mind from the anxieties it had expressed about the links . . . This, in my opinion, just will not do'.[53]

Warner took the view that what was at stake in this case was a rule of natural justice, the *audi alteram partem* principle. He therefore requested the documentation service, located within the Court's Library and Research Division, to carry out a comparative study on the right to be heard in administrative proceedings in the laws of the Member States.[54] The study enabled him to demonstrate that most Member States recognized this principle[55] and advised the European Court of Justice to ensure its observance under EC law. He concluded that on balance 'the right to be heard forms part of those rights which "the law" referred to in Article [220] of the Treaty upholds, and of which, accordingly, it is the duty of this Court to ensure the observance'.[56] The European Court of Justice agreed with Warner's conclusion but did not make any reference to the laws of the Member States. The Court adopted the rule as part of EC law from the nature of the procedure set out in Regulation 99/63.[57] The European Court of Justice stated that the Regulation:

> applies the general rule that a person whose interests are perceptibly affected by a decision taken by a public authority must be given the opportunity to make his point of view known. This rule requires that an undertaking be clearly informed, in good time, of the essence of conditions to which the Commission intends to subject an exemption and it must have the opportunity to submit observations to the Commission.[58]

Warner's Opinion in this case must be recognized as a significant contribution to the procedural safeguards developed by the European Court of Justice in its judgments which protect undertakings under investigation by the Commission for alleged infringements of the EC competition rules.

Another Opinion on a procedural matter was delivered in the *National Panasonic*[59] case where the Court was asked to determine the duties of the Commission when

[53] Ibid, 1087. [54] J Usher, *European Court Practice* (1983), 238.

[55] Opinion in Case 17/74 *Transocean Marine Paint Association v Commission* [1974] ECR 1063, 1088–89. [56] Ibid, 1089.

[57] Regulation 99/63 on the hearings provided for in Art 19(1) and (2) of Council Regulation No. 17 [1963–64] OJ Spec Ed 47.

[58] Case 17/74 *Transocean Marine Paint Association v Commission* [1974] ECR 1063, para 15 of the judgment. [59] Case 136/79 *National Panasonic (UK) Ltd v Commission* [1980] ECR 2033.

carrying out an on-the-spot inspection under Article 14 of Regulation 17/62.[60] What were the duties imposed on the Commission when carrying out these investigations? How far were the duties imposed on the Commission when seeking information under Article 11 of Regulation 17/62[61] also to be applied in respect of an Article 14 inspection? The parties contended that the two procedures should have the same safeguards, namely the Commission should first give notice to the undertakings concerned that it intended to carry out an on-the-spot inspection and then issue a formal decision on arrival at the location if necessary. It was also argued on behalf of the parties that they should have had an opportunity to be heard before the inspection was carried out. The parties considered their rights of defence to have been infringed and relied in particular on Article 8 of the European Convention on Human Rights (ECHR) which protects the right to private and family life and is extended to legal persons.

Both the Court and the Advocate General concluded that the two procedures had different purposes and the powers granted to the Commission were not subject to the same conditions.[62] If the Commission had to give notice before initiating an Article 14 inspection it would defeat the object of this provision which is to prevent documentation held on the premises of the undertakings from being destroyed or removed.[63] There was also agreement, though not for the same reasons, that there had been neither an infringement of Article 8 ECHR nor of the right to be heard. Warner found no evidence provided by the parties that Article 8 ECHR had been infringed. He also reminded the European Court of Justice that the right to be heard rule was a general one subject to exceptions such as, for example, the prevention of destruction of documents.[64] The Court simply stated that the decision to carry out an on-the-spot inspection is not aimed at terminating an infringement or declaring an agreement incompatible with Article 81(1) but simply to gather necessary information.[65]

In this Opinion, Warner took the opportunity to make observations on two matters of procedure with which he was uncomfortable. First, he commented that he found it unusual that the Article 14 investigation lacked a requirement that a warrant be obtained from a national court before the Commission was allowed to enter private premises.[66] This demonstrated his unease with such a right being given to an administrative body or in his words 'officers of a public authority' which was probably influenced by his common law training.

The second observation concerned the attempt by the applicant to rely on passages in reports and statements made by a member of the Commission. These statements were made during a European Parliament debate and suggested that

[60] The corresponding provision in Regulation 1/2003 is Art 20 (powers of inspection).

[61] The corresponding provisions in Regulation 1/2003 are Arts 18 (requests for information) and 19 (power to take statements).

[62] Case 136/79 *National Panasonic (UK) Ltd v Commission* [1980] ECR 2033, para 9 of the judgment and p 2065 of the Opinion.

[63] Ibid, 2069.

[64] Ibid, 2068 and 2069.

[65] Ibid, para 21 of the judgment.

[66] Ibid, 2068.

the authors of Articles 11 and 14 regarded these provisions as laying down similar procedures. Warner dismissed these arguments forcefully, referring back to one of his earlier Opinions[67] and stating that 'what the members of the Council do when they adopt a regulation is to agree the text. They do not necessarily all have the same views as to its meaning'.[68] This is a comment which perhaps remains valid even today!

The last Opinion to be examined in this section is the Opinion delivered in the *Distillers*[69] case. The case concerned judicial review of a Commission decision prohibiting a system of dual pricing under which Distillers charged UK customers lower prices if the spirits they bought were for sale in the UK rather than if they were destined for export. An earlier expressed export prohibition in the notified agreement had been replaced by this dual pricing system. Although Distillers had notified the original agreement they failed to notify this new dual pricing policy. The Commission considered that it had no power to evaluate whether non-notified restrictions could be exempted under Article 81(3).

Both the Advocate General and the Court agreed that, in the absence of notification in accordance with Regulation 17/62, the dual pricing could not be exempted even if the Commission was inclined to do so (which was certainly not the case here).[70] Thus the Court was able to dispose of the case without giving any further thought as to whether the dual pricing system could be granted an exemption or whether the alleged procedural irregularities raised by the applicants to support their claim that the Commission's decision should be annulled.

Warner considered these matters even though the European Court of Justice did not rule on them. As an Advocate General, Warner had to consider all the issues raised in the case, given he could not be sure that the Court agreed with his position that the lack of notification in accordance with Regulation 17/62 was a crucial omission.[71]

The alleged irregularities concerned the documentation placed before the Advisory Committee.[72] There were two main complaints. First, the applicant considered that the Advisory Committee should have been given the minutes of the oral hearing when considering the terms of the Commission's draft decision. Second, the applicant objected to the fact that the copy of the complaint that had

[67] He cited his Opinion in Case 28/76 *Milac v Hauptzollamt Freiburg* [1976] ECR 1639, 1664.

[68] Case 136/79 *National Panasonic (UK) Ltd v Commission* [1980] ECR 2033, 2066.

[69] Case 30/78 *Distillers Company Ltd v Commission* [1980] ECR 2229. Unusually for the Court at the time, there was a four month gap between the delivery of the Opinion and the judgment.

[70] Ibid, 2282 and para 24 of the judgment.

[71] In Case 127/73 *BRT v SABAM* [1974] ECR 51, Advocate General Mayras had reached the conclusion that the preliminary reference was inadmissible. Therefore, he did not consider the actual questions referred to the European Court of Justice by the national court. The European Court of Justice, however, disagreed on the issue of admissibility and instructed Mayras to deliver a second Opinion on the substance. See J Usher, *European Court Practice* (1983) 240–41.

[72] The Advisory Committee consists of representatives of the Member States to whom the Commission's draft decision is submitted for consultation before the decision is adopted formally by the Commission as a collegiate body.

been given to them by the Commission had so much of its content deleted that it was impossible to understand. Yet, the Advisory Committee had been given the whole unedited complaint.

In both instances Warner supported the position of the applicant. He expressed criticism of the Advisory Committee's methods of work which he felt lacked transparency, leaving the undertakings 'in the dark as to what the Committee is told or not told by the Commission and as to the Committee's report'.[73] He had no hesitation in reaching the conclusion that the absence of the minutes was a *prima facie* breach of an essential procedural requirement, and therefore, a valid ground for annulment of the decision under Article 230 EC Treaty.

Another interesting aspect of Warner's Opinion was his strong support for the European Court of Justice being given the widest possible jurisdiction in judicial review proceedings. The Commission had argued that in situations where it is required to make complex assessments of economic factors the Court's power of review was limited. Although Warner accepted that the Commission had a wide discretion imposing conditions on the grant of an Article 81(3) exemption, he considered the Court's competence in reviewing the exercise by the Commission of its powers to be wide.[74]

In contrast, five years earlier, in the Opinion Warner delivered in *Frubo*,[75] a case concerning an agreement between associations of undertakings, his approach was perhaps more cautious as to the European Court of Justice's ability to deal with economic issues. In considering the arguments and economic evidence in support of Frubo's claim that an Article 81(3) exemption should have been granted, Warner stated: 'I do not think that it is for the Court to adjudicate on such arguments, which raise questions purely of economic judgment or opinion'.[76] He went on to cite the judgment in *Consten and Grundig* where the European Court of Justice had stated that judicial review of complex economic evaluations by the Commission must be confined to an examination of the relevance of the facts and of the legal consequences deduced by the Commission.[77] Warner expressed his views strongly in *Frubo* stating that '[i]t is no part of the function of the Court to make economic prognostications'.[78]

In the *Distillers* case Warner was critical of the Commission's 'lack of comprehension of the evidence'.[79] He stated that the Commission's apparent dismissal of whether or not Distillers products were distributed in other Member States seemed to suggest that it considered its policy on parallel imports more important than enabling products to penetrate new markets. Warner commented that was an

[73] Case 30/78 *Distillers Co Ltd v Commission* [1980] ECR 2229, 2292.

[74] Ibid, 2287.

[75] Case 71/74 *Nederlandse Vereniging voor Fruit en Groentenimporthandel, Nederlandse Bond van Grossiers in Zuidvruchten en ander Geïmporteerd Fruit 'Frubo' v Commission* [1975] ECR 563.

[76] Ibid, 597.

[77] Joined Cases 56 and 58/64 *Consten and Grundig v Commission* [1966] ECR 299, para 12 of the judgment.

[78] Opinion in Case 71/74 *'Frubo'* [1975] ECR 563, 597.

[79] Opinion in Case 30/78 *Distillers Co Ltd v Commission* [1980] ECR 2229, 2288.

approach 'which is, in my opinion, incompatible with a proper exercise by the Commission of its discretion under Article 85(3) [81(3)]'.[80]

Issues of substance concerning Articles 81 and 82 EC

In the *Frubo* case already mentioned above, one of the arguments that the applicant raised to challenge the legality of the Commission decision related to the meaning of 'agreement' within Article 81(1) EC. It was contended that this Treaty provision applied to agreements between associations and not to an agreement between the members of an association. This was indeed rejected by Warner and the European Court of Justice but in these earlier years in the evolution of EC competition law the outcome was not a foregone conclusion. Warner explained that for an agreement to fall within Article 81(1) EC it does not depend on whether it creates contractual relations. It may be agreed between the parties that an agreement does not create legal relations and will be binding in honour only. Such 'gentlemen's agreements' are outside the sphere of contract law but within the reach of competition law. He cited the *Quinine* judgment as implied authority for this conclusion.[81]

During Warner's period in office very important judgments on the scope and meaning of Article 82 were delivered by the European Court of Justice. In the mid-1970s the Commission began to adopt a series of decisions applying Article 82 EC Treaty to the market behaviour of undertakings. These decisions were addressed to powerful players in the market who sought judicial review of the decisions challenging, in particular, the Commission's definition of the 'relevant market' upon which dominance under Article 82 had been established. The concept of the relevant market is central to the finding of dominance. Cases, such as *Hoffmann-La Roche*[82] and *United Brands Company (UBC)*,[83] remain highly authoritative on the definition of the concept of a dominant position. Although Warner was not the Advocate General in these cases he contributed to the debate as to the meaning of the relevant market in the *Kali und Salz*[84] case, which was decided a few years earlier. In this case the Commission's decision denying an Article 81(3) exemption was challenged. One of the applicants' challenges was the correctness of the Commission's definition of the relevant market for the purposes of the decision. The Commission had defined the relevant market as straight potash whilst the applicant argued the relevant market was wider and should have been defined as all inorganic potash-bearing fertilizers including compound ones.

[80] Ibid, 2289.

[81] Case 41/69 *ACF Chemiefarma NV v Commission (Quinine cartel)* [1970] ECR 661 cited at p 595 of the *Frubo* Opinion.

[82] Case 85/76 *Hoffmann-La Roche & Co AG v Commission* [1979] ECR 461.

[83] Case 27/76 *United Brands Co and United Brands Continentaal BV v Commission* [1978] ECR 207.

[84] Joined Cases 19 and 20/74 *Kali und Salz AG and Kali-Chemie AG v Commission* [1975] ECR 499.

Warner once again reminded the Court of earlier practice referring to his own Opinion in the *Commercial Solvents* case where he had cited previous decisions of the Court, to support his view that 'a relevant market was one in which the products available were substantially interchangeable'.[85] He dismissed this ground of appeal since he considered that the evidence showed that straight potash was not interchangeable with compound potash even though straight potash was the raw material for the manufacture of compound fertilizers. Thus the test of substitution of one product for another in order to determine the relevant product market was applied right from the beginning and remains the starting point in the process of defining the appropriate relevant market in any competition investigation. Although Warner supported the Commission as far as the definition of the relevant market was concerned, he was critical of the Commission's insufficient reasoning for the decision, a conclusion fully supported by the European Court of Justice. The decision was annulled in a brief judgment.

Warner was also Advocate General in two cases concerning the application of Article 82 EC. The first to be examined is the Opinion he delivered in *BP v Commission*[86] where the Commission found BP to have abused its dominant position on the Dutch motor fuels market by reducing supplies of petrol to an occasional customer during the oil crisis in 1973–74. The Commission acknowledged that the crisis situation was not of BP's making. This fact was reflected in the Commission's decision finding that BP had infringed Article 82 EC, since no fine was imposed on BP.[87] BP however challenged the legality of that decision, particularly the Commission's concept of a dominant position,[88] alleging incorrect analysis of Article 82 EC Treaty. BP was concerned that if the decision were not annulled the company would be susceptible to claims for compensation before national courts. The Warner Opinion is particularly valuable on the concept of dominance since the Court concentrated on reviewing the alleged abuse and did not engage with the issue of whether BP was in a dominant position in the first place.[89]

Warner questioned whether the Commission was right in applying Article 82 'to a situation in which owing to an emergency causing a temporary scarcity of supplies of a particular commodity, the customers or the "normal" customers of each supplier may become dependent on him. I do not think so'.[90] He was of the

85 Ibid, 525.

86 Case 77/77 *Benzine en Petroleum Handelsmaatschappij BV and ors v Commission* [1978] ECR 1513.

87 Both Warner (ibid, 1531) and the European Court of Justice (ibid, para 13 of the judgment) agreed that the fact that the Commission had not imposed a fine on BP, did not deny the existence of BP's interest in seeking an annulment of the Commission's decision.

88 In his Opinion Warner also stated that the Commission had considered, during its investigation, the possibility that the few oil companies operating on the Dutch market had joint dominance within the meaning of Art 82 EC. This is not surprising as in the *Italian Flat Glass* Decision [1989] OJ L33/44, the Commission, for the first time, found that several undertakings had a joint dominant position.

89 Case 77/77 *BP v Commission* [1978] ECR 1513, para 18 of the judgment.

90 Ibid, 1537.

opinion that in these circumstances it was the responsibility of the government, not private undertakings, to allocate supplies.

As far as the dominant position of BP was concerned, Warner did not agree with the Commission's conclusion that a dominant position existed where, owing to the petrol crisis, customers became dependent on the supplier.[91] He cited the definition of a dominant position as set out by the European Court of Justice in the then recently decided *United Brands*[92] case but distinguished that judgment on the facts. Unlike the situation when undertakings are in a dominant position, BP could not disregard the attitude of its customers when distributing its scarce supplies. Once the emergency was over customers would remember how they were treated and so BP was justified in treating different types of customers in different ways. Warner concluded that in a crisis situation BP was not dominant within the meaning of Article 82 EC Treaty.[93]

On the issue of abuse Warner also disagreed with the Commission's reasoning. The Commission considered BP had abused its dominant position by applying dissimilar conditions to equivalent transactions. BP, in Warner's view, were not concerned with the terms on which a trader supplies different customers but with the selection of which customers to supply and what quantities to supply to each one. Warner referred to the refusal to supply in the *Commercial Solvents* case being an abuse but distinguished the situations. In the BP situation '[i]t would be inequitable because it would virtually ignore the special claims of a supplier's contractual and regular customers'.[94] He concluded that 'this kind of case is outside the ambit of Article 86 [82] altogether'[95] and that it was legitimate for BP to act in this manner even if they had a dominant position within the meaning of Article 82 EC Treaty. The European Court of Justice found on the facts that the complainant was an occasional customer and went on to conclude that BP had not treated this customer unfairly. In this case, the reasoning of Warner and of the Court on whether BP had committed an abuse is almost identical.

The final Opinion to be considered in this section is the one Warner delivered in *Greenwich Film v SACEM*,[96] a preliminary reference from the Cour de Cassation in France. The European Court of Justice was asked to rule on the application of Article 82 EC Treaty in respect of performance in non-Member States of contracts entered into in one of the Member States by parties within the jurisdiction of that Member State.

A preliminary matter that was raised was the extent to which the European Court of Justice could rule on issues not raised by the national referring court. Contrary to the Commission's view, Warner advised the Court that its ruling should be confined to the questions referred. The case had come to the European

[91] Ibid. [92] Case 27/76 [1978] ECR 207.

[93] Case 77/77 *BP v Commission* [1978] ECR 1513, 1538. [94] Ibid, 1539.

[95] Ibid, 1540.

[96] Case 22/79 *Greenwich Film Production v Société des Auteurs, Compositeurs et Editeurs de Musique (SACEM) and Société des Editions Labrador* [1979] ECR 3275.

Court of Justice not as a direct action but on a preliminary reference. This is a completely different process from one where the undertaking is directly challenging a decision of the Commission. In a direct action the scope and nature of the European Court of Justice's competence is wider. In a preliminary reference the European Court of Justice is being asked by a national court to interpret a specific Community provision or rule or to make a declaration of validity in respect of a Community measure, in order to enable the national court to deliver judgment in national litigation. In a direct action the European Court of Justice is being asked to interpret and/or apply Community law but also deliver the judgment on the case.

Nevertheless, Warner was willing to give a wide interpretation to the questions asked by the national court. An important matter which had not been asked by the national court, but raised in the written submissions, concerned the effect on the assignment of intellectual property rights should an infringement of Article 82 EC be confirmed. In this context, however, he considered that, since the national court had asked a question related to the performance of contracts, the European Court of Justice would not be going beyond its scope by giving some guidance as the answer to this question had already been given by the Court in an earlier case (*BRT v SABAM*).[97] The European Court of Justice followed the advice and basically repeated the same words it had used in the earlier ruling.[98]

The European Court of Justice was also willing to reply to one of the referred questions by reference to earlier decisions and, in particular to the *Commercial Solvents* judgment, where the Court had ruled that the consequences for the effective competitive structure in the common market must be taken into consideration when deciding whether trade between Member States may be affected by the abuse of a dominant position.[99]

As far as the cases where issues of substance were concerned, Warner and the European Court of Justice appear to have worked well together, with similar reasoning and citing case-law authority wherever appropriate.

Concluding observations

Two primary contributions to the competition regime and to the case-law of the European Court of Justice can be observed from Warner's Opinions examined above. First, in his Opinions he encouraged the Court to exercise its powers of review more effectively as far as Commission competition decisions were concerned.[100] Second, he persuaded the European Court of Justice to rule that the right of an

[97] Case 127/73 *BRT v SABAM* [1974] ECR 313, para 14 of the judgment where the European Court of Justice ruled it was for the national court to decide whether, and to what extent, a finding of infringement of Art 82 EC Treaty affected the validity of licensing agreements.

[98] Case 22/79 *Greenwich Film v SACEM* [1979] ECR 3275, para 10 of the judgment.

[99] Ibid, para 11 of the judgment.

[100] eg n 41 and text above.

undertaking to be heard when being investigated by the Commission was a principle of EC law.

Warner perceived the role of the Court as an active one when reviewing the Commission's powers and how they exercised them. Warner was trained in a common law system therefore it is likely that he would have had more confidence in a court of law than in an administrative body to protect the interests of individuals.[101] Some of the Opinions examined above do tend to support this observation.

The Commission had been granted extensive powers to carry out investigations and to terminate infringements of the EC competition rules. Where the Commission had been granted a power, such as the power to terminate infringements under Article 3 of Regulation 17/62, Warner had no difficulty in advising the Court that this power enabled the Commission to specify to the undertakings concerned how the infringement should be ended (*Commercial Solvents*). However, when new powers were being sought, such as the power to adopt interim measures, Warner applied a strict literal interpretation to the legislative text and advised the Court not to expand the powers granted to the Commission (*Camera Care*). The Court however disagreed with his conclusion in the *Camera Care* case and applied a teleological method of interpretation, concluding that such a power existed under Article 3 of regulation 17/62. On this occasion, the Court appeared, more concerned to ensure the effectiveness of the competition enforcement regime, than to interpret the legislative provision conferring powers on an administrative body restrictively.

Warner was also critical of the reasoning of the Commission in its competition decisions (*Kali und Salz* and *Distillers*) and of the Commission's submissions (*Miller International*). In *Distillers* he commented that one of the reasons put forward by the Commission was 'a statement of a conclusion rather than a statement of a reason'.[102] He was particularly critical of the Commission's submission in the *Distillers* case that the Court's powers of review of competition decisions were limited as these involved making complex assessments. On the other hand he did admit in *Frubo* that whether an exemption should have been granted was not a question for the Court as it involved questions purely of economic judgments.

Warner's Opinions also sought to persuade the Court to penalize the Commission where they did not act with due diligence (*Commercial Solvents*). He was particularly critical of the delay in the Commission's investigation in the *Commercial Solvents* and *Frubo* cases. However, in the *Commercial Solvents* case, he failed to persuade the

[101] Warner often did not support the Commission's claims as to their power. In the *Camera Care* case he disagreed with the claim that the Commission had inherent power to adopt interim measures; in the *Miller International* case he refuted the Commission's statement that undertakings had an obligation to know about the Commission's competition decisions (p162); in the *Kali und Salz* case he referred to Advocate General Dutheillet de Lamothe in Case 22/71 *Béguelin Import Co v GL Import-Export SA* [1971] ECR 949 in support of his conclusion that the Commission's Notice in respect of Minor Agreements has no binding effect.

[102] Case 30/78 *Distillers Co Ltd v Commission* [1980] ECR 2229, 2288–89 where very strong language is used.

Court to annul the fine on this ground but he succeeded in persuading the Court to reduce it in view of the Commission's delay.[103] In *Frubo* he accused the Commission of 'seriously and largely unexplained delays'.[104] In *Distillers* he was critical of the secrecy and lack of transparency of the workings of the Advisory Committee and the disparity of treatment by the Commission in respect of access to documents which were made available to the Advisory Committee and to the undertakings under investigation.[105]

As far as the rights of defence are concerned, Warner's well researched Opinion in the *Transocean Marine Paint* case resulted in the introduction of the rule *audi alteram partem* as part of EC law. Today an undertaking has an opportunity to be heard fairly and impartially by a Hearing Officer who is not a member of DG Competition and therefore independent of the officials who are carrying out the investigation.[106] Warner also sought to introduce a scale of levels of fines to reflect the various degrees of gravity of the infringement (*Miller International*). Although the European Court of Justice did not respond to the proposal, it does not mean that it did not have an impact on the Commission to be more transparent. After all now we have guidelines on setting fines.[107]

In respect of Warner's Opinions on the substance of Articles 81 and 82, there are no significant differences between his reasoning and that of the European Court of Justice. His Opinions on the meaning of 'dominance' and 'abuse' within the context of Article 82 EC Treaty were helpful to a general understanding of the direction that EC competition law should take but not in the specific cases (*BP* and *Distillers*) as the Court found it unnecessary to rule on these concepts in these cases.

The first common law trained practitioner to hold the office of Advocate General at the European Court of Justice, Warner, was indeed a strong supporter of the Court's powers when reviewing decisions of the Commission adopted in the exercise of delegated powers in the area of competition law enforcement. He was concerned to safeguard the undertakings' rights of defence when being investigated by the Commission for alleged infringements of the EC competition rules. But his most significant contribution was to persuade successfully the European Court of Justice that 'the law' which they must apply include principles of natural justice.

[103] Joined Cases 6 and 7/73 *Instituto Chemioterapico Italiano SpA and Commercial Solvents Corp v Commission* [1974] ECR 223, paras 51 and 52 of the judgment.

[104] Case 71/74 *'Frubo'* [1975] ECR 563, 593. [105] See n 73 and text above.

[106] It may not be too speculative to suggest that Warner's Opinion in the *Transocean Marine Paint* case was the prompt that led to a major reform of the oral hearing stage of the Commission's investigation in the early 1980s when the position of Hearing Officer was created with some independence from the case handlers. The Commission had been often accused of being investigator, prosecutor and judge when enforcing the EC competition rules.

[107] Guidelines on the method of setting fines imposed pursuant to Art 23(2)(a) of Regulation No. 1/2003 [2006] OJ C210/2.

Part III

Some fundamental concepts of Community law and the Opinions of the Advocates General

8

The Advocates General and the development of the principle of direct effect

Introduction

This chapter discusses the Opinions of a number of Advocates General in the cases relating to direct effect. It is not the intention of the chapter to examine whether the Court followed the Opinion of the Advocate General in a specific case. It is well known, for example, that Advocate General Roemer and the Court in *Van Gend en Loos* disagreed as to whether Article 25 EC was capable of creating direct effect.[1] Rather, the purpose of the chapter is to analyse the concept of direct effect from the standpoint of the Advocate General. How did the Advocate General approach the case? What kind of thinking influenced him? Is it clear from the Opinions that the Advocates General understood the constitutional significance of the questions before the Court?

Students of Community law nowadays perhaps take the concept of the direct effect of Community law for granted, unaware of the originality and impact of the Court's recognition of the European Community law as a 'new legal order of international law'. It is also sometimes forgotten that the case-law of the Court met with vehement criticism and led to an intense dialogue with the courts of some of the Member States, particularly over the question of the direct effect of directives. Indeed the present author remembers vividly that tutorial so many years ago with JDB Mitchell when she stated that she found it impossible to understand how a provision of Community law could create direct effects if it was not directly applicable and his response—'you are right'. How wrong we both were! By taking a historical point of view it may be possible to assess the contribution of the Advocates General through what was difficult and uncharted terrain.

Precisely because of the constitutional significance of this line of case-law, in particular in charting the relationship between the Community and the national legal orders, one might expect the legal reasoning of the Court to be clear and convincing, all the more so bearing in mind the heightened political sensitivity surrounding these crucial issues at the national level. After all, the Court's rulings

[1] Case ECR 1-26/62 *N.V. Algemene Transpoert—En Expeditie Onderneming Van Gend En Loos v Nederlandse Tariefcommissie* [1963] ECR 1.

would have major implications for the legal orders of the Member States. In their function of assisting the Court in some of these difficult cases one might also expect the Advocate General to provide reasoned arguments for the Court to consider. The Court's audience in these cases is the Member States. However, the reality has often not met up to such expectations. In many cases on direct effect the Court's reasoning can best be described as thin and the contribution of the Advocate General to the debate at times as limited. On the latter point, this is not simply a question of whether the Court follows the Advocate General, since an Opinion which provides a firm counter-factual argument might also be useful to the Court, but whether the quality of the argument assists the Court in coming to its decision.

The case-law on direct effect is enormous and it is not possible to examine each and every case. This chapter examines the development of the concept of direct effect in each of the five decades since the case of *Van Gend en Loos* in 1962. The chapter focuses on one key issue in each decade and the Opinions of the Advocates General in the seminal cases in that decade. In the 1960s, the key issue was the establishment of the principle itself as a constitutional principle and the corresponding Opinion is Roemer's in *Van Gend en Loos*. In the 1970s, direct effect was extended to directives and the two key cases of *Van Duyn* and *Ratti* will be examined.[2] Advocates General Mayras and Reischl gave Opinions in these cases. In 1986, the definitive case of *Marshall* appeared to settle the point that directives could not create horizontal direct effect with Advocate General Slynn giving his Opinion in that case.[3] Three Advocates General: Van Gerven, Jacobs and Lenz argued in the 1990s that the time had come to recognise the horizontal direct effect of directives in *Marshall II*, *Vaneetveld* and *Faccini Dori*—the Court disagreed.[4] In the first years of the new century, it appears that some Advocates General are arguing for a new approach to invocability of Community provisions which might have the effect of minimizing the distinction between horizontal and vertical direct effects. This new approach is based on the concept of primacy of Community law and the corresponding obligations on the courts of the Member States to reconcile differences between the two legal orders. The Opinions of Advocates General Léger, Geelhoed, Ruiz-Jarabo Colomer, Tizzano and Kokott in (respectively) *Linster, Caballero, Pfeiffer, Mangold* and *Adeneler* are examined to explore this new approach.[5]

[2] Cases 41/74 *Van Duyn v Home Office* [1974] ECR 1337; 148/78 *Ministero Pubblico v Ratti* [1979] ECR 1629.

[3] Case 152/84 *Marshall v Southampton and South-West Hampshire Area Health Authority (Marshall I)* [1986] ECR 723.

[4] Cases C-271/91 *Marshall v Southampton and South-West Hampshire Area Health Authority* [1993] ECR I-4367; C-316/93 *Vaneetveld v Le Foyer* [1994] ECR I-763; C-91/92 *Faccini Dori v Recreb* [1994] ECR I-3325.

[5] Cases C-287/98 *Luxembourg v Linster* [2000] ECR I-6917; C-442/00 *Caballero v Fogasa* [2002] ECR I-11915; Joined cases C-397/01 and C-403/01 *Pfeiffer v Deutsches Rotes Kreuz Kreisverband Waldshut eV* [2004] ECR I-8835; Cases C-144/04 *Mangold v Helm* [2006] ECR I nyr; C-212/04 *Adeneler v ELOG* OJ C179/8.

Origins of a constitutional principle—the 1960s

Most authors see the case of *Van Gend en Loos* as the origin of the concept of direct effect and it not surprising given the dramatic constitutional language that is employed by the Court in laying down the principle of direct effect. However, the debate about the effects of the Treaty within the internal legal orders of the Member States had begun before the date of the judgment on 5 February 1963. The first case referred to the Court of Justice under the procedures provided for in procedures provided in Article 234 EC was *Bosch*.[6] This case related to the effects of Article 81 EC on anti-competitive agreements existing at the time of the entry into force of the first Regulation implementing Articles 81 and 82 of the EC Treaty, Regulation 17/62. Advocate General Lagrange advised the Court that the 'provisions of Article 81 of the Treaty are fully and directly applicable in the Member States at least from the entry into force of the Implementing Regulation'.[7] His argument was based on the importance of the competition rules in the creation of the Common Market and the clarity of the provisions of the Treaty in respect of competition, which leave no doubt as to their effect. Once the transitional provisions provided for in the Treaty (Regulation 17) had been made, the Treaty provisions on competition were applicable in their entirety. Lagrange further reasoned that the Treaty 'by virtue of its ratification, is incorporated into national law, and for this reason 'it is the function of national courts to apply its provisions'.[8] The Court did not refer in its own reasoning to the direct applicability of Article 81(1) but, nonetheless, it held that anti-competitive agreements between firms not notified to the Commission and which did not have provisional validity under the terms of Regulation 17 'are automatically void'.[9] Thus the Court recognized the direct effect of Article 81 within the national legal order.

Lagrange did not make explicit in his Opinion the assumptions on which he concluded that Treaty provisions could be applicable in their entirety within the legal orders of the Member States but this statement does appear to take as read that the Member States would accept a monist interpretation of the Treaty. He argued that by ratifying the Treaty it had become incorporated into the legal orders of the Member States, its provisions were therefore part of the national legal order; in other words, they were self-executing. His assumption was shared outside the Court. For example, writing in August 1962, Norman Marsh, then Director of the British Institute of International and Comparative Law, wrote in a preface to the Common Market Law Reports that 'In so far as the Treaties and the instruments made under them are intended to be self-executing, that is to say, to have effect as part of the internal law of the member-States, they have in many cases to be interpreted and applied by the national courts of those States'.[10] And in

[6] Case 13/61 *De Geus v Bosch* [1962] ECR 56. For further discussion of this case see chapter 4.
[7] Ibid, 71. [8] Ibid, 65. [9] Ibid, 55. [10] N Marsh, preface (1962) CMLR vii.

November 1962 the Italian *Consiglio di Stato* ruled that 'the E.E.C Treaty envisages that its regulations might be invoked not merely by member-States and by bodies or institutions of the Community, but also by any interested person'.[11]

The possibility that provisions of the Treaty could create effects within the internal legal orders of the Member States was, therefore, part of the contemporary debate about the effects of membership of the (then) EEC. The framing of the question from the *Tariefcommissie* in the second preliminary reference to be referred to the Court, the case of *Van Gend en Loos*, as whether Article 25 of the Treaty has direct application and creates rights for individuals that must be protected by the courts of the Member States suggests that the Dutch court itself accepted that certain provisions of the Treaty could create direct effect but it was unsure whether Article 25 was one of them.

The facts of *Van Gend en Loos* are well known. Van Gend en Loos imported into the Netherlands a quantity of chemicals and was charged an import duty of 8 per cent, based on a Dutch law incorporating the terms of a protocol agreed between the Dutch, Belgian and Netherlands governments and coming into force on 1 March 1960. Van Gend en Loos argued that this was an increase in import duties after the entry into force of the EEC Treaty and a violation of Article 25 of the Treaty.

Although Roemer and the Court came to a different conclusion on the direct effect of Article 12, this does not mean that his Opinion did not raise significant constitutional issues which needed to be addressed. The starting point for his analysis was the provisions of the Dutch Constitution which gave primacy to international conventions over provisions of national law. According to Dutch law, a provision of an international convention which has 'general compulsory effect' would have primacy over a provision of Dutch domestic law. The conflicting Dutch law would be invalid due to the constitutionally defined hierarchy of norms. By contrast, a provision which requires the Member States 'not to make contradictory legal rules' would not result in a ruling of invalidity. A finding of direct effect therefore had serious constitutional ramifications for the Member States. The Court would, in effect, be asking the courts of the Member States to rule on the compatibility of domestic law with Community law, a jurisdiction which the European Court itself did not possess and, because of the different approaches to constitutional law in the six Member States, a jurisdiction which was different in terms of the powers of the national courts. The Netherlands, Luxembourg and France accepted the primacy of international conventions which created general obligatory rules. Belgium, Italy and Germany did not. The courts of the Member States would therefore come to different conclusions as to how to apply Community law leading to unequal application of Community law.

[11] *Societa Biscotti Panettoni Colussi di Milano v Minestero del Commercio con L'Estaro* [1963] CMLR 133.

Roemer was not completely opposed to the idea that provisions of the Treaty could create rights for individuals that must be protected by the national courts. He cited with approval the Commission's analysis of the Treaty regime, in particular the profoundly innovatory nature of the Treaties, which requires them to be interpreted not solely on the basis of the law of nations. He agreed that Community law is not restricted to contractual agreements between States. The distinctiveness of Community law lay in the creation of new institutions, capable of taking administrative action and creating legal rules, 'which directly create rights in favour of and impose duties on Member States as well as their authorities and citizens'.[12] He then cited a number of Treaty articles which are intended directly to have an effect on national law, including in this, with some foresight, the provisions relating to the free movement of people, services and capital. By contrast, some provisions 'speak expressly of the obligations of the Member-States'. The terminology of the Treaty, the content of the obligation and the context of the provision must be taken into account in assessing the effects of such provisions. For example, where a Treaty provision called for regulations to be made later, then direct effect could not result. He concluded, therefore, that large parts of the Treaty contain obligations for the Member States but do not have direct internal effect in the law of the Member States.

Roemer supported this argument by reference to the system established by the Treaties to enforce Community law. It is the function of the Commission to enforce against the Member States the obligations imposed by the Treaty, and for the Member States to take the measures required to comply. Had it been intended by the drafters of the Treaty that Community law would have direct application over national law in the sense of predominance over it then the sanction included in the Treaty would have been a declaration of nullity of national provisions.

Turning to Article 25, Roemer accepts that it contains a legal obligation which does not require any measures to be taken by the Community institutions. To that extent he conceded the 'direct legal effect of Article 25'.[13] However, Article 25 expressly mentions the Member States as the 'recipient of the commands' of the provision. He compares this provision to others in the Treaty that are similarly worded. Thus he suggests that one of the tests for direct effect is the wording of the provision. For example, he states that there are no words in Article 25 such as 'prohibited' or 'without effect' which would indicate that it is meant to be applied directly by the authorities of the Member States. He then went on further to examine the contents and purpose of Article 25. At that stage in Community law, customs matters were regulated largely by national law and to accord direct application to Article 25 would imply supervision over national law which is not explicit in the provisions of Article 25. He looked at the purpose of Article 12 and argued that it had a complex nature which would mitigate its direct effect. Member States were in the process of harmonizing their customs laws to create the Common Market.

[12] *Van Gend en Loos*, Opinion of AG Roemer, 20. [13] Ibid, 22.

In this developing and complex legal environment to accord direct effect to Article 25 would create legal uncertainty for undertakings which would prefer to rely on the certainty of national law in their commercial activities. Therefore, on the basis of its wording, content and purpose Article 25 could not create direct effect.

Roemer's Opinion is characterized by its deference to the constitutional traditions of the Member States and to the Member States themselves as authors of the Treaty. There was not at that time, and there is not to date, any provision in the Treaty which refers to the direct effect of Community provisions or any provision which sets out the relationship between a directly effective Community provision and conflicting domestic law.[14] Roemer's solution was to look to the different constitutional traditions and explore, on the Court's behalf, their implications. The referring Court was Dutch. It had asked for an interpretation of a Treaty Article in order to assist in determining a case before it. If Article 25 was sufficiently precise to have general compulsory effect, then the Dutch courts would deal with this by declaring incompatible national law to be invalid. The Dutch Court had no need to ask what would happen in the event of a conflict between Community law and national law. Roemer recognized this but was also aware that a declaration of invalidity was not open to all the courts of the Member States because of their different constitutional traditions. His Opinion recognizes the implications in national constitutional law of a finding of direct effect, whereas the Court ignores these implications. It could only come to the decision it did precisely by ignoring the Opinion of the Advocate General on this point. His analysis of the constitutional traditions of the Member States revealed the absence of a European-level constitutional law. In order to avoid the problems raised by Roemer there would have to be a clarification of the hierarchy of norms as between Community law and conflicting national law, and a clear statement of the duties of the national court in case of such a conflict. Roemer was aware of these difficulties and this led him to be cautious in his analysis of both the concept of direct effect as it applied to the Treaty and specifically as it applied to Article 25. By contrast, the European Court turned a blind eye to the constitutional consequences of its ruling and, rather than deferring to national constitutional traditions and the canons of international law, preferred a ruling which would try to realize the obligations undertaken by the Member States. It was only in the later cases of *Costa v ENEL*, when the Court ruled that Community law takes precedence over conflicting national law, and of *Simmenthal* where it required national courts to set aside conflicting national rules to apply directly effective provisions of Community law that the Court began to resolve the constitutional problems raised by Roemer.[15]

[14] Except Art 34 TEU which denies direct effect to framework decisions. This has not stopped the Court from applying the doctrine of consistent interpretation to framework decisions. Case C-105/03 *Pupino* [2005] ECR I-5285 and the discussion in M Fletcher, 'Extending "Indirect Effect" to the Third Pillar: the significance of *Pupino*' (2005) 30 ELR 862.

[15] Cases 6/64 *Costa v ENEL* [1964] ECR 585; C-106/77 *Amministrazione delle Finanze dello Stato v Simmenthal* [1978] ECR 629.

Roemer undoubtedly understood the constitutional significance of the questions put to the Court in *Van Gend en Loos*. What he seems not to have appreciated was the willingness of the Court to break down hitherto accepted boundaries of national constitutional law and international law. In creating the conditions under which individuals could invoke provisions of Community law in the national courts, the European Court of Justice sought to deepen the legal integration of the Member States in the European project in two ways: first, by demonstrating the power of Community law to protect the interests not just of the Member States and the Community institutions but also of individuals; second, by calling on the vigilance of individuals to ensure compliance with Community law. Whereas for Roemer direct effect was a legal question of interpretation, for the Court it was a means of furthering European integration.

Direct effect of directives—the 1970s

In the early 1970s the Court extended its case-law on direct effect, beyond provisions of the Treaty, to decisions and to regulations. In *Grad* the Court ruled that decisions were capable of creating direct effect.[16] The Court based its reasoning on the principle of effectiveness (*effet utile*). Accepting that regulations, because of their quality of direct applicability as provided for in the Treaty, are capable of creating direct effects does not rule out the possibility that other provisions of Community law could produce similar effects.[17] The Court held that it would be incompatible with the binding effect of decisions to rule out the possibility that they might create direct effects. Particularly where Community law imposed an obligation to act in a particular way, the effectiveness of a decision would be weakened if individuals could not invoke its provisions in the courts of the Member States. This is so even though the effects of a decision might not be identical to those of a regulation.

Two years later, the Court ruled that regulations were capable of creating direct effects. Given the debate in *Grad*, it is hardly surprising that the Court held in *Politi* that ' by their very nature and their function in the system of the sources of Community law, regulations have direct effect and are as such, capable of creating individual rights which national courts must protect'.[18]

[16] Case 9/70 *Grad v Finanzamt Traunstein* [1970] ECR 825.

[17] The Court uses the terminology of direct effect and direct applicability almost interchangeably. However it is accepted that there are two distinct concepts. Direct applicability refers to the quality of a provision of Community law which is automatically part of the national legal orders of the Member States with no requirement that the Member States take action to incorporate it. Direct effect refers to the invocability of a Community provision of Community law before the national courts. See below for a discussion of the ability to plead substitution and the ability to plead exclusion.

[18] Case 43/71 *Politi v Ministry of Finance of the Italian Republic* [1971] ECR 1039. See also Cases 84/71 *Marimex v Italian Ministry of Finance* [1971] ECR 89; C-93/71 *Léonesio v Italian Ministry for Agriculture* [1972] ECR 287.

It was only a matter of time before the question of direct effect of directives would be raised before the Court. Although binding on the Member States as to the results to be achieved, directives leave the choice of form and methods of implementation to the Member States. They envisage a two-stage process of legislation; first at the level of the Community and then at the level of the Member State (or region or local authority as the case may be). Logically therefore it is impossible to attribute direct effect when only the Community institutions have fulfilled their part of this two stage process. Failure on the part of the national authorities to complete the legislative process is a breach of Community law and infringement proceedings can be brought against the State under Article 226 EC to ensure compliance.

In fact in *Grad* the Court had already attributed legal effects to a directive, in that case in conjunction with a decision. The decision set out the obligation on the Member States and the directive provided the date by which national implementing action should have been taken. The Court ruled that in these circumstances the directive made the original decision legally complete and the obligations contained in the decision created direct effect only after the expiry of the period laid down in the directive. In *SpA SACE* the Court ruled that a provision in a directive, in conjunction with directly applicable Treaty provisions and a decision of the Council, 'has direct effect in the relations between the Member States, as the party to whom the directive is addressed, and its subjects'.[19] Thus the Court had indicated its openness to arguments that directives, despite the two stage legislative process provided for in the Treaty, might create direct effect after the expiry of the implementing period laid down in the directive and that the direct effect of a provision of a directive might be limited to the legal relations between the Member State and its citizens (vertical direct effect).

It was in *Van Duyn* that the Court was first asked to rule on the direct effect of a 'free-standing' provision of a directive.[20] In this case a woman was refused entry to the UK to take up a post with the church of scientology on the basis of public policy arguments. She challenged this ruling in part on the basis of Directive 64/221, Article 3(1) which stated that such a refusal must be based exclusively on the personal conduct of the person concerned.

Mayras produced an uninspiring Opinion in this case which lacked any clear legal reasoning. Without any discussion about the nature of directives and solely on the basis of the two cases cited above, Mayras advised the Court that directives were capable of creating direct effect. The key question being 'whether the wording, nature and general scheme of the provisions in question are capable of creating direct effects between the Member States to which the directive is addressed and their subjects'.[21] Applying the tests of clarity and precision, the sufficiency of the provision in question and the limitations on the discretion of the Member

[19] Case 33/70 *SpA SACE v Italian Ministry of Finance* [1970] ECR I-1223, para 18.

[20] Case 41/74 *Van Duyn v Home Office* [1974] ECR 1337.

[21] Ibid, 1355.

States, Mayras concluded that the provision in question met the test for direct effect. Mayras made no reference to the principle of effectiveness to justify his Opinion which is surprising given the Court's own reasoning in *Grad* and, in fact, effectiveness was the basis of the Court's reasoning in *Van Duyn* itself.

It was in *Ratti* that certain of the implications of this development were drawn out.[22] The case concerned two directives relating to the labelling and packaging of solvents. The first had not been implemented in time in Italy and the time limit for implementation of the second had not expired on the date the relevant events took place. Criminal proceedings were brought against Ratti who had labelled his products in accordance with the directives, partly because he traded in Germany where the directives had already been implemented, but who was then prosecuted because his goods did not meet the requirements of Italian law.

The starting point for Advocate General Reischl's analysis in this case was the distinction between regulations and directives—only the former were generally applicable in the sense of becoming immediately integrated into the domestic legal order; the latter creating obligations only for the Member States. Directives could produce legal effects similar to regulations but, according to Reischl, that is the exception to the rule. Member States who do not comply with the obligation to implement directives cannot then rely on their own internal rules against an individual; that individual is entitled to rely on the directive. Reischl is here offering an argument based on a form of personal bar (estoppel) which subsequently became an important element in the thinking of the Court. Reischl clearly argued that the direct effect of directives is not automatic. It occurs 'when a Member State does not comply with its obligations and consists in the fact that the State is deprived of the possibility of relying as against individuals and undertakings on its own failure to comply with Community law . . . it is the expiry of the period laid down in the directive for the adaptation of national law which is material'.[23] The legal effects of directives can only be invoked by individuals after the implementation period has expired since up until this point the Member State retains its discretion to implement the directive in the way that it sees fit.

Although in both these cases the Court can be said to have followed the Opinion of the Advocate General, in that the same conclusions were reached, only Reischl offered any real analysis of the distinct nature of directives in the scheme of the Treaty. Mayras's Opinion is thin, the reasoning is lazy and there is no recognition of the significance of the case in constitutional terms. By comparison Reischl understood that the Court was taking a significant step and sought to impress upon the Court that allowing individuals to invoke provisions of unimplemented directives was the exception to the rule. As an exception to the rule, Reischl needed to provide the Court with a convincing legal argument to justify departure from the words of the Treaty, which clearly distinguished the legal effects of regulations and of directives. His Opinion shows caution and respect for

[22] Case 148/78 *Ministero Pubblico v Ratti* [1979] ECR 1629. [23] Ibid, 1653.

the wording of the Treaty and the division of powers contained in the Treaty between the Community legislature, on the one hand, and the Member States on the other. The Court relied on this line of reasoning in *Ratti* and in subsequent cases.[24]

Limiting the horizontal direct effect of directives—the 1980s

In 1976 in *Defrenne v Sabena* the Court opened the door to the horizontal direct effect of Community law allowing individuals to invoke provisions of the Treaty, not against the State but against other individuals.[25] This well-known case related to Article 119 of the Treaty (now Article 141) which required the Member States to ensure and maintain the concept of equal pay for men and women. Defrenne, a member of the cabin crew of Sabena, argued not only that Article 141 was sufficiently clear, precise and unconditional to meet the tests of direct effect but that Article 141 could be relied upon against her employer. She argued that, although the Member States are bound by this provision, it did not mean that women workers must wait for the State to introduce legislation before they could rely on Article 141. Article 119 could only bring about change to the extent to which the principles of equal pay are actually applied in practice. Both the UK and Irish governments who intervened in this case argued against this position. The UK government argued that 'the normal principles of equity' would be defeated if an obligation could be imposed on individuals in consequence of the default of a Member State, and also this would contradict the wording of the Treaty. Ireland relied on the wording of the Treaty to argue against horizontal direct effect on the basis that directives imposed obligations specifically and exclusively on the Member States. The Commission too argued that as regards individual persons Article 141 could not be regarded as having direct effect.

Advocate General Trabucchi supported the arguments put forward by Defrenne. His legal reasoning was very weak. He argued that as the objective of Article 141 was to abolish discrimination in pay it follows that the obligation falls not only on the Member States but also on other, private, employers. This is despite the wording of the Article which imposed an obligation only on the Member States to ensure that equal pay was achieved and maintained. He argued by analogy that the Court should apply the same reasoning to equal pay as it had to discrimination in relation to free movement of persons. Citing *Walrave* to the effect that the provisions of the Treaty relating to free movement of persons and the right of establishment prohibit discrimination in rules arising from whatever source and regulating gainful employment, Trabucchi argued that this same

[24] A formula subsequently repeated by the Court in subsequent cases, for example, Case 8/81 *Becker v Finazampt Munster-Innenstadt* [1982] ECR I-53.

[25] Case C-43/75 *Defrenne v Sabena* [1976] ECR 455.

approach be adopted to the principle of equal pay.[26] Finally he argued that as questions of equal pay were of direct concern to individuals Article 141 must create horizontal direct effect. However, none of these are substantial or convincing arguments as to why obligations clearly imposed on the Member States should be transferred to private employers. Nor is there any discussion of the constitutional significance of this interpretation of the Treaty allowing as it does provisions of Community law to be invoked in disputes in the courts of the Member States involving the legal relationships of private parties.

If the reasoning of Trabucchi is weak on this point then the reasoning of the Court is non-existent. Having determined that Article 141 was sufficiently clear and precise to meet the tests of direct effect in certain circumstances, it then asserted that it was 'not possible to sustain any objection that the application by national courts of the principle of equal pay would amount to modifying independent agreements concluded privately or in the sphere of industrial relations such as individual contracts and collective labour agreements'.[27] It went on, without giving any further reasoning that 'in fact, Article 119(141) is mandatory in nature, the prohibition on discrimination between men and women applies not only to the action of public authorities, but also extends to all agreements which are intended to regulate paid labour collectively, as well as to contracts between individuals'.[28]

Defrenne immediately provoked the following question: if Treaty articles could be invoked in the legal relations between individuals, could other provisions of Community law be similarly invoked? Given that the Court was willing to accord direct effect to directives after the expiry of the implementation period, could directives be invoked in the legal relationships between private parties? In *Marshall* the Court ruled that horizontal direct effect could not be ascribed to directives.[29] The case concerned Directive 76/207 EEC on the equal treatment of men and women in working conditions and the question was whether Marshall could rely on the provisions of that directive to challenge her compulsory retirement at the age of 63 from employment with a health board when men were retired at 65. On this question Advocate General Slynn argued that 'a directive not addressed to an individual cannot of itself impose obligations on him'.[30] In the context of a lengthy Opinion his reasoning on this key issue was brief. Directives do not have to be notified to an individual and are published in the Official Journal only for information; an individual would therefore not know that obligations were imposed on him by the directive. Individuals can rely on the direct effect of a directive in actions against the State since the State cannot rely on its own failure to implement a directive to deny individual rights but this principle cannot be transposed to private parties since they have no influence on the implementation of directives.

[26] Case 36/74 *Walrave & Koch v Association Union Cycliste Internationale* [1974] ECR 1405.

[27] Ibid, 1475, para 38.

[28] Ibid, 1476, para 39.

[29] Case 152/84 *Marshall v Southampton and South-West Hampshire Area Health Authority* [1986] ECR 723.

[30] Ibid, 734.

To accord horizontal direct effect to directives would blur the distinction between regulations and directives.

Although Slynn does not say so, he is in fact agreeing with Reischl that direct effect of a directive is the exception to the rule and, for that reason, the Court should respect the boundaries between regulations and directives provided for in the Treaty. It is interesting that Slynn makes no reference to Reischl's Opinion to support his own submissions and merely relies on existing authority to limit individuals' rights to invoke Treaty provisions. He offers the Court no alternative view. Perhaps Slynn understood that the Court had reached the limits of its interpretative capacity and that the concept of direct effect had its limitations. The Court's statement in *Marshall*, that the problem of inconsistency of rights between individuals working in the public and private sectors was for Member States to implement directives correctly and on time, does suggest that the Court itself was respectful of the distinction drawn in the Treaty between regulations where the Community alone has legislative powers and directives where there is a shared authority. In that sense *Marshall* was a defining point and one where both the Advocate General and the Court seemed at one.

Challenging the limitations of horizontal direct effects—the 1990s

Three Advocates General, Van Gerven, Jacobs and Lenz, argued in the 1990s that the Court's ruling in *Marshall I* should be revised.[31] Before examining their arguments in these cases, it is important to recall some key legal developments that had taken place since 1986 when *Marshall* was decided by the Court. In *Von Colson* the Court first articulated the duty of consistent interpretation (or indirect effects). The courts of the Member States are required, insofar as is possible, to interpret national legal provisions in conformity with Community law so as to achieve consistency between national and Community law.[32] Thus although an individual might not be able to rely on the direct effect of a provision of a directive, the national court nonetheless might achieve the same result by way of interpretation. As discussed below, this duty has subsequently been expanded and clarified by the Court. A second legal development was the Court's expansive interpretation of the concept of the State to include a variety of bodies that one might not automatically consider to fall within the traditional understanding of the term.[33] The effect of this case-law was to expand the impact of vertical direct

[31] Cases C-271/91 *Marshall v Southampton and South-West Hampshire Area Health Authority (Marshall II)* [1993] ECR I-4367; C-316/93 *Vaneetveld v Le Foyer* [1994] ECR I-763; C-91/92 *Faccini Dori v Recreb* [1994] ECR I-3325.

[32] Cases 14/83 *Von Colson and Kamann v Land-Nordrein Westphalen* [1984] ECR I-1891; C-106/89 *Marleasing* [1990] ECR I-4135.

[33] Case C-188/89 *Foster and ors v British Gas* [1990] ECR I-3313.

effect. A significant third development, discussed extensively in chapter 9, is the case-law on State liability. Individuals might be able to sue their own State for compensation if they are denied rights because of the State's failure to implement a directive properly or on time.[34] All three developments meant that the distinction drawn between horizontal and vertical direct effect began to lose its importance in practice. However these developments did not resolve all the problems created by the horizontal/vertical direct effect distinction.

Neither Van Gerven in *Marshall II* nor Jacobs in *Vaneetveld* needed to address the question of horizontal direct effect of directives in their Opinions since the cases before the Court did not raise this question specifically. However each of them did so. It is tempting to see in this coincidence some kind of collusion between the Advocates General as a way of influencing the Court collectively so as to demonstrate a weight of opinion in favour of change. Certainly Lenz quoted his colleagues in *Faccini Dori*, where the question of horizontal direct effect of directives was raised directly before the Court, in support of his own arguments. Van Gerven's arguments were succinct, Jacobs' lengthy and Lenz's comprehensive. Collectively they failed to convince the Court.

Van Gerven was the first Advocate General to argue for change.[35] He regarded some of the Court's case-law as distorting and inconsistent—in particular he was concerned about the Court's extension of the concept of the State which he saw as a somewhat artificial device to extend the direct effect of directives to bodies with an intangible link to the State. Bodies which had no control over the implementation of Community law were nonetheless being held responsible for the Government's failure to act.[36] These same bodies might be in competition with others in the private sector leading to an unfair public/private distinction. Van Gerven also criticized the Court's case-law on the duty of consistent interpretation as he saw in that duty a problematic extension of judicial powers Although he did not expressly say so, it was clear that Van Gerven saw the development of that line of cases as the Court's attempt to subvert the distinction between horizontal and vertical direct effect. For him, the better approach would be to allow the national courts to apply the relevant provisions of unimplemented directives rather than to distort the delimitation of judicial powers in the Member States. Finally, he argued that distortions of the conditions of competition were created between Member States which had implemented directives as against those which had not since economic operators in compliant States faced a heavier regulatory burden.

Jacobs attempted systematically to demolish any arguments that had been raised against the horizontal direct effect of directives. His arguments, in addition to those he shared with Van Gerven, can be grouped into four categories; Treaty based

[34] Joined Cases C-6/90 and C-9/90 *Francovich and ors v Italy* [1991] ECR I-5357.

[35] Case C-271/91 *Marshall II* [1993] ECR I-4367, 4387.

[36] Jacobs agreed with this argument calling it 'singularly inapposite' to impose an obligation on a health board which could not conceivably have responsibility for the failure of the legislature.

arguments, effectiveness, the democratic deficit and the rule of law. Jacobs was not convinced that the Court was consistent in its assertion that it looked to the wording of the Treaty to justify limiting the horizontal direct effects of directives. He argued that Article 249 did not exclude the possibility that individuals might derive rights directly from the provisions of directives and, in any case, strict adherence to the wording of Treaty articles would have led the Court to deny horizontal direct effects to Article 141. So the wording of the Treaty did not form an insurmountable obstacle. Furthermore, the extension of horizontal direct effects to directives would not blur the distinction between regulations and directives as, within the period for implementation, the Member States would still retain the discretion as to how directives were to be implemented. In any case, in practice the distinction was becoming blurred with directives, far from setting out general principles, being often very detailed and leaving little by way of discretion to Member States: in short directives were beginning to resemble regulations. Jacobs also argued that the effectiveness of Community law would be enhanced if individuals could invoke the provisions of unimplemented directives in the national courts and, moreover, that this would enhance the distinctiveness of Community law as against public international law, the latter being characterized by its lack of enforceability.[37] He dismissed arguments based on the democratic deficit reasoning that although the European Parliament had initially a limited role in enacting directives that role had now expanded and the argument that the legislature would be bypassed by enhancing the role of the courts was no longer relevant. Finally, he turned to the absence of a requirement to publish directives. Without explaining the significance of this argument in any depth, he dismissed it by stating that directives are routinely published and, following the entry into force of the Treaty on European Union, publication of directives in the Official Journal was now obligatory.

The Court had no need to address the arguments placed before it by either Van Gerven or Jacobs but in *Faccini Dori* it had to address the question of horizontal direct effect of directives. *Faccini Dori* concerned the failure on the part of Italy to implement Directive 85/77 concerning the protection of the consumer in respect of contracts negotiated away from business premises. By definition it was intended to regulate the legal relationships between private parties rather than the legal relations between a private party and the State. Faccini Dori entered into a contract for the pursuit of a language course at Milan railway station. She later wished to cancel her order and, in the absence of implementing legislation in Italy, relied on Article 5 of the Directive which allows consumers a period of seven days to renounce the contract where the contract has been entered into away from the premises of the company concerned. Faccini Dori was ordered, by the Italian judge, to pay the sums agreed since she did not have a right of cancellation under

[37] Advocate General Lenz subsequently used the argument of effectiveness in Case C-91/92 *Faccini Dori v Recreb Srl* [1994] ECR I-3325.

Italian law. The Italian court referred the case to the European Court of Justice asking whether in the period between the date for implementation set out in the Directive and the actual date of implementation by the Italian authorities the provisions of the Directive were sufficiently precise to create direct effect and, if so, could they be relied on by a consumer in proceedings against a trader.

This was the perfect setting for a discussion of the principle of horizontal direct effects. There were two opposing camps. The Court had sought the views of the Member States. Six Member States; Denmark, France, Germany, Italy, the Netherlands, and the UK, along with the Commission, argued that the Court's case-law should be maintained. Only the Greek government argued against this position. In favour of overruling *Marshall* were, as noted above, two of Lenz's Advocate General colleagues, Van Gerven and Jacobs. They had one ally in the Court who had declared his hand. Judge Schockweiler had written in support of the horizontal direct effect of directives.[38] Given the imbalance of power in these circumstances, Lenz would have to be exceptionally persuasive in his arguments if he wished to influence the Court to allow the horizontal direct effect of directives.

Lenz conceded that he would need to discover a new rationale to justify the horizontal direct effect of directives. The personal bar (estoppel) argument which justified the vertical direct effect of directives could not be used in cases where private parties were involved. Whereas vertical direct effect created a right for an individual against a specific Member State, to hold that a provision of a directive could create horizontal direct effect would have legal effects beyond the State to whom the directive was addressed and create obligations *erga omnes*. He concluded that 'the provision of a directive producing horizontal effects would participate in the primacy of Community law, which would be desirable in the interest of the uniform, effective application of Community law'.[39]

He also advised the Court that the rule of law required that horizontal direct effect should only be attributed to directives adopted after the Treaty on European Union came into effect. Legal certainty requires that the individual on whom a burden would be imposed should be aware of his obligations. Lenz argued that 'the basic condition for a burden imposed on the citizen by legislative measures is their constitutive publication in an official organ'.[40] This was first provided for by the Maastricht Treaty which inserted Article 191 into the EC Treaty, requiring the publication of directives in the Official Journal and therefore the condition was met when the Treaty entered into force on 1 November 1993. For reasons of legal certainty horizontal direct effect could only be recognised for measures whose publication was obligatory and therefore constitutive.

Lenz's arguments are similar to those proposed by Van Gerven and Jacobs. He supported the 'drive to do justice' on behalf of the individuals who would benefit

[38] Quoted by Advocate General Lenz in *Faccini Dori*, 3339.

[39] *Faccini Dori*, 3341, para 56. More recently, Advocates General have argued that primacy of Community law requires the courts of Member States to disapply conflicting national rules. See, in particular, Léger in *Linster* discussed below.

[40] *Faccini Dori*, 3343, para 64.

under provisions of directives but who were abandoned 'to the whim of a Member State in default of its obligations'.[41] He was concerned with discrimination in the context of the conditions of competition, in the context of disparities between individuals who had legal relationships with private bodies and those who had legal relationships with public bodies within a legal system, and in the context of disparities between legal systems. Such disparities offended against the principle of a Single European Market. He was one of the first Advocates General to use the new citizenship provisions to argue that all citizens should be equal before the law to reinforce these arguments.[42]

Like Jacobs, Lenz responded to the range of arguments that had been put forward to defend the status quo. For example, he denied that the wording of Article 249 EC would be offended—Member States retained the right to implement directives, but a legal obligation was imposed on them from the date the directive was published. A combination of their failure to implement a directive and the decision not to accord horizontal direct effect to directives would be to attribute a lesser legal quality to directives as a form of Community law. Like Jacobs, he was not convinced by arguments based on the democratic deficit. National parliaments have freedom to choose the form and methods of implementation both during and after the period for implementation provided for in the directive. The argument that Member States would become careless in their transposition of directives (because they would rely on the Court's finding of direct effect) was dismissed with the counter-argument that it might encourage governments to transpose directives within the time frame required to forestall the involvement of the courts.

All three Advocates General understood the constitutional importance of the arguments they placed before the Court. Van Gerven, in particular, was concerned that the Court's case-law on consistent interpretation would do violence to the traditional doctrine of separation of powers within the legal orders of the Member States. The principle of consistent interpretation requires the courts of the Member States to rule on the validity of national law which is often not within the limits of the national court's jurisdiction. The Advocates General, it could be argued, provided the Court with sufficient and acceptable legal justifications to enable it to overturn *Marshall I*. However, given the constitutional importance of the question and given that the Court's audience is the Member States in these constitutional cases the Court needed to justify any change politically. The early 1990s was not the time for the Court to engage in constructivist interpretations of Community law.[43] From a political perspective, it is not surprising that the Court did not seize the opportunity offered by Lenz to review its case-law. The Court reinforced its decision in *Marshall I* that a directive was binding only on the Member State to whom it is addressed. A Member State cannot rely on its own

[41] Ibid, 3339, para 48.
[42] The development of the concept of citizenship by the Court is discussed in chapter 10.
[43] For more on this point see chapter 10.

failure to comply with Community law. To extend that case-law to relations between individuals 'would be to recognize a power in the Community to enact obligations for individuals with immediate effect' whereas it has competence to do so only where it is empowered to adopt regulations.[44] Thus consumers, like Faccini Dori, could not derive a right of cancellation from Directive 85/577 EEC as against traders.

A new Approach to invocability?—The 21st century

In January 2000, Advocate General Léger gave a very authoritative and powerful Opinion in *Linster* which concerned the question of whether individuals might rely on the provisions of an untransposed directive, in this case Directive 85/337/EEC on the effects of certain public and private projects on the environment, to request a national court to review the legality of national provisions which affect their interests and which do not comply with the provisions of the directive in question.[45] The national court asked whether it had the power to review the legality of national provisions only in the light of directly effective provisions.

Léger's analysis, based on past case-law and academic writing, of the legal effects of untransposed or incorrectly transposed directives is innovative. Léger reviews the previous case-law on direct effect. The Court had ruled that the direct effect of directives is an exception to the principle that the legal effects of directives arose from the implementing national measures. Individuals could rely on the provisions of a directive only against the State which failed to implement it correctly or on time since the State was the defaulting party. Only provisions of directives which are sufficiently precise and unconditional could create direct effect. Léger explains that this is because 'a rule of law is all the easier to apply where there is no doubt regarding its content'.[46] However Léger also points to another tradition, albeit not the predominant tradition, in the case-law of the Court. The Court had ruled that the national court should, in ruling on the legality of national provisions, examine the way in which the Member State had exercised its discretion in implementing a directive to ensure that it had not exceeded the bounds of its discretion.[47] In these cases the Court does not necessarily apply the tests of precision and unconditionality but instead invites the national court to examine 'the powers allocated by the directive between the Community and the Member States'. These cases, he argued, should be seen as raising issues of primacy of Community law rather than its direct effect.

To make sense of these traditions Léger suggests that the key is in the nature of the proceedings brought by the individual which will determine the use to be

[44] *Faccini Dori*, 3356, para 24.

[45] Case C-287/98 *Luxembourg v Linster* [2000] ECR I-6917, OJ 1985 L 175/40.

[46] Ibid.

[47] For example in Case 51/76 *Verbond Nederlands On demimingen v Inspecteur des Invoerrechten en Accijnzen* [1997] ECR 113.

made of provisions of a directive. An individual may 'plead substitution' before the national court. This means that in place of an existing national rule which conflicts with the provisions of a directive, or where there is no national rule because of the failure of the Member State to transpose a directive, the national court is asked to apply the Community rule to define the rights of the individual. For the national court to apply the Community rule it must be clear and precise. Where it is not clear and precise the court cannot substitute the Community rule. In these circumstances the European Court has provided alternative means to secure the effectiveness of Community law. The principle of consistent interpretation requires the national court to seek a solution to the dispute in conformity with the requirements of Community law in so far as it has discretion to do so. Where both direct effect and the principle of consistent interpretation fail to secure the rights for which the directive provides, the individual may 'plead reparation' against the defaulting State under principles of State liability.

In other forms of proceedings an individual may seek to rely on the provisions of a directive to challenge the legality of a national rule. In these cases the individual seeks to 'exclude' the national rule (the ability to plead exclusion) rather than to assert a right. These cases raise questions of hierarchy of laws and the national court is entitled to review the compatibility of the subordinate rule (the national provision) to ensure that the Member State has kept within the limits of the discretion left to it under the terms of the directive. In these circumstances the terms in which the provisions of the directive are couched are less relevant. The relevant provision need not necessarily meet the tests of precision and unconditionality before being invoked by an individual in the national court. Direct effect, which is the requirement of the ability to plead substitution, can be uncoupled from the possibility of relying on a directive to plead exclusion. Léger argued that this approach provides individuals with the right to challenge the legality of national rules 'irrespective of the terms in which [directives] are couched' on the basis of hierarchy of norms. At the same time it respects the definition of a directive in Article 249 EC and reduces the harm caused to the effectiveness of Community law by the failure of a Member State to comply with its obligations. If his argument were to be followed the national court would not be limited to reviewing the legality of a conflicting national rule only against directly effective provisions of Community law but against the requirements of any Community law on the basis of primacy.

In *Caballero*[48] the Court appears to be following the course of action indicated by Léger rather that the Advocate General in the case, Geelhoed. Caballero challenged the manner in which Spain had implemented Council Directive 80/987 EEC on the approximation of laws of the Member States relating to the protection of employees in the event of the insolvency of their employer. In the event of the insolvency of their employer, individuals awarded compensation payments

[48] Case C-442/00 *Caballero v Fogasa* [2002] ECR I-11915.

following a conciliation procedure were not entitled to claim such payments whereas those awarded compensation following judicial proceedings were. The Court ruled that fundamental rights, including the principle of equality and non-discrimination, form part of the general principles of Community law which are binding on the Member States when they implement Community rules. The Spanish government had not put forward arguments to justify the discrimination in the case. The function of the national court in this situation was to set aside the discriminatory national provision 'without having to request or await prior removal by the legislature'.[49]

Geelhoed had based his Opinion on the fact that the provisions of the Directive in question were sufficiently precise and unconditional for application by the national courts but the Court ignored these arguments. Its ruling is based on the obligation on the Member States to respect the principle of equality when they implement directives. The principle of equality is the basis for the national court to exclude the conflicting national provision.

Pfeiffer concerned the transposition of the working time directive in Germany.[50] Germany had transposed the directive into German law but had introduced an exemption not provided for by the directive when it exempted 'duty time' from the calculation of the working week. A number of individuals working for the Red Cross brought actions against their employer for overtime payments and/or for a declaration that they were not required to work the extended hours. There was no discussion in this case as to whether the Red Cross was an emanation of the State, despite the activities being undertaken as part of the emergency apparatus in Germany. The case essentially was, therefore, one between individuals. The case was assigned to the sixth Chamber and Ruiz-Jarabo Colomer gave his Opinion in May 2003. He advised the Court that the disputed provision was sufficiently clear and precise to enable individuals to rely on it in the national courts. However, as the case was between individuals, the employees in question could not rely on its provisions. In these circumstances the Court had held that it was the duty of the national court to seek an interpretation of national law in such a way as to conform to the aims of the directive. He then stated, using *Simmenthal II* as authority: 'where it is impossible to provide an interpretation which conforms to the directive concerned, the national court must ensure the full effectiveness of Community law by setting aside on its own authority, where appropriate, any conflicting provisions of national law. The national court is not obliged to request or await the actual setting aside by the legislative authorities or by means of any other constitutional process'.[51]

If the Court had followed this Opinion it would, in effect, be allowing individuals to rely on the provisions of a Directive in a case against another private

[49] Ibid, para 43.

[50] Case C-403/01 *Pfeiffer v Deutsches Rotes Kreuz Kreisverbond Waldshut eV* [2004] ECR I-8835.

[51] The provision in issue in *Simmenthal* was a Regulation. See Case C-106/77 *Amministrazione delle Finanze dello stato v Simmenthal* [1998] ECR 629, para 58.

party. The passage quoted does not provide convincing arguments as to why the Court should change the direction of its case-law. As it stands, the Advocate General is asserting that it is the duty of the national court to set aside a provision of national law which conflicts with the directive. Applying a Léger-type analysis, Ruiz-Jarabo Colomer is misinterpreting the Court's previous case-law by confusing a pleading in substitution with one of a pleading of exclusion. In view of the importance of this issue, the case was remitted to the Grand Chamber and Ruiz-Jarabo Colomer was asked to deliver a second Opinion, specifically on the effects of an incorrectly transposed directive. In his second Opinion he stated that he was seeking a solution based on the primacy of Community law and the duty of cooperation of Member States under Article 10 EC. He again stated that the provisions of the directive in question were sufficiently clear and precise but that the case-law of the Court meant that individuals could not rely on those provisions in cases against other private parties. In those circumstances it was the duty of the national court to seek an interpretation of the national provisions in conformity with Community law and gave several examples where the Court had, in effect, directed the national court to the correct interpretation even to the extent of not applying a rule of national law. In effect, Ruiz-Jarabo Colomer was arguing that the Court's extensive interpretation of the duty to achieve an interpretation in conformity with Community law was so extensive as to have provided an alternative to horizontal direct effect of directives. He did not wish to see a retreat from this position; otherwise the primacy of Community law would be eroded. Neither was he arguing for the horizontal direct effect of directives. What he wanted was for the national court to find a mechanism to interpret national law to conform with the Directive. This seems a retreat from his earlier Opinion where he suggested that the national court should set aside any conflicting provisions of national law.

The Court, in *Pfeiffer*, whilst making no reference to Léger's Opinion in *Linster* nor to the distinction between pleadings of substitution or exclusion, nonetheless ruled that there are two aspects to the question of whether, if the Directive has been incorrectly implemented, Article 6(2) thereof may be taken to have direct effect. In doing so there is some echo here of Léger's analysis. The relevant passage is worth stating in full:

> As is clear from its wording and from the context in which it occurs, there are two aspects to the question; the first concerns the interpretation of Article 6(2) of Directive 93/104 for the purpose of enabling the national court to decide whether the relevant rules of national law are compatible with the requirements of Community law, whilst the second concerns whether, if the Member State concerned has transposed Article 6(2) into national law correctly, that provision satisfied the conditions which would enable an individual to rely on it before national courts in circumstances such as those in the main proceedings.[52]

[52] Case C-403/01 *Pfeiffer v Deutsches Rotes Kreuz Kreisverband Waldshut eV* [2004] ECR I-8835.

In respect of the import of Article 6(2) the Court ruled that the Directive precluded legislation of the kind in question which permitted the 48-hour maximum period of weekly working time to be exceeded. As regards the second aspect, the Court ruled that Article 6(2) satisfies the criteria for direct effect but that even 'a clear, precise and unconditional provision of a directive seeking to confer rights or impose obligations on individuals cannot of itself apply in proceedings exclusively between private parties'.[53] However it is the responsibility of the national court to provide the legal protection derived from Community law and to ensure that Community law is effective. In doing so, the national court must 'consider national law **as a whole** in order to assess to what extent it may be applied so as not to produce a result contrary to that sought by the directive'.[54] In the present case that means that the national court must do whatever lies in its jurisdiction to ensure that the directive is fully effective. The Court therefore supported the Advocate General's view that there should be no retreat from its case-law, although whether this kind of ruling is helpful to the national Judge is far from clear.

Mangold raised the issue of the legal effects of a provision of a directive before the time limit for transposition had expired as well as the question, similar to that raised in *Pfeiffer*, of the effects in proceedings between individuals of incorrectly transposed directives. Tizzano was Advocate General in this case. Germany had introduced legislation to promote the employment of older workers. It exempted contracts of employment for older workers from the legislation on fixed-term contracts. There was evidence to suggest that employers were reluctant to give open ended contracts to older workers. German legislation required that an objective justification be required for the use of fixed term contracts but that no such objective justification was required in respect of contracts with older workers; older workers initially being defined as over 60 in its 1985 legislation, later reduced to 58 and then 52 by subsequent legislative amendments. Meanwhile Germany was required, by December 2006, to implement Directive 2000/78 laying down a general framework for combating discrimination on the grounds of, *inter alia*, age. Helm offered a position to Mangold in June 2003. It was a fixed-term, part-time contract. Mangold was 56 at the time of the employment contract and the German provisions exempted employment contracts with workers over 52 from the fixed-term contract legislation. There was some evidence to suggest that the parties to the dispute had manufactured the circumstances in order to challenge the validity of the German provision fixing the age limit.

For the purposes of this chapter the relevant question was whether Article 6(1) of Directive 2000/78, which authorized Member States to derogate from the principle of non-discrimination for reasons which are objectively justified and proportionate to the legitimate aim pursued, precluded a national provision which allows workers over 52 to be employed on fixed term contracts where there is no objective reason for the use of a fixed-term contract. Tizzano approached this

[53] Ibid, para 109. [54] Ibid, para 115, emphasis added.

question by arguing that the general principle of equality is binding on Member States when they implement Community law and can therefore be used by the Court in reviewing national rules falling within the scope of Community law.[55] The general principle of equality requires that comparable situations must be treated in the same way unless there is an objective justification and the difference is appropriate and necessary to secure a legitimate aim. He argued that this general principle was the same principle to be found in the directive so the German legislation could be scrutinized for conformity with either the general principle or the provisions of the directive. The former was preferable since 'being a general principle of Community law imposing an obligation that is precise and unconditional, it is effective against all parties and, unlike the directive, could therefore be relied upon directly by Mr Mangold'.[56] Examining the provisions of German law, Tizzano advised the Court that there was an objective justification for the legislation but that the manner in which the objective was pursued was disproportionate because of its effects on substantial numbers of older workers. It did not therefore meet the tests of being appropriate and necessary.

Tizzano is arguing for the recognition of the horizontal direct effect of general principles of Community law and says so explicitly. 'There is no doubt' he says 'the national court would have to disapply a national rule held contrary to that principle which is regarded as having direct effect'.[57] The general principle argument has the benefit that individuals could rely on their Community rights against the State and against other private parties. This result could not be achieved on the basis of Directive 2000/78 because of the distinction in the case-law of the Court between horizontal and vertical direct effect. In the event of incompatibility between the German legislation and provisions of the directive the national court could not disapply the national rules but instead would be obliged to seek a consistent interpretation. Tizzano appears to be taking the Court's decision in *Caballero* even further. Whereas in *Caballero* the Court ruled that fundamental rights could be the basis to plead exclusion, Tizzano now appears to argue that fundamental rights may form the basis of a plea of substitution.

The Court's reasoning is somewhat confused but it seems that it accepted Tizzano's argument that the principle of non-discrimination on grounds of age must be regarded as part of the general principle of equality and thus part of directly effective Community law. As a general principle of Community law, its observance cannot be made conditional upon the expiry of the period laid down in the directive. In these circumstances, the responsibility of the national court is to ensure the legal protection which individuals derive from Community law and set aside any national provision which conflicts with that law.[58] This appears to mean that the Court accepts that individuals can rely on a general principle of

[55] Whether the general principle of equality includes the prohibition of discrimination on the grounds of age is a moot point. See A Arnull's editorial, 'Out with the old . . . ' (2006) 31 ELR 1.

[56] Case C-144/04 *Mangold v Helm* [2005] ECR I-9981, Opinion of AG Tizzano, para 84.

[57] Ibid, para 101.

[58] Ibid, para 77.

Community law in the same way as they might on a provision of the Treaty. However the operational part of the judgment is far from clear since the Court states that it is Article 6(1) of Directive 2000/78 which must be interpreted so as to preclude national legislation of the kind in question and that the responsibility of the national court is to guarantee the full effectiveness of the general principle of non-discrimination in respect of age.

Adeneler is another case relating to fixed term contracts.[59] One of the questions referred by the national court was the following:

> Must a national court—as far as possible—interpret its domestic law in conformity with a directive which was transposed belatedly into national law from:
>
> (a) the time when the directive entered into force, or
> (b) the time when the time-limit for transposing it into national law passed without the transposition being effected, or
> (c) the time when the national measures implementing it entered into force?

Kokott argued that the duty arises even before the expiry of the period for implementation on the basis that directives are binding on the Member States from the date they enter into force as to the result to be achieved. The Court had ruled that Member States were prohibited from frustrating the object of a directive in the transposition period by introducing measures which might jeopardize the attainment of the objectives of the directive.[60] She argued that, as well as this negative duty, a positive duty could also be discerned from Article 10 EC. When a directive enters into force the positive duty to achieve the result of the directive applies to all the authorities of the Member States including the courts. That does not mean that the courts should refrain from applying conflicting national law but that the courts should seek a consistent interpretation within the transposition period. The transposition period is to allow the legislature to accommodate national law to the provisions of the directive; it is not a period of grace that the national courts are granted.

The Court was more circumspect. It held that the duty of consistent interpretation arises only where a provision of a directive lacks direct effect, either because it is insufficiently precise or because the dispute is between individuals. That obligation arises only after the period for the transposition of the directive has expired. However, the Court also ruled that 'from the date upon which a directive has entered into force, the courts of the Member States must refrain as far as possible from interpreting domestic law in a manner which might seriously compromise, after the period of transposition has expired, attainment of the objective pursued by that directive'. Thus the Court did not agree with Kokott but it did extend the scope of the duty of consistent interpretation by requiring the national courts, even before the period of transposition has ended, to refrain from an interpretation of national law inconsistent with the objectives of a directive.

59 Case C-212/04 *Adeneler v ELOG* OJ C179/8.
60 Case C-129/96 *Inter-Environnement Wallonie* [1997] ECR I-7411.

Judge Lenaerts has recently argued that 'the debate on how and when individuals can invoke EU law has not abated' and that the Court itself is 'torn between various models, each with its own advantages and drawbacks'.[61] Given that he was one of the Judges in *Pfeiffer* this comment might give an insight into the deliberations of the Court. It does suggest that the inconsistencies in Community law brought about by the ruling in *Marshall* that directives could not be invoked between private parties are still to be resolved. It could be argued that the Advocates General in the cases discussed here are trying to reduce the inconsistencies inherent in Community law at present. In *Linster* Léger attempted to uncouple the Court's case-law on direct effect from its case-law on the duty of the national court to ensure that the Member State has remained within the bounds of the discretion left to it by Community law when it implements directives. In *Cabellero*, the Court appeared to apply this distinction when it ruled that fundamental rights bind the Member States as they implement Community law. Therefore the national court, in examining how the Member State has exercised its discretion, should take fundamental rights into consideration. In *Pfeiffer*, the Court (without using Léger's language of substitution and exclusion) held that it is not possible to plead substitution in cases between individuals but extended the duty on the national courts to consider national law as a whole in order to seek an interpretation in conformity with Community law. *Mangold* could be read as meaning that the Court now accepts that general principles of Community law are capable of creating direct effect; this is certainly how sections of Tizzano's Opinion read. However, the judgment of the Court in *Mangold* is both unclear and contradictory. Finally the Court in *Adeneler* imposed a restriction on the national courts to refrain from interpreting national law in a way that would ultimately jeopardize the attainment of the objective of a directive.

Lenaerts and Corthaut read these cases, and others, to mean that the concept of direct effect needs now to be seen in context as being only one way in which provisions of Community law can be invoked in the national courts. They argue that the principle of direct effect has its limitations and that those limitations 'should not spill over to limit the application of alternative forms of invoking EU law: consistent interpretation, state liability and primacy of EU law'.[62] They would go further to argue that 'there is no need to examine whether the conditions for direct effect are fulfilled whenever the validity of a norm of national law is assessed in the light of a higher norm of EU law, irrespective of whether judicial review takes place during direct or indirect review proceedings'.[63] The Court has not gone this far, and neither have the Advocates General. In the cases discussed above the Advocates General appear to be encouraging the Court to find ways in which the national court can apply the provisions of Community law in cases involving proceedings between private parties whilst holding technically to the distinction

[61] K Lenaerts and T Corthaut, 'Of birds and hedges: the role of primacy in invoking norms of EU law' (2006) 31 ELR 287.
[62] Ibid, 314.
[63] Ibid.

between vertical and horizontal direct effect. The duty of consistent interpretation has been expanded. There is the possibility that the Court has ruled that general principles of Community law can create direct effect although its judgment is *Mangold* is, frankly, incomprehensible.

These cases serve more than anything to underline the need for some consistent approach from the Court and some clear thinking. The case-law is confusing. Therefore it might also be time for the Advocates General to try collectively to come to a coherent sense of what is required and to argue each case consistently.

Concluding observations

A term that has been used throughout this chapter, and that is also used by other authors, is European constitutional law, or the chapter refers to the constitutional significance of the case-law. The European Union, of course, does not have a constitution in the sense that the term is understood at the level of the Member States. The European Union 'constitution' is found within a series of international treaties. It has been the function of the Court to determine what rules underpin the European constitution and it has done so in an evolutionary manner in responding, in the main, to questions on the interpretation of Community law raised by the national courts. Had there been a 'real' constitution the issues discussed in this chapter would not have been a matter for the courts. The hierarchy of norms between provisions of European and national law, the jurisdictional scope of the national courts and so on would be matters provided in the constitution. However, because the constitutional principles have developed over time and unsystematically, inconsistencies have become built into the system.

Several of the Advocates General discussed in this chapter realized the constitutional significance of the issues before the Court. Roemer certainly set out the key issue in his Opinion, in particular the implications for the legal orders of the Member States to which he deferred. In the 1970s Reischl played an influential role in providing the justification for the direct effect of directives in applying a form of personal bar (estoppel) type of argument. This was helpful for the Court and his arguments have been used subsequently. The 1980s was the decade when the limitations of the direct effect principle first began to become clearly apparent and the inconsistencies of the distinction between vertical and horizontal direct effect on private parties raised questions about the wisdom of this distinction. Slynn proved to be an Advocate General who deferred to the wording of the Treaty. Van Gerven, Jacobs and Lenz sought in vain in the 1990s to influence the Court in the direction of recognising the horizontal direct effect of directives. They understood the constitutional significance of their arguments. Lenz, in particular, saw a possible erosion of the primacy and effectiveness of Community law when directives were not implemented correctly or on time. In the first decade of the new century the Advocates General are still struggling to make sense of

Europe's constitutional law. This group of Advocates General do not defer to the Treaty in the same way as Roemer or Slynn, and appear to be willing to try to push the boundaries of the case-law. However, some of the judgments of the Court seem to be an uneasy compromise between the arguments of these Advocates General and the very constitutional provisions laid out by the Court. Perhaps in the next few years it will be the function of the Advocates General collectively to analyse for the Court a coherent and consistent European constitutional order.

9

The contribution of Advocates General to the development of the principle of State liability in the European Community's legal order

Introduction

Francovich and Bonifaci v Italy (*Francovich*) was the first case where the European Court of Justice expressly ruled that '[I]t follows that the principle whereby a State must be liable for loss and damage caused to individuals as a result of breaches of Community law for which the State can be held responsible is inherent in the system of the Treaty'.[1] The *Francovich* case was decided in 1991, almost 30 years after the European Court of Justice stated in the *Van Gend en Loos* case that:

> the Community constitutes a new legal order of international law for the benefit of which the states have limited their sovereign rights, albeit within limited fields, and the subjects of which comprise not only Member States but also their nationals. Independently of the legislation of Member States, Community law therefore not only imposes obligations on individuals but is also intended to confer upon them rights which become part of their legal heritage. These rights arise not only where they are expressly granted by the Treaty, but also by reason of obligations which the Treaty imposes in a clearly defined way upon individuals as well as upon the Member States and upon the institutions of the Community.[2]

It was inevitable that this new legal order would develop remedies and sanctions to protect and enforce the individual rights which the European Court of Justice had declared in the *Van Gend en Loos* case to have been conferred by the EC Treaty. The initial steps were taken in *Van Gend en Loos* itself by the Court ruling that some

[1] Joined Cases C-6/90 and C-9/90 [1991] ECR I-5357, para 35. For further literature on this case see, for example, the case note by G Behr in (1992) 29 CML Rev 557 and the following: PP Craig, '*Francovich*, remedies and the scope of damages liability' (1993) 109 LQR 595; D Curtin, 'State liability under Community law: a new remedy for private parties' (1992) 21 ILJ 74; M Ross, 'Beyond *Francovich*' (1993) 56 MLR 55; F Snyder, 'The Effectiveness of European Community Law: Institutions, Processes, Tools and Techniques' (1993) 56 MLR 19; J Steiner, 'From Direct Effects to *Francovich*: Shifting Means of Enforcement of Community law' (1993) 18 ELR 3; C Harlow, '*Francovich* and the Problem of the Disobedient State' (1996) 2 ELJ 199.

[2] Case 26/62 [1963] ECR 1, 12.

provisions of the EC Treaty have direct effect and confer rights on individuals which national courts are obliged to protect. Then in *Costa v ENEL* the European Court of Justice stated that: 'the law stemming from the Treaty, an independent source of law, could not, because of its special and original nature, be overridden by domestic legal provisions, however framed, without being deprived of its nature as Community law and without the legal basis of the Community itself being called into question'.[3] This ruling established the principle of supremacy of Community law over national law. The principle of State liability giving rise to a right to compensation thus joined the doctrines of direct effect and supremacy as core principles of Community law.

Given that by the early 1960s the principles of 'direct effect' and 'supremacy' of Community law were established, it is surprising that it should have taken so long for the principle of State liability to be acknowledged in the case-law of the European Court of Justice. Until the *Francovich* case there had been few cases where the issue of State liability had been raised and/or even discussed.[4] The first time this matter was *directly* raised was in the mid-1970s in *Russo v AIMA*.[5]

The slow pace of the development of a State liability principle in Community law is probably due, first, to the restrictions imposed on the European Court of Justice in Article 234 preliminary references[6] and, second, to the generous application of the 'direct effect' doctrine. The development of Community law principles owes much to the willingness of national courts to seek a preliminary judgment (under Article 234 EC) from the European Court of Justice. Since the *Van Gend en Loos* judgment individual litigants may bring actions in the national courts relying on the direct effect of a particular Community provision in order to seek an immediate remedy before a national court.[7] Thus the issue of State liability is more likely to arise in Article 234 proceedings than in direct actions before the European Court of Justice. The development of Community law principles depends heavily on national litigation, the ability of the national courts to identify

[3] Case 6/64 [1964] ECR 585, 594.

[4] Case 23/59 *FERAM* [1958–59] ECR 245; Case 6/60 *Humblet v Belgium* [1960] ECR 559; Case 14/60 *Meroni and ors v HA* [1961] ECR 161; Case 13/68 *SpA Salgoil v Italian Ministry for Foreign Trade* [1968] ECR 453; Case 39/72 *Commission v Italy* [1973] ECR 101; Case 60/75 *Russo v AIMA* [1976] ECR 45; Case 33/76 *Rewe-Zentralfinanz etc v Landwirtschaftskammer* [1976] ECR 1989; Case 45/76 *Comet BV v Produktschap* [1976] ECR 2043; Case 52/76 *Benedetti v Munari* [1977] ECR 163; Case 158/80 *REWE -Handelsgesellschaft v Hauptzollamt* [1981] ECR 1805; Case 199/82 *Amministrazione delle Finanze dello Stato v ApA San Giorgio* [1983] ECR 3595; Cases 106 and 120/87 *Asteris AE and ors v Hellenic Republic and EEC* [1988] ECR 5515.

[5] Case 60/75 [1976] ECR 45, discussed below.

[6] An Art 234 procedure arises from litigation before a national court in which, in order for the national judge to be able to decide the case, it is found necessary to have an interpretation of Community law or a declaration of validity of a Community measure. The European Court of Justice has exclusive jurisdiction to rule on these issues and the Art 234 procedure enables the national court to seek a ruling on the relevant Community law from the European Court of Justice. The national court then applies the European Court of Justice ruling (which is binding upon the requesting national court) to the facts of the case and delivers judgment in the national proceedings.

[7] The range of national remedies is more favourable than Community ones, and of course, may include a remedy in damages.

Community law matters and on the willingness of these courts to seek a preliminary reference from the European Court of Justice.

It is not, therefore, surprising that, after the European Court of Justice had finally made it clear that an action for State liability was available to individuals, it would take several further Article 234 references before the criteria for liability of different kinds of breaches of Community law were established.[8] In an Article 234 ruling the European Court of Justice limits itself to answering the specific questions of Community law referred to it by the national court. Issues that are raised by jurists, commentators and even Advocates General, are not (and cannot be) ruled upon until those questions are specifically referred to the European Court of Justice by the national court.

The impact of the direct effect doctrine on the slow pace of the development of State liability in the Community legal order is subtle and difficult to assess. The doctrine enables natural and legal persons to rely on directly effective provisions of Community law before national courts and to force the Member State to abide by Community law. Since the *Van Gend en Loos* case there have been major developments in the application of the doctrine of direct effect. Not only has the doctrine been extended to secondary Community measures, namely decisions and directives,[9] but the European Court of Justice case-law has expanded the impact of the doctrine indirectly in several ways. For example, in the cases of directives when the principle can only be relied on vertically, (that is against the Member State itself) a very wide Community law meaning has been given to the concept of a 'State'.[10] Similarly, indirect effect has been achieved by imposing on the national court a duty to interpret national law in a manner compatible with Community law wherever possible.[11] In the case of compatibility with directives the obligation on the national courts is imposed irrespective of whether the period prescribed for its implementation has expired.[12]

[8] In Art 234 proceedings a list of questions from the national court is submitted to the European Court of Justice and all parties, generally, limit their submissions to the specific questions referred to the Court. In direct actions there is more opportunity for issues to be raised which have not to have been considered by all the parties. For an acknowledgement of the restrictiveness of the Art 234 procedure in the context of State liability referral see paragraph 29 of the Opinion of Advocate General Léger in C-66/95 *Ex parte Sutton* [1997] ECR I-2163 where he refrained from dealing at all with the question of State liability for breach of Community law since the questions formulated by the national court did not raise the issue. However the European Court of Justice (Full Court) felt no such inhibitions. See also the Opinion of Advocate General Jacobs, para 113 in C-112/00 *Schmidberger* [2003] I-5659.

[9] Case 9/70 *Grad* [1970] ECR 825; Case 41/74 *Van Duyn* [1974] ECR 1337 and Case 8/81 *Becker* [1982] ECR 53. For a detailed analysis of the principle of direct effect see chapter 8.

[10] See Case C-188/89 *Foster v British Gas* [1990] ECR I-3313; Case 152/84 *Marshall* [1986] ECR 723.

[11] Case 14/83 *Van Colson* [1984] ECR 1891. In *Marleasing*, C-106/89 [1990] ECR I-4135, the European Court of Justice stated that in applying national law, whether the national provisions had been enacted before or after the directive, the national court, as far as possible, was required to interpret national law in the 'light of the wording and the purpose' of the directive.

[12] Case 80/86 *Kolpinghuis Nijmegen* [1987] ECR 3969.

These developments provided individuals with access to national courts where their Community rights could be protected. The objective of the litigants was to establish their rights, not to be compensated for losses. Most of the cases concerned employment and social matters where individuals were fighting for rights and the actual losses were not very large. It was in the mid-1980s, in *Bourgoin*,[13] that a UK court for the first time faced a claim in damages against a public body. The case was settled however and did not reach the European Court of Justice.[14] It was only 10 years later, in *Francovich* that the European Court of Justice was given the opportunity to consider directly and thoroughly whether a Member State should be liable in damages to an individual for a breach of that State's Community obligations.

Since the *Francovich* case there have been several important cases including, *Brasserie du Pêcheur, Factortame III*,[15] *ex parte BT*,[16] *Lomas*,[17] *Dillenkofer*[18]and *Köbler*[19] which have further clarified and refined the criteria upon which a Member State may be held liable, as a matter of Community law, to compensate those who have suffered harm as a result of that State's breach of Community law. The *Francovich* case and the cases that followed have resulted in a vast amount of academic literature analysing the reasoning of the judgments and Opinions of the Advocates General as well as discussing the consequences of these decisions.[20] With notable exceptions,[21] not much has been written on the pre-*Francovich* case-law or on the evolution of this significant principle of Community law.

The objective of this chapter is to analyse the European Court of Justice case-law on State liability with particular reference to the Opinions of the Advocates General. Given that the European Court of Justice rarely refers to the Opinions of the Advocate General, it is impossible to assess with confidence the impact such Opinions may have on the judges deliberating the case. An attempt, however, will be made to identify the contribution that the Opinions have made towards the recognition and development of a Community law principle of State liability giving rise to compensation.

[13] *Bourgoin v Ministry of Agriculture, Fisheries and Food* [1986] QB 716, CA.

[14] The Court of Appeal confirmed that a private right to damages existed under English law for misfeasance in public office.

[15] Joined Cases C-46/93 *Brasserie du Pêcheur SA v Germany* and C-48/93 *R v Secretary for Transport, ex p Factortame Ltd and ors (Factortame III)* [1996] ECR I-1029.

[16] Case C-392/93 *R v HM Treasury, ex p British Telecommunications plc* [1996] ECR I-1631.

[17] Case C-5/94 *R v Ministry of Agriculture, Fisheries & Food, ex p Hedley Lomas (Ireland)* [1996] ECR I-2552.

[18] Joined Cases C-178/94, C-179/94, C-188–190/94 *Dillenkofer and ors v Germany* [1996] ECR I-4845.

[19] Case C-224/01 *Köbler v Austria* [2003] ECR I-10239.

[20] See n 1 above and J Temple Lang, 'New legal effects resulting from the failure of the State to fulfil obligations under European Community law: the *Francovich* judgment' (1992) 16 Fordham International Law Journal 1; D Curtin, 'State liability under Community law: a new remedy for private parties' (1992) 21 ILJ 74; R Caranta, 'Governmental liability after *Francovich*' (1993) 52 CLJ 272.

[21] T Tridimas, 'Member State Liability in Damages for Breach of Community Law: an Assessment of the Case Law' in J Beatson and T Tridimas (eds), *New Directions in European Public Law* (1998).

The chapter will be structured as follows. First, Advocate General Mischo's Opinion and the European Court of Justice's judgment in *Francovich* will be examined with reference to the pre-*Francovich* case-law. This exercise will focus on the origin and nature of the principle of State liability within the Community's legal order and on the conditions for liability which have to be met for a successful Francovich-type action, that is, an action for non-implementation of directives. The pre-*Francovich* case-law will be analysed with a view to identifying how far Mischo was influenced by the earlier case-law including the Opinions of other Advocates General.

Second, Advocate General Léger's Opinion in the *Lomas* case and Advocate General Tesauro's Opinions in the *Brasserie du Pêcheur/Factortame III*, *ex parte BT* and *Dillenkofer* cases will be analysed particularly in the context of the origin and nature of the State liability principle under Community law and the conditions of liability for legislative, administrative and judicial failures of the State.

Third, a selection of the subsequent Opinions and European Court of Justice judgments will be considered, focusing in particular upon those which have helped to refine the *conditions* of liability, notably that that there must be a 'sufficiently serious' breach for the Member State to incur liability for damages sustained as a result of the infringement of Community law. The chapter concludes with a general appraisal of the Advocates General's contribution to the creation and development of this principle of Community law.

Francovich: The principle of State liability

In the *Francovich* case the European Court of Justice ruled expressly that compensation for harm caused to an individual by breaches of Community law committed by the State is a 'principle of Community law'.[22] The legal basis of this principle is to be found in Article 10 EC [23] which requires the Member States to take all appropriate measures to ensure the fulfilment of their obligations under Community law.[24] This doctrine of effectiveness of Community law, which is founded on the EC Treaty and clearly applied in the case-law of the European Court of Justice,[25] embodies two central elements: the principle of equivalence

[22] Joined Cases C-6/90 and C-9/90 [1991] ECR I-5357, para 37 of the judgment.

[23] Art 10 imposes on the Member States a strict duty to: 'take all appropriate measures, whether general or particular, to ensure fulfilment of the obligations arising out of this Treaty or resulting from action taken by the institutions of the Community. They shall facilitate the achievement of the Community's tasks.They shall abstain from any measure which could jeopardize the attainment the objectives of this Treaty'.

[24] Joined Cases C-6/90 and C-9/90 *Francovich* [1991] ECR I-5357, para 36 of the judgment and paras 33 point 3 and 37 of the Opinion.

[25] For example, Case 6/60 *Humblet v HA* [1960] ECR 559 where the Court ruled under Art 86 ECSC (which corresponds to Art 10 EC) the Belgian authorities were obliged to nullify the 'effects' of wrongful tax assessments.

and the requirement of adequacy. The element of 'equivalence' requires all remedies available under national law also to be available under the same conditions for breaches of directly applicable Community law provisions. The doctrine of 'adequacy' is self-explanatory, requiring the remedy to be adequate in relation to the harm sustained. Where there is conflict between these two elements, the requirement of adequacy prevails.[26] These elements are particularly relevant when the European Court of Justice is asked to determine the compatibility with Community law of national procedural rules which have an impact on the Community rights of individuals.

The *Francovich* case concerned the failure of the Italian Government to implement Directive 80/987 EEC which provides for the protection of employees in the event of the insolvency of their employers.[27] The European Court of Justice had confirmed in *Commission v Italy*[28] that Italy was in breach of its Treaty obligations for failing to implement the Directive. The plaintiffs, having failed to obtain any payment for arrears of salary from the insolvent employers, sought reimbursement of these sums (or damages) from the Italian State. The national courts before whom the two cases were brought, sought an Article 234 preliminary ruling.

Both the European Court of Justice and Advocate General Mischo concluded that Directive 80/987 did not meet the conditions for direct effect[29] and, therefore, the plaintiffs could not rely directly on the provisions of the Directive before the national courts.

Nevertheless, the European Court of Justice had found Italy to have been in breach of Community law. It was also clear that the plaintiffs had been injured by that failure. The national court therefore asked expressly whether, in these circumstances, individuals could claim compensation for the loss suffered as a result of the Member State's breach of Community law. Advocate General Mischo concluded that Community law provided for State liability in these circumstances. He relied primarily on the obligation on Member States under Community law to ensure the effectiveness of Community law in all cases where rights have been conferred on individuals, irrespective of whether the measures conferring those rights have direct effect.[30] The right to receive compensation complemented other rights conferred on individuals by Community law.

Furthermore, he opined that a failure to implement a Community measure or an incorrect implementation of that measure not only deprives Community law of its effect but the Member State concerned also commits a breach of its Treaty obligations under Article 10 EC. In addition, where a judgment of the European Court of Justice exists confirming that breach, the Member State concerned has a

[26] Case C-213/89 *Factortame I* [1990] ECR I-2433.

[27] [1980] OJ L283/23.

[28] Case 22/87 [1989] ECR 143.

[29] The conditions were set out in Case 41/74 *Van Duyn* [1974] ECR 1337 and confirmed in Case 8/81 *Becker v Finanzamt* [1982] ECR 53.

[30] Joined Cases C-6/90 and C-9/90 *Francovich* [1991] ECR I-5357, para 33 points 1 and 2 of the Opinion.

duty to take all appropriate measures to make good its default including giving compensation for the harm caused to individuals as a result of the unlawful act.[31] The European Court of Justice implicitly agreed with the Advocate General's conclusions ruling that a Member State is required to make good loss or damage caused to individuals by failure to transpose the directive in question.

How revolutionary was Mischo's Opinion? State liability had been raised in only a few cases before the *Francovich* case. *Russo v AIMA*[32] was the first case which *directly* related to the issue of State liability. However there are a few earlier cases where the issue of State liability was raised either by the Court or by the Advocate General. State liability was first mentioned by Advocate General Lagrange within the context of the ECSC Treaty in the *FERAM*[33] and *Meroni*[34] cases. These were actions brought in accordance with Article 40 ECSC where the plaintiffs sought compensation from the High Authority (HA). In these cases, the discussion focused on the conditions, under French law, for the State to incur liability for the wrongful act of one of its administrative organs. State liability was also raised by the European Court of Justice itself in the *Humblet*[35] case, an action against the Belgian State, in respect of the Protocol on Privileges and Immunities of the European Coal and Steel Community where the plaintiff sought relief for an alleged breach of Community law. The *Humblet* case is considered to be the first case where the Court enunciated State liability as a principle of Community law. The other pre-*Russo v AIMA* cases are the *Salgoil*[36] case, an Article 234 reference, and *Commission v Italy*,[37] an Article 226 action.[38] Mischo in his *Francovich* Opinion cited only *Humblet* and *Salgoil* of these pre-*Russo* cases in support of his reasoning. After *Russo v AIMA* (and before the *Francovich* case) few cases referred to State liability.[39]

The origin and scope of the action

*Pre-*Francovich *pioneers*

As stated above, the first case where the matter of State liability was raised directly was in the mid-1970s in *Russo v AIMA*.[40] The Pretura di Bovino sought an Article 234 preliminary ruling, asking the European Court of Justice, *inter alia*, whether a principle existed in Community law which would allow private persons, in the circumstances of this particular case, to be compensated for the harmful pecuniary

[31] Ibid, para 33 points 3 and 4 of the Opinion.
[32] Case 60/75 [1976] ECR 45.
[33] Case 23/59 [1959] ECR 245.
[34] Cases 14/60 et seq. [1961] ECR 161.
[35] Case 6/60 [1960] ECR 559.
[36] Case 13/68 [1968] ECR 453.
[37] Case 39/72 [1973] ECR 101.
[38] Art 226 enables the Commission to bring a Member State before the European Court of Justice where it has concluded that the Member State has failed to fulfil a Treaty obligation. This action is only available after the Commission has issued a reasoned opinion (after giving the Member State concerned an opportunity to submit its observations) and the Member State has failed to comply with it within the period specified by the Commission.
[39] Listed n 4 above.
[40] Case 60/75 [1976] ECR 45.

consequences which resulted from the unlawful action of the Member State. Russo, an Italian producer of durum wheat, was injured by a 1973 decision of the Italian government to freeze wholesale and retail prices of certain products, including pasta (a product of durum wheat). The Italian government had authorized AIMA, the National Body for Interventions on the Agricultural Market, to acquire and stock durum wheat for subsequent sale in the domestic market. The purpose of the authorization was to guarantee supplies to the pasta industry at a price which would in turn ensure that that industry was profitable, despite the set maximum prices for the finished product.

At a time when the world market price was considerably higher than that fixed under Community rules, AIMA purchased large quantities of durum wheat on the world market and sold it to pasta producers for about lit 13,000 per quintal, considerably less than the purchase price and, significantly, considerably less than both the target price (lit 16,400) and the intervention price (lit 15,000) under provisions of the common organization of the market in cereals. The Community rules precluded the export of durum wheat to third countries. The consequence of AIMA's action was that Russo suffered a financial loss since he had to sell his durum wheat below the price he had expected to receive under the system of common organization of the wheat market. The Court held in paragraph 6 that 'an individual producer may claim that he should not be prevented from obtaining a price approximating to the target price and in any event not lower than the intervention price'.

On the question of liability, Advocate General Reischl urged the line of reasoning which was followed by the European Court of Justice, namely, that where harm is caused through an infringement of Community law by the State, the latter is liable for the harm caused in accordance with the provisions of national law on the liability of the State. Reischl expressed the view that the liability of a Member State, 'as a general rule', was a matter for the national courts 'which must, on the basis of the general obligations imposed upon Member States in Article 10 of the Treaty as regards their national legal order, draw the consequences flowing from their State's membership of the Community'.[41] He cited *Commission v Italy*[42] in support of his view.

Commission v Italy was an Article 226 action brought by the Commission asking for a declaration that Italy was in breach of its Treaty obligations by failing to introduce, *inter alia*, a system of premiums for slaughtering cows as required by secondary legislation. Whilst the case was being prepared, Italy complied with its obligation and therefore pleaded that Article 226 proceedings were no longer warranted. In rejecting the plea the European Court of Justice stated: 'a judgment by the Court under Articles 226 and 228 of the Treaty may be of substantive interest in establishing the basis of a responsibility that a Member State can incur as a result of its default, as regards other Member States, the Community or private parties'.[43]

[41] Ibid, 62. [42] Case 39/72 [1973] ECR 101. [43] Ibid, para 11.

It is worth noting that the issue of State liability or responsibility of the State was raised by the Court itself, in support of its ruling that despite the fact a Member State has met its Treaty obligations by the time a judgment is delivered, it is still appropriate for the Court to confirm the original breach. No such argument was raised by Advocate General Mayras although he urged the Court to continue with the proceedings, but on other grounds. He made no reference to the fact that private parties who wish to pursue an action for compensation before a national court would find a declaration of infringement a useful piece of evidence! Advocate General Reischl in *Russo v AIMA*, having quoted from *Commission v Italy*, went on to conclude that the responsibility that a Member State may incur as a result of its default is a logical step from the principle that Community law is supreme and directly effective. He concluded that the liability of the Member States for the consequences of their infringement of Community law arises out of the obligation to provide effective protection of the individual rights created by Community law. He cited the *Salgoil*[44] case in support of this reasoning.

The *Salgoil* case, an Article 234 reference, concerned a claim for compensation for the damage allegedly suffered by the plaintiff company owing to the refusal of the Italian authorities to grant a licence to import a certain quantity of fuller's earth impregnated with fatty substances. The Court ruled that the relevant EC Treaty article has direct effect and therefore creates rights for individuals which need to be protected by Member States by ensuring for those individuals 'direct and immediate protection of their interests'. However the Court went on to state that it is 'for the national legal system to determine which court or tribunal has jurisdiction to give this protection and, for this purpose, to decide how the individual position thus protected is to be classified'.[45]

By now the fundamental principles of the Community's legal order, the doctrines of direct effect and supremacy of Community law, had been established by the European Court of Justice. Since the *Salgoil* case concerned a breach of a directly applicable provision of the EC Treaty, it is not surprising the focus of liability was centred on the rights of individuals derived from Community law.

Advocate General Gand, did not contribute much to the debate in the *Salgoil* case. He merely concluded that the individual rights conferred by Community law must be protected by national courts and the State has no discretion to oppose the exercise of these rights. He cited the Court's judgment in the *Molkerei-Zentrale*[46] case to support his position that although Community law needs to be applied with the same force in all the Member States, this does not prevent national courts applying the most appropriate of the various measures available under national law in order to protect the individual rights conferred by Community law.

The *Humblet* case was not cited in *Russo v AIMA* but it is an important case to examine when tracing the origins of State liability as a principle of Community

[44] Case 13/68 [1968] ECR 453. [45] Ibid, 463. [46] Case 28/67 [1968] ECR 148.

law. In *Francovich* the Court held that the principle of State liability in Community law has its origins[47] in two paragraphs in the *Humblet* case where the Court stated as follows:

> In fact if the Court rules in a judgment that a legislative or administrative measure adopted by the authorities of a Member State is contrary to Community law, that Member State is obliged, by virtue of Article 86 of the ECSC Treaty, to rescind the measure in question and to make reparation for any unlawful consequences which may have ensued. This obligation is evident from the Treaty and from the Protocol which have the force of law in the Member States following their ratification and which take precedence over national law.
>
> Consequently if in the present dispute the Court were to rule that the tax assessment in question was unlawful, it would necessarily follow that the Belgian government would be obliged to adopt the requisite measures to cancel it and to reimburse to the applicant any amounts which were wrongfully collected.[48]

The *Humblet* case was a direct action brought against Belgium by an official of the High Authority. The action was based on Article 16 of the then Protocol on the Privileges and Immunities of the European Coal and Steel Community. The official sought a declaration that the Belgian tax authorities were acting contrary to the Protocol in seeking to take into account the emoluments paid to Humblet.

In *Humblet*, the principle of State liability was raised only by the Court, not by Lagrange. The closest he got was to state that where an individual relies on a European Court of Justice judgment before the national court, the latter must 'deduce the legal consequences for their own decision under national law'.[49]

However, *Russo v AIMA*'s ruling was not the end of the matter. A few years later Advocate General Reischl in *Benedetti v Munari*[50] commented that the EC Treaty contained provisions only on the liability of Community institutions. The national court had asked the European Court of Justice whether there was a duty on a national intervention agency to compensate for resulting damage where its conduct was in breach of Community legislation. The European Court of Justice found it unnecessary to answer the question but Advocate General Reischl considered this to be a matter for national law. Although infringement of Community law led to obligations to compensate, in the then state of integration of Community law, he concluded that it was for national law to enforce this duty. As for damages this was considered to be, as a general rule, a matter for the national court.

In later cases, such as *San Giorgio*[51] and *Asteris*,[52] both the Advocates General (Mancini and Slynn respectively) and the European Court of Justice continued to regard the rights of individuals derived from Community law as the main source for the existence of State liability as a Community law principle.

[47] Joined Cases C-6/90 and C-9/90 [1991] ECR I-5357, para 36 of the judgment.

[48] Case 6/60 [1960] ECR 559, 569, parts of which were quoted by Mischo in *Francovich*, para 63 of the Opinion.

[49] Opinion in Case 6/60 [1960] ECR 559 at 586.

[50] Case 52/76 [1977] ECR 163.

[51] Case 199/82 [1983] ECR 3595.

[52] Joined Cases 106-120/87 [1988] ECR 5155.

Mischo's Opinion in Francovich

Mischo's approach, predictably, was to review the case-law of the Court in search of the appropriate solution. The European Court of Justice had made it clear in the *Salgoil*[53] case that Treaty provisions granted individual rights which needed to be protected in the national legal orders of the Member States in the same manner as rights conferred by national law (doctrine of equivalence). Thus the Member States have no discretion as to putting into effect the protection of a right conferred by EC law. The Court however left the national legal systems to decide procedural details such as which courts would have jurisdiction to give the protection and how the cause of action should be classified. What was important was to ensure that the protection was available and effective. In the *Salgoil* case the approach of the European Court of Justice and Advocate General Gand was very much from the viewpoint of the enforcement of individual rights rather than State liability for wrongful conduct.

Mischo examined whether, as Community law then stood, the liability of the State for failure to comply with its Community obligations was a matter for national law alone or a matter of Community law. Mischo concluded that the European Court of Justice had already 'implicitly held that the question of principle whether a Member State can be liable is a matter for Community law'.[54] This conclusion was far from clear, given the wording used by the European Court of Justice in earlier rulings, particularly in two *Rewe* cases. The first *Rewe* case[55] concerned recovery of a charge on phyto-sanitary inspection which had been levied unlawfully by the State. The European Court of Justice implied that the liability of the State was a matter for national law.[56] Mischo dismissed this interpretation, not by distinguishing the facts, namely that in the *Rewe* case the action concerned recovery not State liability, but by concluding that this interpretation was incorrect. He submitted that the Court's words should be read in context: that the Court's reference to the national legal system was made with regard to the obligation of the Member State to designate appropriate national courts to hear such actions and to national procedural rules which govern the action.

Similarly, Mischo dismissed another European Court of Justice statement in the second *Rewe* case where the European Court of Justice stated that the EC Treaty 'was not intended to create new remedies in the national courts to enforce the observance of Community law other than those already laid down by national law'.[57] He was satisfied that this statement in no way contradicted his view that, once an action for damages exists as a form of action in the national legal order, a Member State cannot

[53] Case 13/68 [1968] ECR 453. The plaintiff, Salgoil, had brought an action against the Italian Ministry in the national court seeking compensation for the damage allegedly suffered by it as a result of a refusal by the Ministry to grant Salgoil an import licence contrary to the EC Treaty's free movement of goods provisions.

[54] Joined Cases C-6/90 and C-9/90 *Francovich* [1991] ECR I-5357, para 46 of the Opinion.

[55] Case 33/76 [1976] ECR 1989. [56] Ibid, para 5.

[57] Case 158/80 [1981] ECR 1805, para 44.

deny individuals the possibility of bringing such an action against the State for breach of EC law. The Member State cannot rely on the fact that it is the State itself which is alleged to be liable, as such a restriction would impair the effectiveness of a Community law provision with direct effect. This was indeed the judgment in the *Factortame I* [58] case where the European Court of Justice confirmed that the non-availability of an interim injunction against the State under national law (English law in this case) could not be allowed to prevent the granting of such a remedy in a situation where the effectiveness of Community law so demanded.

All the above cited cases concerned directly applicable provisions of Community law. However, in the *Francovich* case, it was a non-directly applicable Community measure—a directive—which was in issue. This was a situation not faced by the European Court of Justice before. Advocate General Mischo's approach was to examine whether there were any reasons which might require that national courts be given jurisdiction to deal with State liability in relation to Community measures whose provisions do not have direct effect.

He concluded that in this context there was no difference between directly and non-directly applicable Community law since the rationale behind the remedy is that the non-implementation deprives Community law of its desired effect.[59] The European Court of Justice had always been consistent in holding that Community law imposes a duty on a Member State to take all appropriate measures to enable Community law to be applied where that Member State has failed to fulfil its Treaty obligations. In the *Francovich* situation, the European Court of Justice had already ruled that Italy was in breach by not implementing the directive and, by such an omission, had deprived Community law of its effect.[60] The declaratory nature of these rulings did not excuse Italy from its obligation to take the necessary measures to comply with the judgment.

Mischo quoted approvingly from the *Humblet* judgment where the European Court of Justice confirmed the obligation on the State to take the necessary measures to comply with the judgment and, where appropriate, to make good the harmful consequences of the default.[61] Furthermore, he cited the *Humblet* case in observing that the obligation to comply with, and make reparation for the effects of a breach of, Community law derives directly from Articles 10 and 249 of the Treaty.

Mischo also argued convincingly, relying on a prior judgment,[62] that as regards a directly applicable measure, the individual's rights accrue from the actual provisions of Community law having direct effect in the internal legal order: judgment of the European Court of Justice in infringement proceedings is not required.

[58] Case C-213/89 [1990] ECR I-2433.

[59] Joined Cases C-6/90 and C-9/90 *Francovich* [1991] ECR I-5357, para 60 of the Opinion.

[60] Case 22/87 [1989] ECR 143.

[61] Joined Cases C-6/90 and C-9/90 *Francovich* [1991] ECR I-5357, para 63 of the Opinion, quoting a passage from p 569 of *Humblet*.

[62] Joined Cases 314–316/81 and 83/82 *Procureur de la Republique v Waterkeyn* [1982] ECR 4337, para 15.

The conditions (including remedies) for liability pre-*Francovich*

What kind of a wrongful act suffices for the State to incur liability under Community law? As already noted the first case where liability for wrongs was discussed was in the *FERAM* case where the action was brought against the HA, an administrative organ of the Community.

In the *FERAM* case, the proceedings were brought under Article 40 ECSC against the HA, but for a wrongful act committed by a Dutch official from a Dutch Ministry. The official issued documentation which fraudulently certified that ferrous scrap was of a kind which would entitle the owners to an equalization payment. The agencies to whom the HA had delegated powers to administer the equalization scheme acted on the documentation and paid out. In fact the ferrous scrap originated in the Community and did not qualify for the payment. The recipients were competitors of *FERAM* therefore the latter claimed injury and compensation.

The Court concluded in *FERAM, inter alia*, that the wrongful act committed by the Dutch official could not be imputed to the HA and that the HA had acted appropriately in leaving the issue of the certificates to the Dutch Ministry. Thus the action was dismissed as unfounded.

The case is interesting for the comments on conditions of liability which Advocate General Lagrange made when discussing how the HA's liability should be determined. Lagrange pointed out that under French law, unlike German and Belgian law, the concept of wrongful act or omission has its basis in public rather than civil law. This means that for there to be a wrongful act or omission by the State there is no need for a particular named official to be identified.[63] It also means that by basing the liability in public law the European Court of Justice would be able to list the conditions required for liability since the action would not be governed by national civil law procedures. In Lagrange's view the categorization of the action in public law was important since:

> [i]n this constant battle between the needs of the State and the protection of the rights of the individual the essential consideration to be borne in mind is the nature of the service in question, the special problems peculiar to its operation, the quick decisions which its operation may require etc. It is for this reason that, according to the circumstances, the decisions of the courts require, in order that liability may be put in issue, either a 'manifest wrongful act of particular gravity' (for example, . . . for which the law confers the widest discretionary powers on the administration) or, more commonly, a 'serious error' the most common examples are. . .[64]

[63] Under English law, an action for damages against the Crown was allowed in *Bourgoin v MAFF* based on an old cause of action, misfeasance in public office, which grants a private right to damages. This cause of action also requires a similar identification of the wrongdoer. Such a requirement was eliminated in *Factortame I*, Case C-213/89 [1990] ECR I-2433.

[64] Case 23/59 *FERAM* [1959] ECR 245 at 255.

The interesting analysis of Lagrange lies in the fact that he sought guidance as to the conditions of the liability of the HA, a supranational institution, from national law rules on the liability of public bodies.[65]

Soon after, in the *Meroni* case, Lagrange stated:

> it is incorrect to say that under French law there must usually be a *serious wrong* to render the public authority liable: on the contrary, more often than not an ordinary wrong suffices. On the other hand it is true that the required degree of seriousness *varies* according to the nature of the service, the extent of the difficulty encountered in guaranteeing it, and, on the other hand, to the extent of the protection which the interests which have suffered damage deserve. In each case a balance must be struck between the public interest and private interests.[66]

In the above quote there is already an understanding that the criteria for liability may vary depending on various circumstances.

As early as 1968, in the *Salgoil* case, it was recognized that the national law must provide an effective remedy for breach of a directly applicable Community law provision. Advocate General Gand stated that 'since the law created in favour of persons subject to national jurisdiction by the various provisions which are directly applicable must be identical everywhere, this law cannot be affected by criteria arising under national law'.[67] While this does not mean that there have to be identical remedies throughout the Member States it does require that directly applicable provisions of Community law must be effective in all Member States.

In *Russo v AIMA* the European Court of Justice confirmed that the action of the Italian government was incompatible with Community law. As far as the question of damages was concerned the Court gave some guidance to the national court affirming that:

> [I]t is for the national court to decide on the basis of the facts of each case whether an individual producer has suffered such damage.
>
> If such damage has been caused through an infringement of Community law the State is liable to the injured party of the consequences in the context of the provisions of national law on the liability of the State.[68]

It is interesting to note that there was no attempt by Advocate General Reischl to consider parallels with the jurisprudence then in existence on the Community's non-contractual liability. The Commission had argued in its submissions that the liability of the State should follow the same lines as the Community's own non-contractual liability, which would suggest some common criteria. The Advocate General on the other hand argued simply for the right of individuals to be compensated for harm caused as a result of the infringement of Community law

[65] This approach contrasts with the one adopted by Mischo in *Francovich* as discussed below. See also Case C-352/98P *Laboratoires Pharmaceutiques Bergaderm SA v Jean-Jacques Goupil* [2000] ECR I-5291 at paras 41 and 42 of the judgment for evidence of a convergence between Community and Member State liability.

[66] Case 14/60 [1961] ECR 161 at 174.

[67] Case 13/68 [1968] ECR 453 at 470.

[68] Case 60/75 [1976] ECR 45 at 56.

by a Member State. The obligation to do so had already been confirmed by the European Court of Justice.[69] He was satisfied, 'as a general rule', to leave the discharge of that obligation in the hands of the national legal order. The Advocate General relied on the Court's earlier case-law[70] to argue that this was a matter for the national legal system and for the national courts. In its submissions, the Commission recognized expressly that this solution presupposed that national law provided procedures for the protection of these Community law rights. Reischl acknowledged that it was desirable to avoid the risk of unequal treatment of individuals under the various national legal systems which applied to them. He stated that it was necessary to establish principles, as the Court had already done on various occasions, upon which uniform and effective methods of enforcing individual rights under community law can be established.[71]

The cases decided after *Russo v AIMA* which are particularly relevant to establishing conditions of liability were *Rewe-Zentralfinanz v Landwirtschaftskammer*[72] and *Comet BV v Produktschap.*[73] Both cases concerned an action for recovery rather than an action for damages but the conditions of liability were considered to be the same for both types of action. Both the European Court of Justice and Advocate General Warner concluded that the matter of enforcing State liability (including procedural conditions) should be left to national law. In these two cases the national courts, by way of a reference for a preliminary ruling, asked the European Court of Justice to rule whether a State, in proceedings brought in its own courts, could plead a limitation period prescribed by its own law so as to prevent a trader recovering an amount unlawfully charged by that State. The first case was a reference from Germany and the second from The Netherlands.

Warner delivered a single Opinion covering both cases as similar issues had been raised. He had no hesitation in stating that 'it is for the national law of each Member State to determine the nature and extent of the remedies available in the courts of that State and to give effect to those rights'.[74] He relied on well established authority[75] to support his conclusion that it is for the internal legal system to determine the legal process whereby the claim is secured.

Finally, Advocate General Reischl (in *Benedetti v Munari*[76]) commented that the EC Treaty has provisions only on liability of Community institutions not on the liability of the State. He had no doubt that infringement of Community law led to the obligation to compensate for harm caused but, in the current state of integration, the conditions of liability were to be governed by national law.

Thus it can be seen that in the pre-*Francovich* case law, notwithstanding Reischl's acknowledgement (in *Russo v AIMA*) of the need for common principles through which to ensure uniform and effective enforcement of individual rights

[69] Case 13/68 *Salgoil* [1968] ECR 453. [70] Case 34/67 *Luck* [1968] ECR 245.
[71] Case 60/75 *Russo v AIMA* [1976] ECR 45 at 62. [72] Case 33/76 [1976] ECR 1989.
[73] Case 45/76 [1976] ECR 2043. [74] Case 33/76 [1976] ECR 1989, p 2002.
[75] Including, *inter alia*, Case 6/60 [1960] ECR 559; Case 28/67 [1968] ECR 148; Case 34/67 [1968] ECR 245; Case 13/68 [1968] ECR 453. [76] Case 52/76 [1977] ECR 163.

under Community law, the consistent position (of both the Advocates General and the Court) was that the conditions of liability should be left to the national legal system. Although the Commission had suggested in *Russo v AIMA* that State liability should follow the same lines as the Community Institutions' non-contractual liability this suggestion had not been adopted, or explored, by either the Court or its Advocates General. Thus, prior to the *Francovich* case, the case-law of the European Court of Justice did not have much to say about the conditions of liability, except that these were matters for national law.[77]

It is also worth noting that there is some conflation between the conditions giving rise to a right to a remedy, and the remedy itself, both of which appear to be left to national law and considered as questions of conditions of liability. Arguably, separating this into two questions: the first concerning the establishment of conditions giving rise to liability/the right to a remedy and the second concerning the remedy itself would have permitted the establishment of common principles (in the first stage) such as Reischl advocated, without encroaching on the national jurisdiction to determine the appropriate remedy the Court and Advocates General were clearly keen to conserve.

The conditions for liability: Mischo's Opinion

Mischo's approach to this issue was to resort to those conditions under which the Community incurs liability as a result of the breach of Community law committed by one of its institutions, the so-called non-contractual liability.[78] He concluded that: 'In this case it would seem appropriate that the grant of damages by a national court for breach of Community law by a Member State should be subject to the same conditions as the grant of damages by the Court of Justice for infringement of that same Community law by a Community institution'.[79]

In this, Mischo also relied upon the fact that the Article 288 rules are said to flow from general principles common to Member States. In reviewing the European Court of Justice's case-law, Mischo identified some rulings of the European Court of Justice on the conditions of liability of the State which he considered supportive of his conclusions. He cited the *Asteris*[80] judgment as authority for the proposition that where the Community has been held not liable under paragraph 2 of Article 288 EC in respect of an illegal act of one of its institutions, then the State or one of its authorities which merely implements the Community

[77] Examples of relevant case-law: Case 13/68 *Salgoil* [1968] ECR 453; Case 60/75 *Russo v AIMA* [1976] ECR 45; Advocate General Reischl in Case 52/76 *Benedetti v Munari* [1977] ECR 163; Case 33/76 *Rewe-Zentralfinanz etc v Landwirtschaftskammer* [1976] ECR 1989; Case 45/76 *Comet BV v Produktschap* [1976] ECR 2043.

[78] Para 2 of Art 288 EC. The European Court of Justice case-law specifies three conditions for liability: illegality of the conduct; actual damage; and causal link. See for example, Case 4/69 *Lutticke v Commission* [1971] ECR 325.

[79] Joined Cases C-6/90 and C-9/90 *Francovich* [1991] ECR I-5357, at para 71, relying on Case 281/84 *Zuckerfabrik* [1987] ECR 49.

[80] Cases 106-120/87 [1988] ECR 5515.

illegal legislative measure (and was not responsible for the unlawfulness) cannot be held liable on the same grounds.

Mischo accepted that the procedural and evidentiary rules, as well as the assessment of the harm suffered, were matters for national law. The differences in the procedural rules in the various systems of national law must be accepted, subject to two well-established overriding conditions repeated in the *San Giorgio* [81] case. First, the national rules must not be less favourable than those for similar claims of an internal nature (doctrine of equivalence). Second, the rules must not be of such a nature as to make it virtually impossible to obtain compensation for the harm suffered (doctrine of adequacy).

As the conditions of liability were not in issue in the *Francovich* case, the Court made no comment on Mischo's suggestion that the conditions for non-contractual liability of the Community were appropriate to a finding of State liability for breach of EC law. The European Court of Justice limited itself to commenting that the conditions for liability depended on the nature of the breach echoing Lagrange's analysis in the *Meroni* case in respect of liability under French administrative law.[82] However, in the case where the breach is a failure to implement a directive, the European Court of Justice was specific that three pre-conditions are necessary for liability of the State to be established: first that the directive intends to confer rights on individuals; second, that these rights are clearly identifiable from the provisions of the directive; and thirdly, that there is a causal link between the breach and the loss suffered. Since the European Court of Justice had already confirmed the illegality of Italy's conduct, there would be no difficulty for the national court to find that there had been a sufficiently serious breach for liability to arise.

Comment on the Opinions delivered up to and including *Francovich*

What influence did Advocates General, such as Lagrange and Reischl, have in determining that Member States should be liable to individuals for harm caused by breaches of Community law?

Although at first sight it would appear that State liability in Community law does not owe much to the Advocates General, this may not be quite right.[83] The Reporting Judge in the *FERAM*, *Humblet* and *Meroni* cases was Judge Riese. The Reporting Judge is responsible, *inter alia*, for the drafting of the judgment which is then deliberated by all the judges. Given the detailed analysis by Lagrange in his *FERAM* Opinion, it is not inconceivable, although admittedly speculative, that Judge Riese, being so directly concerned with the earlier case, was well aware of Lagrange's analysis in the *FERAM* case when preparing the draft judgment in the

[81] See Case 199/82 [1983] ECR 3595. See also Cases 33/76 *Rewe-Zentralfinanz etc v Landwirtschaftskammer* [1976] ECR 1989; 45/76 *Comet BV v Produktschap* [1976] ECR 2043; 68/79 *Just* [1980] ECR 2043.

[82] Case 14/60 [1961] ECR 161.

[83] In several often cited cases, namely *Humblet*, *Commission v Italy* and *Salgoil*, the issue was raised primarily by the Court itself.

Humblet case. In fact, in *Meroni*, Lagrange himself refers back to the general considerations he submitted in his *FERAM* Opinion which he believed 'the judgment appears to have taken into account by implication'.[84]

Lagrange, in the *FERAM* case, sought a remedy more from the point of view of the liability of the Member State for wrongdoing rather than from any 'rights' which individuals may have derived from the Community's legal order. He relied heavily on French administrative law on the liability of national administrative organs. French law provides no mandatory remedies for administrative wrongs, therefore damages would be an appropriate solution to achieve effectiveness of Community law. It may be significant however that this case predates the establishment in the mid 1960s of the doctrines of direct effect and supremacy of Community law (*Van Gend en Loos* and *Costa v ENEL*).

In contrast, by the time that State liability was considered in *Russo v AIMA*, Advocate General Reischl was able to rely on the principles of supremacy and direct effect of Community law to underpin State liability as another principle of Community law. Thus, from then on, the focus is on the effective protection of Community rights conferred on the individual and not on the conduct of the Member State which caused the harm. The European Court of Justice similarly viewed State liability as the natural consequence of the breach of individual rights granted by Community law.[85] Mischo referred to *Russo v AIMA* in refuting the argument of the intervening Member States that the European Court of Justice had held that the issue of liability was a matter for national law. Mischo interpreted the *Russo v AIMA* ruling as laying down a Community principle of State liability requiring the harm suffered to be compensated but leaving the national law to govern the procedure and assessment of damages. To return to the two-stage analysis presented above, this could suggest that the conditions for liability are a matter for Community rather than national law.

What influence did Advocate General Mischo's Opinion have on the Court's ruling in the *Francovich* case? There were two main elements to the European Court of Justice's ruling. First, the Court overturned the assumption made in respect of earlier statements from the Court that State liability was a matter for national law. It was stated in very clear terms that the principle of State liability is 'inherent in the Treaty'.[86] Second, the ruling focused on imposing liability (and a sanction in damages) on the Member State for its breach of Treaty obligations which resulted in harm caused to individuals.[87] This can be seen to echo Lagrange's view in the *FERAM* case as well as Mischo's Opinion.

The shift that can perhaps be identified in Mischo's Opinion, adopted in the *Francovich* judgment, is the change of emphasis from the need to establish rights

[84] Cases 14/60 et seq. [1961] ECR 161 at 174.

[85] Joined Cases C-6/90 and C-9/90 *Francovich* [1991] ECR I-5357, para 33 of the judgment.

[86] Ibid, para 35.

[87] C Harlow, '*Francovich* and the Problem of the Disobedient State' (1996) 2 ELJ 199, 205, citing other commentators.

directly granted to individuals by Community law (*Salgoil, Asteris* and *San Giorgio*) to the establishment of liability of the Member States within the Community's legal order for failing to make Community law effective. Member States which are in breach of Treaty obligations by failing to implement a directive, and cause harm to individuals as a consequence, must provide a remedy in damages.[88] The similarity with Lagrange's approach to this point in the *FERAM* case is unsurprising in view of the fact that in neither case was there direct effect of the relevant provision.

As far as conditions of liability are concerned, the *Francovich* judgment is unhelpful as there was no dispute as to fault or causation. Apart from the Court's statement that the criteria under which the liability resulted in compensation would depend on the nature of the breach of Community law which gave rise to the harm, (reminiscent once again of Lagrange's approach in *Meroni)*, the judgment did not take liability much further than that already established in *Factortame I* and *San Giorgio*[89] cases. The influence of Mischo's Opinion, in equating the conditions of State liability with those established for non-contractual liability of the Community, has to be assessed in the context of the post-*Francovich* case-law[90] since the European Court of Justice found it unnecessary to rule on the conditions of liability on this occasion.

What can be stated with certainty is that the Court rejected Mischo's advice that the consequences of the judgment should be limited to those individuals who had already started proceedings before national courts and to future litigants.

Post-*Francovich* developments: the Opinions of Advocates General Léger and Tesauro delivered in 1996

By the beginning of the 1990s, confirmed by the *Francovich* judgment, State liability for breach of Treaty obligations for failure to implement a directive was established as a fundamental principle of the Community's legal order. The principle was inherent in the system of the EC Treaty and could be relied on in cases where the Member States had failed in their Treaty obligations by not implementing directives within the prescribed period of time, even where the provisions of those directives did not meet the conditions for direct effect.

Given that the provisions of the directive in the *Francovich* case had no direct effect, it was not clear whether the principle of State liability in Community law also applied to situations where individuals had alternative remedies as, for example, where the provisions of Community law which had been breached by

[88] See Harlow, ibid 206, suggesting that the source of the European Court of Justice's sanction theory of liability is probably from French administrative law.

[89] Case 199/82 [1983] ECR 3555.

[90] This approach can be traced to the Commission's submissions in *Russo v AIMA* and repeated in *Francovich* (see above, pp. 228 and 231).

the Member State have direct effect. The direct effect doctrine grants rights to individuals which they are able to enforce directly before national courts. If the *raison d' être* behind the adoption of the doctrine was intended to fill a lacuna in the remedies available for breaches of Community law, then there was no reason for its extension to directly effective provisions. Similarly, if State liability's main function is to protect Community rights conferred on individuals, those rights can be protected before national courts where the rights in question arose from provisions of Community law which have direct effect. On the other hand, if State liability's purpose is to sanction a Member State's breach of Community law obligations/failure to make Community law effective (which would be consistent with both Lagrange and Mischo), arguably it should make no difference whether the right in question is directly effective.

Furthermore, there were several unanswered questions, particularly in the context of the conditions for liability. European Court of Justice case-law prior to the *Francovich* judgment was consistent in suggesting that these conditions were a matter for national law. In the *Francovich* case, however, some conditions of liability were set out as a matter of Community law; the question remained: were these confined to liability for non-implementation of directives? The European Court of Justice had clearly stated that the conditions of liability depended on the nature of the breach but the *Francovich* judgment added nothing substantive to the debate as the issue was not of significance in the context of the facts of the case, given that the European Court of Justice had already ruled that the Member State, Italy, was in breach of the EC Treaty. What are the conditions where the breach does not concern directives? Are the conditions to be determined by national law or would Community law lay down some uniform minimum conditions? There were therefore important matters related to this cause of action which remained unanswered and upon which the Court would need (and receive) guidance from its Advocates General in future referrals.

After the *Francovich* case the next major development of the State liability doctrine was a cluster of cases in 1996 which enabled the European Court of Justice to clarify the outstanding issues discussed above. The Court was asked to establish whether and on what terms there exists an obligation on the State to compensate individuals who have suffered loss or damage as a result of national legislative and administrative acts or omissions inconsistent with Community law. The Opinions in these cases were delivered by Advocate General Léger in the *Lomas*[91] case and Advocate General Tesauro in the *Brasserie du Pêcheur/Factortame III*,[92] *Ex parte BT*[93] and *Dillenkofer*[94] cases.

Both Advocates General strongly argued for wide application of the State liability principle and for minimum conditions of liability to be formulated by Community

[91] Case C-5/94 [1996] ECR I-2553.

[92] Joined Cases C-46/93 and C-48/93 [1996] ECR I-1029.

[93] Case C-392/93 [1996] ECR I-1631.

[94] Joined Cases C-178/94, C-179/94, C-188, C-189 and C-190/94 [1996] ECR I-4845.

law. These Opinions made a major contribution to the understanding and development of the doctrine. All these cases were heard before a Full Court, Léger delivering his Opinion in June 1995 followed soon after by Tesauro's three Opinions which were delivered on the same day towards the end of 1995. However, the European Court of Justice judgments themselves were delivered in a different date order. The first judgment was delivered in the *Brasserie du Pêcheur/Factortame III* and *Ex parte BT* cases in March 1996 (on the same day), followed by the judgment in the *Lomas* case in May and in the *Dillenkofer* case in October.

In the *Lomas* case the issue concerned State liability for harm caused by the conduct of a national administrative authority contrary to Community law (an administrative failure). Lomas had applied for a licence to export live sheep to Spain. The licence was refused on the basis that Spanish slaughterhouses did not meet the requirements imposed by the relevant Community directive. The European Court of Justice ruled that the refusal to issue the licence amounted to a quantitative restriction prohibited by Article 29 EC and was not justified under the derogation of Article 30 EC. As to the question of liability the European Court of Justice adopted its earlier judgment delivered in the *Brasserie du Pêcheur/Factortame III* cases that a right to reparation must be recognized where certain conditions of liability are met.

In the *Brasserie du Pêcheur/Factortame III* cases the issue of State liability arose in circumstances where national law was applied in breach of Community law (legislative failures).[95] In the *Brasserie du Pêcheur* case, Germany had failed to amend German law which prohibited the marketing of beers imported from other Member States under the label 'beer' contrary to the EC Treaty provisions on the free movement of goods. The European Court of Justice had already ruled that Germany was in breach of its Treaty obligations, namely Articles 28 to 30 EC, by maintaining this national law and also by imposing a prohibition on certain additives in beer which made the importation of beer from other Member States more difficult.[96] The question arose therefore as to whether damages were available for loss suffered as a consequence of maintenance of national law. In the *Factortame III* case the issue for the European Court of Justice was whether damages could be recovered from the UK for loss suffered due to the adoption of a national law which had been found by the Court to be incompatible with the EC Treaty.[97]

In the *Ex parte BT* case the European Court of Justice was asked similar questions but in the context of the incorrect implementation of a directive and, finally, in the *Dillenkofer* case, the European Court of Justice was given an opportunity to reconsider *Francovich* since the issue raised was the same, namely the failure of Germany to implement a directive (legislative failure).

[95] The national courts in these cases were debarred from awarding damages by their national laws.

[96] Case 178/84 *Commission v Germany* [1987] ECR 1227.

[97] Case C-246/89 *Commission v UK* [1991] ECR I-4585.

Advocate General Tesauro's Opinion in the *Brasserie du Pêcheur/ Factortame III* cases provides a detailed, thorough and coherent analysis of the origins of the Community's principle of State liability. This Opinion, together with the ones he delivered on the same day in the *Dillenkofer* and *Ex parte BT* cases, also provide an exhaustive appraisal of the appropriate conditions of liability for different breaches of Community law which the European Court of Justice should determine. However, five months before Tesauro's Opinions, it was Advocate General Léger in the *Lomas* case who delivered the first direct Opinion since the *Francovich* judgment on the scope of the Community's principle of State liability.

Tesauro's Opinions have had more exposure probably because of the circumstances. First, in one day, Tesauro delivered Opinions on various aspects of State liability in four preliminary references from courts in the UK and Germany.[98] In contrast, Léger delivered only one Opinion on State liability in the relevant period. Second, as sometimes happen with European Court of Justice cases, the *Lomas* judgment was delivered two months after the European Court of Justice had delivered its judgments on the *Brasserie du Pêcheur/Factortame III* and *Ex parte BT* cases. Thus the European Court of Justice judgment in the *Lomas* case reiterates and follows the judgments in the other cases. However one may ask whether Léger's Opinion influenced Tesauro's. There is no express reference by Tesauro to Léger's opinion save for a footnote to the effect that the Opinion of Léger in *Lomas*, then pending before the European Court of Justice, 'also considers some aspects relevant to these proceedings'.[99] This indicates that Tesauro was aware of Léger's Opinion, and had taken note of its existence at least.

These Opinions have to be considered in the context of European Court of Justice judgments delivered in the intervening period on the direct effect of directives. Repeated attempts to change the European Court of Justice's case-law so as to allow horizontal direct effect failed and the European Court of Justice confirmed expressly in the *Faccini Dori*[100] judgment that provisions of directives have no horizontal effect. This meant that, even where the provisions of a directive have direct effect, individuals can rely on these provisions only against the State and not against a private party. In cases such as *Wagner Miret*[101] and *Faccini Dori* itself, the Court cited the principle of State liability as the way in which, in the latter situation, the individual could obtain a remedy. The remedy would be compensation from the State where the State was in breach of its Treaty obligations. The European Court of Justice repeated the ruling in *Francovich*, stating that the Member State was obliged to make good the loss or damage sustained as a result of failure to

[98] *Brasserie du Pêcheur/Factortame III, Ex parte BT* and *Dillenkoffer*.

[99] Footnote 19 of Tesauro's Opinion in Joined Cases C-46/93 and C-48/93 *Brasserie du Pêcheur/Factortame III* [1996] ECR I-1029.

[100] Cases C-91/92 [1994] ECR I-3325. See also during this period, C-192/94 *El Corte Ingles* [1996] ECR I-1281.

[101] Case C-334/92 [1993] ECR I-6911. In none of these cases (C-91/92; C-192/94 and C-334/92) did Advocate General Lenz refer to State liability as a possible avenue for the individual to seek a remedy when unable to rely on the direct effect doctrine. It was the European Court of Justice which mentioned the possibility in the judgment.

implement a directive where the provision in question met the conditions for liability set out in the *Francovich* judgment.

Is the principle of State liability a general or specific principle of Community law?

Both Léger and Tesauro, in the *Lomas* and *Brasserie du Pêcheur/Factortame III* cases respectively, focused on establishing that the principle of State liability in Community law was not limited to a *Francovich*-type situation (a failure to implement a directive) but of general application. As Tesauro's views on this issue in the *Dillenkofer* and *Ex parte BT* cases merely repeated or referred to what he had concluded in his Opinion in the *Brasserie du Pêcheur/Factortame III* cases delivered later on the same day, the analysis in this context will focus upon the latter Opinion.

Léger's approach in the *Lomas* case was to consider the scope and nature of the Community's principle of State liability established in the *Francovich* judgment in order to determine whether this principle is a general one or limited to a State failure to implement a directive. The *Francovich* judgment is authority only for the case of failure by a Member State to implement a directive the provisions of which were not directly effective. He acknowledged that defining the scope of the principle widely enough to make a State liable for loss and damage caused to individuals as a result of all kinds of breaches of EC law is a 'key question'[102] in Community law. The Court was being asked to take a huge step in widening the scope of its earlier *Francovich* ruling in circumstances where, as Léger noted, the issue had been submitted to the negotiators of the Maastricht Treaty without receiving an answer. Léger, despite the silence of the Community legislature, advised the Court to rule that a Member State which infringes EC law ought to incur liability in the same way as the Community may incur liability for loss and damage caused by its institutions or agents in the exercise of their functions.[103]

Léger's Opinion is lengthy, systematically identifying the 'arsenal of rights'[104] the European Court of Justice had established over the years and concluding that another right, namely to bring an action for damages against a State which has acted in breach of EC law, had been affirmed in *Francovich*. He emphasized the trend in the European Court of Justice's case-law to require 'real and effective'[105] judicial protection for individuals. Furthermore the fact that the doctrine of supremacy of Community law allows national law to be 'disapplied'[106] must also require compensation for damage caused by its application.[107]

He argued that an action against the State for breach of Community law is an 'indispensable adjunct' to the principle laid down in the *Simmenthal* ruling[108] that

102 Case C-5/94 *Lomas* [1996] ECR I-2553, para 51 of the Opinion. 103 Ibid, para 52.
104 Ibid, para 64. 105 Cited Case C-271/91 *Marshall II* [1993] ECR I-4367.
106 Case C-221/89 *Factortame II* [1991] ECR I-3905.
107 Case C-5/94 *Lomas* [1996] ECR I-2553, para 68 of the Opinion.
108 Case 106/77 *Simmenthal* [1978] ECR 629, cited at para 69 of the Opinion in *Lomas*.

national legislation that is contrary to Community law is inapplicable.[109] State liability is based on illegality, namely the failure of the State to respect the supremacy of Community law. In the *Francovich* case that failure was non-implementation of a directive within the prescribed period.

Léger relied on existing case-law[110] where the Court had already stated that the right to rely on a directly applicable provision of the Treaty before a national court is *only* a minimum guarantee and not sufficient in itself to ensure full and complete implementation of the Treaty. That the State is liable where failure to transpose a directive exists is not only an effective sanction; it also allows the individual indirectly to take immediate benefit of the right conferred by the directive despite the failure to transpose. Where an individual brings an action for damages against a State on the grounds that the State has breached a directly effective provision of Community law, the first two *Francovich* conditions are automatically satisfied: the rights were granted for the benefit of individuals and the content of the rights are identifiable.[111] Léger concluded that an action for damages is a corollary of direct effect:[112]

> an action for damages against a State is not only a remedy for imperfect direct effect. It is not limited to the situation in the *Francovich* case. It is a vital component of the judicial protection of individuals relying on Community law, from the moment when the provision or decision occasioning the damage is capable of giving rise to rights on the part of individuals.[113]

Thus Léger drew wrongful conduct (the State's breach) together with the need for effective protection of individuals' rights. Therefore, in Léger's view, all organs of the State, the legislature, the executive and the judiciary may be liable for loss sustained owing to their actions in breach of Community law.[114]

In practice therefore there is not a great deal of distinction on whether the principle of State liability is a consequence of wrongful conduct or the need to protect the rights of individuals. However, if the emphasis is primarily on wrongful conduct (breach) the question of 'fault' of the Member State (discussed below) becomes more pertinent to the issue of liability.

What about Tesauro's views on this issue? How different was his approach from Léger's and what approach did the European Court of Justice take? There is nothing in Tesauro's approach or reasoning in his Opinion in the *Brasserie du Pêcheur/Factortame III* cases which would link it to Léger's. It appears that Tesauro considered the nature of the principle of State liability quite independently of Léger's own analysis in the *Lomas* case. Tesauro's starting point for his analysis was to note that State liability for loss or damage caused in breach of a legal duty is a

[109] There was a widespread view at the time that a State should not be liable for acts or omissions of the legislature since the latter reflected the sovereignty of the State.

[110] Case C-120/88 *Commission v Italy* [1991] ECR I-621 cited at para 75 of the Opinion in *Lomas*.

[111] Case C-5/94 *Lomas* [1996] ECR I-2553, para 88 of the Opinion.

[112] Ibid.

[113] Ibid, para 94.

[114] Ibid, para 114.

recognized principle of all legal systems in Europe. He acknowledged the necessary limits that exist, particularly in the context of legislative activity, in order to provide a balance between opposing competing interests: the injured party's interest in recovering the loss or damage suffered and the State's interest in not being hindered in the performance of its legislative tasks. Tesauro also acknowledged the change that had taken place in how the State is perceived: no longer absolutely sovereign but subject to the rule of law. The consequence was a shift of emphasis from focusing on the *conduct* of the wrongdoer to the *rights* of the injured party. Thus State liability, and particularly the obligation to make reparation, is a means of sanctioning the State for unlawful conduct and thus achieving an effective judicial protection of individual rights.[115] This is consistent with Léger's Opinion.

Given that States can incur liability under national laws when causing damage by legislative activity, even though under strict conditions, then it was logical and reasonable for Tesauro to conclude that Member States should be liable for sufficiently serious infringements of Community law which cause harm to individuals.

As to the source of the Community's principle of State liability Tesauro referred to the European Court of Justice's judgment in the *Francovich* case that the principle is 'inherent in the system of the Treaty'. He then proceeded to unpick the European Court of Justice's ruling by reviewing the pre-*Francovich* case-law (*Humblet* and *Russo v AIMA*) so as to determine whether the principle of State liability merely closes the lacuna in the protection of individuals' rights.[116] Tesauro puts the key question thus:

> In particular, it has to be determined whether Community law requires a guarantee in terms of compensation even where provisions having direct effect are infringed or whether the fact that in that event an individual may rely directly on the provision in question and therefore ensure that the right claimed is guaranteed by that means rules out that possibility. [117]

Tesauro concluded persuasively that the principle is a general one. Earlier case-law supported his view that the fact that provisions infringed are *directly effective*, does not deprive the individual of financial protection.[118]

Both Léger and Tesauro emphasized the effectiveness of Community law as the paramount reason for the Community's State liability principle. Léger identified the doctrine of supremacy of Community Law,[119] together with the Article 10 EC obligation to cooperate, as the source of this principle. Tesauro, on the other hand, examined the legal systems in Europe to conclude that the principle of State liability is part of the traditions of all these legal systems. As far as State liability for infringement of Community law is concerned, he relied directly on the European

[115] Joined Cases C-46/93 and C-48/93 *Brasserie du Pêcheur/Factortame III* [1996] ECR I-1029, para 12 of the Opinion.

[116] Ibid, paras 15 to 22.

[117] Ibid, para 23.

[118] See for example, Case C-188/89 *Foster v British Gas* [1990] ECR I-3313, para 22.

[119] Established by the European Court of Justice in Case 6/64 *Costa v ENEL* [1964] ECR 585.

Court of Justice's judgment in *Francovich* itself. The European Court of Justice deliberately specified the principle of State liability as being inherent in the EC Treaty and therefore it applies whenever Community law is infringed. No distinction was made in the *Francovich* judgment between legislative or executive infringements. In respect of the failure to implement a directive, the European Court of Justice merely emphasized that redress was particularly indispensable in that type of legislative failure since the individual would have been deprived of *any* protection where the directive has no direct effect.[120]

Thus Tesauro commented that: 'far from being a moment of eccentricity in the case-law of the Court, *Francovich* was completely consistent with a logical extension of a value which has been upheld on several occasions without question in Luxembourg: effectiveness of Community provisions and hence complete judicial protection'.[121]

Therefore State liability is not dependent on whether the provision of Community law which has been breached has direct effect. It is a self-standing cause of action.

Although Léger and Tesauro did not appear to agree exactly as to the source of this principle of Community law, they both concluded that effectiveness of Community law and the judicial protection of rights conferred on individuals by Community law was of paramount importance and the key objective of the principle.

The European Court of Justice's judgment in the *Brasserie du Pêcheur/Factortame III* cases appears closer to Léger's approach than to Tesauro's. The Court emphasized that 'the right of individuals to rely on the directly effective provisions of the Treaty before national courts is only a minimum guarantee'.[122] Its purpose is to ensure the supremacy of Community law. Full effectiveness of Community law requires that individuals whose rights have been infringed can recover from the State any loss or damage suffered as a result. Where the individual is entitled to rely on a Community right before the national court, 'the right to reparation is the *necessary corollary of the direct effect* of the Community provisions where the breach has caused the damage sustained'. It is unlikely to be coincidence that the language used by the Court is in this instance identical to Léger's.[123]

The Court agreed with the Advocates General that the Community's principle of State liability applies in any case where 'a Member State breaches Community law, whatever the organ of the State whose act or omission was responsible for the breach'.[124]

[120] Joined Cases C-46/93 and C-48/93 *Brasserie du Pêcheur/Factortame III* [1996] ECR I-1029, para 25 of Tesauro's Opinion.

[121] Ibid, para 32.

[122] Joined Cases C-46/93 and C-48/93 [1996] ECR I-1029, para 20 of the judgment. See also para 85 of Léger's Opinion in *Lomas*, Case C-5/94 [1996] ECR I-2553.

[123] Joined Cases C-46/93 and C-48/93 *Brasserie du Pêcheur/Factortame III* [1996] ECR I-1029, para 22 of the judgment (emphasis added). See also para 88 of Léger's Opinion in *Lomas* for the same expression.

[124] Joined Cases C-46/93 and C-48/93 *Brasserie du Pêcheur/Factortame III* [1996] ECR I-1029, para 32 of the judgment.

The conditions of liability: liability for legislative and administrative failures

The pre-*Francovich* case-law clearly stated that the conditions for a Member State to incur liability for a wrongful act were to be determined by national substantive and procedural rules. However the *Francovich* judgment changed that position.

The European Court of Justice expressly listed in *Francovich* three conditions before the State may incur liability under Community law to make reparation for its failure to implement a directive within the prescribed period. It was not absolutely clear however whether the national court could add further conditions. Another outstanding issue was whether the *Francovich* conditions applied to all other types of State infringement of Community law or whether other conditions were required as a matter of Community law. Should the conditions for the Community's non-contractual liability under paragraph 2 of Article 288 EC, established by the European Court of Justice in its case-law apply to similar national legislative failures?

Without a doubt the significant European Court of Justice judgment on the conditions of liability is the one delivered in the *Brasserie du Pêcheur/Factortame III* cases which preceded the judgments in the other three referrals.[125] In these cases the perpetrators of the unlawful acts or omissions were the national legislatures. What criteria should be applied in order to determine whether the unlawful act or omission of a legislature gave rise to liability in damages?

In the *Francovich* case Advocate General Mischo had argued that State liability for breach of Community law should be as for liability of Community institutions under Article 288 EC.[126] The Court however did not follow that advice and set out the three conditions which have already been identified above.

Nevertheless, the European Court of Justice ruled in *Brasserie du Pêcheur/Factortame III* that where the Member States have a wide discretion 'comparable to the Community institution when they adopt legislation pursuant to Community policy' then three conditions have to be met: 'the rule of law infringed must be intended to confer rights on individuals; the breach must be sufficiently serious; and there must be a direct causal link between the breach of the obligation resting on the State and the damage sustained by the injured parties'.[127] In adopting this solution the Court followed to a certain extent the solution preferred by Tesauro.

What were the options available to the European Court of Justice and how did Tesauro and Léger advise the Court? The first option was to leave to the national courts to apply their own national laws. As already noted, this option was rejected

[125] Although the unlawful act in *Lomas* concerned an administrative failure, nevertheless Léger, in his Opinion, also discussed the conditions of liability in a wider context (no doubt because it was the first Opinion on this subject after *Francovich*). Given that the ruling of the Court appears at times to follow Léger's Opinion, some of Léger's conclusions will also be discussed in this section.

[126] Joined Cases C-6/90 and C-9/90 [1991] ECR I-5357, at para 71 of the Opinion.

[127] Joined Cases C-46/93 and C-48/93 [1996] ECR I-1029, para 51 of the judgment.

as it would endanger the effectiveness of the protection of individual rights, the very objective of the Community's principle of State liability. Furthermore, the *Francovich* judgment had already stipulated minimum conditions at Community level for one particular unlawful act, namely the State's legislative failure to implement a directive. It is thus clear from *Francovich* that the European Court of Justice agreed with Tesauro and Léger that the Court had competence to review the degree of protection that the national legal systems provide in order to ensure that effectiveness of Community law rights conferred on individuals is guaranteed.[128] The Court's judgment also confirmed that the liability was inherent in Community law even as regards the conditions for the obligation to make reparation and thus not all the legal inferences from the infringement of Community law are left to national law.

The second option was to apply the conditions of *Francovich* to all acts or omissions of the Member States in breach of Community law. Little support was found for this option. In the *Francovich* case the Court did not have to decide whether the unlawful conduct was sufficiently serious for liability given that the Member States had no discretion on whether to implement the directive and the European Court of Justice had already ruled that the Italy was in breach of its Treaty obligations. Other breaches would have to be assessed differently.

A possible third option, which would have required the European Court of Justice to lay minimum conditions for each type of breach of Community law, was not seriously considered. The final option was to apply the system of rules which the European Court of Justice had created in respect of the Community's non-contractual liability under Article 288 EC, particularly in relation to liability for the Community's legislative failures. However, Community liability and State liability for a breach of Community law are not totally comparable. There is a fundamental difference: Community institutions adopt primary legislation whilst Member States, acting within the field of Community law, have reduced discretion and even sometimes no discretion at all. Both Tesauro and Léger, for different reasons, were not totally supportive of transposing the conditions for the Community's non-contractual liability to State liability. Essentially, Léger's view, recognizing the significance of the fundamental difference in the discretion available to the States as compared with Community Institutions, was that it would be inappropriate to transpose directly the Article 288 EC conditions of liability. Léger was concerned that the conditions for non-contractual liability of the Community, which was marked by 'diversity',[129] should not be transposed to State liability for breaches of Community law. Nevertheless, Tesauro supported this solution in some narrow circumstances: for example he concluded that where Member States have a wide discretion, State liability should be assessed under the same restrictive

[128] Para 22 of Tesauro's Opinion in Joined Cases C-46/93 and C-48/93 *Brasserie du Pêcheur/Factortame III* [1996] ECR I-1029 and para 150 of Léger's in *Lomas*, Case C-5/94 [1996] ECR I-2553.

[129] *Lomas*, Case C-5/94 [1996] ECR I-2553, para 129 of the Opinion.

conditions as applied to the Community institutions. The European Court of Justice's solution was closer to Tesauro's since it expressly focused on the wide discretion exercised both by the Member States and Community institutions when adopting legislative acts. The Court ruled that whether the breach is sufficiently serious is determined by establishing whether the Member State 'manifestly and gravely disregarded the limits of its discretion'.[130]

Nevertheless, both Tesauro and Léger found that the decisive test for liability depended on the degree of discretion available to the Member State.[131] Léger stated that:

> the main lesson to be drawn from the *Francovich* judgment [is that]: the nature of the wrongful act or omission required in order for the State to incur liability depends on the nature of the Community obligation incumbent on it and on the nature of the breach committed. If the Member State commits a breach of Community law in an area in which it has no discretion, it must incur liability more readily than where it acts in an area in which it has a broad discretion.[132]

Tesauro also suggested some factors for the national court to take into consideration when deciding whether the breach is 'manifest and serious'.[133] The Court then provided a list of factors but only the first two were also mentioned by Tesauro in his Opinion, namely clarity and precision of the rule breached and the measure of discretion left by that rule to the national authorities. Other factors listed by the Court are: whether the infringement and the damage caused was intentional or involuntary; whether the error of law was excusable or inexcusable; the fact that the position taken by a Community institution may have contributed towards the omission and the adoption or retention of national measures or practices contrary to EC law.[134] None of these were mentioned directly by the Advocates General in their Opinions.

However whether the infringement and damage caused was intentional or involuntary is another way of considering fault. Both Advocates General concluded that fault in a subjective sense is not necessary.[135] The European Court of Justice, although agreeing with that conclusion, stated that the concept of fault in national law may be relevant for the purpose of determining whether the breach of Community law is serious, but the obligation to compensate cannot be conditional on a finding of fault.

[130] Joined Cases C-46/93 and C-48/93 *Brasserie du Pêcheur/Factortame III* [1996] ECR I-1029, para 55 of the judgment; para 81 of Tesauro's Opinion. The actual words used by the Court came from para 132 of Léger's Opinion in *Lomas* where he quoted from the judgment in Cases C-104/89 and C-37/90 *Mulder v Council and Commission* [1992] ECR I-3061. This was one of the cases which refined the *Schoppendedt* formula establishing the conditions of liability under the second paragraph of Art 288 EC.

[131] Para 78 of Tesauro's Opinion in *Brasserie du Pêcheur/Factortame III* and para 169 of Léger's Opinion in *Lomas*.

[132] Para 169 of the Opinion in *Lomas*.

[133] Para 84 of Tesauro's Opinion in *Brasserie du Pêcheur/Factortame III*.

[134] Para 56 of the judgment in *Brasserie du Pêcheur/Factortame III*.

[135] Léger viewed the concept of fault as contrary to the principle of effectiveness—see para 62 of the Opinion in *Lomas*.

In particular, the European Court of Justice specified that a breach will also be sufficiently serious if it has continued after a judgment establishing the infringement or after a preliminary ruling or settled case-law which makes it clear that the conduct in question constitutes an infringement.[136] In these circumstances a sort of strict liability is imposed on the State. The European Court of Justice also specified that the conditions for liability in Community law are necessary and sufficient to found a right to obtain redress. Nevertheless the Member States may incur liability under less strict conditions based on national law.[137]

As far as damage and causal link conditions are concerned, the rules to be applied are national ones as long as the conditions consistently set out in the Court's case-law are satisfied: the criteria must not be less favourable than the criteria applied to similar claims based on national law and must not be such as in practice to make it impossible or excessively difficult to obtain reparation.[138]

In *Ex parte BT*,[139] Tesauro had to consider, *inter alia*, the conditions of liability for a legislative failure, namely the incorrect implementation by the UK of a provision in one of the public procurement directives.[140] So what should be the conditions of liability where a directive has been implemented within the prescribed period but incorrectly? Were the *Francovich* conditions appropriate? An alternative solution would be to require fault.[141] Other issues, common to all the cases, have already been discussed above.

As far as the correct implementation of directives is concerned, the Member States are given discretion as to the method and means of achieving the objectives set out in the directive. How serious must the breach be before liability is incurred? Was the interpretation of Community law given by the UK national authorities manifestly wrong? Tesauro advised the Court that in the circumstances of this referral, there was no doubt that the incorrect implementation of this public procurement directive, which resulted from a misunderstanding of the meaning of one of its provisions, could not be regarded as manifestly wrong. The content of the provision in the directive was not clear and precise. The *Francovich* judgment was clearly distinguishable since in that case the non-implementation itself was a manifest and serious breach.

[136] At para 57 of the judgment in *Brasserie du Pêcheur/Factortame III*. This is of course consistent with the facts of *Francovich*. See also paras 164 and 176 of Léger's Opinion in *Lomas*.

[137] Para 66 of the judgment in *Brasserie du Pêcheur/Factortame III*.

[138] Ibid, para 83 of the judgment. These two reservations are of course well established in the case-law of the Court.

[139] Case C-392/93 *R v HM Treasury, ex p British Telecommunications plc* [1996] ECR I-1631.

[140] Directive 90/531 [1990] OJ L297/1 concerning public procurement contracts in the utilities sector. The UK implemented incorrectly Art 8(1) of the Directive by excluding from the scope of the legislation certain telecommunication services.

[141] The Commission submitted in *Ex parte BT* that the same conditions listed by the European Court of Justice in *Francovich* should also apply to this situation but they argued in *Brasserie du Pêcheur/Factortame III* that the conditions should be the same for Member States as for the Community!

It is clear from the European Court of Justice's judgment in the *Ex parte BT* case that the Court accepted Tesauro's advice fully. The ruling is short which is not surprising given the fact that the Court had delivered its judgment in the *Brasserie du Pêcheur/Factortame III* cases several months earlier. The Court simply reiterated the three conditions for liability in situations where the Member State concerned is acting in a field in which it has a wide discretion in taking legislative actions. The conditions set out for liability in the *Brasserie du Pêcheur/Factortame III* cases are therefore also applicable in situations where the infringement lies in incorrect implementation of directives.

Although it is for the national court to decide whether the conditions of liability are met in each individual case, the European Court of Justice decided in the *Ex parte BT* case that the Court had all the information necessary to assess whether a sufficiently serious breach of Community law had taken place on this occasion. Had the UK manifestly and gravely disregarded the limits in the exercise of its powers? Given that the rule breached was not clear and precise, that there was no case-law on this provision to guide the UK and that the interpretation adopted by the UK was plausible and shared by other Member States, the European Court of Justice concluded that the breach was not of sufficient seriousness to incur a financial liability. (The reasoning employed here can be related to a finding of lack of fault.)

In the case of a breach due to the failure to implement a directive, the most relevant Opinion is Tesauro's in the *Dillenkofer*[142] case. Given that the liability of the State in the context of non-implementation of a directive had already been established by the European Court of Justice in the *Francovich* judgment, this Opinion is perhaps the least significant. However, this case did give the Court another opportunity to consider the consequences of their ruling in *Francovich* in slightly different circumstances. In the *Dillenkofer* case the plaintiffs in the national litigation sought compensation for losses suffered due to the failure of Germany to implement the so-called 'Package Tours' directive.[143] If the directive had been implemented within the prescribed period the plaintiffs would have been protected against the insolvency of the travel operators. Under German law they had no entitlement to a claim for damages.

The pre-conditions set out in the *Francovich* judgment applied. Tesauro and the European Court of Justice had no difficulty in establishing that the directive conferred rights on individuals.[144] Those rights were precise and capable of determination even though the provisions of the directive were not directly effective as the Member States had a wide discretion as to the means of achieving the objective of the directive. One particular issue which needed clarification was whether the failure to implement the directive within the prescribed period was sufficient in

[142] Joined Cases C-178/94, C-179/94, C-188-190/94 *Dillenkofer and ors v Germany* [1996] ECR I-4845.

[143] [1990] OJ L158/59.

[144] cf Case C-222/02 *Paul and ors v Germany* [2004] ECR I-9425 discussed below.

itself to impose liability on the State or whether it was necessary to show that the State had committed a 'manifest and grave' breach of its obligations before liability could arise. If the latter, do claimants have to prove 'fault' for the breach to be sufficiently serious to impose a financial liability on the State?

Tesauro's analysis of the *Francovich* judgment led him to the conclusion that a State is liable to pay damages whenever the infringement consists of a failure to implement a directive within the prescribed period.[145] Although the European Court of Justice had stated in *Francovich* that liability depended on the nature of the breach, in these circumstances, the liability can be described as strict: the failure to implement presupposes the existence of fault. Thus the European Court of Justice and the Advocate General were in total agreement. No prior European Court of Justice declaration of the State's breach of its Treaty obligations was necessary.

As for administrative failures, the first judgment of the European Court of Justice concerning the conditions for liability of this type of breach was in the *Lomas*[146] case. Given that the European Court of Justice had already ruled on similar issues in the *Brasserie du Pêcheur/Factortame III* and *Ex parte BT* cases, there is nothing surprising in the judgment. The conditions of liability set out in the earlier rulings apply equally when the unlawful act or omission has been committed by the State's administrative organs.

As already stated above, Léger strongly rejected analogies with the Community's non-contractual liability under Article 288 EC. In his view the actions do not have the same foundations and the rules for liability established by the Court for Article 288 liability are unsatisfactory, too stringent and offer insufficient protection for individuals. Léger cited the well-known formula: namely that although State liability is a principle of Community law, substantive and formal conditions are governed by national rules. The common conditions being: breach of rights, damage and causal link. The Court however was not inclined to dismiss totally the analogy with the Community's liability for wrongful acts or omissions of its institutions.

Appraisal of the contribution of Tesauro and Léger to these judgments

Once again it is difficult to reach definitive conclusions but some observations can be made. The Advocates General were fully aware of the significance of their advice to the Court to extend the scope of the *Francovich* judgment to other acts or omissions of the State where the conditions for transposing a breach into liability would not be so straightforward as for the non-implementation of directives. The detailed analysis of the nature and source of the principle of state liability for

[145] Para 28 of the Opinion in Joined Cases C-178/94, C-179/94, C-188-190/94 *Dillenkofer and ors v Germany* [1996] ECR I-4845.

[146] As already stated above, the Opinion was delivered before Tesauro's Opinion in *Brasserie du Pêcheur /Factortame III.*

breach of EC law undertaken by Léger and Tesauro, in particular tying it back to earlier case law, and founding it in general principles and the Treaty, no doubt contributed to its acceptance as a general principle of Community law by the national legal orders.

In addition the Advocates General were in agreement that the Court should lay down some minimum conditions for liability under Community law in order to ensure some degree of uniformity. However, national courts should retain their competence to apply those conditions according to their national laws. Yet in certain significant respects the views of the Advocates General differed. For example as to the degree to which the Article 288 EC conditions of liability could be transposed to State liability.

Ultimately, Tesauro appears to have been more persuasive than Léger. Léger rejected an analogy with the conditions of liability set out by the European Court of Justice in its case-law on the Community's non-contractual liability. The Court, however, adopted similar conditions of liability to those imposed on Community institutions when adopting legislation, at least where the Member State breaches of Community law are in situations where the Member State is exercising a wide discretion. This is more akin to Tesauro's own conclusions.

However the factors set out by the Court as guidance to national courts are more precise than Tesauro's and they are not fully comparable with those to be taken into account when establishing the liability of Community institutions.

Post-1996 developments

Although there have been a number of preliminary references post-1996 seeking interpretation of various aspects of the principle of State liability, none have questioned the principle itself nor the conditions for liability set out by the Court in the *Brasserie du Pêcheur/Factortame III* judgment. The national courts appear to have accepted the extension of the European Court of Justice's competence to an area of law which, until the 1990s, had predominantly been thought to be totally within the national jurisdiction. Furthermore, with the notable exception of Léger, the Advocates General and the European Court of Justice in these cases often claimed that the order for reference provided *all* the necessary information to enable the European Court of Justice to offer 'guidance' to the national court as to whether the breach was sufficiently serious. This is a usurpation of the national court's competence. In a preliminary reference, the assessment as to whether the Member State's breach is sufficiently serious for liability to arise is a matter for the national court not the European Court of Justice.

As already stated above, there have been a number of referrals from national courts seeking further and particular guidance as to how to apply the conditions of liability. Given that the European Court of Justice has placed liability for unlawful legislative acts or omissions squarely on the margin of discretion granted to the Member State by Community law, it is not surprising that most of these preliminary references sought further clarification on the meaning of 'sufficiently serious breach'. Only those rulings and Opinions which have added to the understanding of the principle will be mentioned below.[147] An important, albeit unsurprising, case on State liability considered below is the *Köbler* judgment where the European Court of Justice confirmed that the State may incur liability in damages for judicial failures.[148]

Legislative failures

As far as legislative failures are concerned no significant referrals have arisen in respect of the State's liability for failure to implement a directive. The liability is strict and the *Francovich* and *Dillenkofer* judgments are definitive. The Court has also regularly taken the opportunity to remind national courts of their obligations under Community law.[149] It is only when an interpretation of national law compatible with Community law is impossible that individuals, who have suffered damage as a consequence of the non-transposition or incorrect implementation of the directive, may claim compensation as confirmed in the *Dillenkofer*[150] judgment.

The most interesting cases post 1996 on legislative failures for incorrect implementation of directives are the *Rechberger* and *Svenska Staten*[151] cases. The *Rechberger* case raised the issue whether a failure to implement an article of a directive is a sufficiently serious breach in itself which does not require the national court to consider the factors set out for guidance in the *Brasserie du Pêcheur/Factortame III* judgment. Advocate General Saggio had no hesitation in concluding that the Member State's liability cannot be reduced to a quantitative element.[152] The European Court of Justice agreed with Saggio that the Member State had no margin of discretion as to the entry into force of this article of the directive.[153] The fact that the Member State had implemented correctly all the other provisions of a directive does not excuse the Member State from liability.[154]

[147] Referrals seeking guidance as to the meaning of casual link have been rare. See for example, Case C-140/97 *Rechberger* [1999] ECR I-3499 (discussed below) where it was argued that the causal link had been broken by the imprudent conduct of a third party. Neither Advocate General Saggio nor the Court hesitated to stress that the liability arises from *the State's* breach of Community law.

[148] Case C-224/01 [2003] ECR I- 10239. See for details of the case, M Breuer, 'State liability for judicial wrongs and Community law: the case of *Köbler v Austria*' (2004) 29 ELR 243.

[149] Case C-106/89 *Marleasing* [1990] ECR I-4135 where the European Court of Justice imposed an obligation on national courts to interpret national law, whether adopted before or after the directive, as far as possible, in the light of the wording and purpose of the directives in question.

[150] See for example Case C-54/96 *Dorsch Consult* [1997] ECR I-4961 (Full Court; AG Tesauro) at paras 43 to 45 of the judgment and para 49 of the Opinion; Case C-131/97 *Carbonari* [1999] ECR I-1103 (5th Chamber; AG Jacobs) at paras 48 to 52 of the judgment where the same point was made.

[151] Cases C-140/97 *Rechberger* [1999] ECR I-3499 and C-150/99 *Svenska Staten v Stockholm* [2001] ECR I-493.

[152] Case C-140/97 *Rechberger* [1999] ECR I-3499, at para 39 of the Opinion.

[153] Ibid, para 51 of the judgment.

[154] Ibid, paras 41 of the Opinion and 52 of the judgment.

The *Svenska Staten* case was heard by the Fifth Chamber and the Opinion was delivered by Advocate General Jacobs. The main question on State liability was whether the fact that the provisions of the tax directive in question had direct effect (thereby conferring rights on individuals which could be relied on directly against a Member State before a national court) would reduce the seriousness of the breach since a separate action for damages would not be necessary. Jacobs advised the Court that the 'right to reparation cannot be excluded on the ground that the provision infringed may be relied upon directly before the national courts'.[155] The Court agreed with Jacobs in recognizing that the action for State liability in these circumstances may be unnecessary[156] but it confirmed that the action for State liability is independently available.[157] Jacobs proceeded systematically to consider each factor set out by the Court in the *Brasserie du Pêcheur/ Factortame III* judgment against the facts of the case. He advised the Court that the breach in this case was sufficiently serious to establish liability. Significantly, the European Court of Justice ruled that in the circumstances of the case the failure of the State constituted a serious breach[158] rather than leaving it to the national court to rule on this issue. Similarly, in other cases, both the Advocates General and the Court have been willing to undertake the assessment as to whether the breach is sufficiently serious, rather than leaving it to the national referring court. The Court found in these cases that it had all the necessary information to verify whether the Member State concerned had breached Community law in a sufficient serious manner so as to incur liability for the harm caused.[159]

Another case concerning a legislative failure was the *Norbrook*[160] case where Léger expressly acknowledged that the European Court of Justice had 'clearly and

[155] Case C-150/99 *Svenska Staten v Stockholm* [2001] ECR I-493, at para 50 of the Opinion.

[156] Ibid, para 35 of the judgment.

[157] Ibid, para 36 of the judgment.

[158] Ibid, paras 40 to 42 of the judgment.

[159] See for example, Case C-283/94 *Denkavit* [1996] ECR I-5063 (5th Chamber; AG Jacobs) where the incorrect implementation of a tax directive was found not to be a sufficiently serious breach for the State to incur liability in damages. The factors taken into account in this case included the fact that other Member States had taken the same view following discussions within the EU Council. In addition there was no existing case-law on this directive which might have provided some guidance to the Member State. Another example is Case C-319/96 *Brinkmann* [1999] ECR I-5255 (2nd Chamber; AG Jacobs) where the interpretation given to a provision of a tax directive by the Member State was found not to have been manifestly and gravely contrary to the wording of the directive. The provision concerning the imposition of tax on tobacco was not clear and precise in the context of the facts of the case. In addition there was evidence that several other Member States took the same view of the meaning of the provision. Cf Case C-302/97 *Konle* [1999] ECR I-3099, where Advocate General La Pergola, having advised the Court that it was for the national court to carry out the assessment, went on to suggest that the error of law in this case was excusable (at paras 25 and 26 of the Opinion). The European Court of Justice, however, on this occasion referred the assessment back to the national court (at para 59 of the judgment). A similar situation arose in Case C-63/01 *Sidney Evans* [2003] ECR I-14447 where Advocate General Alber concluded that the breach was sufficiently serious (para 157 of the Opinion) but the Court (5th Chamber) referred the assessment back to the national court (para 88 of the judgment).

[160] Case C-127/95 *Norbrook Laboratories Ltd v Ministry of Agriculture, Fisheries and Food* [1998] ECR I-1531 (5th Chamber).

precisely reiterated the conditions under which a Member State incurs liability for breach of Community law'.[161] As the provisions of the directive in question were clear and precise the incorrect implementation of the provisions by the Member State was a manifest and grave disregard of the limits on the exercise of the Member State's powers. Thus individuals have a right to reparation for the harm caused by the breach.[162] The European Court of Justice once again repeated the standard paragraphs on State liability with which we have now become familiar[163] and concluded that where the discretion is reduced or even non-existent, 'the mere breach of Community law may be sufficient to establish the existence of a sufficiently serious breach'.[164] It was for the national court to determine whether the conditions have been met.

Administrative failures

As far as administrative failures are concerned there have been some issues referred to the European Court of Justice which are of interest. The first one to be considered is in the *Haim*[165] case where the Court was asked to consider liability where the damage was caused by a public-law body. Can such a body, which has acted in breach of Community law, be held liable as well as the Member State? Mischo recognized this was a novel question for the European Court of Justice but not a difficult one to resolve given the consistent case-law of the Court as to the procedural autonomy of the Member States.[166] As long as the damage sustained by the individual is compensated in full, it is for national procedural laws to determine the conditions under which Community rights are asserted before national courts. The national court also asked whether the breach, which in this case was the decision of an official with no discretion in taking that decision in breach of Community law, was sufficiently serious for the State to incur liability. Mischo placed emphasis on the statement of the European Court of Justice in earlier rulings that a breach in such circumstances may be sufficient but is not necessarily so. The factors listed in the *Brasserie du Pêcheur/ Factortame III* judgment have to be taken into account by the national court. Nevertheless, given that all the information necessary to make that evaluation was before the Court, Mischo advised the Court to follow his conclusion that the official in question had committed an excusable error. Haim's situation was exceptional, given that although he was a national of another Member State, his qualifications had been obtained in a third country. In addition, the breach of Community law had occurred before the European Court of Justice ruled on the obligation of Member States to go beyond qualifications and to evaluate also the practical experience of those seeking to establish in the host State when determining whether these Community nationals have met the required conditions.[167] The Opinion was followed by the Court.

[161] Ibid, para 130–31 of the Opinion.
[162] Ibid, paras 133–35 of the Opinion.
[163] Ibid, paras 106 and 107 of the judgment.
[164] Ibid, para 109 of the judgment.
[165] Case C-424/97 *Salomone Haim v Kassenzahnärztliche Vereinigung Nordrhein* [2000] ECR I-5123.
[166] Ibid, para 20 of the Opinion.
[167] Case C-340/89 *Vlassopoulou* [1991] ECR I-2357.

Another case of interest is *Larsy*[168] where the question referred on State liability concerned the failure of an administrative body. The administrative action, in breach of Community law, resulted in Mr Larsy losing a full pension entitlement. Was the breach in question sufficiently serious? Advocate General Léger recalled the Court's case-law which had consistently stated that, where the legislative choice is reduced or non-existent, liability is incurred more readily, and the mere infringement may be enough for the breach to be sufficiently serious. The Court had also maintained that the national court has to proceed to evaluate the breach in accordance with the established factors. The European Court of Justice followed the Advocate General's conclusions but, unlike Léger who advised that the evaluation should be left to the national court, the European Court of Justice decided that it had all the necessary information to be able to carry out the assessment.[169] The Court concluded that, in the circumstances of the case, the national administrative body had no substantive choice. The breach had persisted despite a preliminary ruling which made it clear that the conduct in question constituted a breach.

Another interesting case is *Paul and ors*[170] which concerned the content of rights conferred on the depositor under Directive 94/19/EC on Deposit Guarantee Schemes.[171] In particular, can the Directive give rise to a claim for compensation for damage arising as a consequence of alleged lack of supervision by national authorities? The questions referred to the European Court of Justice included whether Articles 3 and 7 of the Directive confer on the depositor, in the event that his deposit is unavailable, both the right to be compensated by a deposit-guarantee scheme up to the amount specified in Article 7(1) and a further right (beyond that amount) to claim damages for loss suffered as a consequence of misconduct of the national authorities. Furthermore, does the Directive confer rights on the saver/investor such that the competent national authorities must not only take 'prudential supervisory measures' but also incur liability for any misconduct?

Advocate General Stix-Hackl was unequivocal that the Directive does not confer rights on individuals beyond that specifically provided for (up to 20,000 Euros in the event that a deposit is unavailable)[172] and nor do the subsequent Banking directives. It is notable that Stix-Hackl referred to the *Francovich*[173] and *Brinkmann*[174] judgments with reference to the requirement that for liability to be invoked rights must be conferred on individuals. Both the Court and the Advocate

168 Case C-118/00 *Gevais Larsy v Inasti* [2001] ECR I-5063.

169 Ibid, para 40 of the judgment. It is worth noting that in his Opinion in Case C-446/04 *Test Claimants in the FII Group Litigation v Commissioners of the Inland Revenue*, Opinion of 6 April 2006, Advocate General Geelhoed explored the question of whether a breach is sufficiently serious and concluded, referring with approval to AG Fenelly (in Joined cases C-397/98 and C-410/98 *Metallgesellschaft and ors v Commissioners of Inland Revenue* [2001] ECR I-1727) that 'the crucial question in deciding whether a breach . . . is sufficiently serious is the question whether the error of law was, viewed objectively, excusable or inexcusable', at para 138.

170 Case C-222/02 *Paul and ors v Germany* [2004] ECR I-9425.

171 [1994] OJ L135/5.

172 Case C-222/02 *Paul and ors v Germany* [2004] ECR I-9425, at paras 94–101 of the Opinion.

173 Joined Cases C-6/90 and C-9/90 [1991] ECR I-5357.

174 Case C-319/96 *Brinkmann* [1999] ECR I-5255.

General noted that although the objectives of the Directive include the protection of depositors, this is only one objective and it does not constitute the conferral of rights upon the investors.[175] The Court referred to the *Brasserie de Pêcheur and Factortame III*[176] and *Dillenkofer*[177] judgments, and found, like the Advocate General, that liability can only arise 'where the rule of law infringed is intended to confer rights upon individuals' and that the directives in issue 'cannot be regarded as conferring on individuals . . . rights capable of giving rise to liability on the part of the State on the basis of Community law'.[178]

The findings of the Court (and the Advocate General) may be significant in that the emphasis upon the requirement of an *intention* to confer rights on individuals, and the consequent application of this condition, may perhaps be more restrictive than the application of the condition that the directive 'confer rights' in the *Dillenkofer*[179] case.

Judicial failures

As far as judicial failures are concerned, the European Court of Justice has now had the opportunity to confirm that a Member State may be held liable in damages for a breach of Community law by its judiciary. In the *Köbler*[180] case the Austrian Supreme Administrative Court asked whether Member States are obliged under Community law to make reparation for damage caused to individuals by breaches of Community law attributable to national courts adjudicating at last instance. The Austrian court had dismissed an action brought by Köbler who claimed compensation for loss suffered due to indirect discrimination contrary to Community law without making a reference to the European Court of Justice.

The European Court of Justice found that the judgment of the Supreme Administrative Court was based on an incorrect reading of the earlier European Court of Justice judgment. Thus it constituted a breach of Community law but the Court decided, on the facts, that the breach could not be described as 'manifest and grave'. The preliminary issue, as to whether a Member State may incur liability for damage caused by a national court when it acted in breach of Community law, was not seriously doubted in view of the fact that national courts have a decisive role in ensuring the effectiveness of Community law. Léger's conclusion that the State may incur liability for judicial failures was predictable given that in the *Lomas* Opinion he had already expressed his view unequivocally on this issue.[181]

[175] Judgment at para 40; Opinion at para 124.

[176] Joined Cases C-46/93 and C-48/93 [1996] ECR I-1029.

[177] Joined Cases C-178/94, C-179/94, C-188-190/94 *Dillenkofer and ors v Germany* [1996] ECR I-4845.

[178] Case C-222/02 *Paul and ors v Germany* [2004] ECR I-9425, at para 51 of the judgment.

[179] Gerrit Betlem; Carmen Pérez González; Marie-Pierre Granger; Birgit Schoißwohl, Comment on Paul and Others, Post-Francovich Judgments by the European Court of Justice, Francovich Follow-up, at <http://www.eel.nl/index.asp?c_nr=5&sub_categorie=169&ssc_nr=868&anker=Francovich%20 Follow-Up>. (Accessed: 29 August 2006.)

[180] Case C-224/01 [2003] ECR I-10239.

[181] Case C-5/94 *Lomas* [1996] ECR I-2553, at para 114 of the Opinion.

The outstanding interesting issue was whether the conditions for liability stipulated for legislative and administrative failures were to be applied without modification to judicial failures. If there are sensitivities in the context of imposing liability on States for legislative failures, the position is even more delicate in the context of judicial failures. The independence of the judiciary from the executive control is one of the fundamental principles of the modern State.

Advocate General Léger's advice was not wholly followed by the Court. Léger considered that the conditions which applied to legislative and administrative failures could not be transposed for acts or omissions of a national supreme court because of the specific nature of the judicial protection. He favoured an adaptation of the factors to be considered in determining whether the judicial breach is 'sufficiently serious' for the State to incur liability for the ensuing damage. In his view, the question to be asked was whether the error of law at issue was excusable. The answer would depend on factors such as the clarity and precision of the legal rule infringed, on the existing case-law of the European Court of Justice and on the specific circumstances of each case. In this referral the Austrian Supreme Court, as a Court of last instance, had failed to make a preliminary reference in disregard of its obligations under Article 234 EC. Thus Léger concluded that the breach was inexcusable given that the European Court of Justice had not yet ruled on the precise issue raised by the facts of the case.

However, the European Court of Justice stated that State liability for an act or omission of a court of last instance can only be incurred in 'exceptional circumstances' where the national court manifestly committed a breach of Community law. Furthermore, to establish that the breach was manifest the factors listed in the *Brasserie du Pêcheur/Factortame III* judgment also applied to this situation.

The main difference between Léger and the European Court of Justice was thus that the former viewed the judicial failure to make a reference to the European Court of Justice by a national court of last instance, as particularly inexcusable and, therefore, would impose automatic liability. Such a failure is comparable to the State liability for non-implementation of a directive where the mere fact of non-implementation is deemed a sufficient serious breach of Community law. The Court, however, considered the finding that the error of law was inexcusable to be one of various factors that have to be assessed by the national court.[182] The national court will have to assess all the factors in order to determine whether the breach was manifest and, therefore, sufficiently serious for the State to incur liability for damage.

[182] It is worth noting at this point Geelhoed's (subsequent) Opinion in Case C-446/04 *Test Claimants in the FII Group Litigation v Commissioners of the Inland Revenue*, Opinion of the 6 April 2006, in which he held that the question of whether a breach is sufficiently serious turns on whether it is indeed objectively excusable or not. This could indicate that Geelhoed favours a more rigorous approach to 'sufficient seriousness'. However, it could alternatively simply indicate that the European Court of Justice is inclined to ensure wider discretion in respect of the actions (and consequent potential liability) of national judiciary.

In *Commission v Italy*[183] the question for the Court was whether the State is liable for the action of its administrative and judicial authorities in relation to the repayment of taxes levied in breach of Community law. (The practice of the relevant authorities rendered repayment impossible or excessively difficult for the taxpayer.) Thus the issue was whether 'national legal practice contrary to Community law can give rise to a declaration that a Member State has failed to fulfil its obligations under Article 226 EC'.[184] In his Opinion in this case, which was delivered after Léger's in *Köbler*, but before the judgment in that case, Advocate General Geelhoed unequivocally endorsed Léger's analysis in the *Köbler*[185] case. Geelhoed continued by referring to the European Court of Justice's case law to support his conclusion that whatever organ of the State is responsible for a breach of Community law, the State will be liable.[186] Significantly Geelhoed addressed the question on the independence of the judiciary but argued that this, far from precluding State liability, simply: 'means that the courts must settle specific disputes without external influence, in particular from other organs of the State. However in other respects the judiciary functions as part of the apparatus of the State within the bounds laid down by the national constitution and national legislation'.[187]

Geelhoed concluded that, since wrongful interpretation and application of Community law by national courts deprived individuals of the enjoyment of their rights under Community law and endangered the uniform application of Community law, the State should be liable for such a breach by its national courts.[188] However, he also contended that not all judicial errors are sufficient in this respect, and that it was necessary to specify the conditions under which liability could arise. Notably he identified various factors which may be relevant to this question: the first being the status of the national judgments concerned—thus he concluded that an individual judgment of a lower court will not necessarily undermine the effect of Community law within the internal market, although it may discourage individuals from bringing an action or lodging an appeal. In contrast, case law of the Supreme national court may well have such an undermining effect.[189] Another relevant factor to be considered is whether the particular failure constitutes a structural phenomenon: whether it is a one-off, or consistent with a trend in national case law. Is it a new development or does it reflect established practice? In Goelhoed's opinion, the most important factor in the assessment is the effect of the national judgment upon the achievement of the Community's objectives.[190]

[183] Case C-129/00 [2003] ECR I-14637.
[184] Ibid, para 3 of the Opinion.
[185] Ibid, para 49.
[186] Ibid, paras 50–56.
[187] Ibid, para 56.
[188] Ibid, para 60.
[189] The European Court of Justice confirmed in Case C-173/03 *Traghetti del Mediterraneo SpA v Repubblica Italiana*, judgment delivered on 13 June 2006, nyr, that a Member State is liable for damage caused to an individual by a manifest infringement of Community law attributable to a Supreme Court. The European Court of Justice ruled that a Member State cannot limit State liability solely to cases of intentional fault and services misconduct on the part of the national court.
[190] Case C-129/00 *Commission v Italy* [2003] ECR I-14637, paras 63–67 of the Opinion.

In its judgment the Court simply stated, relying on *Commission v Belgium*,[191] that: 'a Member State's failure to fulfil obligations may, in principle, be established under Article 226 EC whatever the agency of that State whose action or inaction is the cause of the failure to fulfil its obligations, even in the case of a constitutionally independent institution'.[192]

This case can be viewed as being significant as it is in fact the first one in which the Court of Justice has found a Member State liable for the actions of the national court.

The subsequent case of *Kühne & Heitz*[193] does not strictly concern the question of State liability, but does deal with the status of judgments of national courts which conflict with Community law. In particular, this case gave rise to the question of whether a judicial decision which has become final should be reopened in light of a subsequent preliminary ruling of European Court of Justice. Advocate General Léger simply applied *Larsy*[194] (which concerned administrative decisions). In the *Larsy* case, the national decision was not final, unlike in the *Kühne & Heitz* case but had the status of *res judicata*. In Léger's view this distinction was not decisive: the decisive factors were the principles of primacy of Community law and direct applicability together with Article 10 EC and the Court's case law in the *Simmenthal, Factortame* and *Francovich*[195] judgments. These cumulative factors required that the national judgment should be reopened in light of Community law. Significantly, Léger did not consider that application of this conclusion infringed the principle of procedural autonomy.[196]

In its judgment the European Court of Justice considered the issue of legal certainty and concluded that 'Community law does not require administrative bodies to be placed under an obligation, in principle to reopen an administrative decision which has become final in that way'.[197] However, the Court continued that in view of Netherlands national law, which provides that administrative bodies have the power to reopen an administrative decision which has become final in this way, and the particular facts of the case, the administrative body was, as a consequence of Article 10 EC, under an obligation to reopen the decision which had become final. Thus in this case, although ultimately both reached the conclusion that the decision should be reopened, the European Court of Justice, in founding its decision upon the particular facts, was rather more cautious than its Advocate General who was comfortable in imposing an obligation under Community law to reopen the decision.

The post-1996 cases show that while no significant divergences have arisen in the approaches of the Advocates General and the European Court of Justice, there

[191] Case 77/69 *Commission v Belgium* [1970] ECR 237.

[192] Case C-129/00 *Commission v Italy* [2003] ECR I-14637, para 29.

[193] Case C-453/00 *Kühne & Heitz NV v Productschap voor Pluimvee en Eieren* [2004] ECR I-837.

[194] Case C-118/00 *Gevais Larsy v Inasti* [2001] ECR I-5063.

[195] Case C-453/00 *Kühne & Heitz NV v Produktschap voor Pluimvee en Eieren* [2004] ECR I-837, at paras 66–67 of AG Léger's Opinion.

[196] Ibid, paras 68–73 of the Opinion.

[197] Ibid, para 24 of the judgment.

are some indications that the European Court of Justice is slightly more reticent in recognising State liability and, in particular, has been slightly more willing in recent cases to emphasize the discretion of the Member States, in particular in relation to the question of whether the breach is sufficiently serious. Only Léger consistently refrains from undertaking an assessment of whether the criteria for liability have been met. In the *Norbrook* case, at least, the Court and Léger agreed to leave that issue to the national court!

Concluding observations

The principle of State liability was firmly established in the Community's legal order only in 1991, in the *Francovich* judgment. However, the European Court of Justice confirmed, early in its case-law, the importance of the effectiveness of Community law which is one of the key elements in the origin of this principle. Furthermore, the principle was found to have been inherent in the EC Treaty as the natural consequence of Article 10 EC which imposes an obligation on Member States to comply with Community law. It is therefore striking that it took over 30 years before the principle of State liability was recognized expressly by the European Court of Justice.[198]

The contribution of Advocates General, in the pre-*Francovich* case-law, to the establishment and evolution of the principle of State liability in the Community's legal order can only be assessed by examining it on various levels. As regards the establishment of a Community principle of State liability in damages per se, the contribution of the Advocates General in the early case law is disappointing.[199] It was the Court, rather than the Advocates General, which seemed to be more aware of the need to ensure Member States were accountable to individuals for harm caused by their failure to comply with Community law. For example, in *Commission v Italy*[200] the Court, not Advocate General Mayras, commented on the usefulness to a private party of an Article 226 declaration that a Member State is in breach of a Treaty obligation where that breach has caused harm which may give rise to an action for compensation before the national court.

As early as the *Humblet* judgment,[201] delivered before the doctrines of supremacy and of direct effect of Community law had been established, the European Court of Justice recognized the need for a Member State to be liable for harm caused to an individual as a result of the Member State's breach of Community law. Advocate General Lagrange himself made no reference to a principle of State liability in Community law in the Opinion he delivered in the *Humblet* case even though, in the Opinions he had delivered earlier in the *FERAM* and *Meroni* cases,

[198] See text above at p 216. [199] See also commentary above at pp 231–233.
[200] Case 39/72 [1973] ECR 101, see text above at p 233.
[201] Case 6/60 [1960] ECR 559, see text above at p 224.

he discussed at length the conditions under French law for State liability for the wrongful act of an administrative body.[202] Yet his failure to return to the principle of State liability in the *Humblet* case may have reflected the Court's lack of engagement with it in the *FERAM* case. As will be discussed below, Lagrange's contribution in the *FERAM* case certainly cannot be lightly dismissed. In founding the principle in public law, thus allowing the European Court of Justice to list the conditions for liability (since these would not be governed by national civil procedure) Lagrange appears to be clearly indicating that this is a Community principle.

The position of Advocate General Reischl in *Russo v AIMA*,[203] the first case where State liability was raised directly before the European Court of Justice (an Article 234 reference) is rather nuanced. While he maintained the traditional view that State liability for breach of Community law was a matter to be governed by the national law he had no doubt that Member States were liable to compensate for such harm, and that this was a Community law obligation. Thus Reischl appears to indicate that there was a Community law principle of State liability, the enforcement of which was left to national law. The source of that liability arose in his view out of the need to protect individual rights created under Community law. In his subsequent Opinion in *Benedetti v Munari*, Reischl confirmed his view that although infringement of Community law gives rise to an obligation to compensate, the conditions of State liability should be governed by national law[204] (he expressly commented on the fact the EC Treaty contained provisions only on the liability of Community institutions).

Thus, until the *Francovich* judgment, an evaluation of the case-law indicates that the Advocates General made a limited contribution to the creation and development of State liability as a principle of the Community's legal order. While Reischl and Lagrange were clear that State liability arose from State failure or error, and Lagrange went as far as to state that by founding the principle in public law the European Court of Justice could list the conditions for liability, broadly the Advocates General (and the European Court of Justice) were happy to leave the criteria and consequences to national law. In the *Francovich* case, however, Mischo had a leading role in persuading the Court that a failure to comply with Community obligations, such as a failure to implement a directive, was a matter for Community law and not to be left entirely to national law. His analysis of the Court's case-law, emphasizing the duty of the Member State to ensure effectiveness of Community law, led him to the conclusion that there was no difference between directly and indirectly applicable Community law as far as State liability was concerned. Furthermore, the rights accrued to individuals to seek compensation for harm caused by the Member State's breach of its obligations arise from the EC Treaty itself and not as a consequence of a European Court of Justice judgment confirming that a Member State is in breach of its Treaty obligations. Thus EC

[202] See text above at pp 231–233 for further comment.
[203] Case 60/75 [1976] ECR 45, see text above at p 222.
[204] Case 52/76 [1977] ECR 163, see text above at p 224.

law, not national law, governs the principle of State liability for harm caused to an individual due to a Member State's breach of EC law.[205]

Mischo, therefore, was the first Advocate General to be seen to contribute directly and significantly to the establishment of State liability as a principle of Community law. Somewhat controversially, he also asserted that this had been previously established by the Court. In the context of non-implementation of directives whose provisions do not have direct effect, the State liability solution was perceived as an effective alternative to an Article 226 EC infringement action since it allows individuals to seek redress directly against a State. Thus the effectiveness of Community law is equally ensured. State liability is also available as a remedy where, as in the case of *Faccini Dori*,[206] the directive has direct effect but the individual concerned may not rely on its provisions in litigation between private parties. Where the provisions of the directive have direct effect, the individual can also rely directly on the rights conferred on him by the directive and seek a remedy before the national court which may include damages.

As for the conditions of liability, the earlier Opinions—such as those delivered by Lagrange in the *FERAM* case are of undoubted significance. Lagrange relied mainly on French law, emphasizing the requirement of a 'serious error' or a 'manifestly wrongful act of particular gravity'. In the *Meroni* Opinion he clarified his position, stressing that an 'ordinary wrong' would suffice in some circumstances, that there was no absolute rule and the required degree of seriousness should vary according to a number of factors.[207] This indeed is how the European Court of Justice went on to rule in the *Brasserie du Pêcheur/Factortame III, ex parte BT* and *Dillenkofer* cases.

As early as *Russo v AIMA* the Commission submitted that the conditions of liability for a Member State should follow the same lines as for non-contractual liability of the Community. However, the Advocates General, with the exception of Lagrange, consistently maintained that the conditions of liability were a matter for the national legal order.[208] Then in the *Francovich* case, Mischo reversed this position arguing for the same conditions for liability as those developed by the European Court of Justice when considering a case for damages resulting from an infringement of Community law by a Community institution. Procedural and evidentiary rules, as well as the measure of damages, should continue to be governed by national law subject to the doctrines of equivalence and adequacy. The European Court of Justice, however, did not follow Mischo's advice and went on to specify three conditions which have to be met before a non-implementation of a directive gives rise to State liability. It also stated that liability would be dependent on the nature of the breach, echoing Lagrange in the *Meroni* Opinion.

The Opinions of Tesauro and Léger in the middle of the 1990s are undoubtedly of significance.[209] Both opinions comprehensively analysed the nature and scope of the principle, concluding that it was a principle of general application

[205] Joined Cases C-6/90 and C-9/90 [1991] ECR I-5357, text above at p 225.

[206] Case C-91/92 [1994] ECR I-3325.

[207] Above text at pp 227–228.

[208] See for example Reischl in Case 60/75 *Russo v AIMA* [1976] ECR 45.

[209] See also above commentary at pp 246–247.

and not simply limited to a *Francovich*-type situation. Thus the principle applies whenever harm is caused due to a sufficiently serious breach of EC law caused by a legislative, administrative or judicial failure. Léger in the *Lomas* Opinion emphasized the European Court of Justice's case-law requirement of effective judicial protection for Community rights granted to individuals. An action for damages is the corollary to direct effect and a 'vital component of the judicial protection of individuals'.[210] Liability is founded on illegality, namely the failure of the Member State to respect the supremacy of Community law.

Tesauro's approach is also similar to Léger's, acknowledging the change of emphasis from the State's conduct to the rights of individuals. In the same manner that the State incurs liability under national law when it causes damage, then it is also appropriate for the Member State to incur liability when it causes harm as a result of its breach of Community law.[211]

As to the conditions of liability, Léger's position is different from Mischo's. His analysis of the Community's non-contractual liability under Article 288 EC led Léger to the conclusion that State liability has a different foundation and, therefore, it is inappropriate to transpose the conditions of liability developed for harm caused by the Community to that caused by the Member State's administrative failure where it acted in breach of Community law. Both Léger and Tesauro however were in agreement that the decisive test for liability depends on the degree of discretion left to the Member States. Tesauro was less negative than Léger in considering the criteria developed by the European Court of Justice for the Community's non-contractual liability, Tesauro considering it in context of legislative failures and Léger considering it in the context of administrative failures. Where a Member State has a wide discretion Tesauro was willing to accept that the Member State's liability should be assessed under the same restrictive conditions as applied to the Community's institutions. This was indeed the conclusion reached by the European Court of Justice. However as to the relevant factors to be taken into account in deciding whether the breach was sufficiently serious, the European Court of Justice listed several more factors than those listed by Tesauro.

The Opinions of Léger and Tesauro were delivered in a relatively short period and raised broadly similar issues. There is, however, no evidence in the Opinions that the Advocates General discussed the issues together. Should there have been? Perhaps not, since an Advocate General is expected to deliver his *independent* conclusions. Nevertheless, one may ask whether the European Court of Justice would have been better served by some discussion in Tesauro's Opinion of the matters raised by the earlier Opinion from Léger, where the latter discussed similar issues. Significantly, both emphasized effectiveness of Community law (a consistent concern throughout the case law and Opinions) and judicial protection of individual rights. However, they were not entirely in agreement as regards the source of the

[210] At paragraph 94 of the Opinion in *Lomas*, Case 5/94 [1996] ECR I-2553.

[211] Above text at p 239.

principle. As regards the conditions of liability, both focused on the degree of discretion available to the relevant actor. The Court ultimately appeared to move closer to Tesauro's approach. All cases were heard before the Full Court but each with a different Reporting Judge.[212] There is some evidence to suggest that the Reporting Judge in the *Brasserie du Pêcheur/Factortame III* cases was aware of Léger's Opinion in *Lomas* since the wording in the former judgment is on several occasions identical to Léger's.[213]

The post 1996 case-law is also interesting for several reasons. First, the European Court of Justice appears more willing than the Advocate General to consider the question of State liability where it has not been raised specifically by the national referring court. For example in the *Sutton*[214] case, Léger refused to consider the question of State liability since it had not been one of the questions referred for interpretation by the national court; it had only been raised in the submissions of one of the parties. The European Court of Justice, however, considered the issue of State liability given that it was mentioned in the order for reference.[215] On the other hand, the Court, and more recently also the Advocates General, regularly remind the national courts in the post-1996 State liability cases of their obligation to interpret national law in accordance with Community law as ruled in the *Marleasing*[216] case. Thus the Court, having established the principle of State liability as part of the Community's legal order, seems keen to encourage other means of ensuring the effectiveness of Community law.

In the *Paul* case both the Advocate General and the European Court of Justice adopted what can be viewed as a strict interpretation of the requirement of an intention to confer rights on individuals, and certainly it is arguable that this interpretation represents a pulling back from the approach in the *Dillenkofer* judgment. One case does not make a trend, however, and it is possible to discern a distinction between the approach of the Court and that of the Advocates General to the imposition of liability (and certainly to the founding of liability in Community law) in the *Köbler* and *Kühne & Heitz*[217] cases.

Second, the overwhelming majority of Advocates General with the notable exception of Léger have been willing to reach conclusions on the seriousness of the breach although they feel the assessment of liability should be left for the national court as it is not a matter of interpretation. The European Court of Justice's approach to this issue is difficult to rationalize. In cases concerning the non-implementation or incorrect implementation of tax directives (*Denkavit, Brinkmann* and *Svenska Staaten*) the Court has consistently followed Jacobs and determined itself whether the breach was sufficiently serious for the Member

212 The Reporting Judge is responsible for drafting the ruling of the Court.

213 Above, nn 122 and 123.

214 Case C-66/95 [1977] ECR I-2163.

215 Ibid, paras 28–35 of the judgment. A similar situation arose in Case C-131/97 *Carbonari* [1999] ECR I-1103 where Léger was also the Advocate General in the case.

216 Case C-106/89 *Marleasing SA v La Comercial Internacional de Alimentacion SA* [1990] ECR I-4135.

217 See below.

state to incur liability. Similarly, in cases concerning administrative failures (*Haim* and *Larsy*), the Court proceeded in the same manner even though Léger, in the *Larsy* Opinion, had concluded that the issue should be left to the national court. A similar approach from Advocates General La Pergola and Alber (*Konle* and *Sidney Evans*) was not followed by the European Court of Justice which referred the issue back to the national court to assess. However, in the *Norbrook* judgment, the Court followed Léger's view and left the issue to be determined by the national court.

As far as a judicial failure is concerned Léger again took a different position from the European Court of Justice in the *Köbler* case. Léger concluded that the criteria adopted for legislative and administrative failures are not appropriate in the case of a judicial failure. He preferred to consider whether the failure was excusable or inexcusable. Léger concluded that the breach was inexcusable in the case of a non-referral by a Court of last instance. His advice, however, was not followed by the European Court of Justice which ruled that a Member State incurred liability for harm caused by a breach of Community law by one of its judicial organs *only* in exceptional circumstances and that, on the facts the failure was not manifest and grave in this case. Significantly in the subsequent case of *Kühne & Heitz*, Geelhoed, unlike the European Court of Justice, was willing to recognize an obligation founded in Community law, breach of which could ultimately give rise to liability. The Court found that such an obligation existed on the facts, but was based in national law. Do these cases indicate perhaps a Court which is now rather more cautious than its Advocates General in imposing liability? This would not be inconsistent with the restraint suggested by the *Paul* judgment (although that restraint was shared by the Advocate General). It is also arguably consistent with the Court's keenness to encourage other means of ensuring the enforcement of EC law.

Thus, in conclusion, the contribution of the Advocates General to the establishment and development of the principle of State liability is not easily summed up. It is on the one hand disappointing that the Advocates General, as a group, were not more pressing as regards the establishment of a Community principle of State liability (as opposed to accepting this as a matter for national law). On the other hand the contribution of a few, notably Lagrange, Reischl, Mischo, Tesauro and Léger to both the establishment and the delimitation of the principle has been substantial. There is, furthermore, some evidence to suggest that the Advocates General may now be pushing the limits further, while the Court displays more caution.

There is no doubt that the combination of a number of different Advocates General producing Opinions on this subject in a relatively short period (1991–96), and some (for example, Léger) producing several on the subject, has also contributed to a careful, reasoned and balanced approach to the development of this principle by the Court. Furthermore the very thoroughness of some of those Opinions and the analysis contained within them (notably Tesauro's and Léger's in the 1990s) undoubtedly contributed to the acceptance of this cause of action. There is no sense, in the emergence of the principle of State liability, of the creation of principle 'on the back of an envelope'. The combination of breadth of reasoning, depth of knowledge and analysis indicates rather a healthy development of principle. This is not insignificant given that State liability in damages was potentially highly controversial for the creation of a new remedy in Community law, yet it has been relatively readily accepted. The emergence of the principle of State liability could perhaps have been faster, yet that might have undermined those very strengths which undoubtedly assisted its acceptance.

10

The Advocates General and the concept of citizenship

Introduction

The case law of the European Court of Justice regarding citizenship has been subject to intensive scrutiny.[1] Particularly in the last decade, the Court has been seen as bringing about fundamental change to the rights of European citizens. In this chapter we ask the question of whether the Advocates General who have assisted the Court in a selected number of these cases have been instrumental in persuading the Court to interpret the citizenship provisions of the Treaty in a more radical way than earlier commentators had suggested might be possible. Or, on the other hand, have the Advocates General sought to act as a restraining influence, reminding the Court of the difficult genesis of these provisions and the reluctance of the Member States to agree to any but the most skeletal of provisions? If they did seek to influence the Court in engaging in a constructivist approach, did the Advocates General demonstrate a political awareness in their Opinions or did they seek merely to make sense of the Treaty framework and the relevant and sometimes conflicting secondary legislation?

The citizenship provisions as they are currently framed represent a compromise agreed at Maastricht between those States, such as Spain, who favoured deepening political integration and others, such as Denmark and the UK, who were reluctant to concede further ground towards a deeper political process. These provisions of the Treaty were so sensitive that they led to the referendum in Denmark at the time of the ratification of the Treaty being lost, in the first referendum, to the 'No'

[1] M Everson, 'The Legacy of the Market Citizen' in J Shaw and G More (eds), *New Legal Dynamics of the European Union* (1995); S O'Leary, *The Evolving Concept of Community Citizenship: from the Free Movement of Persons to Union Citizenship* (1996); J Shaw, 'The Interpretation of Union Citizenship' (1998) 61 MLR 293; S Fries and J Shaw, 'Citizenship of the Union: First Steps in the European Court of Justice (1998) 4 EPL 533; T Faist, 'Social Citizenship in the European Union: Nested Membership' (2001) 39 JCMS 37; C Jacqueson, 'Union Citizenship and the Court of Justice: Something New Under the Sun?' (2002) 27 ELR 260; M Dougan, 'Free Movement: The Work Seeker as Citizen' (2002) 4 CYEL 121; G Davies, 'The High Water Point of Free Movement of Persons: Ending Benefit Tourism and Rescuing Welfare' (2004) 26(2) JSWFL 211; E Spaventa, 'From Gebhard to Carpenter: Towards a (Non) Economic European Constitution' (2004) 41 CMLR 74; K Hailbronner, 'Union Citizenship and Access to Social Benefits' (2005) 42 CMLR 1245.

vote. They are, therefore, written in fairly precise terms, spelling out what the Member States at the time had agreed. Part Two of the Treaty, Articles 17 to 22, contains those provisions that relate to citizenship and which establish citizenship of the Union as a concept and provide that any person having the nationality of one of the Member States holds citizenship of the Union. Citizenship of the Union complements and does not replace national citizenship. Citizens are to enjoy the rights provided for in the Treaty, listed in Articles 17 to 21 (as the rights to move and reside freely within the territory of the Member States), subject to the limitations and conditions laid down in the Treaty and the measures adopted to give it effect: to vote and stand in local and European elections, the right to consular and diplomatic protection, and the right to petition the European Parliament.

As is clear from the interventions of several of the Member States in the citizenship cases, these provisions were neither intended nor understood, at the time of their negotiation, as being capable of leading to an expansion of the rights of citizens beyond those already provided for in the Treaties and in secondary legislation. The relatively tight drafting of the provisions suggests that this interpretation reflects the intergovernmental bargain achieved at Maastricht, and a comparison with the original Spanish proposal confirms this. The Spanish proposal defined citizenship in terms of a new status: 'the personal and indivisible status of nationals of the Member States, whose membership of the Union means that they have special rights and duties that are specific to the nature of the Union and are exercised and safeguarded specifically within its boundaries'.[2] According to this formula, Union citizenship would be a new status conferring special rights specific to the Union and bypassing the Member States. It was this formula that was deemed unacceptable during the negotiations, and so the more circumscribed provisions outlined above were adopted. However, it is clear that the meaning to be ascribed to these provisions was likely to be contested.

This chapter examines some, but by no means all, the cases in which the Court was asked to interpret Articles 17 and 18 EC[3] seeking to examine what influence, if at all, a number of Advocates General had on the Court. It is important to remember the changing political and legal environment in which they were decided because, however influential an Advocate General might seek to be, the Court must remain aware of the complex and changing environment in which it interprets the Treaty provisions. The period 1990–2005 was particularly eventful. The tension between the Member States in relation to the deepening of the Union became forcibly apparent with the Treaty Establishing the European Union in 1992. The desire of some of the Member States to create a political union with a

[2] Quoted in D Chalmers, C Hadjiemmanuil, G Monti, and A Tomkins, *European Union Law* (2006) 567.

[3] Consolidated Version of the Treaty Establishing the European Community, Arts 17 and 18 (formerly Arts 8 and 8a respectively).

single currency and with a greater commitment to shared political values was thwarted by other Member States, of which Thatcher's United Kingdom was the clearest and most forceful example, who were determined to pull back and retreat into a much looser area based on market principles. Successive Treaty amendments and enlargements also brought their own tensions and certainly a feeling that Europe was constantly in flux. Finally, rejection of the EU Constitution by the French and the Dutch in 2005 showed that both European political leadership and the project to re-engage with Europe's citizens had seemingly failed.

Against this background, the European Court has itself reacted in different ways. Douglas-Scott suggests that the 1990s saw a threat to the Court's 'interpretative autonomy' in the constraints placed on the jurisdiction of the Court by Maastricht and Amsterdam.[4] She cites the then President of the European Court of Justice, Judge Rodriguez Iglésias, who, in 1996, stated that the Court should act as guardian of the Constitution and not become a motor of integration. Under these circumstances it is therefore to be expected that in any early cases coming before the Court, relating to what are now Articles 17 and 18EC, that it might not be persuaded to interpret those provisions in any but a restrictive sense.

One of the most interesting analyses of the Court's case-law in relation to the citizenship cases is provided by Dora Kostakopoulou,[5] who argues that the Court's citizenship jurisprudence developed in three phases in the period 1993–2003. She characterizes these phases as 'judicial minimalism' (1993–97), 'signalling intentions' (1998–00), and 'engineering institutional change' (2001–03). She argues that in the early phase 'European Judges saw radical change as difficult, premature and costly in view of post-Maastricht reactions and governmental opposition. As a consequence, the conceptual resources inherent in the institution of Union citizenship were not utilized'.[6] The second phase, 'signalling intentions', saw the Court bringing citizens within the 'scope of the protection provided by the non-discrimination clause' of the Treaty.[7] This phase also coincided with the Commission's proposals for new legislation on residence rights and on updating existing secondary legislation relating to free movement of workers. Kostakopoulou argues that this 'discursive interaction and the Commission's entrepreneurship' provided impetus for judicial activism. That activism underpinned the Court's decision in *Martínez Sala* (discussed below).[8] Perhaps this phase also shows the importance of the Commission/Court dialogue, given that the Court was apparently persuaded by the arguments made by the Commission in the oral proceedings in *Martínez Sala* to come down in favour of the rights of citizens lawfully resident in one of the Member States.[9] The third phase, 'engineering social change' saw the Court expanding the concepts of citizenship to determine the

[4] S Douglas-Scott, *Constitutional Law of the European Union* (2002) 221.

[5] D Kostakopoulou 'Ideas, Norms and European Citizenship: Explaining Institutional Change' (2005) 68 (2) MLR 233.

[6] Ibid, 245.

[7] Ibid, 246.

[8] Case C-85/96 *Maria Martínez Sala v Freistaat Bayern* [1998] ECR I-2691.

[9] S O'Leary, 'Putting Flesh on the Bones of European Citizenship' (1999) 24 ELR 68.

extent and content of citizenship rights. In this phase the Court became, in Kostakopoulou's terms, 'an institutional designer and agent of change', which gave meaning, specificity and value to concepts of European citizenship.[10] This phase continues today.

This is an interesting framework in which to analyse the case-law of the Court, and it also provides a framework for an analysis of the approach of the Advocates General and their influence on the Court. Did the Advocates General urge judicial minimalism in the early cases? Did they provide an analytical framework that persuaded the Court to shift to a phase of engineering social change? Kostakopoulou argues that the case-law of the Court must be seen in the context of a Court influenced by 'exchanges and interactions with the broader socio-political structures and other institutions', where the European Court of Justice participates in a 'reflexive European circuit'. Can the Advocates General be seen as part of the 'reflexive European circuit', where 'normative frames, ideas, and information about the positioning of other institutions circulate and crosscut organizational boundaries', within which the Court reaches its decisions on citizenship cases?[11] In her analysis, Kostakopoulou does not position the Advocates General within this reflexive European circuit, perhaps seeing the Advocates General as an integral part of the Court itself and the Court as a single actor.[12] However, this chapter, using Kostakopoulou's phases as a means of classifying the Opinions of the Advocates General in some of the key cases, particularly in those cases where the Court began to indicate its intentions to use the citizenship provisions as a means of enlarging the rights of citizens, attempts to position the Advocates General *within* that circuit. The question here, therefore, is: did the Advocates General urge the Court to view the provisions of the Treaty as a means to engineer change and did they provide the Court with plausible legal justifications for interpreting the citizenship provisions in an expansive and constructivist way?

Contextual background

Before examining the case-law of the Court regarding the citizenship provisions, it is worth recalling some salient points of Community law which provide the background against which some of the cases below arose in the national courts.[13] The rights of economically active citizens, nationals of one of the Member States, to

[10] Kostakopoulou, n5 above, 263. [11] Ibid, 246.

[12] Iyiola Solanke argues against seeing the Court as a single monolithic actor in 'The Advocate General in Context: Cause Lawyer, Networker or Mediator?' Paper presented to the conference, The Transformation of Europe, IISL, Oñati, 7–9 June 2006. She cites the following: J Weiler, 'The Reform of European Constitutionalism' (1997) 35 JCMS 95 and M P Grainger, 'The Future of Europe: Judicial Interference and Preference' (2005) 3 CEP 155.

[13] For extensive treatment of these issues see C Barnard, *The Substantive Law of the EU: The Four Freedoms* (2004).

move to and reside in another Member State were recognized within the original Treaty of Rome. These rights include the right to seek and take up offers of employment under Article 39 EC,[14] the right of establishment under Article 43 EC,[15] and the right to provide and receive services under Article 49EC.[16] To facilitate the exercise of these rights, a number of regulations and directives were adopted by the Council which, for example, regulated the administrative procedures governing the right of entry and residence of economically active persons or provided for the situation of workers' families.[17] Since these were all matters falling within the scope of application of the Treaty, any discrimination on the grounds of nationality was prohibited by Article 12EC.[18] The Court of Justice interpreted these provisions so as to give maximum protection for economically active citizens and their families viewing them as fundamental freedoms in the operation of the single market. An example of the Court's expansive interpretation is the case of *Cowan*, where the Court, in applying the principle of equal treatment, ruled that a British tourist in France, as a recipient of services, was entitled to access to a compensation scheme for victims of crime on the same basis as French nationals.[19]

The Community legislator extended the rights of movement and residence to non-economically active nationals of the Member States with three directives in 1990.[20] Citizens who could demonstrate that they had sufficient financial resources and sickness insurance and who, therefore, would not be a financial burden on the host State could move to and reside in that State. As will be seen in the discussion below, some of the Member States understood the citizenship provisions introduced by the Maastricht Treaty as simply consolidating these provisions and adding nothing new in so far as the rights of movement and residence were concerned: hence the inclusion in Article 18 EC[21] of the reference to 'the limitations and conditions laid down in this Treaty and by the measures adopted to give it effect'. It is the interpretation of this particular provision that has proved controversial.

[14] Art 39 EC (formerly Art 48).

[15] Art 43 EC (formerly Art 52).

[16] Art 49 EC (formerly Art 59).

[17] For example, Council Regulation 1612/68 (EEC) of the Council of 15 October 1968 on free movement for workers OJ Sp.Ed 1968 L257/2 475, Council Directive 64/221 of 25 February 1964 on the co-ordination of special measures concerning the movement and residence of foreign nationals which are justified on grounds of public policy, public security or public health OJ Sp. Ed. 1964, 850/64 117.

[18] Art 12 EC (formerly Art 6).

[19] Case 186/87 *Cowan v Le Tresor Public* [1989] ECR 195.

[20] Council Directives 90/364/EEC of June 28, 1990 on the right of residence OJ 1990 L180/26; 90/365/EEC of June 28, 1990 on the right of employees and self-employed persons who have ceased their occupational activity OJ L180/28; 93/96/EEC of October 29, 1993 on the right of residence for students 1993 OJ L317/59—the original Directive 90/366 was annulled by the Court on the grounds that the wrong legal base had been used, the provisions of the Directive remained in force. All these directives, plus some of the earlier legislation, have now been subsumed in Directive 2004/38/EC of the European Parliament and of the Council of April 29, 2004 on the right of citizens of the Union and their family members to move and reside freely within the territory of the Member States OJ 2004 L158/77.

[21] Art 18 EC (formerly Art 8a).

The Case-law of the Court

Judicial minimalism

None of the Advocates General who have been involved in the citizenship cases have advocated a reductionist approach to the provisions inserted into the EC Treaty by the Maastricht Treaty that relate to citizenship. Advocate General Lenz in *Faccini Dori* used the citizenship provisions to try to persuade the Court to revise its case-law on the horizontal direct effect of directives.[22] Advocate General Léger too invoked the citizenship provisions in *Boukalfa* when he urged the Court to use the full scope of the citizenship provisions, saying that these provisions had considerable symbolic value with the ultimate conclusion being that European citizens should be treated equally, irrespective of their nationality.[23] In *Stöber and Pereira*, La Pergola appeared to support Léger's opinion regarding the citizenship provisions arguing for an expansionist interpretation of Article 18EC.[24] The Court, however, did not rely on the citizenship provisions in deciding these cases. The Advocates General in these cases appeared to be less constrained than the judges in their interpretation of the citizenship provisions, paving the way for the Court to move into a more active phase and acting as innovators of new Community principles.

Signalling intentions

In that key period in the late 1990s, described by Kostakopoulou as a period where the Court signalled its intentions to interpret Articles 17 and 18EC to expand the rights of European citizens, three Advocates General suggested to the Court that the time had come to read the citizenship provisions in an expansive way in order to reinforce the rights of Union citizens. Advocate General Jacobs in *Bickel and Franz*, Advocate General Cosmas in *Wijsenbeek*, and Advocate General La Pergola in *Martínez Sala* all argued that these provisions should be seen as an expansion of the constitutional protection of the rights of Union citizens.[25] This is not to say that the Court followed the line of argumentation put forward by the Advocates General, particularly in *Bickel and Franz* and *Wijsenbeek*, but that the Court was exposed to a line of legal reasoning attempting to justify an interpretation of these provisions which contradicted the views of the Member States and which would reinforce and secure the constitutional importance of these provisions.

[22] Case C-91/92 *Faccini Dori v Recreb Srl* [1994] ECR ECR I-3325. The case is discussed extensively in chapter 8.

[23] Case C-214/94 *Boukalfa* [1996] ECR I-2253.

[24] [1997] ECR I-511.

[25] Cases C-274/96 *Horst Otto Bickel, Ulrich Franz* [1998] ECR I-7637; C-378/97 *Ariël Wijsenbeek* [1999] ECR I-6207; C-85/96 *Maria Martínez Martínez Sala v Freistaat Bayern* [1998] ECR I-2691.

The Opinion of Advocate General La Pergola, delivered in July 1997 in *Martínez Sala* is a defining Opinion in the development of the citizenship case-law and it undoubtedly influenced the Court. Martínez Sala, a Spanish national living in Germany since the age of 12, had worked in Germany for a number of years, albeit with some interruptions. During this period she had had residence permits, although latterly, largely due to the failure of the German authorities to actually supply a residence permit, she simply had a letter stating that she had applied for the renewal of her permit. On the birth of her second daughter she applied for a child-raising allowance but was refused on the ground that she did not possess a valid residence permit. The German authorities had made no move to deport Martínez Sala and, in any case, could not have done so under the terms of the European Convention on Social and Medical Assistance of 11 December 1953 to which both Germany and Spain were Contracting Parties. Martínez Sala argued that she had suffered discrimination on the grounds of nationality contrary to Community law.

La Pergola advised the Court that, on the facts presented to the Court, she could neither be deemed to be a worker within the meaning of Article 7(2) of Regulation 1612/68,[26] nor could she be considered an employed person within the meaning of Regulation 1408/71.[27] These issues were, however, for the national court to determine. If she could be brought within the ambit of either of these Regulations, she would be able to apply for the child-raising benefit on the same terms as nationals of the Member States, as the allowance in question constituted a social benefit.

Thus far the Opinion of La Pergola could be described as being a perfectly competent and logically argued Opinion, the legal reasoning being based on existing legal authorities and analysis of the text of the legislation. However, the German court had also asked whether it was compatible with the (unspecified) law of the European Union for German legislation to require an individual who was permitted to reside in Germany to have a formal residence permit before being able to apply for the child-raising allowance in question. La Pergola pointed to the obvious issue: if Martínez Sala was not a worker, then 'what other status is afforded by the legal order of the Union' for preventing such discrimination?[28] It is clear from his Opinion that the Court was faced with two very different interpretations of Article 18[29] at the oral hearing. The Commission invited the Court to read Article 18 as creating a right to move and reside freely throughout the Union, and to recognize that the reference to 'limitations and conditions' in the Treaty did not affect the existence of that right but the conditions under which it might be exercised. Pitted against the Commission's arguments were the collective governments of Germany,

[26] Regulation (EEC) 1612/68 of the Council of 15 October 1968 on the free movement for workers within the Community OJ Sp. Ed. 1968 L 257/2, p 475.

[27] Regulation (EEC) 1408/71 of the Council of 14 June 1971 (as amended) on the application of social security schemes to employed persons, to self-employed persons and to members of their families moving within the Community, OJ 1997 L28/1; OJ 1972 L74/1.

[28] Case C-85/96 *Maria Martínez Sala v Freistaat Bayern* [1998] ECR I-2691, para 14.

[29] Art 18 EC (formerly Art 8a).

France and the UK, all of whom argued that Article 18EC simply reiterated existing law, and that its function was to bring together all the existing rules scattered in various directives and weld them together into a single provision. Article 18EC, therefore, should be read as a summary of existing law. Faced with these two very divergent approaches to the interpretation of Article 18EC, La Pergola opted to follow the Commission, although his arguments differed from the Commission in certain key respects.

Germany had argued that Martínez Sala's right to reside in Germany stemmed not from Community law, since she was no longer a worker, but from the German law implementing its international obligations under the 1953 Convention on Social and Medical Assistance. La Pergola denied this. He argued that Martínez Sala's right of residence derived from Community law under Article 18. In a very elegant summary of what he believed to be the position he stated:

> The right to move and reside freely throughout the whole of the Union is enshrined in an act of primary law and does not exist or cease to exist depending on whether or not it has been made subject to limitations under other provisions of Community law, including secondary legislation. The limitations provided for in Article 8a [now Art 18] itself concern the actual exercise but not the existence of the right.[30]

La Pergola argued that free movement of persons, which he described as a liberty, was already embodied in the treaties, specifically by the Single European Act which created an area without frontiers. Article 18EC added to these provisions by extracting 'the kernel' from the free movement provisions and by defining the right to move and reside as a 'primary right'; the first such right ascribed in the Treaty to the status of citizenship. The status of citizenship is created by the Treaty and can only be lost by the individual ceasing to hold the nationality of one of the Member States of the Union. It is therefore 'the fundamental legal status' guaranteed by Community law. Arguing against Germany, therefore, La Pergola stated that Martínez Sala's right of residence derived from her status as a citizen of the EU and not from any German legal provision.

He then extended his argument to the principle of non-discrimination. He reasoned that the principle of non-discrimination on the grounds of nationality under Article 12EC applies across all the provisions of the Treaty, including Article 18EC, which itself alters the scope of the Treaty by creating a new individual legal standing where discrimination is prohibited. Where a Community citizen is resident in another Member State, the right not to be discriminated against 'continues to exist for as long as he is resident there'. That right derives from Article 18EC and not from any provision of secondary Community law. In the particular case, Martínez Sala was resident in Germany, and thus La Pergola was able to avoid a head-on clash with the governments intervening in this case when they argued that Article 18EC

[30] Opinion of Advocate General La Pergola in Case C-85/96 *Maria Matínez Sala v Freistaat Bayern* [1998] ECR I-2691, para 18.

did not create any new rights of residence or movement. He did not go so far as to state that all Community citizens derive a new right of entry and residence from Article 18EC, and he was therefore able to argue that it did not matter whether the right to reside derived from the directives on the right of residence or from German law. Where the right to reside exists, the limitations provided on the right to equal treatment can only be those expressly provided for in the Treaty, such as the right to vote in general elections, which is a right reserved specifically to nationals of the Member States. He argued that it was for the Court to determine, in each specific case, how the status of citizenship of the Union could be relied on by persons complaining of unequal treatment.

Applying his logic to the case of Martínez Sala, La Pergola argued that, by requiring a Union citizen to be in possession of a permit before being eligible for a child raising allowance without any objective justification for such a requirement, the German legislation was discriminatory. The right to the benefit arises not from the residence permit but from the right of residence; the permit being declaratory and not constitutive in character.

La Pergola helpfully distinguished his approach from that of the Commission, although both came to the same conclusion in the case in point. The Commission had argued that Mrs Martínez Sala has a right of residence in Germany deriving from the Treaty and she retained that right until the Member States limited its exercise under the terms of one of the residency directives. La Pergola rejected this view: equality of treatment is justified by the status of citizen, governed by Article 18EC. He further argued that by taking this approach he is consistent with the Court's approach in *Cowan*,[31] where the Court had held that a recipient of services in a Member State was entitled to equal treatment. A Community citizen who had moved to Germany could be seen as a recipient of services and therefore entitled to equal treatment. La Pergola wondered whether the Court should move on from *Cowan* to argue that a person, such as Martínez Sala, a potential recipient of a range of services, should also now be entitled to rely on the status of citizen to assert the right to equal treatment.

La Pergola's Opinion is not an exercise in perfect logic—it is a persuasive reading of a skeletal text that gives meaning to the text in the context of the Treaty. His argument rests on the assumption that the citizenship provisions add to the existing freedoms and do not merely replicate them. In making this assumption, which was directly contradicted by the Member States intervening in this case, La Pergola established, in the interpretation of and direction of Community law, a tension between the Member States, on the one hand, and the Court and the Commission on the other. Through his Opinion, La Pergola invited the Court to shift the balance of control away from the Member States, extended the reach of the principle of non-discrimination on the grounds of nationality, and subjected national legislative provisions, as well as existing Community law, to judicial review.

[31] Case 186/87 *Cowen v Le Tréson Public* [1989] ECR 195.

What weakens this particular Opinion is La Pergola's discussion of *Cowan*. Having argued for a constructivist interpretation of Article 18EC, he sought further justification for his position in the case-law of the Court deriving from the freedom to provide and receive services. This section of the Opinion reads like an alternative line of argument in order to justify the application of the principle of non-discrimination. The argument seems to be that a citizen resident in a host Member State is a recipient of a number of services and, for that reason, not because of his fundamental status as a citizen of the Union, is entitled to equal treatment. In the context of an otherwise powerful Opinion relating to citizenship, this section is unconvincing. Such an argument could well have been made without any reference to citizenship on the basis of pre-existing provisions and case-law. Perhaps La Pergola intended to provide the Court with an alternative solution although, as Advocate General Tizzano was later to demonstrate, this argument is untenable[32]; La Pergola did not explore other possible lines of argument which could have achieved the same result. For example, there is the argument that Article 18EC required the host State to provide a residence permit, despite the fact that the terms of the article do not appear to impose positive obligations on Member States. Another line of argument would be to argue that Article 18EC was directly effective, although La Pergola did not address the issue of direct effect and neither did the Court. To do so, in this case, would have required an understanding of the scope of the direct effects of Article 18EC, which is written in terms of a right to move and reside and not in terms of a right to access social benefits.

It is clear that the Court was influenced by the Opinion of La Pergola in this case. The judgment itself reads clearly and singularly. The Court agreed that it had insufficient information to determine whether Martínez Sala was a worker or was employed and then turned to the meaning to be attributed to Article 18EC. Like La Pergola, the Court did not rule that Article 18 created a new right to reside in a Member State but, instead, focused on the status of citizenship. It was not necessary to decide if Article 18 created a new right of residence for Martínez Sala since she was authorized to reside in Germany in any event. As a citizen lawfully residing in Germany, Martínez Sala came within the personal scope of the Treaty provisions on European citizenship. Attached to the status of EU citizen is the right not to suffer discrimination on the grounds of nationality within the material scope of the Treaty, and thus Martínez Sala could rely on Article 12 EC[33] to challenge the refusal to grant her the child raising allowance.

La Pergola had provided arguments for the Court to justify a particular interpretation of the citizenship provisions, provisions whose meaning (or meanings) was contested. His reasoning was based on the premise that an individual in the situation of Martínez Sala appeared to lack a clear status in law and that her position needed recognition. She had been a worker in the past, had received social assistance in the past, she could not be removed from her host State and she did

[32] In Case C-200/02 *Man Levette Chen and Kunqian Catherine Chen v Secretary of State for the Home Office* [2004] ECR I-9925, discussed below.

[33] Art 12 EC (formerly Art 6).

not have a residence permit because of the failure of the administration of the host state. Her status was still not clear, and yet there was a clear Community law dimension due to the fact that she was a Union citizen who had exercised her rights to move and reside in another Member State. La Pergola's argument is that an individual, having exercised the right to move and reside, could rely on the status of citizen to claim equal treatment. It is the force of that argument that was accepted by the Court in the case itself and has been subsequently applied in a variety of different circumstances.

Advocate General Jacobs gave his Opinion in the joined cases of *Bickel and Franz* after La Pergola delivered his Opinion in *Martínez Sala* but before the Court gave judgment in that case.This case concerned the rights of German citizens to have a criminal case against them heard in German in an area of Italy where local residents could decide the language of the case. This particular circumstance arose in the Trento-Alto Adige region where, in order to protect the linguistic minorities residing in Italy, the official languages of the courts were both Italian and German. The Court did not decide this case on the basis of the citizenship provisions but on the basis of Article 49EC,[34] but Jacobs did point out to the Court that 'where a citizen exercises his right to move and reside within the territory of the Member States, his situation falls within the scope of the Treaty for the purpose of the prohibition of discrimination on the grounds of nationality'.[35] In this line of argument he is restating the La Pergola thesis.

It was Advocate General Cosmas, in the case of *Wijsenbeek*, who confronted those Member States who argued that Article 18EC did not create any additional rights but merely reflected existing Community law. This case concerned a challenge to the right of Member States to require individuals to present their passports or other form of identity on arrival on their territory; a Member of the European Parliament who refused to present his passport on returning from Strasbourg to Rotterdam was subject to criminal proceedings. The national court wished to know if Article 18EC precluded national legislation which required the production of a passport. Neither the Advocate General nor the Court was willing to interpret Article 18EC to preclude such legislation; however, from the point of view of presenting the Court with a conceptual framework for understanding the citizenship provisions, Cosmas' Opinion makes interesting reading. The central tenet of his argument was that Article 18EC must mean something, and that to argue otherwise would undermine the constitutive task of the Community legislature, would ignore the dynamic evolution of the Community, and would run counter to the spirit and wording of Article 18EC. He argued that the use of the term 'rights' and 'citizen of the Union' showed the constitutional nature of these provisions. Prior to the Maastricht Treaty, individuals derived rights from Community law based on their function in attaining one of the objectives of the Treaty, whereas Article 18EC had created rights for individuals of a substantive nature, benefiting

[34] Art 49 EC (formerly Art 59) on the provision of services.
[35] Case C-274/96 *Horst Otto Bickel, Ulrich Franz* [1998] ECR I-7637.

the holder of the right and not the Community. For Cosmas this was a paradigm shift, as rights were now accorded to individuals, not pursuing economic activities, but based on their status as a citizen of the Union. With a degree of foresight he stated that this reading of the text would need to result in a revision of our understanding of the cases and legislation on free movement and the questioning of received solutions.

Cosmas advised the Court that Article 18EC created direct effects. It created the right to move and to reside freely, and the Council was empowered to 'facilitate' this right. Thus the right existed independently of any secondary Community law, and this right to free movement was linked to the fundamental right of personal freedom requiring the Member States to refrain from introducing obstacles to that right except where these could be justified. The Community authorities are similarly obliged to respect the citizen's rights. The right to free movement is subject to the limitations and conditions laid down in the Treaty, but this phrase did not call into question the direct effect of Article 18EC. That said, the phrase could, however, be interpreted in two ways. One interpretation was that the rights created by the Treaty could only be exercised within the framework of existing rules of Community law, while the other option was to say that existing provisions were now subject to judicial scrutiny in order to examine if the restrictions and limitations previously provided for were justifiable in the face of the fundamental right to move and reside freely. Cosmas favoured the latter interpretation. The Court remained silent on most of the matters raised by Cosmas in this Opinion, nonetheless they had before them an extension of the arguments placed before the Court by La Pergola and a strong legal justification for reading the citizenship provisions in a way which would give constitutional meaning to these provisions.[36]

If it is true that in the late 1990s the Court signalled its intentions to explore the possible interpretations of the citizenship provisions, then it is equally true that in those years the Court heard arguments from its Advocates General on the possibilities of these provisions. In particular, La Pergola provided a justification and legal reasoning for the coherent development of rights of residence and movement within a framework of non-discrimination. Cosmas too flagged up the underlying constitutional importance of the provisions. This suggests that the Advocates General should be factored into that reflexive European circuit feeding ideas into the Court; they might not influence the outcome of a particular case, although La Pergola clearly did in *Martínez Sala*, but they can be considered as forming part of the interactions between the key actors within the Community. In that sense, the Advocates General were heard not only by the Court. The Commission, too, intervened in all these cases and was influenced by the Advocates General at a time when the Commission was responsible for drafting legislation in support of citizens' free

[36] In her Durham lecture, Advocate General Juliane Kokott makes a similar argument that the citizenship provisions cannot be read as being purely declaratory in character. She argues that introducing Article 18 EC would have been a redundant exercise if this was the case. See J Kokott, 'EU citizenship—citoyens sans frontiers?, European Law Lecture at the Durham European Law Institute, 2005.

movement rights. Without the input of the Court and the Advocates General that legislation would look very different.

Engineering institutional change

The principle of non-discrimination

Cosmas was correct in stating that, if the Court were to read the citizenship provisions as constituting a new approach to the rights of movement and residence, the Court would be required to look afresh at its own previous case-law and the existing secondary legislation. In the period following *Martínez Sala* the Court was faced with a number of questions relating both to the application of the principle of non-discrimination and on the rights of residence.

A number of these cases involved individuals who, having exercised their right to move and reside in the territory of one of the Member States, wished to know if they could access certain social benefits normally reserved to citizens of the host country or to workers and their families under the terms of Community law. Examples of these cases are *Grzelczyk* (Advocate General Alber), *D'Hoop* (Advocate General Geelhoed), *Collins* (Advocate General Ruiz-Jarabo Colomer) and *Bidar* (Advocate General Geelhoed).[37] Kostakopoulou characterizes cases such as *Grzelczyk* and *D'Hoop* as cases where the Court engineered institutional change, and so these cases are particularly interesting in examining the extent to which the Advocates General contributed to the reasoning of the Court. A working hypothesis could be that, where the Court is determined on a course of action that requires it to look afresh at its own case law, the Advocate General in a particular case is unlikely to be able to assist the Court until such time as he discerns a pattern in the Court's thinking. His role can be then characterized as consolidation. An alternative hypothesis is that an Advocate General has the opportunity to do the fresh thinking for the Court and suggest a new way forward. His role in these circumstances can be characterized as innovation.

Grzelczyk concerned a French national who went to live in Belgium to study for a University degree. For three years he paid for his studies by working in part-time jobs but, in his fourth year, he applied for assistance in the form of the minimex (a non-contributory benefit ensuring a minimum subsistence level). He was refused this benefit as, while Belgian students could receive it, migrant students were not eligible. Directive 93/96/EEC relating to students' rights of residence required a student to declare that he had sufficient resources to maintain himself for the course of his studies, and so the referring Court asked whether it was contrary to the principles of European citizenship for entitlement to the mimimex to be

[37] Cases C-184/99 *Rudy Grzelczyk v Centre public d'aide sociale d'Ottignies-Louvain-la Neuve* [2001] ECR I-6193; C-224/98 *Marie-Nathalie D'Hoop v ONEM* [2002] ECR I-6191; C-138/02 *Brian Francis Collins v Secretary of State for Work and Pensions* [2004] ECR I-2703; C-209/03 *R (on the application of Dany Bidar) v London Borough of Ealing, Secretary of State for Education and Skills* [2005] ECR I-2119.

granted only to 'workers' eligible under Regulation 1612/68EEC and not to all European citizens. In addition, the Court wished to know whether Articles 12 and 18 EC and Directive 93/96EEC were to be interpreted as meaning that after a student's right of residence has been acknowledged by the host State he cannot be excluded from entitlement to the minimex.

The main thrust of Alber's Opinion was that Grzelczyk might be in a position to exercise two sets of residence rights concurrently; one determined by his position as a worker, the other on the basis of his status as a student. As a worker he would be entitled to the minimex but, as student, according to Alber, he would not. This argument rests on his interpretation of Directive 93/96/EEC that recourse to social assistance would be a ground for terminating a student's rights of residence. Alber reasoned that to accept otherwise would mean that the provisions of Directive 93/96/EEC would have to be set aside 'because it infringed a higher rule of law'.[38] Under those circumstances, the student would need to assert his rights of residence on the basis of the Treaty alone.

Alber stated that citizenship affords to the citizen an original right of residence but argued that this right of residence is not unlimited; thee directives on residence rights do impose limitations on the exercise of those rights, including the obligation not to become a burden on the public finances of the host State. This was a limitation tolerated by Community law. It is for the Member State to determine the circumstances under which an individual becomes such a burden and their right to residence is terminated. In this Alber was reflecting the arguments of the Commission and of some of the Member State but he was not followed by the Court. The Court held that: 'Union citizenship is destined to be the fundamental status of the nationals of the Member States, enabling those who find themselves in the same situation to enjoy the same treatment in law irrespective of their nationality, subject to such exceptions as are expressly provided for'.[39]

A citizen of the Union who is lawfully resident in one of the Member States is able to rely on the principle of non-discrimination in situations falling in the material scope of the Treaty, including where a citizen exercises the right to move and reside in the territory of a Member State. The Court then stated that amendments to the Treaty had introduced both the concept of citizenship and a new chapter devoted to education and training. In light of these amendments the Court felt able to distinguish *Brown* (in which the Court had previously held that access to maintenance grants for students was outside the scope of Community law) and to hold that, in principle, Article 12EC can apply to a student who is resident in the territory of a host Member State.[40] Whilst accepting that Directive 93/96EEC regulates the exercise of the right of residence, the Court interpreted the Directive as not necessarily excluding a student from social assistance automatically, stating that the Directive implied 'a certain degree of financial solidarity'

[38] Case C-184/99 *Rudy Grzelczyk v Centre public d'aide sociale d'OHignies-Louvain-la Neuve* [2001] ECR I-6193, para 112.
[39] Ibid, para 31.
[40] Case C-197/86 *Brown v Secretary of State for Scotland* [1986] ECR 3205.

between the citizens and the Member States'.[41] This degree of financial solidarity derived from EU citizenship meant that the student could enjoy the social benefit but only for so long as the student did not become 'an unreasonable burden' on public finances.

The Court's interpretation is very far removed from that offered by Alber in his Opinion. Alber offered a lengthy exposition of the state of Community law as it stood, drawing on the existing case-law of the Court and the confusing and contradictory legislative provisions. His attempts to persuade the Court to accept the concept of overlapping status as a means of reconciling these conflicts was not accepted and neither was his final conclusion in relation to Grzelczyk himself. Alber appears not to have caught the mood of the Court in his Opinion and seems completely out of step with it. Indeed, the Court's judgment in *Grzelczyk* owes more to the Opinion of La Pergola in *Martínez Sala* than to Alber, a fact that might be explained by the coincidence of the Reporting Judge in both *Grzelczyk* and *Martínez Sala* being Judge David Edward.

In the case of *D'Hoop*, however, it is possible to discern more of an interaction between the Advocate General and the Court. D'Hoop, a Belgian national who had completed her secondary education in France, had returned to Belgium to pursue her university education. On graduation she was refused a tide-over allowance that was designed to assist unemployed graduates to access special training schemes. Belgian legislation required that a person receiving such an allowance should have completed their secondary education in a school run by, subsidized, or otherwise approved by one of the Belgian communities. The referring Court wished to know whether the refusal of the tide-over allowance to a Belgian national who had completed her secondary education in France was contrary to Community law. Whether or not Geelhoed's Opinion in this case could have been said to have assisted the Court is a moot point. Comparing the Opinion and the judgment one can see that the Court took a very different starting point for its reasoning than the Advocate General had. The Court examined the specific reason underlying the refusal by ONEM (the employment office) to grant the tide-over allowance to D'Hoop. The refusal was based on the fact that her education in France was completed before 1991. Any alleged discrimination therefore took place before the provisions on citizenship came into force. The Court rejected that view stating that the provisions on citizenship are applicable from the date they came into force and are applicable to instances of current discriminatory treatment. Geelhoed had not addressed this specific point which became the starting point for the Court's reasoning. Repeating that Union citizenship is destined to be the fundamental status of Community nationals, the Court ruled that those citizens who found themselves in the same situation within the material scope of the Treaty are entitled to the same treatment. Situations falling within the material scope of Community law include those involving the right to reside in a Member

[41] Ibid, para 44.

State other than their own. Citizens who exercise their right to reside in a Member State other than their own should not be disadvantaged, on their return, as against individuals who had not exercised their free movement rights. This is particularly true in the field of education where the mobility of teachers and students is encouraged. The inequality of treatment suffered by D'Hoop was therefore contrary to Community law.

Geelhoed had come to the same conclusion but his Opinion is by no means as clearly stated as the judgment of the Court. Having looked at alternative scenarios, he stated that D'Hoop could neither benefit from the provisions relating to free movement of workers nor be seen as a recipient of services in France as education did not fall within those provisions. He argued that D'Hoop had been resident in France for a purpose envisaged by the Treaty, and so came within the scope of the Treaty, therefore the principle of non-discrimination should apply. He reminded the Court of developments in Community law relating to education, a point that was picked up by the Court, as was his analysis of the application of the equal treatment principle to nationals of a Member State who had exercised their Community rights as against those who had not. Thus it can be seen that Geelhoed, albeit from a different starting point, demonstrated a line of legal reasoning that could be applied in this case. He also engaged with arguments put forward by the Commission as to the kinds of criteria that might be used to justify the exclusion of a citizen of the Union from access to such a benefit. The Commission had argued that a State could not be compelled to pay a tide-over allowance to every student who had completed their studies in one of the Member States, and that a State was entitled to require that there be a connection with the host Member State. Geelhoed did not deny this, but pointed out that the requirement in question ignored the genuine link between a Belgian national and one of its own citizens. The Court agreed that the state concerned was entitled to ensure a real link between the applicant and the geographical employment market concerned but also agreed that the residence requirement in question went beyond what was necessary to ensure such a link. In this case therefore there was a dialogue between the Advocate General and the Court.

Both Grzelczyk and D'Hoop could legitimately show a link between themselves and the State against whom they were claiming assistance. However, in *Collins*, the existence of such a link was extremely tenuous, and caused Ruiz-Jarabo Colomer some difficulties in extending the principles developed by the Court to cover this case. Brian Francis Collins, born and educated in the USA, came to the UK in 1978 to spend a semester in a UK University. He later returned to the UK doing casual and part-time work and during that period he acquired Irish nationality; thereafter he had dual Irish and American nationality. In 1981 he returned to the USA and, between 1981 and 1998, he worked in the USA, as a volunteer in central Africa, and as a teacher in South Africa. He returned to the UK in May 1998 to seek employment in the social services sector and, nine days later, claimed job seeker's allowance as he had insufficient resources to maintain himself. He was refused the allowance on the grounds that he was not habitually resident in the UK, and appealed against that decision. The referring Court wished to know whether Collins was a worker within the meaning of Regulation 1612/68EEC, whether he derived a right of residence pursuant to Directive 68/360EEC or whether any other principle of Community law required the UK to pay the job seeker's allowance to an individual in these circumstances.

Whilst both the Court and the Advocate General agreed that Collins could not be classified as a worker on the basis of work performed in the UK some 17 years before his application for the allowance, and that he should be considered to be in the same situation as any other Community national in search of work, they disagreed on the consequences for such an individual in terms of application for an allowance of the kind in question. Ruiz-Jarabo Colomer based his analysis on the earlier case-law of the Court, in particular *Martínez Sala* and *Grzelczyk*. In both these cases the individuals concerned had been lawfully resident in the host State for a considerable period of time. Ruiz-Jarabo Colomer argued that these cases should be read in the light of the specific factual circumstances—circumstances which did not apply to Collins, who had not established a link or connection with the UK. In these circumstances, a Member State was entitled to refuse a person in his situation access to welfare benefits; this is justified as a means of avoiding 'welfare tourism' and to prevent abuse. This line of reasoning was consonant with the previous case-law of the Court and its reference to the 'link' between the applicant and the national labour market.

The Court, however, took another tack in this case. It held that a citizen lawfully resident in the territory of a Member State can rely on the non-discrimination principle in all areas falling within the material scope of Community law, repeating that citizenship of the Union is destined to be the fundamental status of the nationals of the Member States. Given these developments, the Court held that it was not now possible to exclude from the scope of Article 39(2) EC[42] financial advantages intended to facilitate access to the labour market. In doing so the Court overruled its earlier case-law of *Lebon* by interpreting Article 39(2) in light of the citizenship provisions,[43] and thus Collins was entitled to apply for the job-seeker's allowance. Member States were entitled to require a link between the person seeking work and the employment market, and such a link could be demonstrated by showing that the person concerned had actually sought work 'for a reasonable period'. However, the criteria to be used must be specified in advance and subject to judicial scrutiny. The Court did not specify the length of time which would constitute a 'reasonable period'; in particular, there was no indication of whether it was the same reasonable period during which a national of a Member State is entitled to remain in a host State whilst seeking work. Up until

[42] Art 39(2) EC (formerly Art 48).

[43] Case C-316/85 *Centre public de l'aide sociale de Courcelles v Lebon* [1987] ECR 2811. See also O Golynker, 'Jobseekers' rights in the European Union: challenge of changing the paradigm of social solidarity' (2005) 30 ELR 111.

this point the Court had maintained a distinction between the types of benefits available to a job seeker. Under the terms of Regulation 1612/68EEC, a job seeker was entitled to access services which would enable him to find work but was not entitled to social and tax advantages. The latter were available only to those who had entered the labour market. Interpreting Article 39(2)EC to include access to financial advantages intended to facilitate access to the labour market, because 'to do otherwise was not possible, in light of the citizenship provisions', the Court seems to have been prepared to weaken the concept of the link between an applicant and the host State. The Advocate General cannot have known that the Court would wish to follow this direction, particularly in light of its own very recent case-law and he certainly did not advocate such a development.

Where the Advocate General and the Court were in harmony was in the case of *Bidar*.[44] This case concerned loans made on favourable rates to students in English universities. Bidar had come to the UK as a child with his mother, who at first was gravely ill and subsequently died, leaving Bidar in the care of his grandmother. He attended school in the UK and was accepted to study economics at University College London. He was denied a student loan on the basis that he was not 'settled' in the UK for the purposes of the Education (Student Support) Regulations 2001. These stated that a person could only be regarded as 'settled' if he had lived in the UK for a period of 4 years, but also that the time spent for the purposes of full-time education did not count in calculating the period of residence. The key question, therefore, was whether or not student loans fell within the material scope of the EC Treaty.

Geelhoed's approach was to begin with an overview of Community law, including the case-law of the Court in relation to student finances, citizenship and social benefits, providing a summary for the benefit of the Court. In addressing the specific issues raised by the case, Geelhoed distinguished two groups of students. The first are those who go to a Member State for the purpose of study, who fall within the ambit of Directive 93/96EEC. Geelhoed stated that Bidar would have difficulty in claiming a grant or loan because of the limitations concerned in the Directive, particularly the requirement that a student must make a declaration that he had sufficient resources to support himself. The second group of students, of which Bidar could be considered a representative, were EU citizens who had previously exercised their right to move and to reside in the territory of a Member State other than their own. These students should not be considered students within the meaning of Directive 93/96EEC. The question arises whether maintenance grants or loans might be payable to such Union citizens. Relying on the arguments in *Grzelczyk*, and the inclusion of provisions relating to student mobility in the Treaty, Geelhoed asserted that assistance with maintenance costs fell within the substantive scope of the EC Treaty. In coming to this conclusion Geelhoed was

[44] Case C-209/03 *R (on the application of Dany Bidar) v London Borough of Ealing, Secretary of State for Education and Skills* [2005] ECR I-2119.

arguing against the Commission and the seven Governments who intervened in this case, all of whom had argued that maintenance grants and loans did not fall within the material scope of Community law.

In coming to its decision the Court followed the logic of Geelhoed's argument, concentrating on the rights of citizens lawfully resident in a Member State, of whom Bidar was one. Bidar had lived in the UK and completed his secondary education there without previous recourse to social assistance. He was therefore able to rely on Article 12 EC to access benefits on the same terms as UK nationals. Agreeing with Geelhoed that developments in Community law now meant that loans or grants intended to cover maintenance costs of students now fell within the scope of Community law, particularly Article 12 EC, Bidar, having a lawful right of residence, was entitled to the loan. This conclusion is without prejudice to the fact that other students who travel to another Member State to study cannot base any right to maintenance grants on Directive 93/96EEC. Thus the Court maintained the distinction, proposed by Geelhoed, between the two distinct groups of students.

The national court had also asked for clarification of the criteria to apply to determine whether the conditions for granting assistance to students to cover their maintenance costs are objective and independent of nationality. Geelhoed argued that conditions which are more 'cumbersome' for EU citizens must be seen as indirect discrimination on grounds of nationality. They must, therefore, be objectively justified under Community law. Geelhoed, citing *D'Hoop* and *Collins*, argued that Member States had a legitimate aim in ensuring a genuine link between the recipient of allowances and integration with the labour market, but in terms of student grants, the link which needed to be established was the 'degree of affinity' between the applicant and the educational system and the degree of integration into that society.[45] A person like Bidar must be deemed to have integrated into UK society. Geelhoed argued that a residence requirement could only be the starting point for determining eligibility, and the Court followed this reasoning. It ruled that it is legitimate for a State to grant assistance only to students 'who have demonstrated a certain degree of integration into the society of that State',[46] thus echoing the words of the Advocate General. It also agreed with Geelhoed that a residence requirement, which precluded a national of another Member State lawfully resident in a host State from obtaining the status of a settled person where that person has a genuine link with the society of the State, is prohibited by Article 12 EC.

These cases tell us something about the contribution of the Advocate General to the way in which the Court engineered institutional change in these cases. In the cases of *Grzelczyk* and *Collins* the Court was willing to overrule its own previous case-law and change the parameters of Community law. The Court must have taken such a step after considerable deliberations and with a clear intention of

[45] Ibid, para 60. [46] Ibid, para 57.

change Community law. In each case the Court specifically referred to its intention to overrule its own case-law, namely *Brown* and *Lebon* respectively. In these circumstances it is difficult for the Advocate General to assist the Court as the Treaty demands. In *Grzelczyk*, Alber stayed within the parameters of existing law whilst attempting to provide a coherent framework, a theory of concurrent status, which would enable the Court to make sense of existing Community law. As we know, the Court broke free of Community law by means of a new interpretation. Alber could not have 'read the Court's mind' and it is no criticism to say that he was out of step with the Court's thinking. Similarly, Ruiz-Jarabo Colomer in *Collins* applied existing (and very recent) case-law to deny Collins's right to a job-seeker's allowance. Again, he was not to know that the court was willing to rethink its previous approach and to take a different direction. His Opinion, perfectly logical within the existing parameters of Community law, ultimately did not influence the Court to stay within those boundaries. It also appears, from reading his Opinion, that he had a certain sympathy for the views of the Member States when faced with a potential financial burden from individuals who apparently had no connection with either the host State or the State whose nationality they had acquired. By contrast where Community law is, relatively speaking, more settled, as was the case in *Bidar*, the Advocate General can assist the Court by applying existing rules to the factual situation before the Court (consolidation). Also, where there is a sometimes uncertain situation, as in *D'Hoop*, the Advocate General may, by his analysis, have some input into the Court's reasoning. When the Court is determined to pursue a path of engineering institutional change, however, it seems difficult, on the evidence of these examples, for the Advocate General to lead the Court in a particular direction.

Rights of residence

In the cases discussed above, the individuals concerned were resident in the territory of one of the Member States, and were not seeking to assert a right to reside in that territory. In yet other cases, however, the Court was asked to determine whether Article 18 EC creates an independent right of residence for individuals who are not economically active, and who do not fall within the ambit of one of the three residence Directives. Three of these cases are discussed here: *Baumbast* (Advocate General Geelhoed), *Akrich* (Advocate General Geelhoed) and *Chen* (Advocate General Tizzano)[47]

In *Baumbast*, the referring court asked the question whether Mr Baumbast, an EU citizen, could enjoy a directly effective right of residence in another Member State pursuant to Article 18(1)EC.[48] Mr Baumbast, a German married to a

[47] Cases C-413/99 *Baumbast v Secretary of State for the Home Department* [2002] ECR I-7091; C-109/01 *Secretary of State for the Home Office v Hacene Akrich* [2003] ECR I-9607; C-200/02 *Man Levette Chen and Kunqian Catherine Chen v Secretary of State for the Home Office* [2004] ECR I-9925.

[48] Case C-413/99 *Baumbast v Secretary of State for the Home Department* [2002] ECR I-7091.

Colombian, was a worker in the UK at the time of the marriage. Mrs Baumbast, from her first marriage, had a daughter who had Colombian nationality, and there was a second daughter of the marriage, who had both Colombian and German nationality. Originally employed in the UK, then self-employed in the UK, Mr Baumbast was later employed overseas on temporary contracts by a German company. The family remained in the UK but returned to Germany for medical treatment when required, as Mr Baumbast had comprehensive medical coverage there. It was agreed that the children had a right of residence in the UK under the terms of Regulation 1612/68EEC, since they were attending school in the UK and the adjudicator had held that the UK was obliged to provide the best possible circumstances for their education to continue. As their primary carer, Mrs Baumbast was permitted to stay in the UK because her children had a right of residence; both she and the children were subsequently granted indefinite leave to remain in the UK. Mr Baumbast, however, was denied leave to remain. His status was uncertain—it was agreed by all parties that he was no longer a worker in the UK and also that he could not rely on Directive 90/364EEC concerning the rights of persons not economically active since he did not have medical insurance in the UK as required by the terms of the Directive.

The Immigration Appeal Tribunal referred several questions to the Court in relation to the rights of the children and the primary carer, as well as in relation to Mr Baumbast. The Court answered the questions relating to the children and their mother on the basis of Regulation 1612/68EEC—these points will not be discussed further here—thus leaving the question of whether Mr Baumbast had any status in Community law which would grant him the right to reside in the UK. Geelhoed argued that Article 18 EC has direct effect. Referring to the Opinions of both La Pergola in *Martínez Sala* and Cosmas in *Wijsenbeek*, he stated that the 'clear and unconditional wording' of the first part of Article 18(1) cannot be interpreted in any other way than to say it had direct effect. He supported his argument by analysing the scheme within the Treaty relating to free movement of persons. For economically active persons the Treaty provides a specific framework in Articles 39, 43 and 49 EC. For those who wish to travel or reside within the Community and who are not economically active, the equivalent rights are provided by the three residence directives and, he argued, all these rights, for both the economically active and inactive are now subsumed into Article 18EC. Furthermore, not to accord direct effect to Article 18EC would mean that it would lose its efficiency; although it is couched in general terms, Article 18EC serves the function of securing the right of free movement for all citizens.

As for the substantive content of the rights contained in Article 18EC, Geelhoed argued that the rights provided for were not without limitations, in particular the need to ensure public order, public safety and public health and, significantly, the financial interests of the Member States. But Article 18EC must be seen as having recognizable substance, and the conditions and limitations attached to the exercise of these rights must be both necessary to attain a legitimate objective and proportionate. He further argued that Article 18EC imposed an obligation on the Community legislature to ensure an adequate framework in which Community citizens could exercise their rights, and that in the absence of specific provisions Article 18EC becomes the default provision on which they can rely. In the case of Mr Baumbast, he was an economically active citizen, but no longer economically active in the UK. Geelhoed therefore believed that the restrictions which apply to economically active individuals should be applied by analogy to Baumbast. As economically active individuals are not required to have health insurance, neither should Baumbast.

The Court held that Article 18EC did create direct effect in respect of the right to reside, stating that 'that right is conferred directly on every citizen of the Union by a clear and precise provision of the EC Treaty. Purely as a national of a Member State, and consequently a citizen of the Union, Mr Baumbast therefore has the right to rely on Article 18(1)EC'.[49] In that sense the Court could be seen to be following or agreeing with the Advocate General. The Court also agreed that the right is conferred subject to conditions and limitations which are, however, subject to judicial review and must be in compliance with the general principles of Community law, particularly the principle of proportionality; they therefore must be necessary and appropriate to meet a legitimate objective. In Mr Baumbast's case, the Court held that to require him to have health insurance was disproportionate given his family and economic circumstances. The Court therefore came to the same conclusion as the Advocate General but arrived at its judgment via a different legal reasoning. The Court did not follow Geelhoed's logic that, in cases such as *Baumbast* where there are no specific legislative provisions, the Court should apply, by analogy, detailed provisions applying to other circumstances, but instead relied on the application of well understood principles of Community law and invited the relevant authorities of the Member States, including the courts, to do the same.

Neither did the Court follow the legal reasoning of Geelhoed in *Akrich*. Akrich, a Moroccan, had been deported from the UK and re-entered illegally. He married a Community national in the UK. His wife went to live and work in Ireland and Akrich, at his own request, was deported to Ireland by the UK authorities. Their intention was to rely on the provisions relating to free movement of workers, as interpreted by the Court in *Singh*, to re-enter the UK and to regularize the husband's status.[50] Geelhoed's Opinion is long, sometimes repetitive, and confusing in parts, not to mention that it omits perhaps one of the fundamental issues decided by the Court in *Martínez Sala* in this area, that in order to exercise Community rights under the citizenship provisions a person must be lawfully resident in one of the Member States. As Akrich was not lawfully resident in the UK prior to his deportation to Ireland, he could not thereafter rely on Community

[49] Ibid, para 84.

[50] Case C-370/90 *R v Immigration Appeal Tribunal et Surinder Singh, ex p Secretary of State for Home Department* [1992] ECR I-4265.

law. In this case there is clear divergence between the legal reasoning taken by the Advocate General as against the far greater clarity of the Court in coming to its decision.

By contrast, the Opinion of Advocate General Tizzano in *Chen* provided a template judgment for the Court which appeared to repeat the Opinion in its legal reasoning as well as in the logic and the structure of the argument. *Chen* concerned the case of a Chinese national who went to Northern Ireland to give birth to a second child. Her first child had been born in China and she and her husband wished to circumvent China's one child policy. The husband was a businessman who frequently travelled to the UK, where they had been informed that, in contrast to the UK's own policy, if a child was born in Northern Ireland it would attain, by virtue of Irish law, Irish nationality—even if the child were born in the UK she would not attain British nationality. Mrs Chen applied for, and was denied, a residency permit in the UK and she appealed. The Immigration Appellate Authority referred several questions to the Court effectively asking whether the child, Catherine, was entitled to reside permanently in the UK as either a recipient of services, as a Community national who is not economically active but who has sufficient resources at her disposal to maintain herself or directly on the basis of Article 18 EC. In addition the Court asked whether the mother derived any rights to remain with her daughter.

Tizzano's Opinion is designed specifically to answer the questions raised by the national court and does not digress into any side issues or present a general overview of the law. His starting point is the need to answer the questions posed by the national court and deal with the legal arguments brought to the European Court by the Member States and the Commission. The first way in which the Tizzano assisted the Court was in simplifying the seven questions referred to it by the Immigration Appeal Tribunal into two simple questions; the first relating to the residence rights of the child and the second to the right of the parent. Dealing with each point in turn, he rejected the argument that this was a purely internal situation, citing the Court in *Garcia Avello* to the effect that a national born in the host State is not deprived of their rights purely on the basis that he has not exercised the right to move and reside elsewhere.[51] The child in question was Irish and the dispute therefore fell within the scope of the Treaty. He then asked whether a minor can be vested with Community law rights and, rejecting the argument of the Irish government, he answered this question in the affirmative. Legal capacity in all the legal systems of the Member States is acquired at birth; a minor is a subject of the law and a holder of the rights conferred by law. Under Article 49 EC even very young children may be the recipient of services and Article 18EC also refers to 'every Community national'. Citing *Echternach and Moritz*, he stated that the Court had recognized that minors can be vested with residence rights.[52]

[51] Case C-148/02 *Garcia Avello* [2003] ECR I-11613.
[52] Joined Cases C-389/87 and C-390/87 *Echternach and Moritz* [1989] ECR 723.

Turning to the substantive questions, Tizzano first examined the question whether the child could derive a long-term right of residence as a recipient of services. He argued that she could not, as services in a host State are not utilized on a permanent basis, and thus the recipient of services would have a right of residence only on a temporary basis until those services came to an end, in this case child-care or medical services. Tizzano argued that the child appeared to fall within the terms of Directive 90/364EEC as she had health insurance and sufficient resources, courtesy of her mother, to avoid becoming a burden on the host State. The intervening Member States interpreted this provision to mean that an individual seeking to rely on Community law provisions must have resources in their own right but Tizzano disagreed. The Directive is a means of facilitating the rights of residence under Article 18EC, whereas the UK and Irish governments were interpreting it as a means of limiting the exercise of a fundamental right. By contrast, the Court in *Baumbast* had stated that the limitations and conditions referred to in the Treaty must be applied in light of the principles of Community law, and of proportionality in particular. The interpretation suggested by the intervening governments would unnecessarily hamper the objectives of the Community.

On the mother's right of residence, Tizzano argued that, as a national of a non-Member state, she could not derive a right of residence under any of the Community Directives since she was not dependent on her daughter, but rather her daughter was dependent on her. However, he also argued that the mother derived a right of residence from the rights of her daughter; to argue otherwise would be to deprive the daughter's rights of any useful effect. Again quoting *Baumbast,* Tizzano reminded the Court that it had recognized the right of the primary carer to remain in the host State 'to facilitate the exercise of that right'.[53]

Finally, Tizzano addressed an issue raised by the UK government to the effect that the Chen family had abused Community law by contriving to achieve Irish nationality for their daughter in order to manufacture a right of residence in the UK. All parties had agreed that the family had arranged for the birth of the daughter in Belfast to effect the outcome that Tizzano had now agreed was possible. Tizzano rejected that view and argued that if there was a problem at all, the problem arose out of the criteria used by Ireland to establish Irish nationality. None of the parties had questioned the right of Ireland to establish such criteria, and so the Chen family could not be criticized for taking advantage of Community rights.

The Court agreed with all the points raised by Tizzano and followed his Opinion almost to the letter, even citing with approval his analysis of the capacity of minors to derive rights under Community law. In terms of logic, in terms of authorities cited and in terms of conclusions, the Court was at one with the Advocate General. His Opinion must have been extremely valuable to the Reporting Judge in preparing the draft for the deliberations. This degree of alignment arose because Tizzano began by addressing the question referred by the

[53] Case C-413/99 *Baumbast v Secretary of State for the Home Department* [2002] ECR I-7091, para 75.

national court and he did not digress, waiver or provide an overview of the matters under consideration. He also had at his disposal clear authorities on a number of issues. Furthermore he managed, in this Opinion, to dispose of an argument raised by a number of Advocates General and never referred to by the Court, as to whether the provisions relating to services could provide the basis for a right of long-term residence. This issue had been mooted by several Advocates General such as La Pergola in *Martínez Sala* or Geelhoed in *D'Hoop*, but had always seemed an implausible basis on which to found a right of residence or other citizenship rights. Tizzano appears to have finally put an end to that kind of speculative argument.

These cases again raise the issue of how helpful the Advocate General is to the Court when it is faced with interpreting new areas of Community law. Although Tizzano clearly assisted the Court in the case of *Chen*, at the opposite extreme was the *Akrich* case, where the Court appears to have bypassed the Advocate General entirely. This is perhaps not surprising given the lack of clarity of that particular Opinion. Comparing the Opinions in *Akrich* and *Chen* demonstrates the need for the Advocate General, if he is to provide assistance to the Court, to keep his Opinion both simple and within the bounds of the questions submitted by the national court. Geelhoed, in *Baumbast*, appears to have had some influence upon the thinking of the Court, for example, on the issue of the direct effect of Article 18 EC but, for the rest, the Court appears to have developed its own line of reasoning.

Concluding observations

This discussion of the role of the Advocates General suggests that it is possible for an Advocate General to have a major impact on the thinking of the Court in a particular area of Community law. Whilst all the Advocates General discussed in this chapter form part of the 'reflexive European circuit', not all of them have been able to influence the Court in the same way. La Pergola undoubtedly contributed to the Court's thinking in the groundbreaking case of *Martínez Sala* and influenced the future direction of Community law. In that phase when the Court began to signal its intentions to interpret the citizenship provisions in a very active sense, it had the full support of the Advocates General. Whilst neither Jacobs nor Cosmas could be said to have influenced the Court in the particular cases in which they were involved, they did lay down a marker for future developments. Indeed, Cosmas showed prescience in his analysis. It is more difficult to assess the contribution of the Advocates General when the Court was engaged in engineering institutional change; it is clear that the Court did not rely on the reasoning of the Advocate General in *Grzelczyk. Baumbast, Akrich* and *Collins*. In these cases the Court was laying down new principles and did not rely on existing authorities to reach its judgment; under these circumstances it is not possible for the Advocate

General to 'second guess' the Court's thinking. The judges themselves, in the deliberations, knowingly shift the Community law paradigm in ways that are unforeseen by observers, even intimate observers like the Advocate General or the Commission. In these cases it is not surprising that the Court does not 'follow' the Advocate General since the Court alone leads the process of norm creation. The Advocate General can only attempt to absorb the new interpretations handed down by the Court for use in subsequent cases.

These cases have also demonstrated that the Advocate General can assist the Court best, in the normal course of the work of the Court, when he is able to take existing authorities and apply them logically, clearly and succinctly to the questions referred to the Court by the national judge, as was the case in *Chen* and, to a lesser extent, *Bidar*. It may seem to be stating the obvious that the Advocate General should seek precision and clarity but, in some of these cases, the Advocates General have provided the Court with lengthy and sometimes confusing essays on Community law, with only a brief reference at the end of their Opinions to the questions referred. To busy judges this cannot be helpful, and it is not surprising that many of the points raised do not find a place in the reasoning of the Court. It does not appear that the Court finds the presentation of difficult and abstruse theoretical possibilities to be helpful. It seems to have preferred in these cases the simpler (even if more radical) solution than some of the arguments presented in the Opinions of the Advocates General. For example, Alber's theory of concurrent status did not find favour with the Court although it was an attempt to find a solution to the case within the existing parameters of Community law. When the judges have such an enormous work load, they cannot engage in such abstruse questions and need practical assistance to answer the cases before them.

11
Conclusion

In this book we have attempted to position the work of the Advocate General in the Court of Justice and to assess his contribution to the Court both in terms of his function of assisting the Court and in terms of developing European Community law. These are complex questions and our findings are equally complex. There is no simple answer, for example, to the question of whether the Court follows the Opinion of the Advocate General in coming to a decision on a case. Neither can we state with any certainty that any particular Advocate General has contributed to the development of Community law. Such developments often emerge unexpectedly, in the Court's decision in individual cases. The Court listens to the parties in the dispute, to the lawyers of intervening States, to representatives of the Institutions, particularly the Commission, as well as the Advocate General. The judges read the literature, gauge the reaction to their case-law, interact with national judges and academics, meet students in the Court and respond to questions. The Opinion of the Advocate General is therefore part of that complex *mélange* of information and argument. What we have tried to do in our case studies is to focus on the Opinion of the Advocate General to see if we can discern the dialogue that takes place between the judges and the Advocates General of the Court. We offer some conclusions in this regard. We are also conscious that there has been some debate about the continued role for the Advocate General and we offer some thoughts about the future role of the institution.

The research we have undertaken for this book is merely the tip of the iceberg. It would be useful for similar research to be undertaken, particularly on the establishment and evolution of other principles of EC law such as the principles of supremacy, proportionality and legitimate expectations.

The role of the Advocate General in procedure

There is evidence that the Advocate General is very much involved in the decisions taken by the Court in managing its case-load. The Advocate General is fully involved in judging the importance of the issues raised in the case and how the case should proceed. Thereafter, the primary task of the Advocate General in the Court's procedure remains to deliver an Opinion in open court and to bring the oral procedure to a close. Advocates General do not normally confer with other Advocates General who may also be preparing Opinions on similar issues. The Advocates General do not form a College, they work as individuals. It is probably true to say that, in the earlier years of the Court, when there were just two Advocates General, they did work more closely. However in the larger Court there is less interaction amongst the Advocates General. There is mixed evidence as to whether an Advocate General will discuss the substance of a case, rather than administrative aspects of it, with the Reporting Judge. The degree of interaction probably depends on the personality and relationships amongst particular Advocates General and particular judges. There may well be informal contacts between the respective Legal Secretaries (the French version which is also sometimes used is 'référendaires') in the *Cabinets* of judges and Advocates General. Discussions with the judges' Legal Secretaries indicate that the Opinions of Advocates General are read with a great deal of care and interest by them. Given that it is common for the Reporting Judge to delegate the drafting of the judgment to a Legal Secretary, it is not unreasonable to suggest that the Opinions, particularly of long-standing Advocates General with well established reputations such as Jacobs, Léger and van Gerven, do have a significant impact on the minds of these young, bright but relatively inexperienced jurists. There is no means of discovering whether the Opinions are discussed when the judges deliberate. It is submitted that any in-depth consideration of an Opinion is likely to be confined to the members of the Chambers of the Reporting Judge. However, one may speculate that in Chambers of three or five judges the situation may well be different.

In the Article 300(6) EC procedure the Advocates General are involved in offering assistance to the Court but these proceedings are in camera and the collective Opinion is not publicly available. It is not possible therefore to discern how much discussion and debate there is between the judges and Advocates General in these proceedings. In matters relating to external relations it is perhaps essential that the European Community speaks with one voice but for researchers it is frustrating not to see the advice given to the Court.

Some questions have been raised about the fairness of the Court's procedure under Article 6 of the European Convention on Human Rights since the parties are not given an opportunity to reply to the Opinion. Although Advocates General no longer deliver Opinions in every case, they will continue to do so in cases raising important points of law such as, for, example appeals on law from the Court of First Instance where direct actions by private parties, challenging decisions of Community institutions are heard. There is a convincing case that the Advocate General's role in the decision-making process of the Court is suspect.[1] We conclude that the Court should re-examine its own procedures for compatibility

[1] The right to be heard in Commission competition investigations is a principle of EC law recognizzed by the Court in Case 17/74 *Transocean Marine Paint Association v Commission* [1974] ECR 1063, discussed in ch 7.

with the European Convention on Human Rights, particularly in view of the possibility of the European Union acceding to the Convention.

Does the Advocate General assist the Court?

This question is enormously complex and we offer some tentative conclusions. A preliminary point should be noted. In exercising their function the Advocates General need to address all the issues and arguments that have been raised in the case. They have no means of identifying either how the Court will rule on each individual issue or in what order the Court will consider the issues or indeed whether the Court will rule on all the issues raised. For example, in *Distillers* Warner thoroughly reviewed the complaints from the applicants in respect of alleged procedural irregularities involving the documentation which had been provided to the Advisory Committee before the contested Commission competition decision had been adopted.[2] The Court dismissed the case on a technical matter and therefore did not discuss these issues. However, the criticism of the Advocate General is likely to have had an impact on the Commission, since as a competition authority it must operate fair and non-discriminatory procedures. Thus the views of the Advocate General in this context may have an influence on how the Community institutions operate.

It has been said that only occasionally does the Court reach a conclusion significantly different from that proposed by the Advocate General. We have found numerous instances where the Court reaches the same conclusion as the Advocate General on a particular point. For example, Advocate General van Gerven in *Barber* or in several other sex discrimination cases[3] and Advocate General Jacobs in all except one of the intellectual property cases.[4]

Sometimes both the Court and the Advocate General follow the same line of reasoning in reaching that conclusion. The significance of the Advocate General's reasoning is clearly demonstrated, for example, in Advocate General Warner's Opinion in *Transocean Marine* on the right to be heard.[5] Another clear example of this is the case of *Chen* where the Court repeats almost verbatim both the reasoning and the conclusions of the Advocate General.[6] A more subtle example is the Opinion of Advocate General Reischl in *Ratti* where he introduced a concept akin to personal bar (estoppel) to explain and justify the distinction between vertical and horizontal direct effect.[7] His reasoning has subsequently been maintained by the Court.

[2] Case 30/78 *Distillers Co Ltd v Commission* [1980] ECR 2229, discussed in ch 7.

[3] Case C-262/88 *Douglas Hervey Barber v Guardian Royal Exchange* [1990] ECR I-1889 discussed in ch 5.

[4] The cases are examined in ch 6.

[5] Case 17/74 *Transocean Marine Paint Association v Commission* [1974] ECR 1063 discussed in ch 7, n 52 and text following.

[6] Case C-200/02 *Man Levette Chen and Kunqian Catherine Chen v Secretary of State for the Home Office* [2004] ECR I-9925, discussed in ch 10.

[7] Case C-148/78 *Ministero Pubblico v Ratti* [1979] ECR 1629, discussed in ch 8.

However, in other instances the Court reaches the same conclusion but for different reasons. For example in the 1996 repackaging cases, Advocate General Jacobs had a different approach from the European Court of Justice to the questions referred by the national court.[8] Although the same conclusion was reached, Jacobs' reasoning would have had a different impact on the national litigation as to which party would bear the burden of proof. The starting point for the reasoning of Advocate General Geelhoed in *D'Hoop* and that of the Court were very different, but the outcome of the case for the individual concerned was the same.[9]

In yet other cases, the Court reaches a conclusion that is very different from the Advocate General. There is some evidence to support the view that when the Court lays down new directions for Community law, the Advocates General's contribution has been minimal. The Court reasons quite independently of the Advocate General's conclusions. In these judgments, by their very nature, the Court does not rely on existing authorities. The Court often applies a teleological method of interpretation, developing Community law in a direction not contemplated by the Advocate General. For example, the Court in *Grzelczyk* reappraised its previous case-law by relying on Article 18 EC in a way that was not foreseen by Advocate General Alber.[10] Another example is the judgment of the Court in *Camera Care* where the Court decided the Commission had powers under Article 3 of Regulation 17/62 to adopt interim measures.[11]

Occasionally, the Court appears to come to a conclusion based on a form of reasoning presented to it by an Advocate General in a previous case. This is evident in the examination of the 1996 State liability cases (*Brasserie du Pêcheur/Factortame III, Dillenkofer* and *Lomas*) where the Advocates General Tesauro and Léger delivered Opinions. For example, in *Brasserie du Pêcheur/Factortame III* judgment the Court's reasoning is closer to Léger's Opinion in *Lomas* in some respects but closer to Tesauro's in others.[12] It is also apparent in *Grzelczyk* where the Court's judgment relies more on La Pergola in *Martinez Sala* and ignores Advocate General Alber's complex analysis.[13]

Thus from our studies we can provide examples of very different outcomes. We would argue that such an approach tells only a small part of the story. We believe that in assessing how the Advocate General assists the Court it is immaterial whether the Court actually follows the Advocate General in any particular case.[14]

[8] Case C-427/93 *Bristol-Myers Squibb v Paranova A/S*; C-429/93 *C.H. Boehringer Sôhn, Boehringer Ingelheim KG abd Boehringer Ingelheim A/S v Paranova A/S* and Case C-436/93 *Bayer Aktiengesellschaft and Bayer Danmark A/S v Paranova A/S* [1996] ECR I-3457, discussed in ch 6.

[9] Case C-224/98 *Marie-Nathalie D'Hoop v ONEM* [2002] ECR I-6191, discussed in ch 10.

[10] Case C-184/99 *Rudy Grzelczyk v Centre public d'aide sociale d' Ottignies-Louvain-la Neuve* [2001] ECR I-6193, discussed in ch 10.

[11] Case 792/79R *Camera Care Ltd v Commission* [1980] ECR 119, discussed in ch 7.

[12] Discussed in ch 9, n 122 and text following.

[13] Discussed in ch 10.

[14] But see K Mortelmans, 'The Court under the Influence of its Advocates General: An Analysis of the Case Law on the Functioning of the Internal Market' (2005) Yearbook of European Law 127 for a quantitative approach.

It is certainly the case that the Advocate General can assist the Court in developing reasoning which it can follow in coming to its decision. However the Advocate General can also be of assistance in providing reasoning which the Court rejects. In these cases the Court might see flaws in the reasoning and come to a decision by more careful reasoning. What is important is the dialogic relationship between the Advocate General and the Court. This dialogic relationship does not end with the outcome of any particular case but continues as part of the ongoing conversation on the interpretation of Community law[15] and it takes place over time—as can be seen from the study of the principle of direct effect. It can also take place outside the Court. Judges of the European Court of Justice, much more so than judges from the courts of the Member States, participate in academic and practitioner conferences and events where they are exposed to a wide variety of ideas. Very often, academics would look to the Opinions of the Advocates General as a starting point for a critique of the case-law of the Court.

The Advocates General we have studied have assisted the Court in the following ways:

- By arguing for innovation based on a teleological approach.
- By arguing for consolidation based on existing case-law or legislation.
- By arguing against past case-law.
- By arguing for a strict interpretation.

An Advocate General will not always argue for innovation or for consolidation—much depends on the matter under consideration. Where there is relative clarity in the law he is more likely to argue for consolidation. In new areas of law he might either opt for innovation or a strict interpretation.

Arguing for innovation based on a teleological approach

Advocate General Lagrange, on the occasion of his departure from the Court, indicated that the analysis and summary role of the Opinion 'is a useful complement to the work of the Juge-Rapporteur, expressed in the report of the Hearing'.[16] It may well be that in the early period in the creation of this new legal order the Advocate General's Opinion was more valuable in assisting the Court than it is now. For example, Advocate General Lagrange's comparative law approach, reviewing the national law of the original six Member States and extracting from the analysis common principles which could be transposed to the European legal order, was undoubtedly helpful to the Court. At the time there was no research unit in the Library of the Court to be called upon and the age of databases and web searches was a long way away.

[15] D Kostakopolou discusses the reflexive European circuit in her work on citizenship 'Ideas, Norms and European Citizenship: Explaining Institutional Change' (2005) 86 (2) MLR 233. See ch 10.

[16] Speech delivered at the formal sitting of the Court on 8 October 1964.

Similarly, in the early years when the Community legal order was being created, the Court had difficult cases to decide which would determine the future, the scope and nature of Community law, for example in *Van Gend en Loos* or *Costa v ENEL*.[17] Advocate General Roemer initially appeared to favour an interpretation of the Treaty which deferred to the constitutional traditions of the Member States, whereas the study of Lagrange shows that he delivered unequivocal, strong and well reasoned Opinions in favour of the Court exercising a wide jurisdiction, particularly in the context of preliminary references and actions by the Commission against Member States for breaches of Community law in order to create a specific European constitutional law.

The study of Lagrange's Opinions has confirmed that he contributed much to the creation and development of a Community legal order governed by the rule of law. The legal order created by the EC Treaty has developed so quickly primarily because of the excellent relationship that has been established between national courts and the European Court of Justice. All the fundamental principles of Community law have been established in Article 234EC judgments. This was a novel procedure, unknown in the international legal order. The Opinions of Advocates General Lagrange and Roemer were of importance in encouraging the Court not to interpret admissibility questions too strictly. They fully encouraged the Court to exercise its power to bring Member States to account for breaches of EC law.

However in this respect, the more recent principles and concepts of EC law, such as State liability, the contribution of the Advocates General has to be assessed more carefully. As far as State liability is concerned the contribution of Advocates General in the early case law is disappointing, save for Lagrange who, once he had floated the idea but received no response from the Court, abandoned it. It was the European Court of Justice's judgments rather than the Opinions which seemed more engaged with the need to ensure that Member States were accountable to individuals for harm caused by their failure to comply with Community law. The Advocates General at the time maintained the traditional view that this was a matter for national law. Advocate General Mischo, in the *Francovich* case had a leading role in establishing this principle of State liability.[18] In the meanwhile, effectiveness of Community law had become an important guiding principle in the Court's case-law. Once State liability became recognized as a principle of EC law, Tesauro and Léger can be clearly identified as the main contributors, not only to the exhaustive analysis of the nature and scope of the principle, but also to the development of coherent conditions of liability.

More recently there is evidence that certain Advocates General have adopted a teleological approach to the interpretation of Community Law. For example, it is clear that both Advocates General Léger and La Pergola, perhaps independently or

[17] Case C-26/62 *N.V. Algemene Transpoert—En Expeditie Onderneming Van Gend En Loos v Nederlandse Tariefcommissie* [1963] ECR 1 and Case 6/64 *Costa v ENEL* [1964] ECR 585 discussed in chs 4 and 8.

[18] Joined Cases C-6/90 and C-9/90 *Francovich and ors v Italy* [1991] ECR I-5357, discussed in ch 9.

perhaps after discussions over coffee, encouraged the Court to interpret the citizenship provisions in an expansive way. Although at first seemingly rebuffed, this approach subsequently won the day with the Court although the Advocates General probably formed part of a wider effort to persuade the Court of the possibilities inherent in the concept of citizenship. For example, Advocate General la Pergola acknowledges the influence of the Commission's arguments on his own thinking: the Court may have similarly been influenced.

Arguing for consolidation based on existing case-law or legislation

Cases come to the Court of Justice on identical or similar issues from different routes. Intellectual property law cases are a good example. As shown in chapter 6, some cases come to the Court indirectly as appeals from the Court of First Instance whilst others come directly to the Court as preliminary references from national courts. The Advocate General can discharge an important role in reconciling the judgments and summarizing the case-law and thus assist the Court to develop Community law in a consistent manner.[19] This role is particularly useful where judgments on similar areas of Community law are delivered by Chambers, not necessarily composed of the same judges. The emphasis on various aspects of the cases may be different and lead to submissions that the Court should not follow precedent where on a closer analysis the essence of the judgment is in fact the same.

In other areas of Community law the Court might take different approaches based on the particular facts of the case or the way in which the national judge has framed the question in a preliminary reference. Sometimes the case-law of the Court becomes inconsistent. Under these circumstances it is useful for the Court (and a wider audience) to hear an exegesis of the law to prompt deeper thinking. In such a case an Advocate General might invite the Court to step back and review its case-law to date in order to proceed with more consistency of approach. Advocate General Léger in *Linster* provided one such moment of reflection on the implications of the Court's case law on direct effect and the duty of consistent interpretation.[20] His understanding of the need for consolidation might, however, have fallen on deaf ears in the Court at the time.

Advocate General Tizzano in *Chen* might have seemed quite radical in his interpretation of the law to an outsider unfamiliar with the case-law of the Court.[21] However his Opinion is based on existing case-law. The reason why his analysis in that case was helpful to the Court and, one supposes, to the Reporting Judge, was

[19] Cases C-383/99P *Procter & Gamble Co v Office for Harmonisation in the Internal Market (Trade Marks and Designs)* (*BABY-DRY*) [2001] ECR I-6251 and C-191/01P *Office for Harmonisation in the Internal Market (Trade Marks and Designs) v Wm. Wrigley Jr. Company* (*DOUBLEMINT*) [2003] ECR I-12447.

[20] Case C-287/98 *Luxembourg v Linster* [2000] ECR I-6917.

[21] Case C-200/02 *Man Levelte Chen and Kungian Catherine Chen v Secretary of State for the Home Office* [2004] ECR I-9925.

that he based his Opinion specifically on existing case-law and applied that case-law in a logical and consistent manner, leaving the Court with little alternative but to follow his analysis without revisiting its past case-law. Other examples of the Advocate General providing a useful summary of existing case-law can be found in the Jacobs Opinion in *Bristol-Myers Squibb*[22].

Arguing against past case-law

Our studies have demonstrated examples of how the Advocate General can attempt to persuade the Court to change direction when the full implications of its previous case-law have been realized.[23]

By contrast, in chapter 8 we have shown that, despite the concerted efforts of the Advocates General in the 1990s, the Court was not persuaded of the need to revise its position on the horizontal direct effect of directives. The Court held to what might be described as the 'Reischl position' on this matter. However the very fact that van Gerven, Jacobs and Lenz reminded the Court of the practical problems and inconsistencies created by its case-law might have had an impact on the Court's approach to other potential ways of resolving these inconsistencies, such as the need to refine the duty of consistent interpretation or the principles of State liability.

Arguing for strict interpretation

Some of the Advocates General studied in some of the cases have shown a preference for a strict literal interpretation. This is particularly evident when an interpretation of secondary legislation is being sought. Both Jacobs in *Davidoff v Gofkid* and Warner in *Camera Care* provide examples of this approach. On both occasions the Court applied a teleological method of interpretation which enabled the Court to depart from the text of the secondary legislation and to fill the identified gap.[24]

Ways in which the Advocate General does not assist the Court

The Court of Justice is a busy Court faced with a wide range of issues. In an attempt to reduce its workload a Court of First Instance has been established and judicial panels created. The role of Advocate General appears almost anachronistic in such a busy Court. It is perhaps reminiscent of an earlier time when the Court was faced with far fewer cases. There is also a practical problem for the Court in that although French is the official language of the Court, the documents

[22] Case C-427/93 *Bristol-Myers Squibb v Paranova A/S* [1996] ECR I-3457.

[23] eg Case C-10/89 *SA CNL-SUCAL NV v HAG GF AG (HAG II)* [1990] ECR I-3711, discussed in ch 6.

[24] Both cases discussed in chs 6 and 7.

submitted to the Court have, for a variety or reasons, to be translated into a number of different languages. The sheer cost of such translations is enormous and one response to this problem has been to ask the Advocates General to limit the length of their Opinions, although it must be said that this request appears to have fallen on deaf ears in some instances.

From the point of view of the judges (except as insofar as they are managers of the Court) the key issue is one of time. As has been made clear in this book, the opinion of the Advocate General is made available to all the judges in a particular case. These judges are likely to be involved in a considerable number of cases in any one year. Lengthy Opinions which examine the detail of cases are not helpful to busy judges. The lengthier and more complex an Opinion the less likely it is that the judges, other perhaps than the Reporting Judge, will read the Opinion in any but the most cursory manner. They are far more likely to rely on the Reporting Judge in deliberations to provide guidance in a case. In deliberations the judges are free to raise a variety of questions and are able to discuss different approaches to the solution of the cases before them. Extended essays are not therefore helpful. What is helpful is an Opinion which addresses the question and proposes a solution, supported by analysis of case-law and legislation, even although that solution might not be followed.

The Court of Justice seems to have a preference for avoiding complex reasoning in its judgments even in the most complex of cases. So, for example, the Court was reluctant to accept the entirely logical case by van Gerven that actuarial statistics might infringe the equal treatment principle.[25] It preferred to avoid the implications of his argument in these cases. The Court also preferred the much simpler approach to the principle of non-discrimination in *Grzelczyk*[26] than that suggested by the Advocate General. In difficult cases, clear succinct arguments appear to have more benefit for the Court than abstruse and convoluted interpretations of Community law.

Future

Having undertaken this research and reached the above conclusions, it would surely be disappointing if we did not have some challenges to offer the reader as to the future role of Advocates General. These ideas are presented simply to open up debate. We are fully aware that none of them are unproblematic and we do not propose to set out the positive and negative aspects of each suggestion.

The first, provocative, suggestion is to propose that there is no longer a need for Advocates General at the European Court of Justice. After all, the Community legal order has now reached a degree of maturity where the responsibility for

[25] Discussed in ch 5.

[26] Case C-184/99 *Rudy Grzelczyk v Centre public d'aide sociale d'Ottignies-Louvain-la Neuve* [2001] ECR I-6193, discussed in ch 10.

enforcing Community law is continuously being placed on national courts and national authorities. Recent examples include the development of the principle of State liability for breaches of Community law or the duty on the national Court to interpret national law in conformity with Community law. Many aspects of Community law are settled and clearly understood, so much so that there is repatriation to the national authorities in areas such as competition law. Within such a mature system there may be no need for the post of Advocate General. Other mature systems of law operate without the benefit of an Opinion before the deliberation by the judges. In addition the background research that the Advocate General provides might no longer be needed given that the Court has at its disposal rich sources of legal advice ranging from academic writings to the written submissions of a number of law practitioners often from different legal systems. Furthermore, there is nothing to prevent the Court from appointing one of its members as Advocate General for a specific case where, for example, an issue of constitutional importance is raised or, for example, where the case-law on the issue was not consistent and there was a need for an independent analysis and summary. One of the benefits of dispensing with the role would be cost and time savings, an important consideration given the increased need to translate documents into so many different languages.

A less radical suggestion and one that should be considered seriously is to redefine the role and function of the Advocate General, taking into account that the European Court of Justice is now a much more complex structure consisting of a number of Chambers, a Court of First Instance and a Staff Tribunal. More tribunals or first instance courts such as one for intellectual property law matters are being discussed. Furthermore the enlargement of the EU has led to the necessity of the Full Court no longer consisting of all judges. The Grand Chamber, consisting of 13 judges has replaced the Full Court for most purposes.

The cases being heard by these components of the Court will vary in importance and degree of complexity. As stated in chapter 1 the issues coming before the Court range from minor technical questions of interpretation of secondary legislation to judgments of major significance for natural and legal persons. Perhaps the primary role of the Advocate General should no longer be focused on 'assisting' the Court to reach a judgment in a specific case but to act as a 'guardian of the law' with a right to be heard in cases where the case law is inconsistent or unclear, or the issue raised before the Court is of constitutional importance.

Alternatively it might also be suggested that it is no longer necessary that *all* Advocates General be generalists. The competences of the Community have grown with each Treaty amendment and now there are specialized areas of Community law (and Union law) where it may be advantageous to have the same Advocate General appointed for the same type of case. A specialized constitutional lawyer or commercial lawyer working with the Court on key cases might prove advantageous for the uniform and consistent development of the law.

This is an apt time in the history of the Court and the Community to discuss the position of the Advocate General within the Court structure in view of the debates on constitutional matters and the possibility of even further enlargement which will have a direct impact on the workload of the Court. We have shown that the Advocate General has assisted the Court to develop the Community legal order. However, the role played by the Advocate General in the past may not necessarily meet the needs of EC Law in the future.

The Advocates General of the European Court of Justice

LAGRANGE, Maurice (born 14 May 1900)

Lagrange was the first of the Advocates General, and is credited with defining the role. Born in France in 1900, he held office for two mandates from 4 December 1952 until 8 October 1964. Prior to this he had served over 21 years at the *Conseil d'État*, as well as having taken part in the negotiations of the Treaty of Paris and being involved in the drafting of the Protocol on the Statute of the Court.

ROEMER, Karl (born 30 December 1899)

Germany's first Advocate General, Roemer served from 2 February 1953 until 10 October 1973, which was, effectively, the entire period during which the Advocates General numbered two. During this period, which amounted to almost 21 years, Roemer was considered to be a true architect of European Community Law. Before becoming a member of Court, Roemer had been involved in banking, as well as spending some time on the judicial bench in Cologne.

TRABUCCHI, Alberto (born 26 July 1907)

Prior to his appointment as Advocate General on 9 January 1973, Trabucchi had argued cases before the Court for five years and then served as its 'extra' judge for nearly nine. The position of the 'extra' judge ended in 1973 when the number of Member States increased to nine, and so Trabucchi was appointed by Italy to be Advocate General when their number was increased from two to four. He served a single mandate until 7 October 1976, when he retired at the age of 68.

GAND, Joseph (born 28 February 1913)

France's second Advocate General, Gand, also came from the *Conseil d'État*, where he returned after his single mandate of almost six years, having been sworn in on 8 October 1964. He had three spells as *Commissaire du gouvernement* in the Judicial Division of the Council of State (1947–50, 1957–60 and 1962–64), prior to which he was Director-General of Administration and the Civil Service for two years, from 1959–61.

DUTHEILLET DE LAMOTHE, Alain Louis Georges (born 25 August 1919)

Dutheillet de Lamothe's spell as Advocate General only lasted for 17 months, from 7 October 1970 until he passed away on 2 January 1972. He had previously also served in the *Conseil d'État* and had been seconded to the offices of the Prime Minister (1952), the Minister for National Defence (1952–54) and the Minister for Justice (1969–70). He was also a Senior Lecturer at the Institut d'Etudes Politiques and at the Ecole Nationale d'Administration, where he himself studied. He and was a regular contributor to many legal journals.

MAYRAS, Henri (born 29 March 1920)

Mayras, the fourth Advocate General appointed by France, succeeded Dutheillet de Lamothe on 22 March 1972 and served until ill-health forced him to retire nine years later on 18 March 1981. Mayras had experience of both the *Conseil d'État* and the *Conseil Constitutionnel*, as well as having worked as an academic in both France and Morocco.

WARNER, Jean-Pierre (born 24 September 1924)

The first British appointment as Advocate General, Warner, was bilingual, having a French mother and an English father. He was appointed on 9 January 1973 when the number of Advocates General was increased from two to four, and left the Court just over eight years later to take up a position in the High Court. Prior to this he had practised for 22 years at the Chancery Bar, which had culminated in his appointment as Queen's Counsel in 1972.

REISCHL, Gerhard (born 17 July 1918)

Germany's second Advocate General, and the replacement of the long-serving Roemer, was Reischl, who had previous experience as a judge, civil servant and legislator. Reischl was a member of the *Bundestag* from 1961–72, serving as State Secretary during the last two years before departing for a position as a Member of the European Assembly (now European Parliament). He was sworn in as Advocate General on 9 October 1973 and served until 11 January 1984.

CAPOTORTI, Francesco (born 9 February 1925)

Similar to Trabucchi, who he succeeded as Advocate General on 7 October 1976, Capotorti had also served as the Italian judge of the European Court of Justice, albeit for only eight months. He served one mandate as Advocate General, which finished on 6 October 1982. His background was predominantly academic: he was a Professor of International Law, working in the Universities of Naples, Cagliari, Bari and Rome, although he was a member of numerous delegations to the United Nations.

SLYNN, Sir Gordon (born 17 February 1930)

Sir Gordon Slynn replaced Warner as the British Advocate General on 7 October 1988. His appointment was a notable one because he was the first person, as noted by President Mertens de Wilmars, to have pleaded before the Court, to have referred questions to it for preliminary ruling, and then to serve it as Advocate General; prior to his appointment he had represented the UK before the International Court of Justice, the European Court of Human Rights, and the European Court of Justice. Sir Gordon Slynn served as a judge at the Court after finishing as Advocate General on 10 March 1992.

ROZÈS, Simone (born 29 March 1920)

France's fifth appointment as Advocate General was the first woman to hold the position, and the first female member of the European Court of Justice. Rozès was sworn in on 18 March 1981 and served a single mandate, until 13 February 1984 when she departed to become First President of the *Cour de Cassation*. She was also the first French appointee not to have experience of the *Conseil d'État*; rather, she had been Vice-President of the *Tribunal de Grande Instance*.

VERLOREN VAN THEMAAT, Pieter (born 16 March 1916)

The first Advocate General from the Netherlands, Verloren Van Themaat, was appointed on 4 June 1981 as a *fifth* Advocate General. This move was a direct response to Community enlargement, and the post was understood as being intended to be held in turn by nationals of 'smaller' Member States. Verloren van Themaat was an expert on economics: prior to his appointment he had been a Professor of Economic Law at the University of Utrecht, as well as having served in the Dutch Ministry of Economics. He had also served as Director-General at the European Commission (1958–67).

MANCINI, Giuseppe Federico (born 23 December 1927)

Following the Italian tradition of serving as both Advocate General and judge, Mancini replaced Capotorti as Advocate General on 10 October 1982, and then succeeded Giancinto Bosco as judge exactly six years later. Mancini was a labour lawyer—he was Professor of Labour Law in the Universities of Urbino, Bologna and Rome, as well as Professor of Comparative Private Law at Bologna. Immediately prior to his appointment as Advocate General he served as a Member of the High Council of the Judiciary from 1976–81.

LENZ, Carl Otto (born 5 June 1930)

Otto Lenz, Germany's third appointment as Advocate General, was a legislator before becoming a member of the Court on 11 January 1984. Educated at Cornell University in the United States, Lenz was a lawyer who subsequently chaired both the Legal Committee and the Committee on Community Affairs in the *Bundestag*.

He served three mandates as Advocate General, being reappointed twice before leaving the Court on 6 October 1997.

DARMON, Marco (born 26 January 1930)

Appointed by France on 13 February 1984, Darmon served as Advocate General for more than 10 years, departing on 6 October 1994. Prior to his appointment he had held both judicial and administrative positions in France: he was President of Chamber of the *Cour d'Appel* in Paris, and then Head of the *Direction des Affaires Civiles et du Sceau.*

MISCHO, Jean (born 7 September 1938)

Mischo is unique in two respects: he is the only Luxembourgish national to serve as Advocate General, and the only Advocate General to serve for two separate appointments. The first was from 13 January 1986 until 6 October 1991, while the second occurred over six years later, on 19 December 1997 and lasted until 6 October 2003. Before taking up his first appointment, Mischo held various positions of responsibility in the Ministry of Foreign Affairs of the Grand Duchy, and was Deputy Permanent Representative of the Grand Duchy of Luxembourg to the European Communities.

DA CRUZ VILAÇA, José Luis (born 20 September 1944)

The Court's first Portuguese Advocate General was also the man who negotiated Portugal's accession to the European Community during his time as Secretary of State for European Integration. Da Cruz Vilaça served from 31 January 1986 until 6 October 1988. His mandate was so short because this post was the sixth Advocate General position created, and it only lasted two years and nine months before rotating to Belgium.Prior to being appointed Advocate General he was predominantly an academic. Shortly after leaving the European Court of Justice he became the President of the Court of First Instance, a position that lasted from 1 September 1989 until 17 September 1995.

VAN GERVEN, Walter (born 11 May 1935)

The Belgian Advocate General, Walter Van Gerven, who served a single mandate from 7 October 1988 until 6 October 1994, came from a Flemish region of the country—his selection reflects Belgium's policy in terms of selection of attempting to balance region and language. Van Gerven had both academic and professional experience prior to his appointment: he held professorial chairs in the Catholic University of Leuven, the University of Chicago and the University of Amsterdam, and was Chairman of the Commission on Banking.

JACOBS, Francis Geoffrey (born 8 June 1939)

Jacobs, the third Advocate General to come from the UK was primarily an academic. He was a Professor of European Law at Kings College, London, and had published extensively in the field of European Law. He had also served as the Legal Secretary of Advocate General Warner, as an Official in the Secretariat of the European Commission of Human Rights, and as Queen's Counsel. His three mandates lasted from 7 October 1988 until 10 January 2006.

TESAURO, Giuseppe (born 15 November 1942)

Tesauro succeeded Mancini on 7 October 1988 to become Italy's fourth Advocate General, and he served almost 10 years, until 4 March 1998. Before taking up this appointment, Tesauro had been Professor of International Law and Community Law at the University of Naples and had, since 1964, directed the School specializing in Community Affairs, which was based at the University of Rome. He was also an Advocate before the Court of Cassation and a Member of the Council for Contentious Diplomatic Affairs at the Ministry of Foreign Affairs.

GULMANN, Claus Christian (born 22 April 1942)

Denmark's first Advocate General was Claus Gulmann, who came directly from private practice in Denmark. Gulmann was sworn in on 7 October 1991 and served until 6 October 1997. Directly after completion he was reappointed as a judge and served until 10 January 2006. Also an experienced academic, Gulmann had both held the Chair in Public International Law and been the Dean of the Law School at the University of Copenhagen.

LA PERGOLA, Antonio Mario (born 13 November 1931)

La Pergola joined the Court as perhaps the most accomplished Advocate General, having been an academic, a practitioner, and a politician. Prior to his appointment on 1 January 1995, La Pergola had been: a Professor of Constitutional Law and General and Comparative Public Law at the Universities of Padua, Bologna and Rome; a Member of the Italian High Council of the Judiciary (1976–78); a Member of the Constitutional Court and President of the Constitutional Court (1986–87); the Minister for Community Policy (1987–89); and an Italian Member of the European Parliament (1989–94). He had even served three months as a judge at the Court prior to his appointment as Advocate General, a position to which he returned directly after finishing on 14 December 1999 and where he remained until 3 May 2006.

COSMAS, Georgios (born 14 July 1932)

Greece appointed Georgios Cosmas its first Advocate General on 7 October 1994, and he served a single mandate until 6 October 2000. Educated in Paris, Cosmas had become a full Member of the Greek Council of State in 1973 and a State Counsellor in 1982, a position he retained until 1994. He was also a member of both the Special Court, which hears actions against judges, and the Superior Special Court. Among other positions, Cosmas sat on the High Council of the Judiciary and the High Council of the Ministry of Foreign Affairs.

LÉGER, Philippe (born 10 December 1938)

Léger succeeded Darmon as Advocate General on 7 October 1994. Prior to his appointment he had served as a judge for the Court of Appeal in Paris from 1983 until 1986, when he became Deputy Director of the Private Office of the Minister for Justice. He served as Advocate General of the French Court of Appeal in Paris before becoming Advocate General at the European Court of Justice until 6 October 2006.

ELMER, Michael Bendik (born 26 February 1949)

Elmer was appointed by Denmark to serve the remaining three years of Advocate General Gulmann's term. Due to the nature of the rotating position Elmer could not be reappointed, and so only served from 7 October 1994 until 18 December 1997. Before joining the Court, Elmer had been a member of the judiciary in Denmark, and was the Minister in the Ministry of Justice responsible for Community Law and Human Rights from 1991–94.

FENNELLY, Nial (born 3 May 1942)

Ireland's first Advocate General was unlike the judges it had appointed to the Court in that he was a senior barrister who had been neither Attorney General nor a member of the Supreme Court Justice in Ireland. Rather, Fennelly was a member of the Bar Council and a former president of the Legal Aid Board, a position from which he had resigned in protest over the Irish Government's failure to support legal aid for those who could not afford it. He served as Advocate General from 19 January 1995 until 6 October 2000.

RUIZ-JARABO COLOMER, Dámaso (born 20 June 1949)

Ruiz-Jarabo Colomer was Spain's first Advocate General, taking up his appointment on 19 January 1995. Prior to joining the Court he had been both a judge and the Head of the Private Office of the President of the *Consejo General del Poder Judicial* (General Council of the Judiciary) in Spain, and had served as a judge at the *Tribunal Supremo* (Supreme Court) from 1996. He was also an ad hoc judge to the European Court of Human Rights. Originally a two year appointment so that the new Advocates General could have staggered terms, he is currently in his 11th year of service.

ALBER, Siegbert (born 27 July 1936)

Germany's fourth Advocate General, Siegbert Alber, served a single six-year mandate from 7 October 1997 until 6 October 2003. Having been a law student at the Universities of Tübingen, Berlin, Paris, Hamburg, Vienna, and Cambridge, Alber became a member of the German *Bundestag* in 1969, where he served until 1980.

Elected to the European Parliament in 1977, he became its Vice-President in 1984, a position he retained until 1992.

MISCHO, Jean (2nd appointment, see listing above)

SAGGIO, Antonio (born 19 February 1934)

Saggio was the sixth Advocate General to come from Italy. Prior to his appointment to the Court of Justice he had been both a judge and the President of the Court of First Instance, from 1989–95 and 1995–98 respectively. In Italy his career was also predominantly judicial: he began as a judge in the District Court in Naples then moved to the Court of Appeal in Rome, and then the Court of Cassation. He served as Advocate General at the Court of Justice from 5 March 1998 to 6 October 2000.

TIZZANO, Antonio (born 1 January 1940)

Saggio was succeeded as the Italian Advocate General by Antonio Tizzano, who was sworn in on 7 October 2000 and completed his single mandate on 3 May 2006. Following the Italian tradition, Tizzano's spell as Advocate General was immediately followed by one as a judge at the Court, beginning on 4 May 2006. Prior to joining the Court, Tizzano was a Professor of European Law and Director of the Institute of International and European Law at the University of Rome, and had been a member of the Italian delegation in international negotiations and at intergovernmental conferences, including those on the Single European Act and the Maastricht Treaty.

GEELHOED, Leendert A (born 12 November 1942)

Only the second Advocate General to come from the Netherlands, Geelhoed was sworn in on 7 October 2000. His career prior to his appointment was varied: after a three-year spell as a Legal Secretary at the Court of Justice of the European Communities (1971–74) he returned to the Netherlands for seven years of service as a Senior Adviser, Ministry of Justice (1975–82), after which he became a member of the Advisory Council on Government Policy (1983–90). Immediately before joining the Court he was first Secretary-General of the Ministry of Economic Affairs (1990–97) and then Secretary-General of the Ministry of General Affairs until 2000. His mandate as Advocate General ended on 6 October 2006.

STIX-HACKL, Christine (born 12 June 1957)

Austria's first appointment as Advocate General on 7 October 2000, Christine Stix-Hackl was only the second female appointment since the office began in 1952. She started her career in 1982 as a member of the Austrian Diplomatic Service and then joined the office of the Legal Adviser to the Ministry of Foreign

Affairs as the expert on European Union matters (1985–88). As well as serving in the Legal Service of the European Commission in 1989, Stix-Hackl also participated in the negotiations on the European Economic Area and on the accession of the Republic of Austria to the European Union. She was the Agent of the Republic of Austria at the Court of Justice of the European Communities from 1995 and Austrian Consul-General in Zurich until 2000, when she joined the Court. Her mandate as Advocate General ended on 6 October 2006.

KOKOTT, Juliane (born 18 June 1957)

Juliane Kokott, who succeeded Alber as German Advocate General on 7 October 2003, is Germany's fifth Advocate General but its first female appointment. Prior to joining the Court her career was predominantly academic: she undertook her own law studies at the Universities of Bonn and Geneva, following that with an LL.M from American University/Washington DC, a Doctor of Laws from the University of Heidelberg, and a Doctor of Juridical Sciences (S.J.D.) from Harvard University, and then held chairs at the University of California, Berkeley, and the Universities of Augsburg (1992), Heidelberg (1993), Düsseldorf (1994) and St Gallen (1999). Her specific interests are International Business Law and European Law.

MADURO, Luís Miguel Poiares Pessoa (born 3 January 1967)

After a gap of almost exactly 15 years since de Cruz Vilaça's mandate finished in 1988, Maduro became Portugal's second Advocate General on 7 October 2003. His background was also principally academic: after completing his degree at the University of Lisbon in 1990 and receiving his doctorate from the European University Institute, Florence in 1996, a thesis which earned the Prize *Obiettivo Europa* for the best Doctoral Thesis of the EUI, Maduro held numerous professorial chairs across Europe. Among these were positions at the London School of Economics, the College of Europe in Natolin, the Ortega y Gasset Institute in Madrid, the Catholic University of Portugal, the Institute of European Studies in Macao, and the Universidade Nova in Lisbon.

SHARPSTON, Eleanor (born 13 July 1955)

The UK's first female Advocate General, Sharpston, succeeded the long-serving Jacobs on 6 January 2006. After first studying at Cambridge University and then teaching at Oxford, she was called to the Bar in 1980 and practised as a barrister before working as a Legal Secretary in the Chambers of the Advocate General, and subsequently Judge, Sir Gordon Slynn. Afterwards, she returned to academia and to practise at the English Bar. She is a Fellow of King's College, Cambridge University.

MENGOZZI, Paulo (born 16 June 1938)

Mengozzi, appointed by Italy on 4 May 2006 to succeed Tizzano, had previously been serving for almost eight years as a judge at the Court of First Instance. Prior to that he had been a member of the working group of the European Community on the World Trade Organisation (WTO), a member of the consultative committee of the Commission of the European Communities on public procurement, and the Under-Secretary of State for Trade and Industry during the Italian tenure of the Presidency of the Council. Academically his interests are in the fields of International and European Law: as well as holding positions at the Universities of St. Johns (New York), Georgetown, Paris-II, Georgia (Athens), he was a Professor of International Law and holder of the Jean Monnet Chair of European Community Law at the University of Bologna, and was also the director of the 1997 session on the WTO of The Hague Academy of International Law research centre.

Please note that the subsequent list of books and websites indicate the sources for the compilation of the Advocate General entries.

Books and articles

LN Brown and T Kennedy, *The Court of Justice of the European Communities* (5th edn, London: Sweet & Maxwell, 2000) Appendix III, Members of the Court of Justice

AA Dashwood, 'The Advocate General in the Court of Justice of the European Communities' (1982) 2 Legal Studies 202

SJ Kenney, 'The Members of the Court of Justice of the European Communities' (1998) 5 Columbia Journal of European Law 101–33

Websites

<http://www.curia.europa.eu/en/instit/presentationfr/index_cje.htm>

<http://www.curia.europa.eu/en/instit/presentationfr/composition/membrescour_anciens.htm> (ie the website of the Court of Justice of the European Communities. Accessed: 31 August 2006)

<http://www.cassidy.com/about/biodetail.asp?Id = 131&Office = dc2>. (Accessed: 31 August 2006)

Select Bibliography

Arnull, A. 'Out with the old . . . ' (2006) 31 European Law Review 1

Barav, A. 'Le commissaire du gouvernement pres le Conseil D'Etat Francais et l'avocat general pres la Cour De Justice des Communautes Europeennes' (1974) Revue Internationale de Droit Compare 809

Bengoetxea, J., MacCormick, N. and Soriano, L. M. 'Integration and Integrity in the Legal Reasoning of the European Court of Justice' in G deBurca and J Weiler, *The European Court of Justice* (Oxford: Oxford University Press, 2001)

Bengoetxea, J. *The Legal Reasoning of the European Court of Justice* (Oxford: Clarendon Press, 1993)

Bentley, D. 'An Advocate for the European Court' (1994) 37 International Commercial Lawyer 15

Birch, M. *Primus Inter Pares? An Examination of the Influence of the Advocate General on Judicial Decision Making* Ph. D. thesis (Liverpool, 1999)

Borgsmidt, K. 'The Advocate General at the European Court of Justice: A Comparative Study' (1988) 13 European Law Review 106

Brown, L.N. and Kennedy, T. *Brown & Jacobs: The Court of Justice of the European Communities* (5th edn, London: Sweet & Maxwell, 2000)

Castle, B. *Fighting All The Way* (London: Macmillan 1993)

Chalmers, D., Hadjiemmanuil, C., Monti, G. and Tomkins, A. *European Union Law* (Cambridge: Cambridge University Press 2006)

Colomer, D. 'L'institution de l'Avocat General a la Cour de Justice des Communautes Europeennes' in G.C.R. Iglesias, O. Due, E. Schintgen, and C. Elsen (eds), *Melanges en hommage à Fernand Schockweiler* (Baden-Baden: Nomos Velagsgesellschaft, 1999) 523

Darmon, M. 'The Role of the Advocate General at the European Court of Justice' in Shimon Shetreet (ed), *The Role of Courts in Society* (Dordrecht: Martinus Nijhoff 1988)

Dashwood, A. 'The Advocate General in the Court of Justice of the European Communities' (1982) 2 Legal Studies 202

Davies, G. 'The High Water Point of Free Movement of Persons: Ending Benefit Tourism and Rescuing Welfare' (2004) 26(2) Journal of Social Welfare and Family Law 211

Dougan, M. 'Free Movement: The Work Seeker as Citizen' (2002) 4 Cambridge Yearbook of European Legal Studies 121

Douglas-Scott, S. *Constitutional Law of the European Union* (Harlow: Longman 2002)

Edward, D. 'How the Court of Justice Works' (1995) European Law Review 535

Egge, A. and Stix-Hachl, C. 'Sports and Competition law: a never Ending Story' (2002) European Competition Law Review 81

Everson, M. 'The Legacy of the Market Citizen' in J Shaw and G More (eds), *New Legal Dynamics of the European Union* (Oxford: Oxford University Press 1995)

Faist, T. 'Social Citizenship in the European Union: Nested Membership' (2001) 39 Journal of Common Market Studies 37

Fennelly, N. 'Reflections of an Irish Advocate General' (1996) Irish Journal of European Law 5

Fletcher, M. 'Extending "Indirect Effect" to the Third Pillar: the significance of *Pupino*' (2005) 30 European Law Review 862

Fries, S. and Shaw, J. 'Citizenship of the Union: First Steps in the European Court of Justice' (1998) 4 European Public Law 533

Gardner, J.P. (ed), *The Role and Future of the European Court of Justice* (London: British Institute of International and Comparative Law, 1996)

Golynker, O. 'Jobseekers' rights in the European Union: challenge of changing the paradigm of social solidarity' (2005) 30 European Law Review 111

Gori, P. 'L'Avocat General A La Cour De Justice Des Communautes Europeennes' (1976) Cahiers de Droit Européen 375

Grainger, M.P. 'The Future of Europe: Judicial Interference and Preference' (2005) 3 CEP 155

Greaves, R. 'Judge Edward Acting as Advocate General' in Hoskins and Williams (eds), *A True European: Essays for Judge David Edward* (Oxford, Hart 2003) ch 8

Hailbronner, K. 'Union Citizenship and Access to Social Benefits' (2005) 42 Common Market Law Review 1245

Jacobs, F. 'Advocates General and Judges in the European Court of Justice: Some Personal Reflections' in D. O'Keefe and M. Andenas (eds), *Liber Amicorum for Lord Slynn: Judicial Review in European Law* (Amsterdam: Kluwer Academic Press, 2000)

Jacqueson, C. 'Union Citizenship and the Court of Justice: Something New Under the Sun?' (2002) 27 European Law Review 260

Joliet, R. 'Exegis on *Keck*' in Journal des Tribunaux Droit Europeén (1994) 145 and Columbia Journal of European Law 1995

Kenney, S. 'The members of the Court of Justice of the European Communities' (1998) 5 Columbia Journal of European Law 101

Kerse, C. and Khan, N. *EC Antitrust Procedure* (5th edn, London: Sweet & Maxwell, 2005)

Kokott, J. 'EU citizenship-citoyens sans frontiers?', European Law Lecture presented at Durham European Law Institute, 2005

Kostakopoulou, D. 'Ideas, Norms and European Citizenship: Explaining Institutional Change' (2005) 68(2) Modern Law Review 233

Lagrange, M. *Le role de l'Advocat Général* discourse pronounce a l'audience solennelle de la Cour, 8 October 1964 (Library, ECJ)

Lecourt, R. 'Allocution prononcee par Monsieur Le President Robert Lecourt lors de l'audience solonelle du 9 octobre 1973 a l'occasion du depart de Monsieur 'l'avocat general K. Roemer' (Luxembourg, 1973).

Léger, P. 'De la Nature de l'Avocat General a la Cour de Justice des Communautes Europeennes' in Melanges offerts au Professeur Jean-Claude Soyer (Librairie generale de droit et de jurisprudence)

Lenaerts, K. and Corthaut, T. 'Of birds and hedges: the role of primacy in invoking norms of EU law' (2006) 31 European Law Review 287

McColgan, A. *Discrimination Law: Text, Cases and Materials* (Oxford: Hart, 2000)

Mortelmans, K. 'The Court Under the Influence of its Advocates General: An Analysis of the Case Law on the Functioning of the Internal Market' (2005) Yearbook of European Law 127

Norberg, S. 'The EFTA Court' in R Plender (ed), *European Courts Practice and Precedents* (London: Sweet & Maxwell, 1997)

O'Leary, S. 'Putting Flesh on the Bones of European Citizenship' (1999) 24 European Law Review 68

O'Leary, S. *The Evolving Concept of Community Citizenship: from the Free Movement of Persons to Union Citizenship* (The Hague: Kluwer, 1996)

Örücü, E. 'Law as Transposition' (2002) 51 International Comparative Law Quarterly 205

Ovey, C and White, R. *Jacobs & White: The European Convention on Human Rights* (4th edn, Oxford, New York: Oxford University Press, 2006)

Pavlopoulos, A. *The Advocate General's office and its contribution to the Development of the Law and the Judicial Machinery of the European Communities* (Athens-Komotini, 1986)

Plender, R. (ed), *European Courts Practice and Precedents* (London: Sweet & Maxwell, 1997)

Prott, L.V. *The Latent Power of Culture and the International Judge* (Abingdon: Professional Books, 1979)

Ramsay, L. 'Reforming the European Courts at the IGC' in (2000) Juridical Review 213–25

Rasmussen, H. *On Law and Policy in the European Court of Justice: A Comparative Study in Judicial Policy Making* (Dordkcht, M Nijhoff, 1986)

Reed, (Lord) and Murdoch, J. *A Guide to Human Rights Law in Scotland* (Edinburgh: Butterworths Scotland, 2001)

Schepel, H. and Wesseling, R. 'The Legal Community: Judges, Lawyers, Officials and Clerks in the Writing of Europe' (1997) 3 European Law Journal 165

Schermers, H.G. and Waelbroeck, D.F. *Judicial Protection in the European Union* (6th edn, The Hague: Kluwer Academic Press, 2001)

Schwarze, J. 'The Origin of the European Courts' Statutes and Rules of Procedure' in Plender, R. (ed), *European Courts Practice and Precedents* (London: Sweet & Maxwell, 1997)

Shaw, J. 'The Interpretation of Union Citizenship' (1998) 61 Modern Law Review 293

Solanke, I. 'The Advocate General in Context: Cause Lawyer, Networker or Mediator?' in Paper presented to the conference 'The Transformation of Europe', IISL, Oñati, 7–9 June 2006

Spaventa, E. 'From Gebhard to Carpenter: Towards a (Non) Economic European Constitution' (2004) 41 Common Market Law Review 74

Tridimas, T. 'The Role of the Advocate General in the Development of Community Law: Some Reflections' (1997) 3 Common Market Law Review 1349

Usher, J. *European Court Practice* (London: Sweet & Maxwell, 1983)

van Gerven, W. 'The Role and Structure of the European Judiciary Now and in the Future' (1996) European Law Review 211

van Gerven, W. 'The ECJ's Case Law as a Means of Unification of Private Law' in Fordham International Law Journal (1997) 680–98 (also published in: European Review of Private Law (1998) 293–307 and in AS Hartkamp, MW Hesselink, E H Hondius (eds), *Towards a European Civil Code* (2nd edn, London: Kluwer, 1998)

van Gerven, W. 'A Common Law for Europe: the Future meeting the Past?' (2001) European Review for Private Law 485–503

van Gerven, W. *Bringing (Private) Laws Closer to Each Other at the European Level* (2005) at <http://www.law.kuleuven.ac.be/ccle/pdf/2005-01-18_WvG_.Impact_courts_on_private_law.pdf>
Weiler, J. 'The Reform of European Constitutionalism' (1997) 35 Journal of Common Market Studies 95

The Future of the Judicial System of the EU (Proposal and Reflections) May 1999 and the Contribution by the Court of Justice and the Court of First Instance to the IGC
Report of the Reflexion Group on the Future of the Judicial System of the Communities (7 February 2000)

Index